"According to the Law"

Journal of Theological Interpretation Supplements
MURRAY RAE
University of Otago, New Zealand
Editor-in-Chief

1. Thomas Holsinger-Friesen, *Irenaeus and Genesis: A Study of Competition in Early Christian Hermeneutics*
2. Douglas S. Earl, *Reading Joshua as Christian Scripture*
3. Joshua N. Moon, *Jeremiah's New Covenant: An Augustinian Reading*
4. Csilla Saysell, *"According to the Law": Reading Ezra 9–10 as Christian Scripture*
5. Joshua M. Strahan, *The Limits of a Text: Luke 23:34a as a Case Study in Theological Interpretation*
6. Seth B. Tarrer, *Reading with the Faithful: Interpretation of True and False Prophecy in the Book of Jeremiah from Ancient to Modern Times*

"According to the Law"
Reading Ezra 9–10 as Christian Scripture

CSILLA SAYSELL

Winona Lake, Indiana
EISENBRAUNS
2012

Copyright © 2012 Eisenbrauns
All rights reserved.

Printed in the United States of America

www.eisenbrauns.com

Library of Congress Cataloging-in-Publication Data

Saysell, Csilla.
  "According to the law" : reading Ezra 9–10 as Christian scripture / Csilla
    Saysell.
      p.   cm. — (Journal of theological interpretation supplements ; 4)
  Includes bibliographical references (p.   ) and index.
  ISBN 978-1-57506-703-2 (pbk. : alk. paper)
  1. Bible. O.T. Ezra IX–X—Criticism, interpretation, etc.   I. Title.
  BS1355.52.S29   2012
  222′.706—dc23
                                                          2012027558

The paper used in this publication meets the minimum requirements of the American National Standard for Information Sciences—Permanence of Paper for Printed Library Materials, ANSI Z39.48-1984.♾™

To the memory of my father and to my mother

TABLE OF CONTENTS

ACKNOWLEDGEMENTS xi
ABBREVIATIONS xii
PART I 1
1 INTRODUCTION 3
2 ATTITUDES TO THE "LAW" 6
    2.1   CHRISTIAN APPROACHES 6
    2.2   JEWISH RESPONSES 9
    2.3   CONCLUSION 18
3 THE CONTEXT OF EZRA 9–10 20
    3.1   WIDER CONTEXT: NEHEMIAH 9 20
    3.2   IMMEDIATE CONTEXT: EZRA 7–8 29
    3.3   EZRA 9:1–2: THE CRISIS 31
    3.4   CONCLUSION 32
4 THE ABOMINATIONS OF THE NATIONS 34
    4.1   THE LIST OF NATIONS IN EZRA 9:1 35
    4.2   ABOMINATIONS IN EZRA 42
    4.3   THE IDENTITY OF THE "FOREIGN WOMEN" 45
    4.4   A COMPARISON WITH NEH 13 52
    4.5   CONCLUSION 56
5 ḤĒREM LAW AND EZRA 9–10 58
    5.1   ENEMY ḤĒREM IN THE OT 59
    5.2   PROPERTY ḤĒREM IN THE OT 65
    5.3   DEDICATION AND DESTRUCTION 67
    5.4   ENEMY ḤĒREM IN EZRA 9–10 68
    5.5   ḤĒREM OF PROPERTY IN EZRA 10:8 77
    5.6   CONCLUSION 79
6 HOLY SEED AND INTERMINGLING 81
    6.1   "HOLY SEED": A DISTINCT RATIONALE 82
    6.2   THE BACKGROUND FOR THE HOLY SEED RATIONALE ... 84
    6.3   SIMILAR DEVELOPMENTS IN JEWISH LITERATURE 92
    6.4   NEW RATIONALE: WHY NEEDED? 93
    6.5   CONCLUSION 95

7 PROFANATION AND IMPURITY 96
- 7.1 PURITY TERMINOLOGY 97
- 7.2 SACRILEGE IN EZRA 9–10? 100
- 7.3 THE STATUS OF THE "FOREIGN" WIVES: PROFANE OR IMPURE? ... 113
- 7.4 *MAʿAL* AND PURITY LANGUAGE IN NEH 13:23–31 115
- 7.5 CONCLUSION 120

8 CONCLUSION TO PART I 123

PART II 127

9 INTRODUCTION TO A CHRISTIAN READING OF EZRA 9–10 129

10 EZRA 9–10 IN CHRISTIAN INTERPRETATION 131
- 10.1 OT THEOLOGIES 131
- 10.2 EN COMMENTARIES 142
- 10.3 CONCLUSION 158

11 EZRA 9–10 IN JEWISH UNDERSTANDING 160
- 11.1 JEWISH PERSPECTIVES 160
- 11.2 ACCOUNTING FOR THE DIFFERENCE 165
- 11.3 CONCLUSION 169

12 CONSTRAINTS FROM CANON AND TRADITION 170
- 12.1 EZRA 9–10 IN THE CHRISTIAN CANON 170
- 12.2 LESSONS FROM TRADITION 178
- 12.3 CONCLUSION 180

13 NT PERSPECTIVE: 1 COR 7:12–16 182
- 13.1 JEWISH AND HELLENISTIC BACKGROUND 185
- 13.2 THE NATURE OF SANCTIFICATION 188
- 13.3 HOW SANCTIFICATION IS TRANSMITTED 194
- 13.4 THE PRECEDENT FOR PAUL'S THINKING 196
- 13.5 A CLASH OF LAWS: THE PRIORITIES 199
- 13.6 2 COR 6:14–7:1 202
- 13.7 CONCLUSION 206

14 INSIGHTS FROM ANTHROPOLOGY AND A CONTEMPORARY CASE STUDY 207
- 14.1 THE "HOLY SEED" RATIONALE: A HEDGE 208
- 14.2 THE FOCUS OF PROTECTION 210
- 14.3 A CASE STUDY AND COMPARISON 213
- 14.4 CONCLUSION 216

15 CONCLUSION	218
BIBLIOGRAPHY	226
INDEX OF BIBLICAL CITATIONS	241
INDEX OF AUTHORS AND SUBJECTS	252

Acknowledgements

It is impossible to measure the value of the warmth and security of a loving home, long conversations at the dinner table, where questioning and discussion was encouraged, the benefits of several thousand books at home in various languages, as well as all the support that I have received from my parents over the years. My perceptions and understanding have been profoundly shaped by their words and life and so my deepest gratitude goes to them.

I am thankful to my friends, Paul and Traci Valerio for modeling to me the kind of Christian life that was lived by grace and yet was not without the law of Christ. It triggered in me those first questions about law and grace that led to this study some 15 years later. It was also under Paul's guidance and leadership that in the humid heat of Haifa I discovered the joys of in-depth Bible study and my love of the Old Testament. I am also grateful to have such a long-term friend as Ildikó Szabó, for our many stimulating conversations and for helping me grow personally and intellectually.

Walter Moberly's scholarly work excited me when I first encountered it and awakened in me the desire to study under him. I greatly enjoyed his approach to interpretation, which, I felt, combined rigorous exegesis with the kind of reading that brought biblical texts alive for Christian faith. I learnt much from his wisdom and carefully worked out theology through his lectures, seminars, books and personal supervision. I also thank Robert Hayward for the many fascinating seminars he led on the Targums, Midrash and the Aramaic portions of Ezra, the latter of which first sparked my interest in the Postexilic Period. He has an amazing gift for asking questions that stimulate discussion and his enthusiasm is contagious. I have fond memories of our Hebrew reading classes, which contributed much to my understanding of rabbinic thinking. Loren Stuckenbruck took a personal interest in this project beyond any call of duty and I very much appreciated his encouragement and comments along the way. I am also grateful to Rob Barrett, who first suggested Ezra 9–10 as a way of anchoring my interest in the Law.

My theological training would not have been possible without a lot of financial help and I am touched at the thought of the generous support I received from church and friends over the years. Thank you to you all. I am also grateful to the Arts and Humanities Research Council for their generous scholarship in the last two years of my PhD studies and for the postgraduate scholarship that the Theology Department in Durham secured for me from the university in my first year.

Finally, I thank my husband, Phil, my safe haven and anchor, for being there for me in the big things and the small, including his patient help with formatting issues. I am also grateful for the fun and laughter we share that lifts my heart and keeps me happy. My Best Beloved, you mean the world to me.

Abbreviations

AB	Anchor Bible
ABD	*Anchor Bible Dictionary*
AJS Review	*Association for Jewish Studies Review*
'Abod. Zar.	*'Abodah Zarah*
Ag. Ap.	Josephus, F., *Against Apion*
Ant.	Josephus, F., *Antiquities*
AOTC	Abingdon Old Testament Commentary
BAGD	Bauer, W., W. F. Arndt, F. W. Gingrich and F. W. Danker (eds.), *A Greek-English Lexicon of the New Testament and Other Early Christian Literature*
B.C.E.	Before the Common Era
BDB	Brown, F., S. R. Driver and C. A. Briggs (eds.), *The New Brown-Driver-Briggs-Gesenius Hebrew And English Lexicon with an Appendix Containing the Biblical Aramaic*
b.	*Babylonian Talmud*
BECNT	Baker Exegetical Commentary on the New Testament
BI	*Biblical Interpretation*
Bib	*Biblica*
Bik.	*Bikkurim*
B. Meṣi'a	*Baba Meṣi'a*
BWANT	Beiträge zur Wissenschaft vom Alten and Neuen Testament
BZ	*Biblische Zeitschrift*
BZAW	Beihefte zur Zeitschrift für die alttestamentliche Wissenschaft
CB	The Century Bible
CBQ	*Catholic Biblical Quarterly*
CE	Common Era
DCH	Clines, David J. A. (ed.), *The Dictionary of Classical Hebrew*
DJD	Discoveries in the Judean Desert
DSB	The Daily Study Bible Series
EN	Ezra–Nehemiah
1–2 Esd	1–2 Esdras
Gen. Rab.	*Genesis Rabbah*
Giṭ.	*Giṭṭin*
HALOT	Koehler, Ludwig, and Walter Baumgartner (eds.), *The Hebrew and Aramaic Lexicon of the Old Testament*

HAT	Handbuch zum Alten Testament
HBM	Hebrew Bible Monographs
Hor.	*Horayot*
HTR	*Harvard Theological Review*
ICC	International Critical Commentary
ITC	International Theological Commentary
JAOS	*Journal of the American Oriental Society*
JBL	*Journal of Biblical Literature*
JPS	Jewish Publication Society
JSB	*Jewish Study Bible*
JSJ	*Journal for the Study of Judaism*
JSNT SS	Journal for the Study of the New Testament Supplement Series
JSOT	*Journal for the Study of the Old Testament*
JSOT SS	Journal for the Study of the Old Testament Supplement Series
JSS	*Journal of Semitic Studies*
Jub.	*Jubilees*
KJV	King James Version
Ker.	*Kerithot*
Ketub.	*Ketubbot*
LCL	Loeb Classical Library (London: Heinemann, and Cambridge, MA: Harvard University)
LXX	Septuagint
m.	*Mishnah*
Meg.	*Megillah*
MNTC	The Moffatt New Testament Commentary
MT	Masoretic Text
NASV	New American Standard Version
NCB	The New Century Bible Commentary
NCBC	The New Cambridge Bible Commentary
NKJV	New King James Version
NLT	New Living Translation
NIDOTTE	VanGemeren, Willem A. (ed.), *New International Dictionary of Old Testament Theology and Exegesis*
NIB	Seow, Choon-Leong, et al. (eds), *The New Interpreter's Bible: A Commentary in Twelve Volumes*
NIBCOT	The New International Biblical Commentary on the Old Testament
NICNT	The New International Commentary on the New Testament
NICOT	The New International Commentary on the Old Testament
NIV	New International Version
NJBC	*The New Jerome Biblical Commentary*

NRSV	New Revised Standard Version
NT	New Testament
NTD	Das Neue Testament Deutsch
NTS	*New Testament Studies*
OT	Old Testament
par.	parashah
Qidd.	*Qiddušin*
RB	*Revue biblique*
RSV	Revised Standard Version
Sanh.	*Sanhedrin*
SBL MS	Society of Biblical Literature Monograph Series
t.	*Tosefta*
TDNT	Kittel, Gerhard and Gerhard Friedrich, *Theological Dictionary of the New Testament*
TDOT	Botterweck, G. Johannes, Helmer Ringgren, and Heinz-Josef Fabry (eds.), *Theological Dictionary of the Old Testament*
Tg. Neof.	*Targum Neofiti*
Tg. Onq.	*Targum Onqelos*
Tg. Ps.-J.	*Targum Pseudo-Jonathan*
Ter.	*Terumot*
T. Levi	*Testament of Levi*
TNTC	Tyndale New Testament Commentaries
TOTC	Tyndale Old Testament Commentaries
Tob	Tobit
VT	*Vetus Testamentum*
WBC	Word Biblical Commentaries
y.	*Palestinian Talmud (Yerushalmi)*
Yebam.	*Yebamot*
ZAW	*Zeitschrift für die alttestamentliche Wissenschaft*

PART I

1

Introduction

Well over a century ago Wellhausen in his influential *Prolegomena* (1885) writes:

> In the Priestly Code the work of Moses lies before us clearly defined and rounded off; one living a thousand years after knows it as well as one who saw it with his eyes. It is detached from its originator and from his age: lifeless itself, it has driven the life out of Moses, out of the people, nay out of the very Deity.[1]

And later:

> With the appearance of the law came to an end the old freedom, not only in the sphere of worship, now restricted to Jerusalem, but in the sphere of the religious spirit as well. There was now in existence an authority as objective as could be; and this was the death of prophecy.[2]

In these words is encapsulated much of an earlier belief surrounding the "Law," reflecting a Lutheran dichotomy of law versus grace, a prioritization of prophecy over legal material and implicitly, the setting up of "moral" injunctions (as reflected in the prophets) over against "ritual" regulations (as expressed in the priestly writings).

This overall framework survived well into the twentieth century as M. Noth's theory demonstrates. Published originally in German in 1940, his essay "The Laws in the Pentateuch" presents the notion that law becomes detached from the covenant relationship between Israel and God in the Postexilic Period. Without this anchor in God's redemption, law turns into a free-floating entity, obeyed for its own sake rather than motivated by God's grace.

---

[1] Julius Wellhausen, *Prolegomena to the History of Israel*, trans. J. Sutherland Black & Allan Menzies (Edinburgh: Adam & Charles Black, 1885) 347.
[2] Ibid., 402.

> It is the fate of human institutions which arise out of definite historical situations to decline in the course of history. But the ordinances and statutes, which had had their place in the context of those institutions, obstinately maintain their existence and, after their real basis has disappeared, take on a worth of their own which they had never possessed and which is not their due. Then do men worship dead ordinances and statutes, and regard it as a particular service and a work worthy of reward that they preserve what has been handed down merely because it has been handed down, and allow their lives to be governed by such fossilized laws.[3]

It is not surprising that perhaps due to this general attitude to the "Law" until recently there has been little interest in the stories of Ezra and Nehemiah and what there was mostly concerned itself with historical-critical questions.[4] Today, for various reasons it is problematic to speak of Israelite and Jewish Law negatively and see in Judaism a legalistic and self-righteous system. Thus Christian commentators of the OT are quick to reject the charge of "legalism" in Ezra 9–10; yet they find little theological value in the story.[5] The questions of how the "Law" is to be integrated into a Christian viewpoint and the way in which the message of such a narrative is to be understood continue to be a challenge.

The reasons for this are not hard to find. The narrative of Ezra 9–10 with its "midrashic" interpretation of pentateuchal regulations is closer to later Pharisaic traditions and rabbinic Judaism than to Christianity. Its focus on rigid ethnic separation jars with the perceived "openness" of the NT embracing both Jew and Gentile alike. The necessity of such action as the story presents is justified with notions relating to holiness and purity, categories that Christians often associate with ritual perspectives in the OT, and which in this instance clash dramatically with ethical considerations over the treatment of these "foreign" women. Thus the narrative's Torah-interpretation and observance is a useful "hard case" for testing attitudes to Torah and reflecting on how a controversial OT passage may be understood from a Christian faith perspective.

This book will explore ways in which a difficult OT text can be read as part of Christian Scripture, using the story of Ezra 9–10 as a challenging example with a view to address some larger hermeneutical issues and sketch a broader framework for dealing with such passages. The principles and tools outlined here will inevitably be somewhat specific to the particular concerns in my chosen passage, yet it is to be hoped that they may be applied, albeit with modifications, to other hard texts as well.

---

[3] Martin Noth, "The Laws in the Pentateuch: Their Assumptions and Meaning" in *The Laws in the Pentateuch and Other Studies*, trans. D.R.AP-Thomas (Edinburgh/London: Oliver & Boyd, 1966) 106.
[4] E.g., The commentaries of Rudolph, Batten, Grabbe, Torrey, etc.
[5] See Chap. 10 on Christian interpreters for examples.

My work naturally falls into two parts. Part I will focus on the "exegesis," while Part II will consider avenues of "application." Although, as I have noted, attitudes to the "Law" have changed, there is still an ongoing dilemma about a Christian's relationship to the "Law." For this reason I will briefly consider ways in which Christians have dealt with the "Law" and add some Jewish perspectives. This will be followed by a kind of scene-setting for Ezra 9–10 in two ways. First, I shall look at Israel's own self-understanding of its postexilic position as it is reflected in Neh 9 (and to a lesser extent 10) and secondly, I shall focus on the immediate context of the intermarriage crisis by examining Ezra 7–8 and seeking to answer the question why the author/editor placed the story here rather than after the reading of Torah in Neh 8. Next I shall consider Ezra 9–10 with a particular emphasis on Torah interpretation and observance. In other words, my exegesis will selectively concentrate on answering the question what led the exiles to see intermarriage with "foreign" women as a problem and how they arrived at the particular solution they found through their interpretation and application of pentateuchal laws.

Part II will then build on the picture that thus emerges and move to the challenges of a specifically Christian reading. Again, I will start here with setting the scene and assessing various Christian commentators' views on Ezra 9–10 and its application. As a way of creating distance and perspective I will then consider Jewish understandings of the intermarriage crisis and reflect on the differences between the two traditions (Christian and Jewish). Next I will think of ways in which this OT story is constrained by canon and tradition, which will be followed by a comparison of the Ezran intermarriage crisis with its NT "counterpart," 1 Cor 7:12–16. Finally I will utilize the insights of anthropology to draw out some lessons from Ezra 9–10 and will contrast the Ezran solution with a contemporary case of regulating mixed marriages in a Christian setting and how it compares with a Jewish approach today. The purpose of the exercise is to use various angles in an effort to build up a fuller picture of what is involved in the story and how it might be used for benefit in a Christian context.

2

Attitudes to the "Law"

Law for Christians is, arguably, what Christ is for Jews: the hard nut that resists cracking. It is not surprising that this is so, since Christ for Christians is what Torah is for Jews: the central concern and at the heart of their religion respectively. It is the key distinctive feature for each that causes the most difficulty for the other in a Jewish-Christian dialogue.

Engagement with Jewish understandings of Torah therefore can be potentially enriching for Christians because these categories of thought and perspectives may shed light on aspects of truth in Scripture to which Christians, and Protestants in particular, have been blinded because of their long-entrenched traditions. Below I shall consider two particularly prominent ways in which Christians attempt to integrate "Law" into their overall theology. One we might call the "covenantal framework," the other the method of "theologizing." These I shall juxtapose with some Jewish responses.

2.1 Christian Approaches

2.1.1 *Covenant & Salvation History*

The emergence of covenantal ideas has given Christian theologians a conceptual framework into which the law can be fitted.[6] While for Wellhausen covenant is a negative category which breaks the "natural bond" between God and his people, both for most of its earlier and later advocates the concept becomes a positive term for describing the relationship between YHWH and

---

[6] For a history overviewing the development of covenantal ideas see Ernest W. Nicholson, *God and His People: Covenant and Theology in the Old Testament* (Oxford: Clarendon, 1986) Chaps. 1–4.

Israel. Thus many Old Testament theologies discuss law within the structure of covenant, most obviously Eichrodt's *Theology of the Old Testament*. A variation on the link between covenant and Law is Preuss' solution, which presents the two as divine election and human response/obligation, although his estimate of the Law is mixed; it is both given for life and for good (Deut 10:13) and for extermination and as a curse (Deut 27–28).[7]

The issue for Christian theology in these examples then is ultimately the perceived tension between law and grace. Whether the overarching principle is phrased in terms of covenant or election, both indicate a relationship and point to God's grace in salvation as the motivator for obedience. Perhaps the best known example for understanding law in the context of salvation history is von Rad's *Old Testament Theology*, the scholar whose name is ultimately associated with *Heilsgeschichte*.

It is argued that if this aspect of salvation is not emphasized the result will be legalism, rigidity and outward compliance without sincere inward motivation as best exemplified by the ancient Israelite amphictyony of tribes in Noth's famous theory.[8] As mentioned in the introduction, Noth assumes that the covenant relationship has been lost by the Postexilic Period and that "Law" as an absolute entity moves away from being a grateful response to God's grace.

One other consideration contributes to the strong associations of covenant with *Heilsgeschichte*; namely the perceived similarities of Israel's covenant with ancient Near Eastern suzerainty treaties noted by Mendenhall and later McCarthy.[9] From our point of view, the "historical prologue" in the Hittite treaties is particularly significant because it generally recounts the favors received from the suzerain thereby providing the vassal with a foundation for gratitude for obeying the covenant stipulations. However, more recent assessments caution against an overenthusiastic identification of biblical covenants with suzerainty treaties.[10] Nicholson goes as far as to say that the similarities are more apparent than real.[11] He argues that the terms "father-son," "love," "treasured possession" (סגלה) are all concepts familiar to Israelites from everyday life and they do not need treaty language to add nuance to them. Further, he queries whether Israelites would use a suzerainty treaty form which they were familiar with but which in the case of the Assyrians has led to the

---

[7] Horst D. Preuss, *Old Testament Theology*, trans. Leo G. Perdue (2 vols.; Edinburgh: T&T Clark, 1995–96) 1:80–95.
[8] Noth, "The Laws," 1–107.
[9] See George E. Mendenhall, "Ancient Oriental and Biblical Law," *The Biblical Archaeologist* 17/2 (1954), 25–46; Idem, "Covenant Forms in Israelite Tradition," *The Biblical Archaeologist* 17/3 (1954), 49–76, and Dennis J. McCarthy, *Treaty and Covenant: A Study in Form in the Ancient Oriental Documents and in the Old Testament* (Rome: Biblical Institute, 1981).
[10] Already McCarthy notes that early covenant texts in the Bible do not demonstrate all the features of the suzerainty treaty (*Treaty and Covenant*, Chap. 28).
[11] Nicholson, *God and His People*, esp. 70–82.

despoiling of the land and the subjugation of the people. Would YHWH allow himself to be seen in the same position as the Assyrians were?

While covenantal ideas are perhaps less popular today, the notion of relationship within which God's salvation, that is, prevenient grace, is the motivator for obedience continues to play a part in Christian understandings of the "Law." A recent example is Goldingay's discussion at the beginning of his *Old Testament Theology*, which sets the agenda for all three volumes.

In his introductory section Goldingay sets out the threefold division of his theology.[12] "Volume one concerns the Old Testament's gospel, or how things were, or what God and Israel have done." His second volume on "the Old Testament's faith and hope, or how things are and will be, or who God is and who we are" is based on the Latter Prophets, the Wisdom Books and Psalms. The source for the third volume on ethos is "the instructive material in the Torah" (i.e., the commandments and laws in the Pentateuch). On the same page he also calls this threefold division "narrative, faith and ethics" and alternatively "gospel, faith and lifestyle," the latter of which closely resemble the respective titles of his individual volumes.

It is evident in this structuring that Goldingay consciously patterns his OT theology along NT lines and places the "commandments" within the framework of salvation history. The sequence of "gospel, faith and lifestyle" echoes the progression of a New Testament understanding of salvation as good news that is heard (Rom 10:14), believed (Acts 16:31) and lived out (Phil 1:27).

2.1.2 *"Theologizing"*

A second way in which the "Law" finds a place within a Christian understanding is what I call "theologizing." This is the practice that sees OT "Law" as reflecting values and principles rather than something that Christians should obey in all its intricate detail and entirety. Clearly, this process is easier with what are known as "ethical/moral" laws, which still underlie the Christian ideal of how one's life should be governed as a child of God. Similarly "civil" laws often have a more easily discernible "moral" core and so the transference from particular practice to general principle is relatively straightforward. The most difficult segment of OT law is what has traditionally been described as "cultic/ritual/ceremonial" law. Apart from the prejudice and suspicion of an earlier Protestant scholarship against "ritual," much of what falls under that rubric in the OT does not give a theological explanation of its significance, nor are the practices in themselves self-explanatory.

Two examples of this "theologizing" should suffice. Cranfield asserts that although Christians are no longer "under the Law" in the sense of being condemned by it for their inability to obey it fully, nevertheless, the Law remains the guideline for filling out the details of the more general love

---

[12] John Goldingay, *Old Testament Theology* (3 vols.; Downers Grove, IL: IVP Academic, 2003–2009) 1:28.

command and for understanding God's will better.[13] He specifically addresses the problem of "ritual" law and his solution is to see in those practices a foreshadowing of Christ; an approach that finds its antecedent in the Letter to the Hebrews.

> Whereas for the non-Christian Jew the literal observance of the ceremonial law is still obligatory, the Christian, who knows that the One, to whom all along the law was pointing, has come and has accomplished his saving work, no longer has to observe it literally. The word "literally" in the last sentence is important, for what is being suggested is not [...] that the ceremonial law has simply been abrogated and that the Christian should just ignore it, but that he should honour it by looking steadfastly in the direction in which it was all along pointing and by believing in Christ as he and his work are witnessed to by it.[14]

Similarly Goldingay, in connection with the issues in Neh 5:1–13 makes the following throwaway comment reflecting the same attitude of "theologizing": "[W]e may misunderstand the nature of Moses' Teaching in expecting such provisions [Sabbath year, jubilee year] to be implemented as if they were statutes in a law book. They may be more like visions or ethical statements."[15]

2.2   Jewish Responses

Mechanisms developed by Christians to deal with the "Law" have called forth Jewish scholars who address these and create ways in which to re-think how "Law" works. The scope of this book does not allow for a detailed overview of Jewish responses and my focus is not the issue of "Law" in general but the particular passage of Ezra 9–10. Thus I have chosen two "responses," which will hopefully give a "flavor" of some Jewish perspectives. Levenson's reflections are obviously a reaction to Christian conceptualizations of the "Law" and since he has long been involved in Jewish-Christian dialogue, engagement with his thoughts is a worthwhile exercise. My second choice is a more idiosyncratic essay by Diana Lipton entitled "Terms of Endearment," which was recently published (2008) and is a fascinating and provocative re-thinking of the "Law."

2.2.1   Creation (Levenson)

Levenson addresses both Christian approaches that I set out above: the Christian propensity to connect "Law" with covenant and theologizing. He

---

[13] Charles E. B. Cranfield, "Has the Old Testament Law a Place in the Christian Life? A Response to Professor Westerholm" in *On Romans and Other New Testament Essays* (Edinburgh: T&T Clark, 1998) 114, 111–12, 117.
[14] Ibid., 114–115.
[15] Goldingay, *OT Theology* 1:722.

observes that the association of "Law" and covenant is attractive for Christians because, "A new appreciation of covenant has redeemed law for biblical theology, for covenant gives law a place within a structure of faith and integrates it into the total relationship with God. [...] Covenant subsumes law."[16]

Further, he summarizes well both the two-fold Christian problem and its resolution using John Bright as an illustration.

> A good Paulinist, Bright must steer clear of the heresy of Judaizing. The implication that the laws must be obeyed, whenever possible, cannot be accepted. But across the straits from the Scylla of Judaizing sits the Charybdis of Marcionism, with its bold proclamation that the Jewish Scriptures are irrelevant to the Christian. This, too, must be resisted. Only theology enables safe passage, for by converting law into theology, specific practice into general belief, Bright can grant Paul his doctrine of exemption from Torah without granting Marcion his idea that the Jewish God and the Christian are antithetical. The specifics fade, the laws wither, but Old Testament theology endures forever.[17]

Levenson is witty and right about the motivation behind the Christian conceptualization, although he is not entirely fair regarding Christian practice. Clearly, for a religion that emphasizes faith and grace to the degree Christianity does it is a danger to "theologize away" the need for obedience, yet the NT does not condone such an attitude (e.g., Jas 2:14–26; 1 Cor 6:9–10; Gal 5:14–24, cf. 6:7–8), nor can the church if it wants to heed its own Scriptures.[18] There is also evidence that the church considers certain aspects of the "Law" fundamental to Christian living. Thus, for instance, many denominations incorporate the Ten Commandments into their basic catechism or stress the necessity of "righteous" living in their prayers of confession.[19] Admittedly, the Christian emphasis is

---

[16] Jon D. Levenson, "Theologies of Commandment in Biblical Israel," *HTR* 73 (1980) 18–19.

[17] Jon D. Levenson, "Why Jews Are Not Interested in Biblical Theology" in *The Hebrew Bible, the Old Testament, and Historical Criticism: Jews and Christians in Biblical Studies* (Louisville, KY: Westminster John Knox, 1993) 52–53.

[18] Conversely, the danger for an orthopraxic religion such as Judaism is to lose sight of the wider framework which explains the reasons and motivation behind the practices. See the discussion on prioritising Halakah below.

[19] Examples are numerous. Luther's *Small Catechism* incorporates an explanation of the Ten Commandments and it is assumed that Christians are called to obey them. Martin Luther, *Small Catechism*, n.p. [cited 10 June 2009]. Online: http://bookofconcord.org/smallcatechism.php. Similarly, *The Westminster Shorter Catechism* explicates the Ten Commandments and precedes it with the following Question and Answer: "Q44. What doth the preface to the Ten Commandments teach us? A44. The preface to the Ten Commandments teacheth us, That because God is The Lord, and our God, and Redeemer, therefore we are bound to keep all His commandments." *The Westminster Shorter Catechism*, n.p. [cited 10 June 2009]. Online: http://www.ccel.org/creeds/westminster-shorter-cat.html. *The Book of Common Prayer* (1662) has the following prayer of confession in its Order for Morning Prayer: "Almighty and most merciful Father, We

primarily on "moral-religious" aspects of the "Law" and the theologizing aspect, as we have seen (§2.1.2), comes more to the fore when interpreting "ritual" law.[20]

This is a particular challenge in the case of Ezra 9–10, where the "holy seed" rationale especially, as we shall see, reminds commentators of "ritual" aspects of the law. The instinct to "theologize" in order to avoid the thorny issues of the text leads many interpreters to make their "application" so vague and general that it almost becomes meaningless (see §10.2.3).

It follows from the above Christian interpretative framework that norm (i.e., legal regulations/commandments) is subordinate to narrative since it is the covenant relationship and salvation history that define the context in which laws are to be acted out. Put another way and using Jewish terminology, Haggadah (biblical and rabbinic stories) is more important than Halakah (legally binding regulations) for Christians whereas for Jews Halakah has precedence over Haggadah (see more on this in §11.2.2). For a most extreme form of this latter conviction one might refer to Rabbi Isaac quoted by Rashi in his commentary on Gen 1:1, who allegedly said that the Torah should have started with Exod 12:2 (the Passover legislation) because the purpose of Torah is the commandment. Rashi, however, argues for the benefit of the creation story as justifying Israel's legitimate claim to her land, since the earth belongs to YHWH and he can give it to whomever he wishes. Similarly, Heschel calls for a redressing of the balance in Jewish thinking and the need to recognize the equally important aspect of Haggadah.

> Halacha is an *answer* to a question, namely: What does God ask of me? The moment that question dies in the heart, the answer becomes meaningless. That question, however, is agadic, spontaneous, personal. It is an outburst of insight, longing, faith. It is not given; it must come about.[21]

---

have erred and strayed from thy ways like lost sheep, We have followed too much the devices and desires of our own hearts, We have *offended against thy holy laws*, We have left undone those things which we ought to have done, And we have done those things which we ought not to have done, And there is no health in us: But thou, O Lord, have mercy upon us miserable offenders; Spare thou them, O God, which confess their faults, Restore thou them that are penitent, According to thy promises declared unto mankind in Christ Jesu our Lord: And grant, O most merciful Father, for his sake, *That we may hereafter live a godly, righteous, and sober life*, To the glory of thy holy Name. Amen." *The Book of Common Prayer* (1662), n.p. [cited 12 Oct 2010]. Online: http://www.cofe.anglican.org/worship/liturgy/bcp/texts/. [italics mine]

[20] I am aware of the particular difficulty with the traditional terminology of "moral" and "ritual" laws. Nevertheless, for convenience and for lack of a better option I shall continue to use it here. See my similar discussion on "moral" and "ritual" purity in §7.1.

[21] Abraham J. Heschel, *God in Search of Man: A Philosophy of Judaism* (New York: Farrar, Straus & Giroux, 1955) 339.

Notwithstanding Heschel and others who argue for the importance of Haggadah as well, Levenson's position probably reflects more the majority attitude of Jews, which prioritizes Halakah. Reacting to a Christian trend of theologizing and stressing salvation history Levenson calls for an alternative conceptualization that does not threaten the Jewish emphasis on the importance of norm. In examining the motivation behind various laws, he finds two kinds of reasons which do not connect the commandments with revelation and *Heilsgeschichte*, but with rational thought/wisdom on the one hand and "nature"/creation on the other.[22] For instance, he sees the reasoning for the observance of the Sabbath in Deut 5:14 ("so that your male and female servants can rest like you") "as the particular Israelite realization of universally intuited norms" (p.28), that is, a wisdom that can be rationally discerned without recourse to Israel's salvation history. Under what he terms the "cosmological argument" he refers to Ps 119 & 19 to show that biblical law is of the same order as those of the laws of nature.

The Jewish perspective Levenson demonstrates finds its parallel in recent Christian trends in OT theology, which recognize the need to see beyond a narrow christological focus.[23] A Christian scholar who explicitly relates the "Law" to creation is Fretheim.

> Sinai draws together previously known law and develops new law for this redeemed and called community. In most respects, Sinai is simply a regiving of the law implicitly and explicitly commanded in creation or made evident in common life experience (within Israel and without). The exodus gives Israel some new motivations for keeping the law, indeed empowers Israel to that end, but, as I have already noted above, the law is grounded in Israel's creation-faith, not God's redemptive activity.[24]

---

[22] Levenson, "Theologies," 25–32. My ensuing discussion here uses creation and redemption as the two primary categories which certain laws are associated with even though I am aware that the classic theological terms for the two groups are "natural law" and "revealed law." The latter pair reflects how we know about these laws (from nature or through special revelation), whereas my focus is on motivation for keeping the law and this is better expressed by the terms creation and redemption, hence my reason for using them.

[23] See for instance Barr's discussion on natural theology and his argument with Barth over its negation as well as his examples from Paul, wisdom literature and the Psalms. James Barr, *Biblical Faith and Natural Theology: the Gifford Lectures for 1991, Delivered in the University of Edinburgh* (Oxford: Clarendon, 1993). There are also corresponding trends in systematic theology emphasising the importance of creation for doctrine. E.g., The work of Colin E. Gunton, *Christ and Creation* (Carlisle: Paternoster / Grand Rapids MI: Eerdmans, 1992), Idem., *The One, the Three and the Many: God, Creation and the Culture of Modernity: the Bampton Lectures 1992* (Cambridge: Cambridge University Press, 1993).

[24] Terence E. Fretheim, "Law in the Service of Life: A Dynamic Understanding of Law in Deuteronomy" in *A God So Near: Essays on Old Testament Theology in Honor of Patrick*

Fretheim overstates his case in wanting to make the creational principle all-encompassing and his view that Sinai law is implicit in creation is counter-intuitive. He bases this on the Genesis narrative which, he argues, assumes an implicit knowledge of the Sinai Law in line with creation rather than an anachronistic reading of Sinai Law back into Genesis. Thus Cain should have known that murder was sin (Gen 4:10–13), and Abraham's obedience to the commandments (Gen 26:5, cf. 18:19, 25) is a reflection of this same principle that Sinai Law is integral to creation.[25] Salvation enables Israel to fulfill God's creational purposes by facilitating free and true human life as it was envisaged in creation.

> God's work of salvation has the effect of reclaiming and enabling not only true human life and freedom, but also *responsibility* for the sake of life for all. As a newly redeemed community, Israel stands before God and is in effect addressed as human beings were on the sixth day of creation, called to take up this vocation.[26]

Despite the imbalance in Fretheim's theory, he is right in wanting to bring aspects of creation into the discussion of the Law. However, it is not necessary to play creation against redemption and here Levenson's perspective seems a more balanced one. After all, creation and redemption are sometimes juxtaposed as in the case of the Sabbath law, which is given two rationales. On the one hand, the Sabbath points to God's rest after bringing the world into existence and calls for *imitatio dei* in rest after work (Exod 20:11). On the other, it is also a reminder of redemption from slavery (Deut 5:15). Similarly, Jer 33:20 speaks of God's covenant with day and night. His commitment to uphold creation is then compared to his covenant with Israel and David.

Other examples intertwine the creational and redemptional aspects within Scripture. Thus the future restoration of the covenant between Israel and YHWH is often described in creational terms: new heavens and new earth (Isa 65:17); an Eden-like quality where not only is Israel at peace and free from her enemies, but so is creation. Carnivorous animals will become herbivores (the lion will eat straw, the wolf will dwell with the lamb—Isa 11:6–7; 65:25); the symbol of the arch-enemy in Eden, the serpent, will be so harmless that a nursing child may play at the viper's den and not get hurt (Isa 11:8) and a fresh-

---

D. *Miller* (ed. Brent A. Strawn & Nancy R. Bowen; Winona Lake IN: Eisenbrauns, 2003) 189–90.

[25] Ibid., 186. An interesting alternative reading is given by Moberly, who avoids the simplistic understanding that Genesis is an anachronistic reading of the Sinai Law back into the pre-Sinai narrative. Rather, he suggests that the patriarchal narrative is consciously shaped by the YHWH-istic editor(s) in terms of Torah-obedience but without eliminating all the differences in the worship of Israel's God pre- and post-Sinai. The aim of such a construal is to provide through the story of the patriarchs models and examples even for post-Sinai readers. R. W. L. Moberly, *The Old Testament of the Old Testament: Patriarchal Narratives and Mosaic Yahwism* (Minneapolis MN: Fortress, 1992).

[26] Fretheim, "Law in the Service of Life," 190.

water stream will flow from the sanctuary leading to the growth of trees with healing leaves and edible fruit (Ezek 47:1–12). Conversely, the Mosaic covenant may remind the reader of creation.[27] The ark of the covenant carries two cherubim on top from where YHWH is to speak with Moses (Exod 25:22), which resonates with the cherub holding the flaming sword and guarding the entrance to the Garden and the tree of life (Gen 3:24, compare also the repeated pattern of cherubim and palm trees on parts of the new temple in Ezekiel's vision—Ezek 41:25).

What is the significance of this combination of creation and redemption in connection with the Law? It may demonstrate that the motivation for doing Torah may not be exclusively gratitude for salvation but a recognition that the commandments "make sense," are "reasonable" or that they fit in with the created order, with the laws and patterns discernible in life. In other words, one should not only obey the Law "blindly" because God said so—even if it is done in gratitude –, but recognize the inherent "goodness" and appropriateness of God's Torah. If one overemphasizes blind obedience because of the authority behind the Law, there may be no check on any misunderstandings regarding what is required. If, on the other hand, the final arbiter is the appropriateness of a commandment then humanity may become the supreme authority over what counts as good or evil irrespective of God. Thus the intertwined nature of creational and redemptional motifs in connection with the commandments and in the concept of the covenant may signify that these two principles should be held in balance.

2.2.2   Engagement (Lipton)

Lipton does not engage explicitly with a Christian approach to Law, although she admits that discussions polarizing love and law stimulated her interest in wanting to show that the two are intertwined.[28] Her perspective is also directly relevant to the previous discussion on obedience to the Torah done "blindly" or as a recognition of its appropriateness and goodness. The way she sets out her argument, however, is very different from Levenson's although in a paradoxical way it is also typically Jewish.

She argues against the "sovereign obedience model" of biblical law, which sees God as a supreme and independent being who issues orders and punishes the disobedient.[29] She sets out the "problem" of the "Law" as follows.

---

[27] I do not wish to make here a traditio-historical comment to the effect that the author of Exod 25:22 knew the creation story. Rather, my point is one of reader-response in light of the whole canon of Scripture.

[28] Diana Lipton, "Terms of Endearment: A (Very) Fresh Look at Biblical Law," in *Longing for Egypt and Other Unexpected Biblical Tales*, HBM 15 (Sheffield: Sheffield Phoenix, 2008) 174 fn. 5.

[29] Ibid., 172–73.

> A society in which law reigns supreme over almost every aspect of waking life, and in which death or some form of exclusion features prominently among penalties incurred, would quickly find itself with few surviving members! Two obvious options present themselves. The first is to diminish the significance of the law, or even dispense altogether with its enforcement, focusing instead on the values and ideals it was intended to promote. This represents my understanding of Christianity's response to biblical law. The second option is to maintain law in its pure form whilst granting immense dispensation in its application. This I see as the Jewish approach.[30]

Here we see again the same recognition that Christianity "theologizes" although the motivation for Christians to do so stems less from the fear outlined above and more from the anxiety that a "sovereign obedience model" may skew the loving character of God or create the impression that "salvation" is earned by obedience to the "Law." It is precisely this that the Christian emphasis on salvation history and the covenantal model address. Her second option, what she considers the Jewish approach, demonstrates the particular Jewish difficulty, which comes from wanting to keep the "Law" in its entirety. It also shows up the Christian misconception of an earlier era that considered Jewish obedience to Torah as rigid and inflexible.[31] Jews themselves would not recognize their own practice in this description; rather the vast material known as the Oral Torah suggests precisely that the written Torah cannot be taken woodenly and applied literally, but that there needs to be flexibility and a constant re-contextualization of ancient laws and regulations. The story of Ezra 9–10, as we shall see, and the way the exiles re-interpret a combination of laws to apply them to their specific situation is a good illustration of this principle.

Lipton in her reassessment of Torah also makes a contribution to the discussion on the relationship between Halakah and Haggadah. She argues that narrative underpins law in several unexpected ways. First, the golden calf incident at Sinai suggests that God gives (at least) a second chance to people who break even some of his core commandments. Moreover, the second time he allows greater human participation: "God dictates and Moses writes."[32] Thus the narrative context of the giving of the Law undermines the sovereign obedience model and portrays God as having more flexibility than this model would allow. Further, Moses' involvement in the re-giving of the Law indicates a level of human engagement.

---

[30] Ibid., 173–74. She admits that her characterisation of the Christian response may be an oversimplification and that she should be talking about Paul not Christianity as a whole but maintains that her view above is not without justification. Ibid, 174 fn. 5.

[31] See, for instance, Cranfield who polarises the Jewish position as the "wooden observance of the law's letter" against the "free and joyful aiming at its intention" thought of as the Christian approach. Cranfield, "Has the OT Law," 117.

[32] Lipton, "Terms of Endearment," 174.

Secondly, Lipton argues that biblical accounts often relate stories where the characters break the laws, sometimes major ones, yet by staying within the system they demonstrate that despite the limitations of application, law is not compromised and is still viable. In other words, "biblical law can survive application."[33]

Positively, she conceptualizes "Law" very differently than the usual model of "crime and punishment."

> I see law instead as a vehicle for unending, interactive engagement—that is, a two-way process between people of different status, between people of equal status, and, above all, between people and God. The closest approximation of this dialogic engagement is erotic love, and its ultimate goal, theologically speaking, is intercession. [...] I see intercession as the prophet's central task—standing in the breach to protect Israel from divine anger—and I see law alongside prophecy as a key vehicle of intercession in the Bible.[34]

In Lipton's view, especially Deuteronomy is set up as a record of the loving engagement between God and Moses providing a model for future generations to use "law as an agent of intercession against God's angry attempts to annihilate them."[35] She reflects on this theme of interaction, engagement, and intercession through several rabbinic and biblical texts culminating in an exploration of the Akedah.

On her reading, which she emphatically states is not the only legitimate one, Abraham's unquestioning obedience in Gen 22 is not a virtue but a deficiency because it fails to engage with God and question whether offering up Isaac is the right thing.[36] The fact that without the angelic intervention Abraham would have cut off his own line makes the outcome of such obedience at least ambivalent. Rather, Abraham should have interceded for his son and challenged God on the rightness of offering up Isaac as he did when he interceded at Sodom and Gomorrah. Lipton argues that the second angelic voice promising blessing to Abraham because he has done "this thing" (הדבר הזה—v.16) refers to the replacement of Isaac with the ram rather than to his obedience to the original command. Lipton thus concludes,

> Genesis 22 promotes not obedience but a gradually intensifying engagement culminating in the identification of something that could be offered in place of God's original request. Without the angels this claim would be controversial. With the angels, there can be no question that God did not in fact want what he said he wanted![37]

---

[33] Ibid., 176.
[34] Ibid., 177.
[35] Ibid., 178.
[36] Ibid., 197–211.
[37] Ibid., 212.

There is much to comment on (and argue with) in Lipton's fascinating reassessment of Torah. Her solution to use Haggadah in order to undermine the sovereign obedience model and bring law and love closer together is actually not that different from Christian attempts to use narrative accounts to show a framework of relationship and love in which there is room for a second chance. However, her understanding that biblical stories of breaking the law indicate the viability of the law, seems to me to be open to question.

Her point about engagement in the application of Law, on the other hand, is one that raises interesting possibilities despite some aspects that are rather arguable. What is unclear in her general presentation of law as a means of intercession to ward off an angry God, is why God should be angry in the first place? Surely, the anger of God is not unpredictable but directly connected to disobedience to his will as set out in Torah. Lipton's reading of the Akedah seems equally counter-intuitive as a negative account of obedience, at least from the story's own perspective.

Nevertheless, her insight that human engagement is required in the application of the Law is one well worth considering further. Here I return to the discussion closing the section on Levenson (§2.2.1) and the tension between obedience "because God said so" and obedience as a recognition of the inherent goodness of the commandment. In Lipton's provocative formulation "Obedience to law, is not merely unimportant, but may be negative, at least where it forecloses engagement."[38] Despite what at first glance seems like a thoroughly un-Jewish position (what could be more important than obedience to Torah?), Lipton stands in the rabbinic tradition that constantly calls for a re-assessment and re-appropriation of Torah in ever-changing situations. Her stance chimes in with Michael Fishbane's position, which in a way subjects even God to his own Torah.[39]

> For the well-known Talmudic image of God studying and interpreting his own Torah is nothing if not that tradition's realization that there is no authoritative teaching which is not also the source of its own renewal, that revealed teachings are a dead letter unless revitalized in the mouth of those who study them.[40]

Engagement and re-thinking of Torah regulations are important because a mechanical application of commandments may seem correct in detail and yet clash against the overall spirit and *ethos* of the overall purpose of the Law. This is a particularly crucial point that I shall return to in Part II of this book, namely

---

[38] Ibid., 211.

[39] Similarly, Lipton uses the well-known talmudic story of Rabbi Eliezer and the Carob Tree (*b. B. Meṣi'a* 59b) to show that in a rabbinic debate about Halakah not even a Heavenly Voice can be the final arbiter in the discussion. Ibid., 179–187 (see esp. 187).

[40] Michael Fishbane, "Inner-Biblical Exegesis: Types and Strategies of Interpretation in Ancient Israel" in *The Garments of Torah: Essays in Biblical Hermeneutics* (Bloomington: Indiana University Press, 1989) 19.

the tension between the exiles' desire to obey Torah and the ethical difficulties of the solution they found.

Lipton herself mentions the tension between God's command and the ethical difficulty in the Akedah although she argues that using her model does not call for a choice between God and morality.

> Human engagement over divine commands will inevitably involve an appeal to *moral values acquired independently*, not to mention such aspects of human experience as emotional attachment, and indeed the intention from the outset was that law, as packaged and delivered to Israel, would demand such engagement.[41] [italics mine]

I query Lipton's formulation that morality is acquired independently from the divine commands, although I believe that the overall thrust of her position is closer to what I argue below than what the above quotation would imply. I suggest that a true understanding of "morality" (not narrow moralizing but a sense of right and wrong) grows out of an engagement with God's Law and will and ultimately with God himself. It is this overall sense of what is good and true learnt through ongoing dialogue with him that helps in the details of engagement with specific regulations. Such an understanding of the "spirit" of what is required provides a check on interpretations of individual commandments that might clash with it.

Neither is human experience and attachment something that is outside of the framework God has set. If Law is an expression of God's will and design originally planned for creation then surely this same design is in some sense matched and imprinted on created beings. Thus the love of a father for his son—or to think of Ezra 9–10—that of a husband for his wife is not independent from God's design but a part of it, as it is reflected in God's own experience and emotional attachment to Israel in the father-son, husband-wife imagery so often used in Scripture.

Thus, I argue that the totality of human experience and engagement with God feed into an understanding of what constitutes his will and purpose, which in turn helps to translate that into practical terms in the interpretation and application of individual laws.

2.3 Conclusion

This brief introduction into different approaches to the Law is meant to serve two purposes. First, it aims to create an awareness of the ways in which Christians approach the Law (through the covenant framework and theologizing). Secondly it is to be hoped that the two examples of Jewish responses demonstrate a lively engagement with the commandments, which addresses the heart of the matter and may provide Christians with further thought about ways of understanding the Law. Levenson's explorations into

---

[41] Lipton, "Terms of Endearment," 213.

rationales for commandments rooted in creation may broaden the Christian framework for Law to include aspects other than salvation history. Indeed, implications of an understanding of creation are already making their effects felt in some respects in Christian biblical studies irrespective of Jewish responses. Lipton's fresh look at the question of obedience to Torah offers Christians a new way of thinking about the Law that does not merely involve mechanical obedience but calls for an engagement with God and his will although by the nature of the Christian faith this will inevitably take different forms from Jewish practice.

3

The Context of Ezra 9–10

3.1   Wider Context: Nehemiah 9

Before turning to the story of Ezra 9–10 I wish to consider first the prayer in Neh 9 and to a lesser extent the follow-up action of the exiles in Neh 10 in order to see a postexilic understanding of the Law and Israel's relationship to YHWH. I shall group my observations around four topics: 1) the nature of the covenant, 2) the place of the law, 3) sins of the past and 4) how restoration is envisaged.

From a historical-critical perspective Neh 9 has often been linked to the story of mixed marriages in Ezra 9–10 due to its content of mourning and confession, which would have been a logical response to the crisis described in Ezra 9–10.[42] Although not out of place where it is positioned in the canon now, after Neh 8, there is nevertheless a switch in tone from the explicit call not to grieve but to rejoice and celebrate (Neh 8:9–12) to mourning and confession. On the other hand, there is no reference in Neh 9 to intermarriage, nor any specific mention of the sins corresponding to the commitment of the exiles in Neh 10. The lack of specificity may therefore indicate the independent origin of the

---

[42] W. Rudolph thinks it fits after Ezra 10 (*Esra und Nehemia mit 3.Esra*, HAT 20 [Tübingen: Mohr Siebeck, 1949] 154–55). He attributes the absence of Ezra's name from Neh 9 to the Chronicler, who wanted to minimise the connection of Ezra with the rigorist approach evident in Ezra 9. H. G. M. Williamson (following F. Ahlemann, "Zur Esra Quelle," *ZAW* 59 [1942–43] 89) places it between Ezra 10:15 and v.16, in which case the 24th of the month in Neh 9:1 refers to the 9th month rather than the 7th (*Ezra, Nehemiah*, [WBC 16; Nashville TN: Nelson, 1985] 310). He also notes the use of "seed" in both Neh 9:2 and Ezra 9:2 which may argue for the connection between the two chapters (Ibid., 308–9).

3.1.1 *The Nature of the Covenant*

The word ברית (covenant) is only mentioned twice in Neh 9; the first occurrence relates God's covenant-making with Abraham (וכרות עמו הברית—v.8), the second confirms YHWH's character as a covenant-keeping God (שומר הברית והחסד —v.32). The covenant renewal of the exiles is not called a ברית but a "fixed or sure agreement" (אמנה), although the verb "to cut" is retained from the original expression "to cut a covenant" (אנחנו כרתים אמנה—Neh 10:1[9:38]).[44] These three preliminary observations signify three characteristics of the prayer, which I shall expand on below.

First, it is an important feature of the text that it traces the origins of Israel's relationship with God to Abraham rather than to the exodus events and Sinai. Although Mount Sinai is mentioned (v.13) and the giving of Torah through Moses (v.14) the events there are understood within the ongoing relationship of Israel with her God.[45] The particular emphasis on Abraham is linked with the promise of peoplehood (v.7) and land (v.8); two obvious concerns for the returned exiles. The former is a reference to the name change of Abram to Abraham in Gen 17:5 where the event is connected with the promise that Abraham will be made the "father of a multitude of nations" (כי אב־המון גוים נתתיך). It is noteworthy that outside the patriarchal narratives the only other allusion to the name change from Abram to Abraham is in 1 Chr 1:27 where a genealogical list traces the line of descendants from Adam and concludes with "Abram, that is Abraham" (אברם הוא אברהם). This then leads on to Abraham's descendants and the twelve tribes of Israel over the next few chapters with special emphasis on Judah and the Davidic line (1 Chr 2–3) and a detailed list of the priestly line (1 Chr 6). In 1 Chronicles as in Neh 9 the name change then is implicitly associated with the formation of Israel as a people. Ryle argues that "the change of name corresponds with the institution of the covenant sign of circumcision" and "was a pledge of new relation into which

---

[43] Joseph Blenkinsopp bases his conclusion on this fact and also contrasts the references to an oppressive foreign rule with the more benevolent and providential characterisations in the Ezra–Nehemiah material (*Ezra–Nehemiah: A Commentary* [London: SCM, 1988] 301). D. J. A. Clines similarly concludes the separate nature of the document and its later addition by an editor arguing that Neh 9 is unconnected to Ezra 9–10, since Ezra is not among the signatories in Neh 10 and the confession does not bear signs of Nehemiah's authorship (*Ezra, Nehemiah, Esther* [NCB; Grand Rapids MI: Eerdmans / London: Marshall, Morgan & Scott, 1984] 199–200).

[44] Where the Hebrew (MT) chapter/verse division differs from the English, I give the English numbers in square brackets throughout the book.

[45] Blenkinsopp similarly notes that only the Abrahamic covenant is mentioned in the prayer although he draws no further conclusions from this fact (*Ezra–Nehemiah*, 303).

Abraham and his seed passed."⁴⁶ A further echo of the promise of peoplehood given to Abraham is in Neh 9:23, where the prayer remembers God making Israel as "numerous as the stars of heaven" (cf. Gen 15:5; 22:17).

The land is even more prominent in Neh 9 with numerous references to its promise, possession and the exiles' degraded status on it (vv.8, 15, 22, 23, 24, 25, 35, 36). Interestingly, there is no explicit mention of the Exile except for the vague "you gave them into the hand of the peoples of the lands" (ותתנם ביד עמי הארצת—v.30) and absolutely none of the temporary loss of the land. The assessment that Israel did not serve God in the land (v.35) is followed by the admission that "we are slaves today" (אנחנו היום עבדים—v.36) and repeated at the end of the verse in connection with the land ("we are slaves on it" אנחנו עבדים עליה). Israel's degradation is well reflected above and is echoed in Ezra's confession in Ezra 9:9 in the same statement that "we are slaves" (עבדים אנחנו). In Ezra's prayer, obedience is connected to keeping the land and being able to pass it on as an inheritance for the next generations and by implication disobedience threatens with the potential loss of land (Ezra 9:12).

The Abrahamic covenant's connection with God's promise of the land is well-established in Scripture (Exod 6:4; Lev 26:42; Ps 105:9, cf. v.11) although the word ברית is sometimes replaced by the mention of the oath sworn to the patriarchs to give them the land (הארץ אשר נשבע יהוה לאבתיכם—Deut 1:8, similarly Deut 6:10; 9:5–6; 30:20; 34:4, etc.). Therefore when God remembers or is reminded by his people of the patriarchs, it is an appeal to his gracious character and his faithful commitment to Israel to give her the land (Exod 32:13; Lev 26:42).

When, on the other hand, the Mosaic covenant is referred to it is in the context of expected or failed obedience to the commandments (Exod 19:5; 34:28; Deut 4:13, 23; 17:2; 29:9; 31:16, Pss 25:10; 78:10, etc.). Covenant and commandment are so closely identified in Sinai that when Solomon mentions the place prepared for the ark, he calls the two tablets with the Ten Commandments "the covenant of YHWH" (ואשם שם מקום לארון אשר־שם ברית יהוה—1 Kgs 8:21, cf. Deut 4:13) meaning, of course, the two tablets with the Ten Commandments (hence also the name "the ark of the covenant" ארון ברית־יהוה).

We shall see that the renewed acknowledgement of the exiles is the fact that Israel has disobeyed God again and again, yet it is conspicuous that the Sinai covenant is not mentioned, not even sideways by saying that Israel broke the covenant by not keeping the law. In fact, the idea of breaking the covenant is studiously avoided even though that and its variants are a standard way in the prophetic literature and in the Psalms to express disobedience to the law.⁴⁷

---

⁴⁶ H. E. Ryle, *The Books of Ezra and Nehemiah with Introduction, Notes and Maps* (Cambridge: Cambridge University Press, 1897) 254.

⁴⁷ E.g., Israel did not keep the covenant (שמר—Ps 78:10), she broke the covenant (חפר—Isa 24:5; 33:8; Ezek 16:50, 17:19), forsook the covenant (עזב—Jer 22:9), transgressed the

Although the events at Sinai are evoked, again the covenant is not mentioned, only God's gifts are listed, among them, the Torah. Covenant then in Neh 9 only occurs in connection with YHWH's commitment, not Israel's. This is surely significant and perhaps points to an understanding of the situation, which sees hope for restoration based on God's gracious character and covenant-keeping. Despite Israel's rebellion and arrogance and the present state of affairs ("we are slaves"—v.36) there is no doubt about the enduring nature of the covenant because it is based on God's promise to Abraham for land and peoplehood.

This may also explain why the exiles' agreement is not called a covenant, but an אמנה (9:38[10:1]), since it is a rededication rather than a new commitment.[48] Moreover, the term אמנה echoes the basis of the Abrahamic covenant as this group envisages it ("you found his heart faithful before you" מצאת את־לבבו נאמן לפניך—v.8). The word נאמן alludes to Abraham's faith in believing God's promise in Gen 15:6, but it also plays on the idea of faithfulness and loyalty he exhibited in his obedience to leave his own land and kin behind (Gen 12:1–3), and in his willingness to sacrifice to God what was most precious to him (Gen 22:1–19). BDB observes that the term is associated with righteous attitude (צדק) in human character (Prov 12:17; 1 Sam 26:23; Isa 59:4; Jer 5:1) and with divine mercy/grace (חסד) in God (Pss 89:25[24]; 92:3[2]; 98:3; Hos 2:21–22[19–20]).[49] For the exiles then the word they use for their own commitment may have the same twofold connotation of faith in the mercy of this covenant-keeping God and faithfulness to his commands.

At the same time, the idea of repercussions for disobedience to the law and thereby the covenant is present in the text in a series of divine "reversals" which echo Deuteronomy.[50] Israel entered the land and YHWH gave the Canaanites into their hands (ותתנם בידם—Neh 9:24), but after their continued disobedience they in turn were given into the hands of their enemies (vv.27, 28, 30). They could do to the Canaanites as they pleased (לעשות בהם כרצונם—v.24), but in the end foreign kings ruled over their bodies and their cattle as they pleased (ועל גויתינו משלים ובבהמתנו כרצנם—v.37). They did not serve God (לא עבדוך—v.35), so they became the servants (אנחנו היום עבדים—v.36, cf. Deut 28:47–48) of foreign kings who ate the produce of the land (v.37 cf. Deut 28:33). Their actions in effect call down on them the covenant curses in Deuteronomy. This kind of thinking is further reflected in Neh 10:30[29] where the exiles enter into a curse and an oath to walk in God's law (ובאים באלה ובשבועה ללכת בתורת האלהים), an expression similar to the one in Deut

---

covenant (עבר—Hos 6:7), profaned/violated the covenant (חלל—Ps 55:21[20]), was not faithful to the covenant (אמן—Ps 78:37), etc.

[48] Blenkinsopp suggests that אמונה may be used here to distinguish it from historical covenants where YHWH was directly involved (*Ezra-Nehemiah*, 312).

[49] BDB, 530 אמונה §3.a–b.

[50] The prayer is full of scriptural resonances although deuteronomic thought permeates it more than anything else. For a detailed list of allusions of biblical passages see J. M. Myers, *Ezra, Nehemiah*, (AB 14; New York: Doubleday, 1965) 167–69.

29:11[12], where Israel is gathered at Moab in order to cross over into God's covenant and oath/curse (לעברך בברית יהוה אלהיך ובאלתו).

Nevertheless, even in the description of judgment for disobedience, Israel is a people with a difference. When Pharaoh and his people acted arrogantly against Israel (הזידו עליהם—Neh 9:10) God destroyed them (v.11), whereas when Israel acted arrogantly (ואבתינו הזידו—v.16) against God, he did not abandon them (ולא עזבתם—v.17), nor did he make a complete end of them (לא־עשיתם כלה—v.31).

While the covenant with Abraham is more emphatically associated with God's commitment to make him a people and give him the land, the covenant with Israel stresses the requirement for her commitment to YHWH's covenant stipulations, the Torah. Both covenants, however, have their complementary sides even if the overall stress is on God's commitment in the first and Israel's response in the second. Thus Abraham is called to be blameless (תמים—Gen 17:1) and to keep the covenant expressed in circumcision (Gen 17:9–14) and Israel is promised to be God's "treasured possession" (סגלה), "a kingdom of priests and a holy nation" (ממלכת כהנים וגוי קדוש—Exod 19:5–6) and is restored after the golden calf incident as a result of YHWH's gracious and compassionate character (Exod 34:6, cf. Neh 9:17). In the prayer of confession the two covenants are merged into one in a synthetic way so that Sinai theology is fused with the Abrahamic context and God's commitment outweighs Israel's continued disobedience.

Clines argues that the emphasis on YHWH's covenant-keeping character is an indication that Israel has broken the covenant and can have no claims upon it; she can only appeal to God's uncovenanted mercy.[51] In the light of the above discussion this is hard to believe. The implications of covenant are evident in both their positive and negative effects and thereby show that both God's commitment to Israel and Israel's expected commitment to God are at play in the unfolding story. YHWH's mercy is not given beyond the covenant but in it because of the promise made to Abraham, and Israel is disciplined for her rebellion to God and his Torah again under the covenant.

One further point may be noted, namely that the Davidic covenant is not mentioned at all.[52] This may seem surprising at first glance when the exiles felt themselves to be slaves and the hope of Davidic restoration might have been a comfort and encouragement. At the same time, it is in line with EN's overall tenor, which downplays the role of the Davidic descendant Zerubbabel (see more on this in §4.1.5) and as often noted by commentators, generally seems to have a more positive attitude toward the Persian monarchs.[53] There is evidence

---

[51] Clines, *Ezra, Nehemiah*, 198.

[52] F. C. Fensham, *The Books of Ezra and Nehemiah* (Grand Rapids MI: Eerdmans, 1982) 230.

[53] E.g., Williamson, *Ezra, Nehemiah*, l–li; F. C. Holmgren, *Israel Alive Again: A Commentary on the Books of Ezra and Nehemiah*, (ITC; Grand Rapids, MI: Eerdmans,

in the book that Judah was seen in some quarters as a rebellious province (Ezra 4:15, 19) and the quietist attitude may be an attempt to avoid political conflict or be the result of disillusionment with Davidic hopes. Alternatively, the omission may simply be due to the conviction that restoration was going to come through obedience to Torah rather than political upheaval and a fight for freedom.

3.1.2 The Place of the Law

Given the above way that covenant is portrayed, what place does Torah have in Neh 9? Its first occurrence (vv.13–14) is sandwiched between the pillar of cloud and of fire (v.12) on the one hand, and the bread from heaven and the water from the rock on the other (v.15). The chronological order in which the exodus narrative presents these is disrupted by the insertion of the Law between these two events highlighting thereby its gift nature.[54] Its position is all the more conspicuous because whenever the wilderness experience is reflected on and God's provision is mentioned, the texts refer to the pillars of cloud and fire as guidance (Deut 1:33), the provision of bread and water (Deut 8:3), or both (Pss 78:14–16, 24; 105:39–45), but not to Torah. Yet in the wider canonical context of the OT the concept of Torah connects to guidance on the one hand, it is a light unto Israel's feet (Ps 119:105) teaching Israel in the way that she should go (Ps 32:8). On the other hand, it is also linked to the idea of supernatural bread, a reminder to Israel that "man does not live by bread alone but by every word proceeding from the mouth of the Lord" (Deut 8:3).

The element of instruction is even more prominent in v.20, which follows on the repetition of God's gift of guidance (the pillars of cloud and fire—v.19) and precedes the provision of bread and water (v.20). The verse does not mention Torah but God's Spirit instructing the people (ורוחך הטובה נתת להשכילם). Clines argues that this change in the wording is due to the fact that the law-giving could not be repeated,[55] but this may not adequately explain the modification. After all, it would have been possible to say that the pillar of cloud did not leave and they continued to have God's law to teach them. Rather the replacement of Law with Spirit expresses the close association of YHWH and his Law in the thinking of Neh 9. Thus disobedience to the Law is rebellion against God and grieves his Spirit (Ps 106:33; Isa 63:10). The Spirit's instruction evokes the event of God's Spirit given to the 70 elders in the wilderness in order to help them judge Israel and lighten Moses' load (Num 11:17). The need for the

---

1987) 5; Sara Japhet, "Sheshbazzar and Zerubbabel. Against the Background of the Historical and Religious Tendencies of Ezra–Nehemiah," *ZAW* 94 (1982) 72–74.

[54] Clines, *Ezra, Nehemiah*, 194. Allen similarly observes the out of sequence order and sees in this an effort to give prominence to Torah in the prayer. Leslie C. Allen and Timothy S. Laniak, *Ezra, Nehemiah, Esther*, (NIBCOT 9; Peabody MA: Hendrickson, 2003) 136. Williamson also notes that the author abandons a strict chronological order in vv.12–21 although he concludes from this more generally that the aim is to highlight God's overall graciousness (*Ezra, Nehemiah*, 313–14).

[55] Clines, *Ezra, Nehemiah*, 195.

interpretation of Torah and its proper application in specific situations is implicit in the Spirit's instruction in v.20 and in the admonishment of the Spirit through the prophets in v.30. The concept expresses the dynamic aspect of the law, the importance of having to understand it rightly. This would certainly have resonances for the exiles, who were grappling with questions of how to live in obedience to Torah in a postexilic setting which differed in many ways from Israel's life before the exile.

The interplay of guidance and presence is evident in the combination of Law and Spirit and it parallels the association of the same double feature in the pillar of cloud and fire. While these two elements lead Israel (Exod 13:21–22) they are also an expression of God's presence with his people. One might only need to think of the thick cloud and lightning flashes at the Sinai theophany (19:16) or the cloud of glory in the tabernacle (Exod 40:34) and later the temple (1 Kgs 8:10–12). Similarly, God's Law and his Spirit speak not only of God's guidance but also of his presence with his people.

Another feature that stands out is the repeated emphasis on the laws and commandments being just (ישרים), true (אמת), and good (טובים) in v.13 and the adjective "good" (הטוב) describing the Spirit in v.20. Why this unusually strong emphasis on the positive nature of the Law and God's Spirit? It may well be that the point of this is to stress God's goodness and graciousness in contrast to Israel's ongoing disobedience which is the major theme of the prayer as commentators invariably point out.[56] Is it not self-evident that the laws are good, true and just? Malachi's portrayal of the people feeling burdened by the law (Mal 1:13) springs to mind as the possible background for the need of such emphasis, or Haggai's rebuke that the people are building their own houses instead of YHWH's and excuse themselves by saying that the time has not come for temple building (Hag 1:2). There are also instances in the book of Nehemiah that the response to the law was not always as wholehearted and committed as one might have hoped. Thus the neglect of paying tithes, the selling and buying on the Sabbath, as well as intermarriage with foreigners in Neh 13 may indicate a similar attitude to the ones described above in the prophetic books.

Referring to my earlier discussion under the Jewish responses (§2.2), the emphasis on the true and just nature of the Law may indicate a recognition of the need to acknowledge the inherent goodness and rightness of the commandments in order to obey them wholeheartedly. It is interesting that along with this emphasis there is also a characterization of God as Creator at the beginning of the prayer (v.6). As Clines observes, "Reference to the creation in such summary histories of Israel is unique."[57] The verse does not speak of the design in creation and thus it does not connect the thought directly to the idea of God's good laws built into the fabric of the world. Rather it seems to be an exaltation of God above all on earth and in heaven and a statement of his power

---

[56] Fensham, *The Books of Ezra and Nehemiah*, 230; Williamson, *Ezra, Nehemiah*, 314; Allen, *Ezra, Nehemiah*, 132–33.
[57] Clines, *Ezra, Nehemiah*, 193.

and supremacy. Schneider speculates that it may imply the idea that God had already created the things which he intended to give to Israel, or perhaps it is an expression of his faithfulness, as Clines concludes.[58] Nevertheless, this broadening of vision beyond the narrow focus of Israel and its ongoing history of salvation and deliverance may have implications beyond the obvious main function that it has in the passage.

There is yet another aspect that is significant, namely the specific reference to the Sabbath apart from the other commandments. Clearly this is a crucial point in the exiles' thinking and it is one of the three areas of commitment listed in Neh 10 which the signatories pledge themselves to observe (v.31[30]) and which some later break (Neh 13:15–18).

Overall, we see then that the portrayal of the Law in Neh 9 fits in with what we have seen in the presentation of the covenant. It is a good gift rather than a burdensome obligation and it is closely linked with God's Spirit, an expression of his presence and guidance to instruct Israel in the way that she should go.

3.1.3 Sins of the Past

The list of sins that Israel has committed is a long and repetitive one. Only two refer to specific events: the first mentions the decision to return to Egypt after the spies' report (v.17, cf. Num 14:4), the second the golden calf incident (v.18, cf. Exod 32). Again, the events are out of chronological sequence. The key moment is the first; all the general complaints in v.16 that the people became arrogant (הזידו), stiffened their neck (ויקשו את־ערפם), did not listen to the commandments (ולא שמעו אל־מצותיך) lead up to the reluctance to enter and possess the land. It is significant that this moment is chosen from a long list of episodes, which could have been mentioned and underlines the primary concern of the passage for the possession of the land (cf. also Deut 1, which opens with the account of this same rebellion).

The golden calf and the act of apostasy and idolatry are only highlighted to show that God was nevertheless compassionate to his people. The text, as observed earlier, is silent on the violation of the covenant (§3.1.1) and its graphic demonstration in the breaking of the two stone tablets.

The rest of the list condemning Israel's sins reflects a general attitude of stubbornness and hard-heartedness, the unwillingness to listen to God's commandments (vv.16, 17, 29, 30, 34) and the merciless silencing of his prophets (v.26). The "stubborn shoulder" and "stiffened neck" (ויתנו כתף סוררת וערפם הקשו—v.29) evokes the picture of an "ox who resists the guidance of a yoke,"[59] an apt image, we might say, of Israel's refusal to take on the yoke of Torah. It is this general attitude to the Law and the commandments which is

---

[58] Heinrich Schneider, *Die Bücher Esra und Nehemia* (Bonn: Peter Hanstein, 1959) 214; Clines, *Ezra, Nehemiah*, 193.
[59] Clines, *Ezra, Nehemiah*, 195.

deplored above all else. The ultimate verdict of the prayer is that Israel did not serve God; thereby it identifies the service of God with obedience to Torah. As Williamson puts it, Torah "can stand virtually alongside God himself: to reject the one is to reject the other (vv.26a, 29), while to return to the one is to return to the other (vv.26b with 29a)."[60]

Verses 26–35 relate the cycle of sin, oppression by enemies, cry for help, God's gracious intervention and another cycle of rebellion once rescue came reminding the reader of the cycle well known from the book of Judges.[61] The overall impression one gets is Israel's utter depravity and YHWH's surpassing mercy leading back to the earlier conclusion about the emphasis being on God's covenant commitment.

What is conspicuous throughout the confession is the utterly vague nature of Israel's sin. Apart from the initial reluctance to enter the land and the sideways mention of the golden calf incident, the text does not give any clues as to *how* Israel broke the commandments. As noted earlier, it is not connected at all with the specific commitment the exiles make in Neh 10: there is no mention of Israel breaking the Sabbath, of intermarriage or issues of temple worship. This may be due to the fact that the confession is "imported" into the book and was originally a separate document; nevertheless, the omission of specific sins is peculiar. What is clear overall, however, is that sin is understood here in terms of disobedience to Torah.

3.1.4 Renewal

How then do the exiles in EN envisage renewal? Their answer is well reflected in their actions: they make an agreement to obey Torah from now on. Both the instruction of God's Spirit in 9:20 and the events around the reading of the Law in Neh 8 suggest an emphasis on the understanding and interpretation of the laws as key to obeying them. We see this in the example of the proper celebration of Tabernacles according to the Law, which is the outcome of Torah study (Neh 8:13–18). Further, what is significant for the exiles from the Torah is evident from the content of their commitment: no intermarriage (Neh 10:30[29]), keeping Sabbath (v.31[30]) and provision for the temple service in the form of contributions and tithes (vv.32–39[31–38]). The negative examples of various sins in the book indicate where the exiles' interest and emphases lie: foreigners' presence in the temple (13:1–3, 4–9), the neglect of paying tithes (13:10–14), the breaking of the Sabbath by selling and buying (13:15–18) and mixed marriages (13:23–29). The picture that emerges from both the negative

---

[60] Williamson, *Ezra, Nehemiah*, 316.
[61] The similarity of these cycles to those in the book of Judges is frequently noted by commentators. E.g., Willimson, *Ezra, Nehemiah*, 315; Blenkinsopp, *Ezra-Nehemiah*, 306; Allen, *Ezra, Nehemiah*, 133; R. J. Coggins, *The Books of Ezra and Nehemiah* (Cambridge: Cambridge University Press, 1976) 118; Peter R. Ackroyd, *I & II Chronicles, Ezra, Nehemiah: Introduction and Commentary* (London: SCM, 1973) 302.

and the positive examples is a particular focus on issues that are primarily not ethical.[62]

The common thread in the three main areas of concern as expressed in Neh 10 is the desire to be distinctive as God's people. The Sabbath is a characteristic feature of Israelite religion and the ban on intermarriage is similarly aimed at keeping Israel separate and thereby distinct. Again, questions relating to temple worship are also expressions of Israel's distinctive faith and practice. In anthropological terms all of the above fit into the category of establishing strong boundaries for a group whose identity is in jeopardy or which feels that it is. The above attempts of the exiles to keep distinct and separate becomes a standard feature of the Postexilic Period, but it is noticeable that the food laws do not play any part in EN, although they later become the demonstration *par excellence* for a boundary marker between "them" and "us."

3.2   Immediate Context: Ezra 7–8

Although commentators often raise the question where the episode of the mixed marriage crisis fits best, the answer given usually only involves historical-critical considerations. It is generally assumed that the events in Ezra 9–10 better fit after the reading of Torah in Neh 8 than in its present context,[63] yet the issue *why* the narrator/editor thought it appropriate to include the incident here is not raised. Ezra 9–10 is thus "left without adequate introduction and the motivation for the leaders' confession remains unexplained."[64] A closer inspection of the present narrative context, however, may shed light on the meaning of the episode and provide insight into the reason why it was placed here.

---

[62] The only exception is perhaps Neh 5 and the issue of debt slavery, which is an ethical question, yet it serves in the story more to underline the fact that Israel is called to be a free nation and not to be enslaved to either foreigners or their own kin.

[63] The separation from the "foreign" wives would seem logical as a response to the public reading and interpretation of the Law and would match the tone of mourning and confession in Neh 9. One of the perceived difficulties with the present location of the story is the time between Ezra's first arrival in the 5th month (Ezra 7:9) and the expulsion of the wives in the 9th (Ezra 10:9), which seems inordinately long to commentators (except for Yehezkel Kaufmann, *From the Babylonian Captivity to the End of Prophecy* [vol. 4 of *History of the Religion of Israel;* New York: Ktav Publishing House, 1977] 331) for the negotiations and meetings with various officials described in Ezra 8:36. The reading of the Law in the 7th month (Neh 7:73, 8:14) would partly bridge this gap (so, e.g., Rudolph, *Esra und Nehemiah*, 85; Blenkinsopp, *Ezra-Nehemiah*, 174, etc.). Despite the logic in this argument, if Neh 8 is moved back to Ezra's first arrival in Jerusalem, then Nehemiah's presence as governor is incongruous. If Ezra 9–10 is moved up to Nehemiah's time after the reading of Torah in Neh 8 then what was Ezra doing regarding the Law up until then? Either way, the text is problematic for a historical reconstruction of the events.

[64] Williamson, *Ezra, Nehemiah*, 128.

3.2.1 Ezra 7: The Importance of Torah

The Ezra narrative in chapter 7 opens with the mission of Ezra (v.10) to "study" (Qal לדרוש), "practice" (Qal לעשת) and "teach" Torah (Piel ללמד). Although לעשת literally means "to do" it is also possible to see in this an activity of legal composition or compilation, as indeed Jewish tradition takes the figure of Ezra to be the compiler of Torah. Fishbane justifies this based on לעשת describing scribal activity in Eccl 12:12 and on comparable formulae in Assyrian and Babylonian references.[65] Ezra is commissioned by the king to inquire into the situation in Judah and Jerusalem "according to the law of your God" (בדת אלהך—Ezra 7:14). He is to ensure the smooth operation of the temple service with regular sacrifices offered as commanded by God (Ezra 7:15–23), and to appoint magistrates and judges (Ezra 7:25, cf. 8:36) who know the law and can presumably apply it in making legal-juridical decisions. The effect of all this is the sense that Israel's law and worship is recognized and legitimated in the province.

In this setting of the scene which emphasizes the importance of Torah, there are also resonances of Deut 4:5–8, where the nations come to recognize the wisdom and understanding of Israel as the people whose statutes and judgments are righteous (חקים ומשפטים צדיקים—v.8) and whose God is near to them when they call. A similar theme is evident in the Isaianic vision of future restoration and God's universal reign, when the nations will worship in Jerusalem and "the law will go forth from Zion" (מציון תצא תורה—Isa 2:3; cf. Mic 4:2; Isa 51:4). Perhaps the Persian king's edict in Ezra 7 is presented as a partial fulfillment of these twin themes; the recognition of the true God by the nations and justice administered through God's law. It also ties in with assertions of God's kingship and dominion over all (cf. Dan 4:3, 34; 6:26) and the title typically used to describe him as "the God of heaven" (אלהי השמים—Ezra 1:2; Neh 1:4, 5; 2:4, 20; אלה שמיא—Ezra 5:11, 12; Dan 2:37, 44). As in Neh 9:6 where God is praised as the Creator, here again we see a broader vision that encompasses the nations and the created world.

3.2.2 Ezra 8 & 9: The Priests and the People

It follows from the above that if the nations are in the picture, then the question of how Israel is to live in relation to them develops into a prime concern. It is here that the language of holiness grows in prominence. Israel needs to be a people set apart for God, worshiping only YHWH and faithfully following his commandments (Deut 26:19; 28:9). Implicit in this setting apart as God's consecrated people are both a "coming out" from among the nations and an "entering" into the land God gives, where Israel is to live according to YHWH's laws and not follow the unclean practices of those living there.

---

[65] Michael Fishbane, *Biblical Interpretation in Ancient Israel* (Oxford: Clarendon, 1985) 30–31, 36.

Following this pattern, Ezra 8 opens with a repetition of the "exodus" motif in Ezra 1. Unlike the return under Sheshbazzar in Ezra 1, however, the expedition is led by a priest who can trace his genealogy back to Aaron (Ezra 7:1–5, cf. 1:8) and the temple vessels are equally carried by priests who are set apart/separated (Hiphil בדל) for this purpose. בדל is a key term in the priestly understanding most often denoting the separation of the holy and the profane, the clean and the unclean (Lev 10:10; 11:47; 20:24–26), thereby highlighting the aspect of consecration. In line with this interpretation Ezra in his commission describes both the priests and the vessels as holy (אתם קדש ליהוה והכלים קדש—Ezra 8:28). The whole procedure is reminiscent of Isa 52:11–12, verses which call the exiles to depart, touch nothing unclean, carry the vessels of YHWH in a purified state and which assure them of God's protection (cf. Ezra 8:31).

The opening sentence of Ezra 9 connects the chapter with Ezra 8 ("when these things had been completed" וככלות אלה—v.1) and so do the repetition of the word בדל (this time in the reflexive Niphal) and the concern for holiness (זרע הקדש—v.2). Thus the two incidents are put side-by-side and contrasted. Not merely the priests need to be set apart for their holy task, but the people of Israel as a whole. The return to the land is essential, but so is the requirement to be God's holy people. How this is to be understood is spelt out in more detail in the incident that follows in Ezra 9–10.

3.3   Ezra 9:1–2: The Crisis

Ezra 9 opens with the princes' complaint that the people, the priests and the Levites have not separated themselves from the "peoples of the lands" (עמי הארצות—v.1). Although "separation from the uncleanness of the people of the land" (וכל הנבדל מטמאת גוי־הארץ) is mentioned earlier in connection with the exiles' celebration of the Passover (Ezra 6:21), what this separation entailed is not explained there. In Ezra 9:2 the crisis is the result of intermarriage.[66] It is not clear who these women were apart from the designation that they belonged to the "peoples of the lands" (9:1) or the "peoples of the land" (עמי־הארץ—10:2) and characterized by "abominations" (תועבות) associated with a list of nations (9:1, 14) as well as the further description that they were "foreign women" (נשים נכריות— 10:2).

The exilic leadership reasons against intermarriage on two grounds. Ezra 9:1 enumerates eight groups associated with abominations. Depending on the reading of the last name (Amorite or Edomite), the list includes four or five Canaanite nations that appear to be taken from the intermarriage ban in Deut 7:1–3 or Exod 34:11–16 and three or four other nations who appear in Deut 23:4–9[3–8] in the command forbidding the descendants of these to enter the

---

[66] The word used here for marrying (נשא—v.2) and repeatedly elsewhere in EN (Ezra 9:12; 10:44; Neh 13:25) is late in origin cf. 2 Chr 11:21; 13:21; 24:3, Ruth 1:4. BDB, 671, נשא §3.d

"assembly of YHWH" (קהל יהוה) to a prescribed number of generations. Ezra's prayer (esp. v.12) links the exiles' problem further with Deut 7:1–3 and Deut 23:4–9[3–8]. Although the wording for the intermarriage ban with the Canaanites is not identical in Ezra 9:12 and Deut 7:3, the two are closer than Ezra 9:12 and Exod 34:16 as the table below shows. Both Ezra 9:12 and Deut 7:3 ban the intermarriage of Israelites with foreign men and women and use the verb נתן (give) in the first instance. The difference is that Ezra uses נשא (take, marry) as the second verb, has plurals throughout, as well as negates with אל while Deuteronomy employs לקח (take), singulars and לא respectively.

ועתה בנותיכם אל־תתנו לבניהם ובנתיהם אל־תשאו לבניכם	Ezra 9:12a–b	So now do not **give** your **daughters** to their **sons** nor take their **daughters** as wives **for** your **sons**
בתך לא־תתן לבנו ובתו לא־תקח לבנך	Deut 7:3b–c	You shall not **give** your **daughter** to his **son**, nor shall you take his **daughter for** your **son**.
ולקחת מבנתיו לבניך	Exod 34:16a	Lest you take some of his daughters for your sons

On the other hand, the admonition not to seek their peace and prosperity in Deut 23:7[6], originally referring to the Ammonites and Moabites, is quoted almost *verbatim* and is applied to the Canaanite nations (see table below).

ולא־תדרשו שלמם וטובתם עד־עולם	Ezra 9:12c	and never seek their peace or their prosperity forever
לא־תדרש שלמם וטבתם כל־ימיך לעולם	Deut 23:7[6]	never seek their peace or their prosperity all your days

The second reason for the ban on intermarriages is given in Ezra 9:2 that "the holy seed has intermingled with the peoples of the lands" (והתערבו זרע הקדש בעמי הארצות). The expression זרע הקדש is almost unique in the OT and it is not entirely clear where the legal justification for such an explanation comes from. Neither is it spelt out who "the seed" is (the Israelite spouses, their offspring or both), and what happens to it. Is it defiled or profaned and if either, what is the exact content of such defilement/profanation? Finally, how do the two justifications (the deuteronomic intermarriage ban and the "holy seed" rationale) relate to each other?

3.4 Conclusion

We have seen that the wider context of Neh 9 shows the exiles' main emphasis on the importance of the Law within the context of an ongoing relationship with God that started with the promise given to Abraham about land and peoplehood. I have observed that the prayer is a remarkable blend of Sinai language and Abrahamic covenant and its primary concern is with the land. The Law given at Sinai is seen as an expression of God's gracious gift that is associated variously with guidance, provision, God's Spirit and his presence. The Spirit's instruction may suggest a dynamic aspect to the Law that requires engagement and understanding along the lines considered under "Jewish Responses" (§2.2.2). The emphasis that the laws and commandments are good perhaps reflects an implicit recognition of the fact that wholehearted obedience requires an acknowledgement of the inherent rightness of God's law, which may be connected to ideas of God's design and "law" built into creation (see discussion in §§2.2.1 and 2.2.2). I have also observed that Israel's past sins are seen in terms of her disobedience to Torah and restoration requires a re-commitment to the Law especially exemplified in banning intermarriage, keeping the Sabbath and providing for the ongoing worship in the temple through tithes and other contributions.

The chapters immediately preceding Ezra 9–10 further reinforced and refined this picture by showing how the Persian king's authorization of Ezra's mission to bring and teach Torah in the Trans-Euphrates legitimated Israel's Law and perhaps expressed the future hope of God's universal rule over all nations with his "Law going forth from Zion" (Isa 2:3). Further, the parallels of language and concepts in Ezra 8 and 9 suggested that as the priests separated themselves to carry back the holy vessels to Jerusalem, so the whole people needed to separate from foreign elements in order to be holy.

Finally, I have set out the various questions that need to be answered relating to Ezra 9–10. The exegesis below will explore the background and understanding of the two explanations of why intermarriage was wrong and how they relate to each other. First I shall consider the questions surrounding the laws of Deut 7:1–3 and Deut 23:4–9[3–8] focusing in Chapter 4 on questions relating to the list of nations in Ezra 9:1 and in Chapter 5 on the understanding of the *ḥērem* law of which Deut 7:3 is a part. This will then be followed in Chapters 6 and 7 by a discussion on the "holy seed," its origins in biblical law and the meaning of impurity and profanation in Ezra 9–10.

4

The Abominations of the Nations

As mentioned above, the leaders justify the need for separation in the first instance by using Deut 7:1–3 and Deut 23:4–9[3–8] and it is parts of these two laws that Ezra quotes in his confessional prayer (Ezra 9:12, cf. Deut 7:3; 23:7[6]).

In Deut 7 the rationale for the prohibition of intermarriage with the seven nations in Canaan is the temptation to apostasy/idolatry and the consequence of disobedience is quick destruction (והשמידך מהר—v.4). Israel thus incurs on herself the fate assigned to the "idolatrous seven." In Deut 23 the reason for the exclusion of the Ammonites and Moabites from the assembly of YHWH (קהל יהוה) is their historic obstruction of Israel's way into the Promised Land expressed in the lack of hospitality and in their scheming to have the one cursed whom God has blessed (v.4[3]). The outcome is that Israelites who ally themselves in marriage with those who wished ill on Israel forfeit their right to see their descendants within the assembly of YHWH.

In Ezra 9:1 the prohibition of intermarriage is justified by the association of "abominations" (תועבות) with the nations listed. In Deut 7:25–26 the word is used for idols and to a large extent in the OT "abominations" is connected to apostasy and idolatry (e.g., Deut 7:25–26; 13:15[14]; 17:3–4; 2 Kgs 21:2; 23:13; Isa 41:24; Jer 44:4, Ezek 5:9, etc.). It can also refer to related sins such as child sacrifice (e.g., Deut 12:31; 18:9–10; 2 Kgs 16:3; Jer 32:35) and cultic prostitution (1 Kgs 14:24).

However, it may describe other sins not necessarily connected with idolatry, such as sexual sins (male same-sex intercourse—Lev 18:22, incest and adultery—Ezek 22:11), unethical behavior like having unjust weights (Deut 25:16; Prov 11:1), being greedy for gain (Jer 6:13–15), stealing, murder, swearing falsely (Jer 7:9–10), oppression of the poor and needy (Ezek 16:47), and money loaned on interest (Ezek 18:3). The word may denote eating unclean food (Deut 14:3) or meat with the blood (Ezek 33:26), as well as not keeping the

Sabbath (Ezek 20:4), bringing uncircumcised foreigners into the sanctuary (Ezek 44:6–8) or sacrifices offered by the wicked (Isa 1:13).

The above list makes it clear that idolatry/apostasy is not the sole referent of תועבה not even in Deuteronomy, but that it "refers to something in the human realm that is ethically abhorrent, either as an idea or as an action; above all it is irreconcilable with Yahweh, contrary to his character and his will as an expression of that character, an ethical and cultic taboo."[67]

In order to explore the reason behind the ban on intermarriage and what "abominations" might signify for the exiles I shall examine the list of nations to see what they might have in common and why these nations are included and not others.

4.1 The List of Nations in Ezra 9:1

When compared with the nations mentioned in Deut 7:1 and Deut 23:4[3], 8[7] the list in Ezra 9:1 raises several questions. Deut 7 only forbids intermarriage with the seven nations living in Canaan, in fact, the command is to destroy them (see §5.1.1). This is presumably because the people most likely to influence Israel adversely are those living in closest proximity to her. That this is the implicit logic of the ban in Deut 7 is shown in the laws of warfare in Deut 20:10–18 and the law of the captive woman in Deut 21:10–14. The former commands the utter destruction (החרם תחרימם—v.17) of the seven Canaanite nations but only requires the killing of the men in the cities very far from you (הערים הרחקת ממך מאד—v.15), while the women and children are spared (v.14). The law of the captive woman who is spared does not specify where she is from and the reason for permitting her to become an Israelite's wife is not spelt out but again it is likely that without an extended family she poses less of a threat for Israel's commitment to YHWH.

Deut 23:4–9[3–8] adds four other nations to the list who are not to be exterminated but whose descendants are nevertheless excluded from Israel, which implies a mixed marriage scenario. The Ammonites and Moabites are excluded for ten generations, which seems to be a synonym for "forever" (גם דור עשירי לא־יבא להם בקהל יהוה עד־עולם—v.4[3], cf. also v.7[6] לעולם), while the descendants of Egyptians and Edomites are allowed in after three generations.[68] The reason for the severity or relative permissiveness of the command is justified by particular actions or relationship with these nations.

The combined list of Ezra 9:1 looks like this.

---

[67] Horst D. Preuss, "תועבה," *TDOT* 15: 602.

[68] Jeffrey H. Tigay notes that the idiom "ten times" means "countless times" in the Bible (e.g., Gen 31:7; Num 14:22; Job 19:3; Neh 4:6[12]) and that on the same analogy "for ten generations" is to be understood as "forever" (*Deuteronomy* [JPS Torah Commentary; Philadelphia PA: JPS, 1996]) 211.

לכנעני החתי הפרזי היבוסי העמני המאבי המצרי והאמרי \ והאדמי	Ezra 9:1	Canaanites, Hittites, Perizzites, Jebusites, Ammonites, Moabites, Egyptians, Amorites (MT) / Edomites (1 Esd)
החתי והגרגשי והאמרי והכנעני והפרזי והחוי והיבוסי	Deut 7:1	Hittites, Girgashites, Amorites Canaanites, Perizzites, Hivites, Jebusites
עמוני ומואבי אדמי מצרי	Deut 23:4, 8 [3, 7]	Ammonite, Moabite Edomite, Egyptian

4.1.1 The Seven Nations of Canaan

Of the seven Canaanite nations Ezra 9:1 lists only five (if we take the MT's reading of the last to be the Amorites—האמרי). This is not particularly remarkable, since lists of them elsewhere tend to drop one or two names, most often the Girgashites and sometimes the Perizzites and the Hivites. The sequence of the names also tends to vary.[69]

The reason for the inclusion of the Canaanite nations is obvious since they are the ones most closely associated with "abominations" (תועבות) both in the sense of idolatry and perverse sexual practices (cf. Lev 18). They are also the nations living in closest proximity to Israel, who therefore pose the greatest threat for Israel's allegiance to YHWH.

4.1.2 The Ammonites and Moabites

Although these two nations are mentioned together here, the Ammonites do not feature in the incident to which Deut 23:4[3] refers (Num 22). There is no record elsewhere in the Pentateuch that they opposed Israel,[70] though later they were among Israel's enemies (2Sam 11–12; 2Chr 20:1, 10, 22–23; 2 Kgs 24:2). Perhaps the fact that both Moab and Ammon descended from Lot and in later politics were often in allegiance with each other against Israel (2 Kgs 24:2), as well as their geographical proximity, have led to considering them together. The prohibition against the Ammonites was given particular poignancy by their opposition to the wall building in Nehemiah's time (Neh 2:19; 4:1–8[7–14]), as well as by the reprehensible actions of Tobiah the Ammonite (Neh 6:18; 13:4–5).

---

[69] For a helpful table of biblical texts where the nations of Canaan are listed see P. E. Satterthwaite and D. W. Baker, "Nations of Canaan," in *Dictionary of the Old Testament: Pentateuch* (ed. T. Desmond Alexander & David W. Baker; Downers Grove, IL: IVP, 2003) 598.

[70] Tigay theorises that there may have been a variant tradition about Israel's encounters with Ammon and Moab since Ammon is bypassed in Deut 2:37 and Moab did provide food for Israel in Deut 2:28–29 (*Deuteronomy*, 211).

McConville in particular observes that in the deuteronomic command "The inclusions and exclusions may relate to the Abrahamic formula by which nations are blessed or cursed according to their attitude to Abraham's descendants (Gen. 12:3)."[71] This is borne out by the further comment of the text about the intended curse of Balaam which is turned into a blessing for Israel while the fact that Moab and Ammon's welfare is not to be sought implies the return of the curse onto Moab (and Ammon).[72]

Although Deut 23:4–7[3–6] holds against Ammon and Moab their lack of hospitality to Israel on her way to the Promised Land, the aspect of sexual perversion is implicitly there in the context as well. The Ammonites and Moabites are the descendants of the incestuous relationship between Lot and his daughters (Gen 19:30–38) and the prohibition regarding Ammon and Moab follows closely on the heels of various bans including those who have been emasculated and others from illicit relationships.[73] It is generally assumed that the emasculation referred to here is associated with pagan cultic acts of that nature. It is also likely that those of illegitimate births denote the offspring of incest or adultery. This series of prohibitions for various groups to enter the assembly of YHWH is preceded directly by laws regulating instances of rape, adultery and incest in Deut 22:13–23:2[22:30].

It is also noteworthy that Deut 23:5[4] mentions Balaam. While the verse refers primarily to the hiring of Balaam and God's way of turning the intended curse into a blessing, at the same time, the verse also carries the association of Balaam's counsel to Balak, which led to Israel's sin at Baal Peor (Num 25, cf. Num 31:16). That Deut 23:5[4] alludes to the above incident is argued by Rashi. He notes the unusual wording in v.5, where the reason for the exclusion of Ammon and Moab is introduced with the phrase על דבר אשר (because), even though על אשר as "because" would suffice. Rashi therefore proposes that דבר refers to Balaam's counsel "because of the word" (בדבר בלעם—Num 31:16). The suggestion is that the same people who did not meet Israel's need had no qualms in enticing her into idolatry and immorality. Significantly, the transgression which the people are guilty of in the incident at Baal-Peor is the worship of other gods combined with flagrant sexual immorality.

Thus the inclusion of Ammon and Moab may reflect both their animosity to Israel's well-being as well as their possibly negative influence through idolatry and sexual malpractices associated with them.

---

[71] J. G. McConville, *Deuteronomy* (AOTC 5; Leicester: Apollos / Downers Grove IL: IVP, 2002) 348.
[72] McConville, *Deuteronomy*, 349.
[73] Michael Fishbane, *Biblical Interpretation in Ancient Israel* (Oxford: Clarendon, 1985) 119.

4.1.3 The Egyptians

The source for the inclusion of the Egyptians in the list is generally attributed to Deut 23:8–9[7–8] although it is at odds with the more lenient treatment they receive there. However, this may not be an issue if the intermarriages in Ezra have not gone beyond the third generation in which case the same exclusion applies as in the case of Ammon and Moab. The omission of Edom in the MT's version of Ezra 9:1, on the other hand, raises some more serious doubts whether Deut 23 is indeed the source here.

We have already seen that "abominations" in Ezra 9:1 carry associations of idolatry/apostasy, hostility and sexual immorality. How may these be reflected in the inclusion of Egypt? In general, Egypt is associated with the term "the house of slaves" (בית עבדים—e.g., Exod 20:2; Deut 5:6; 6:12), referring to its oppression of Israel. Outside the Pentateuch, the warnings against Egypt generally deplore political alliances (e.g., Isa 30:2–3; Hos 7:11) and the Deuteronomistic History of Kgs mentions Solomon's Egyptian wife in recounting the king's turning away from YHWH to idols (1 Kgs 11:1–13). While the Pentateuch is not explicit about the idolatry in Egypt, the Exilic-Postexilic Period shows a number of overt links between the two (Jer 24:8; 44:8; Ezek 16:26; 20:7–10; 23:19, 27). With the Exile the growing Jewish community in Egypt was exposed to the danger of idolatrous influences. Even if the threat was not necessarily outright apostasy, intermarriage and syncretism was clearly a reality as the archaeological findings in Elephantine demonstrate.[74]

While sexual immorality is not a sin that one would immediately associate with Egypt, Lev 18:3 is the one pentateuchal text that not only deplores Egyptian ways, but also equates them with the abhorrent practices "abominations" (תועבות—vv.26, 27, 29, 30) of the Canaanites (כמעשה [...] לא תעשו וחקתיהם לא תלכו).[75] Commentators generally associate the deeds referred to here with irregular sexual acts as described in the rest of the chapter.[76] Similarly, the rabbis thought that it was meant to make it clear that מעשה (deed, doing) in the first half of the sentence does not refer to such general acts of these nations as how they plant or build, but to the laws governing relationships, which Israel should not follow because they are abhorrent to YHWH. This

---

[74] See Bezalel Porten, *Archives from Elephantine: The Life of an Ancient Jewish Military Colony* (Berkeley: University of California Press, 1968) 248–252 for intermarriages, 151–186 (esp. 173–179) for syncretism.

[75] H. G. M. Williamson is the only one of whom I am aware who justifies the inclusion of Egypt with Lev 18:3, although he does not draw the overall conclusions regarding the whole list as I am doing below (*Ezra, Nehemiah* [WBC 16; Nashville TN: Nelson, 1985] 131).

[76] E.g., John E. Hartley, *Leviticus*, (WBC 4; Dallas TX: Word, 1992) 293; Jacob Milgrom, *Leviticus 17–22: A New Translation with Introduction and Commentary* (AB 3A; New York: Doubleday, 2000) 1520; Gordon Wenham, *The Book of Leviticus*, (NICOT; Grand Rapids MI: Eerdmans, 1979) 251–52; J. R. Porter, *Leviticus* (Cambridge: Cambridge University Press, 1976) 143.

means that among these people "A man would be married to a man, a woman to a woman, a man to mother and daughter, and a woman to two men (*Sifra Aḥare*, par. 8:8)."[77] Beyond the usual sexual sins Levine also argues that the unusual word חקת ("statutes") here may also have a connotation of idolatry and the worship of other deities (חקות הגוים "the statutes of the nations" 2 Kgs 17:8).[78] This point may connect with the one reference to a non-sexual sin in Lev 18, the mention of child sacrifice to Molech (v.21).

The association of Egypt with sexual immorality is not as unusual as it may seem at first glance when we consider that it had a well-known reputation for incest documented in history. The link between Lev 18 and Ezra 9 is further strengthened by Ezra's prayer (especially v.11), which shows some parallels with Lev 18:24–30.[79] Ezra speaks of the defilement (טמאה) of the land because of the abominations (תועבות) committed in it by the Canaanite nations and his prayer implies the fear that Israel may be dispossessed unless she is faithful to YHWH's Torah (Ezra 9:12). Lev 18:26–30 repeatedly describes the same scenario; the "defilement" of the land (טמאה), "abominations" committed (תועבות) and the consequence (the Land will spew out Israel as it did the Canaanites if she acts as they did). Further, another word Ezra uses for impurity (נדה) is the same one describing the sin of incest in Lev 20:21.

Approaching the question from a different direction it may be possible that Egypt is not meant literally, but figuratively in the same way that the Canaanite nations have a metaphorical connotation: they no longer mean the nations traditionally considered to have inhabited the Land, but the present occupants (i.e., "the people(s) of the land(s)"). By the same token, Egypt may not refer to the historic nation, (although of course it did not cease to exist), but to the country out of which Israel had come in this second exodus, that is, Babylon.[80] In fact, the polemic in Isaiah 40–55 may imply that the idolatrous practices encountered there by Israel have not left the exiles unaffected.

Since the exodus imagery is a repeated motif in the book (Ezra 1:6, 8:25, cf. Exod 3:21–22) this would make the parallel possible, although we have next to no evidence that the exiles had Babylonian wives. Rudolph thinks that judging from Ezra's extreme reaction to the intermarriages in Ezra 9, this was an unexpected shock and therefore not likely to have been an issue in Babylon.[81] He explains the absence of such a problem in exile by the fact that there were

---

[77] Milgrom, *Leviticus 17–22*, 1520.

[78] Baruch A. Levine, *Leviticus*, (JPS Torah Commentary; Philadelphia PA: JPS, 1989) 118.

[79] Fishbane also notes the deliberate allusion in v.11 to Lev 18, but without connecting it to the inclusion of Egypt in Ezra 9:1. In that respect, as mentioned earlier, he follows the standard argument that Deut 23 is the source for the four non-Canaanite nations and he too reads Edomite for Amorite (*Biblical Interpretation*, 119).

[80] As far as I am aware, no one has suggested this.

[81] Wilhelm Rudolph, *Esra und Nehemia mit 3.Esra* (HAT 20; Tübingen: Mohr Siebeck, 1949) 87.

enough Israelite women there, unlike in the Land, where most of the returnees must have been men and had little choice in Israelite women. He refers to Daiches' study (*Jews in Babylonia*), which seems to confirm this assumption in that the latter only finds one example of intermarriage deduced from the name of the wife.[82]

We see then that there might be a combination of associations at work in the list. Egypt's linkage with oppression corresponds to Ammon and Moab's animosity to Israel, while exilic—postexilic prophetic materials connect Egypt more explicitly with idolatry. Finally Lev 18:3 warns of following Egyptian and Canaanite ways, which, as the rest of Lev 18 makes clear, are mainly sexual malpractices described as "abominations."

4.1.4 The Amorites

If one accepts the MT's reading then the final name in the list reverts back to one of the seven nations mentioned in Deut 7, the Amorites. Most commentators focus so closely on the two acknowledged sources (Deut 7:1 & 23:4[3], 8 [7]) for the list of nations in Ezra 9:1 that the MT's reading of "Amorite" as the last name in the sequence is simply dismissed as implausible.[83] Admittedly, 1 Esdras' solution seems more straightforward and elegant in its simplicity, disposing of both difficulties mentioned above: the out-of-sequence listing of the Amorites is eliminated and replaced by the expected fourth nation from Deut 23.

At the same time, the majority of manuscripts have "Amorite" and it is the more difficult reading, which should lead one at least to consider the logic for its inclusion and the omission of Edom. First, even if Deut 23 is the source for the non-Canaanite names in the Ezran list, Edom should ideally precede Egypt in the sequence. Secondly, although Edom and Egypt are treated the same in Deut 23 and this would make it logical to pair them together in the Ezran list, there is precedence in later rabbinics that the two were differentiated presumably on the basis of kinship (Deut 23:8[7] "for he is your brother" (כי אחיך הוא). According to one Halakah and also in the view of Rabbi Asher ben Yehiel (14th c.), a proselyte Edomite could marry a Jewess straightaway, whereas the exclusion for an Egyptian remained valid for the third generation even if he became a proselyte.[84]

---

[82] Samuel Daiches, *The Jews in Babylonia in the Time of Ezra and Nehemiah according to Babylonian Inscriptions* (London: Jews' College, 1910) 34.

[83] Among the many commentators who read "Edomite" following 1 Esdras are: Joseph Blenkinsopp, *Ezra-Nehemiah: A Commentary* (London: SCM, 1988) 175; Rudolph, *Esra und Nehemia*, 86; Fishbane, *Biblical Interpretation*, 116; etc. The one prominent exception is Williamson, who retains the MT's reading on the basis that the inclusion of Edomites would clash with the more lenient treatment they receive in Deut 23 (*Ezra, Nehemiah*, 131).

[84] M. Rosenbaum and A.M. Silbermann, eds., *Pentateuch with Targum Onkelos, Haphtaroth and Prayers for Sabbath and Rashi's Commentary* (London: Shapiro,

Edom could possibly fit into the list on the basis of hostility and ill-will toward Israel to which exilic and postexilic texts testify (e.g., Ezek 25:12–14; 35:15; 36:5; Ps 137:7; Mal 1:4). However, apart from Solomon taking a wife, among others, from Edom (1 Kgs 11:1) there is no particular association of Edom with "abominations" in the sense of idolatry/apostasy or sexual immorality.

Perhaps the absence of Edom from the list in Ezra is an indication, on the one hand, that kinship ties were recognized as important, which put Edom in a different category from Egypt and, on the other, that the primary connotation of "abominations" here was idolatry/apostasy and possibly sexual immorality. If the latter is true then it follows that hostility in itself was a secondary category, which was only important as a first sign of a greater problem, namely, enticement into the worship of other gods.

The position of "Amorite" at the end of the list may be explained using arguments from the historic background of the Postexilic Period. Van Seters reasons that the term "Amorite" referred to the Arabs by the time of Ezra and Nehemiah and not to one of the ancient inhabitants of Canaan.[85] Williamson, who follows the MT's reading, picks up on his theory.[86] If this is so, however, it is odd that the Arabs mentioned in Neh 4:1[4:7] and 6:1 are not called Amorites but הערבי/הערבים. It may be possible though that both terms were used for the same people group and Ezra 9:1 applies "Amorites" to affirm the link with the prohibition in Deut 7, but by placing it in ultimate position indicates its changed meaning.

If the placing of the Amorites at the end of the list is intentional, it may also indicate the encompassing of these non-Canaanite peoples in the sins most prominently associated with the nations in Canaan. The Canaanites, who start the list and the Amorites, who finish it were the two major groups, who were sometimes used individually as umbrella terms for all the inhabitants of Canaan (e.g., Gen 15:16; Exod 13:11). Such an inclusion of other nations may also underline the point that whether from the land or from outside of it, the same sins should fall under the same treatment and be dealt with firmly as Deut 7 suggests.

4.1.5 *The Edomites (1 Esd 8:68)*

Since the overwhelming majority of scholars follow the variant reading of 1 Esd 8:68 it is worth reflecting on the interpretative moves made in the

---

Vallentine & Co, 1946) Appendix for Deut, 218. The editors unfortunately do not reference the Halakah in question. They also note on Rashi's interpretation of Deut 23:8[7] that Dukes' translation of Rashi, following Elias Levitas, attributes this distinction to Rashi himself, although Rosenbaum et al. argue, in my view correctly, that Rashi treats Edom and Egypt the same.

[85] J. Van Seters, "The Terms 'Amorite' and 'Hittite' in the Old Testament," *VT* 22 (1972), 76.

[86] Williamson, *Ezra, Nehemiah*, 131.

process. In a way 1 Esdras' reading of Ezra 9:1 and the likely replacement of "Amorite" with "Edomite" is already a form of interpretation.

1 Esdras diverges from the book of Ezra in the MT in several ways and the changes are not haphazard and incidental but fall into a conscious pattern. First, it reflects messianic hopes for Israel's restoration under a Davidic king and gives Zerubbabel (grandson of King Jeconiah—1 Chr 3:17–19) a more prominent role as personal bodyguard to Darius, whose wisdom gains him the king's favor for the rebuilding of Jerusalem and the temple (1 Esd 4–5, not in MT). In comparison, the MT noticeably downplays Zerubbabel's role omitting his name several times, which is in line with its positive take on the Persian kings and its co-operative stance under their rule (1 Esd 6:18, cf. Ezra 6:14; 1 Esd 6:27, cf. Ezra 6:7). Ezra's explicit mention of Zion being raised by God from desolation (1 Esd 8:81, not in MT) is another indication linking 1 Esdras' hopes to political as well as religious restoration.

The Edomites feature in the book a number of times apart from their appearance in the list of nations. When speaking to the king, Zerubbabel blames them for burning down the temple (4:45) even though 2 Chr 36:19 attributes this crime to the Babylonians. The king in response demands that the Edomites surrender the villages they have seized from the Jews (4:50). The grievances and the hostility toward them echo the exilic and postexilic texts of the MT, which resent Edom's *Schadenfreude* over Israel's downfall and the benefits they derived from it by acquiring land (see p.41). Apart from the replacement of "Amorite" with "Edomite" there is one other modification in the list of 1 Esd 8:68 but one which does not seem to have much significance. Namely, the Ammonites are dropped from the list altogether. It is hard to give an adequate reason for this, unless it is simply a mistake. If the change is deliberate then perhaps its aim is to bring the number of nations down to seven. It may also be that it is dropped because there is no record of Ammon opposing Israel's progress into the land. Alternatively, perhaps Ammon's omission indicates a shift of focus away from them (see especially Neh 2:19; 4:7[13]; 13:1, 23) to an enemy considered more vicious.

4.2 Abominations in Ezra

Having looked at the various nations in the list of Ezra 9:1 as well as the alternative reading in 1 Esd 8:68, it is time to pull our findings together. As a preliminary observation it is worth noting that on the basis of this selective list *all* foreign women are excluded from marriage with Israelites. Thus there seems to be no need to look for exact identifications and there is no exception mentioned on the basis that someone was not from the nations in the list. The precedent for taking these nations as exemplary of evil is already there in 1 Kgs 11:1–2, where the legal source for condemning *all* of Solomon's foreign wives is Deut 23 (perhaps in conjunction with Deut 7), even though the king had women who were not included in either lists (e.g., the Sidonians).

Similarly, Williamson argues that the local inhabitants are not identified with the Canaanites; the list of nations qualifies "abominations" and "thus is meant only as a stereotyped formula, adopted from the law."[87] Hayes phrases it even more radically when she proposes that "The eight parties listed do not actually figure in Ezra's prohibition. They are invoked for purposes of comparison only so as to justify the prohibition of local inhabitants. The latter are as abhorrent in their behavior as these well-known abhorrent peoples and must be avoided."[88]

This understanding of how the nations list functions would also explain why certain other nations such as the Arameans in the north are not mentioned.[89] The text is clearly interested in establishing specifically from Torah why intermarriage with foreigners is unacceptable and is therefore limited to a historic list of nations most of which did not exist by the time of the return from exile. Nevertheless, by referring to their abominations the returnees are able to connect these mostly extinct nations with those of their own time who are considered to be characterized by the same heinous sins.

If the above assumption is correct then the question is what the "abominations" are which hold these listed nations together and which threaten to influence Israel adversely through intermarriage? I suggested that the MT's list is based on three legal sources (Deut 7:1–3; Deut 23:4–7[3–6]; Lev 18:3) rather than solely the commonly held first two and this is reinforced by the allusion to all three in Ezra's prayer (9:11–12). I have argued that all these nations carry the association of idolatry and sexual immorality, even Ammon and Moab through their incestuous ancestry, and the latter also through the events at Baal-Peor. By contrast, Edom, which only fits the list on the basis of its hostility to Israel but not particularly as a source of temptation for apostasy/idolatry is absent and may thereby underline the specifically religious threat implicit in the meaning of "abominations." Finally, the inclusion of nations in the list that are outside Israel as well as inside, living near to her or further afield, has the effect of being all-encompassing.

If these conclusions are along the right lines, however, then we are faced with the dilemma that idolatry is not mentioned explicitly anywhere in EN or specifically in Ezra 9–10. The one instance that perhaps comes closest to implying such a thing is the offer of the peoples of the lands to help build the temple on the basis that they had been worshiping the same God as the exiles since the time of Esarhaddon of Assyria (Ezra 4:1–2). The returnees' rejection of this offer (v.3) and the fact that the altar has only recently been restored in its rightful original place and the sacrificial system re-started (Ezra 3) suggests that the peoples of the land may have been sacrificing in a different place. The

---

[87] Williamson, *Ezra, Nehemiah*, 130.

[88] Hayes, "Intermarriage and Impurity in Ancient Jewish Sources," *HTR* 92/1 (1999), 12 fn. 25.

[89] I am grateful to Walter Moberly for raising this question which made me consider the function of this list more closely. Personal communication.

reference to Esarhaddon denotes the situation described in 2 Kgs 17 when the people resettled in the land after the northern tribes have been taken into captivity. The evidence there points to a people of mixed origins and a syncretistic religion. As Maccoby argues, the "coded" way in which the real issue is indicated is due to the fact that the exiles lived in the Persian empire, which itself practiced "a tolerant syncretism" and it may not have been too pleased to hear of tension as a result of an exclusivist, intolerant monotheism.[90]

Beyond this covert aspect of dealing with the issue of idolatry/apostasy, however, there is also a certain amount of stereotyping going on in the way "abominations" is used. Thus the problem with those approaching the exiles in Ezra 4:1–2—the way the narrative portrays it—is that they have nothing to do with the God of the exiles and therefore could have nothing to do with building him a temple.[91] This same justification is evident in the restoration of the city wall, where again those who do not constitute the community of Israel are not allowed to join in the process (Neh 2:20). This time, however, the reasoning is expanded, so that it becomes clear that building the walls is seen as giving a certain right of ownership in the city and by implication a place among the people of God. The other aspect in these texts is that despite the claim to having common ground (Ezra 4:1–2) the narrative presents them as people who are hostile to the restoration of Israel (Ezra 4:1, 8–16; Neh 3:33–4:17[4:1–23], etc.). This seems to suggest that Israel is not to ally herself with peoples who may pretend to be friendly, but are fundamentally opposed to God's purposes for her. This obstruction of God's plans for God's people is reminiscent of Deut 23:4–7[3–6] and the reason given there for the rejection of the Ammonites and Moabites.

Further encounters with the peoples of the lands specifically through intermarriage lead to encroachment on sacred space, which has to be cleansed from defilement (Neh 13:4–9). Moreover, intermarriage seems to affect the holiness of the Israelite seed (Ezra 9:2).[92] The result of this foreign influence leads to a neglect of the Sabbath (Neh 13:15–18) and of Israel's own language (Neh 13:24). Further, an enemy of Israel, Tobiah, is spoken well of because of the allegiance owed him due to his marriage connections (Neh 6:17–19).

Thus, according to the perspective of the Ezra–Nehemiah narrative the problem is twofold. On the one hand, the peoples of the land as implicitly associated with idolatry and immorality are the enemies of God's purposes and giving them a share in the community of Israel undermines God's plans for her from the inside. On the other, Israel by allying herself with such people ends up

---

[90] Hyam Maccoby, "Holiness and Purity: The Holy People in Leviticus and Ezra-Nehemiah" in *Reading Leviticus: A Conversation with Mary Douglas* (ed. John F.A. Sawyer; Sheffield: Sheffield Academic, 1996), 165–166.

[91] This attitude is a diversion from the building of the First Temple, which was erected with the help of foreign labour either entirely (1 Kgs 5:27–32[13–18]) or at least in part (2 Chr 2:1[2], 17[18]).

[92] More on this in Chap. 7.

abandoning the Law of her God (e.g., the neglect of the Sabbath, tithe, etc.) and loses her distinctiveness that marked her out as YHWH's special possession. Thus "abominations" becomes a convenient term to describe peoples who are unclean by definition because they are not set apart to God as Israel is, and who have the potential to defile her both by virtue of contact with her and by drawing her away from her special calling to obey the Law. In both instances Israel loses her distinctive status.

The way "abominations" is used in Ezra 9:1 reminds one of the later Jewish usage of "idolatry." In the Mishnah all Gentiles are seen as idolatrous, a stereotypical term for them and a kind of shorthand for depicting those outside the community of Israel. It is a way of saying that they are sinners of every description who cannot be trusted to refrain from any evil. Thus *m. 'Abod. Zar* 2.1 states,

> Cattle may not be left in the inns of the gentiles since they are suspected of bestiality; nor may a woman remain alone with them since they are suspected of lewdness; nor may a man remain alone with them since they are suspected of shedding blood. (Danby)

Similarly, elsewhere the idolater was seen to have denied the Torah and its precepts, particularly the Ten Commandments (*Sipre Num* par. 111; 32a). As Neusner comments, "the theory of idolatry, involving alienation from God, accounts for the wicked conduct imputed to idolaters, without regard to whether, in fact, that is how idolaters conduct themselves."[93] I suggest that the word "abominations" functions in the same way in Ezra 9:1 with the association of uncleanness which can defile Israel, but without demonstrating in the narrative the kind of abhorrent practices listed elsewhere in Scripture.

4.3 The Identity of the "Foreign Women"

4.3.1 Foreign?

At this point it is worth considering briefly the identity of these women with whom marriages were unacceptable. Many commentators do not address the issue, while those who do are scattered on a spectrum from treating these women as foreign, alien or consisting partly or entirely of non-exiled Judeans.[94]

---

[93] Jacob Neusner, *Making God's Word Work: A Guide to the Mishnah* (New York: Continuum, 2004) 80.
[94] Williamson explicitly calls them "foreign landlords" (*Ezra, Nehemiah*, 160). Allen and Wijk-Bos both describe them as aliens (Leslie C. Allen and Timothy S. Laniak, *Ezra, Nehemiah, Esther* [NIBCOT 9; Peabody MA: Hendrickson, 2003] 72; Johanna W. H. Wijk-Bos, *Ezra, Nehemiah, and Esther* [Louisville, KY: Westminster John Knox, 1998] 43–44). Joseph Blenkinsopp thinks that foreigners, resident non-Judeans and indigenous Judeans are all part of the group (*Judaism: The First Phase. The Place of Ezra and Nehemiah in the Origins of Judaism* [Grand Rapids, MI: Eerdmans, 2009] 67). C. C. Torrey speaks of "heathens" and "heathenized Jews" (*Ezra Studies* [New York: Ktav,

One way of trying to decide the question is to consider the biblical accounts. These suggest that the majority was taken from the land and only the poorest of the people remained (2 Kgs 24:14; 25:12). Grabbe disputes the impression and suggests that the majority had in fact remained in Judah after a minority was taken to Babylon.[95] These, he assumes, took over abandoned land and are in fact the people the returned exiles describe as "foreigners" or "peoples of the land." He refers to the study of Gunneweg to support his claim that "the peoples of the land" means Israel in the OT and in later rabbinic literature.[96]

It is difficult to prove or disprove this theory about a majority remaining in the land, as we have only the biblical accounts to go on and Grabbe reads between the lines a story that goes against the narrative's explicit claim. If a large group was left in the land rather than a minority (against the statement of 2 Kgs 24:14; 25:12), if they mostly stayed in Judah rather than went to Egypt after Gedaliah's murder (contrary to 2 Kgs 25:26 and Jer 43:5–7), then it is possible that the returnees faced these non-exiled Judeans. However, it is equally plausible to accept the biblical account to be broadly correct, in which case the small number of Judeans left in the land could have been assimilated and the land taken over by the already mixed population living in the former Northern Kingdom and by the neighboring peoples in Edom, Ammon, Moab. This would accord well with the situation as described by EN of a mixed population that is at best syncretistic in its religion if not entirely foreign.

Moreover, the meaning of "the people of the land" does not support the argument that the women were Judeans. As Nicholson, to my mind convincingly, shows the עם הארץ is not in any way a *terminus technicus* but has a general sense of a population living in a given land and the meaning varies within that from context to context. Thus he shows that the same term is used of the inhabitants of Hebron in Gen 23:7, 12–13; of the Egyptians in Gen 42:6; of Israelites in Lev 20:2 and of the indigenous people of Canaan in Num 14:9, etc.[97]

Further, we may note that in EN the only occurrence of עם הארץ in the singular is in Ezra 4:4 where it is set in opposition to the people of Judah

---

1970] 279–80). At the far end of the spectrum Lester L. Grabbe treats them entirely as non-exiled Judeans (*Ezra-Nehemiah* [London: Routledge, 1998] 136–38). A monograph by K. E. Southwood, in the process of being published as I write, equally questions the ethnic component of the intermarriage crisis based on anthropological considerations (*Ethnicity and the Mixed Marriage Crisis in Ezra 9–10* [Oxford Theological Monograph Series; Oxford: Oxford University Press, 2012]). Unfortunately, it will be too late for me to engage with her work in this book.

[95] Grabbe, *Ezra-Nehemiah*, 136–38.
[96] Gunneweg, A. H. J. "Zur Interpretation der Bücher Esra-Nehemiah: Zugleich ein Beitrag zur Methode der Exegese," *Congress volume, Vienna 1980*, VTSup 32 (Leiden: Brill, 1980), 146–61 in Grabbe, *Ezra-Nehemiah*, 137.
[97] Ernest W. Nicholson, "The Meaning of the Expression עם הארץ in the Old Testament," *JSS* 10 (1965) 59–66

(עם־יהודה). If the meaning of *am haaretz* elsewhere is so clearly a reference to God's people, Israel, it is hard to imagine that the exiles would choose such a word to refer to a group that they clearly did not regard a part of Israel/Judah. Moreover, the term is most often used in EN in the plural "peoples of the land/lands." Outside EN, "peoples of the land" (עמי הארץ) occurs 11 times and 8 of these explicitly juxtapose them with Israel in the sense of the "nations" (Deut 28:10; 1 Kgs 8:43, 53; Zeph 3:20; Esth 8:17; 1 Chr 5:25; 2 Chr 6:33; 32:19). The other three references are not quite so explicit though they still seem to speak of the nations (Josh 4:24; 1 Kgs 8:60; Ezek 31:12).

The expression "peoples of the lands" (עמי הארצות) only occurs twice outside of EN. In 2 Chr 13:9 Abijah, the king of Judah admonishes Jeroboam that he and the Northern Kingdom had made for themselves priests like the peoples of the lands, clearly a reference to other nations. In 2 Chr 32:13 Sennacherib, the king of Assyria taunts Hezekiah saying that the gods of peoples of the lands could not deliver them and by implication neither will YHWH save Judah. His utterance equates "the peoples of the lands" with the nations (v.14).

We may conclude then that in its plural forms the expression "peoples of the land/lands" outside of EN always refers to nations other than Israel and there is precedent for the singular to mean non-Israelites as well. Thus the usage of the phrase in EN of denoting a group other than Israel/Judah would accord with the expression's general meaning and usage elsewhere in the Old Testament.

In favor of the position that these women were, at least in part, non-exiled Judeans it may be argued that EN essentially treats the exiles as Israel, the story is their story and we do not read of Judeans living in the land whom the exiles find on their return. The repeated designation of "the sons of the exile" (בני הגולה—Ezra 4:1; 6:19; 8:35; 10:7, 16) as a synonym for Israel clearly underlines this point. There is only one occurrence in EN where there is explicit mention of another group outside the exiles who separated themselves from the impurity of the peoples of the land (Ezra 6:21). This might well refer to non-exiled Judeans who purified themselves or possibly to aliens who converted although from the meager evidence it is impossible to decide the question conclusively. If we take this group to consist of purified non-exiled Judeans then the next question is whether the Ezran group or the author/editor of the material in Ezra 9–10 accepted the same principle of incorporating non-exiled Judeans. Since conversion/purification is not mentioned as an option for any of the women in Ezra 9–10 this presumably means either that the women were all non-Judeans or that the Ezran group did not accept purification as a way of re-integration for non-exiled Judeans. There is thus no conclusive evidence either way.

What else might help to decide the question? The exiles' list of nations might give us some clues even though, as we have seen, it is a stereotypical formula rather than a direct reference to specific nations. If all the unacceptable women were Judeans then it is curious why the list includes not only the indigenous people of Canaan who might be seen as analogous to them but also other foreign nations outside the borders of Israel. The latter makes better sense if there were at least some women among them from other territories. Further, the predominantly plural designation "peoples of the land/lands" rather than the singular "the people of the land" suggests a more heterogeneous group with members who are not all local. Thus the evidence points at least to a mixed entity which, if it included non-exiled Judeans at all, consisted of *bona fide* foreigners as well.

Although we cannot entirely exclude the possibility of non-exiled Judeans among the women in Ezra 9–10, there are two other reasons why this seems to me unlikely. First, it is unquestionably the case that for the postexilic community genealogy and descent plays a huge part in the definition of identity and thus it is hard to imagine that this would have been entirely disregarded in the case of Judeans who have not been exiled. The stress on descent in the Postexilic Period is evident in the preoccupation of Chronicles with genealogical lists and also present in the repeated lists of EN (Ezra 2, 8, Neh 3, 7, 11, 12). Admittedly, there is a special concern for the priesthood and the Levites to prove their ancestry (Ezra 2:62) but the importance of descent for ordinary members of the community is also crucial. We shall see later that in Ezra 9:2 Israel as a holy *people* (cf. Deut 7:6) is replaced by Israel as the holy *seed*, which indicates an emphasis on descent. Further, if the issue is the experience gap of the non-exiled Judeans and a concomitant lack of religious commitment then why is conversion not an option and why are descendants of mixed marriages to be sent away/excluded (Ezra 10:3, Deut 23:4–7[3–6])? The mixed marriage crisis, I argue, supports a definition of Israel that is partly based on descent and partly on religious commitment. Clearly, the former is not enough so that those among God's people who do not comply with the community's decision to deal with the crisis are excluded (Ezra 10:8) and forfeit their right to belong. However, by definition they are counted "in" unless they give reason to be excluded and one would expect similar treatment of non-exiled Judeans.

Secondly, even if we assume, that the criteria for membership is the dual condition of genealogical descent *and* exilic experience, it is curious why the exclusion of a supposedly non-exiled group should happen under the guise of "foreignness," rather than for the real reason. After all, Jeremiah's prophecy of the good and bad figs (Jer 24) could explain the returnees' justification, yet nowhere do we read anything even remotely mentioning the lack of exilic experience as grounds for rejection.

Admittedly not going into exile would certainly have left its mark on the community staying in the land. Not being taken into captivity may have bred in those remaining a sense of complacency as if God had abandoned those who were taken and left in place the innocent, as it were (Ezek 11:15). Thus the full tragedy of the events may not have affected those remaining in place and they may have even profited from the removal of their leaders and the opportunity to gain abandoned land. If so, this certainly would not have led to the kind of reflection and remorse felt by those forcefully taken from the land. Neither would the lower strata of society have necessarily provided the kind of theological thinkers who could lead the community into a renewal in line with faithful Yahwism. If God's people have become deeply syncretistic and idolatrous before the exile, and this is what the OT accounts suggest, then the poorest people remaining in the land would have had neither the motivation, nor the abilities to renew themselves in sole commitment to YHWH. In fact, the kind of thinking that may have been prevalent among those remaining in Judah is reflected in Jer 44:15–19, where the group escaping to Egypt after Gedaliah's murder connect the catastrophe of the Exile with the lack of faithfulness in sacrificing to *other gods*. The neighboring peoples would have very likely moved into the political and social vacuum left in Judah providing the ingredients for the recipe for assimilation.

Thus, I argue, the issue for the returnees is the presumably mixed or foreign descent of those in the land and their lack of religious commitment to YHWH. If there were non-exiled Judeans among the women then they must have been assimilated and mixed both in their descent and their worship.

4.3.2 Why Women?

A notable fact of the intermarriage crisis in Ezra 9–10 is that only "foreign" women are mentioned, despite the deuteronomic prohibition which includes both men and women in the ban (Deut 7:3) and which Ezra quotes in his prayer (Ezra 9:12). It is possible, of course, that the answer is quite simple and prosaic: the only intermarriages found by the leadership were those between an Israelite man and a non-Israelite woman. It could be explained on the basis that most of the returnees were men and the shortage of Israelite women led to this state of affairs.[98] On the count of probability this is obviously more likely than the other way round; nevertheless, it is difficult to believe that there was absolutely no exception to the general setup of non-Israelite woman + Israelite man = intermarriage. We see, in fact, that there were indeed exceptions to the above, where an Israelite woman was married to a non-Israelite man (Neh 6:18).

Another reason for concentrating entirely on the "foreign" women in Ezra 9–10 could have been the difficulty for a woman to initiate divorce, in which case there was no solution for a Jewish woman's marriage to a foreign man.[99] A similarly practical reason for the silence may have been the fact that a

---

[98] This is Rudolph's explanation, although he does not directly ask the "why only women?" question; rather he tries to give a reason why there were *more* intermarriages with non-Israelite women involved. Rudolph, *Esra und Nehemia*, 87.

[99] I have not come across this particular reasoning in the secondary literature at all. There is little that we know of this period and the possibility of divorce may have also depended on the customs and laws of the foreign husband's culture. Instone-Brewer argues that as a general trend in the last two centuries B.C.E. it became increasingly easier for women to initiate divorce but Jewish women were still subject to their husbands in the question of divorce. By the first century C.E. if a Jewish wife wanted divorce she could get one granted she could convince the court that she had sufficient grounds for it (e.g., husband's adultery), in which case the court would put pressure on the husband to initiate the

Jewish woman was expected to adopt her husband's religion as it is assumed to have been the case in the Jewish community of Elephantine (e.g., *AP* 14).[100] Both these arguments, however, are less than satisfactory since they only flag up the difficulty of finding a solution to the problem but do not adequately explain the silence for mentioning such cases.

A further possibility why the text concentrates on foreign women is the assumed greater influence of the mother on the religious education of the children.[101] If this view is correct then a Gentile woman would be more dangerous for the descendants. However, we do not know if women had the kind of influence ascribed to them at this time and the inference is often made from the knowledge of later periods. Besides, the children are considered non-Israelite anyway demonstrated by the fact that they are to be sent away with their mothers (Ezra 10:3). This accords with the later rabbinic ruling for matrilineal descent (*b. Qidd.* 68b), which does not recognize the children of Gentile women in a mixed marriage as Jewish and thus their religious education is of no importance since they are Gentile anyway. Rather, it is the offspring of Jewish mothers who count as Jewish whose religious commitment is endangered by the presence of a foreign father.

Beyond the historical-practical considerations there are also sociological factors drawn into the task of interpretation. Thus Janzen considers the divorces of Ezra 9–10 a form of "witch-hunt," what he calls a "ritualized act of purification," which gets rid of dangerous elements within the community.[102] He argues that a community with strong external boundaries (fear and resistance of foreign influence) and weak internal integration (lack of adherence to the community's social morality) will worry about the latter and look for someone to blame. If there is no obvious candidate, the community will engage in "witch-hunts," blaming people who seem foreign and dangerous not because of what they have done but because of who they are. In his view, these "scapegoats" are more likely to be women than men (see esp. his Chapter 2).[103]

---

process. At the same time, marriage contracts from Elephantine suggest that a Jewish woman there could divorce her husband without much ado but it is difficult to ascertain how widespread this practice was elsewhere or how much it reflects the customs of a small community. David Instone-Brewer, *Divorce and Remarriage in the Bible: The Social and Literary Context* (Grand Rapids MI: Eerdmans, 2002) 72, 76–78, 85.

[100] Blenkinsopp, *Ezra-Nehemiah*, 177.

[101] F. C. Holmgren, *Israel Alive Again: A Commentary on the Books of Ezra and Nehemiah* (ITC; Grand Rapids, MI: Eerdmans, 1987) 73; Blenkinsopp, *Ezra-Nehemiah*, 177.

[102] David Janzen, *Witch-hunts, Purity and Social Boundaries: The Expulsion of the Foreign Women in Ezra 9–10*, (JSOT SS 350; Sheffield: Sheffield Academic, 2002). For a short summary of his thesis see pp.19–21.

[103] Similarly, Harold C. Washington bases his reading of the intermarriage crisis on the social-anthropological theory of Kristeva who considers impurity in Leviticus to be rooted in the abjection of the maternal body. It is the association of the feminine with uncleanness which is the grounds in his view for the special focus on foreign women but

While Janzen's witch-hunt theory has not won universal acceptance, some of his observations are worth considering further. For instance, his description of the returned exiles as having strong external boundaries and weak internal integration is borne out by the evidence of the biblical text. It is easy to see that foreign influence was feared in the Postexilic Period and equally obvious that the Jewish community recently returned from Exile struggled with the lack of religious commitment in its own midst. We need only think of the long delay in re-building the temple blamed by Haggai on the people's lack of incentive (Hag 1:3–4), the initial absence of Levites in the group of those about to return to the Land with Ezra (Ezra 9:15) and the recurring disobedience to Torah particularly in the book of Nehemiah (Neh 5—usury, Neh 13:10–14—neglect of tithing, Neh 13:15–22—breaking of the Sabbath, etc.). Janzen is also correct in recognizing that Israel's lukewarm commitment is blamed largely on the foreign influence in her midst. He also rejects the simplistic view that openly expressed theological statements are merely cynical cover-ups for an internal power struggle. Rather, he argues that "ideology must be persuasive if it is to be successful, and it can be persuasive only if it points people's attention to a world view and social order that they already take for granted."[104] Thus he insists that Ezra and the leadership could only convince the group of the course of action to be taken, if the people themselves felt that the explanation and solution fitted with how they understood the world.

What exactly would this world view be which could give an adequate explanation for the actions taken and which might explain the prominence of foreign *women* as the problem? Israel's narrated history has some examples of the danger that foreign women might pose for God's people, most obviously King Solomon whose wives included among others Egyptian, Moabite, Ammonite and Edomite women (1 Kgs 11:1). Similarly King Ahab married the Sidonian princess Jezebel and engaged in Baal and Asherah worship (1 Kgs 16:30–33) and his sin is attributed to Jezebel's influence (21:25). Although Ezra 9–10 itself does not mention either king, Neh 13:26 cites Solomon's sin and it is possible that he became a standard negative example.

Thus, the way the narrative is shaped reveals the background of the exiles' thinking. The emphasis in Ezra on the leadership as being foremost in this unfaithfulness (9:2—וְיַד הַשָּׂרִים וְהַסְּגָנִים הָיְתָה בַּמַּעַל הַזֶּה רִאשׁוֹנָה) and on the foreign *women* suggests a pattern that is similar to some kings going astray under the influence of foreign wives and leading Israel into sin as a result. The extension of the list of Canaanites with three or four nations (if Edomite is read for Amorite) prominent in the spiritual downfall of Israel's greatest king also heightens the similarity between the two accounts. Thus the story of the mixed marriage crisis highlights the parallels between Israel's past and present situation

---

not men in Ezra 9–10 ("Israel's Holy Seed and the Foreign Women of Ezra-Nehemiah: A Kristevan Reading," *BI* 11 [2003] 427–37).

[104] Janzen, *Witch-hunts*, 8.

and endows the incident with a certain emblematic quality. It is not surprising therefore that the spotlight is put on the foreign women rather than the men.

4.4 A Comparison with Neh 13

Having considered the nations list in Ezra 9:1 and the legal and narrative material that informs it I wish to consider briefly how a similar issue is handled in Neh 13:1–3 and 13:23–31. In Neh 13 we encounter the problem of mixed marriages, as well as the use of Deut 7, 23 and 1 Kgs 11:1–2. There are nevertheless some differences in the way the situation is handled by the two accounts, which makes a comparison worth pursuing.

4.4.1 Neh 13:1–3

Unlike Ezra 9 where Deut 23 is used as a prohibition to intermarry, Neh 13:1–3 quotes it to justify excluding those of mixed descent. Neh 13:1–3 uses Deut 23:4–6[3–5], although the citation is not *verbatim* and it does not include the further section of Deut 23:8–9[7–8] on Egypt and Edom. As in Ezra 9:1 where on the basis of a selective list all "foreign" women are divorced, so here on the basis of the prohibition directed against Ammon and Moab *all* those of "mixed descent" are excluded from Israel (ויבדילו כל־ערב מישראל—v.3). The word used for those excluded is ערב "mixture" rather than "foreign" (נכרי) people and it emphasizes the aspect of mixed descent (cf. Ezra 9:2 where the holy seed is seen to have "intermingled" התערב).[105] The focus therefore seems to be specifically on the offspring of such mixed marriages, rather than on the foreign spouses (unless the latter were already of mixed descent). It is not clear from the Hebrew whether the exclusion mentioned in Neh 13:3 involved the break-up of mixed marriages, although based on the silence of Neh 13:23–31 on any divorce proceedings this is unlikely.

The word ערב is unusual and may have been taken from Exod 12:38 where we are told that "a mixed multitude" (ערב רב) left Egypt with Israel.[106] Admittedly there is no disapproval attached to this group in Exod 12:38. Num 11:4, however, implies that Israel's greediness for meat in the wilderness is incited by a rabble element (אספסף). Although the word is different from the one used in Exodus, two factors indicate that it might refer to the same non-Israelite contingent. First, the Hebrew sentence of Num 11:4 itself distinguishes between the two groups.

---

[105] Commentators generally take ערב to mean "of mixed descent" or "foreign" except Eduard Meyer, who translates it as "Bedouin" here on the basis of vocalising ערב as ʿarav (*Die Entstehung des Judenthums: eine historische Untersuchung* [Halle: Max Niemeyer, 1896] 130). However, as J. M. Myers points out in connection with Meyer's suggestion, "foreign" is more likely in the context (*Ezra, Nehemiah* [AB 14; New York: Doubleday, 1965] 206).

[106] Rudolph, *Esra und Nehemia*, 202; C. F. Keil, *The Books of Ezra, Nehemiah, and Esther* (trans. Sophia Taylor; Edinburgh: T&T Clark, 1873) 286.

והאספסף אשר בקרבו התאוו תאוה וישבו ויבכו גם בני ישראל.	Num 11:4	The rabble who were among them had greedy desires; and also the sons of Israel wept again (NASV)

The אספסף are "among them [i.e., Israel]" (בקרבו) but they are different from the sons of Israel who "also" (גם) wept. Had the "rabble" been a part of Israel one would have expected a sentence like "and the rest of Israel also wept" but there is no such qualification made. Secondly, the LXX translates אספסף in Num 11:4 as ἐπίμικτος ("mixed"); the same word it uses for ערב in Exod 12:38 and in Neh 13:3. Thus the LXX connects the above three passages through the use of the same word. As a further comparison the table below shows the Targum translations for the MT's ערב רב in Exod 12:38 and for אספסף Num 11:4.

	Exod 12:38	Num 11:4
Tg. Onq.	נוכראין סגיאין (many foreigners)	עירברביןֹ (mixed multitude)
Tg. Ps-J.	נוכראין סגיאין (many foreigners)	גיורייא (aliens)
Tg. Neof.	גיורין ערברוביןֹ (mixed multitude of aliens)	ערבובה (mixed multitude)

The above illustrates that the MT's somewhat ambiguous reference to a foreign/non-Israelite element in Num 11:4 as the cause of evil influence is made explicit in the Targums through the Aramaic versions of ערב רב (in Onqelos and Neofiti) and through the use of "alien" (Hebrew גר) in Pseudo-Jonathan. We see then that "foreignness" in these instances is associated with negative "religious-moral" influence that incites rebellion against YHWH.[107] If for the author of Neh 13 ערב carried an association of this mixed multitude in Exod 12:38 and Num 11:4, then it was all the more fitting to use it in the postexilic context, since the intermarriages have similarly eroded the commitment of Israel to God. I have argued in this chapter that the abominations (תועבת) which the "foreign" women are characterized with in Ezra 9 may have an analogous connotation beyond the stereotypical association of idolatry.

---

[107] I use negative "religious-moral" influence here as a descriptive term to express both a threat to religious allegiance (i.e., commitment to YHWH) such as idolatry and the possible moral-ethical implications often associated with turning away from YHWH, such as sexual immorality, social injustice or the like. I recognise the potential difficulty with the use of such an adjective which might easily be misunderstood. "Religious" may be thought of as a term broader than the way I employ it here including such aspects as ritual for instance, while "moral" might be identified with narrow moralising, a stance alien from the Bible's perspective. However, for want of a better word I will continue to use it in the sense defined above. For a further discussion on similar difficulties on terminology see §7.1.

The reasoning behind the exclusion of Ammon and Moab in Deut 23:4–7[3–6] is also appropriate to the wider context of the book of Nehemiah because it shows a remarkable parallel with the events in Nehemiah's time. Fishbane points out the similarities between the hiring (שכר) of two prophets; Balaam on the one hand, Shemaiah on the other (Neh 6:12). In the case of the former the king of Moab was involved, in the latter Sanballat and Tobiah, the Ammonite. In both events divine reversal occurred; the intended curse was turned into a blessing in the first and the life of Nehemiah was protected in the second.[108]

4.4.2   Neh 13:23–31

Neh 13:23–31 deals with a mixed marriage crisis similar to the one in Ezra 9–10. The legal basis for disapproval, as I shall show below, is Deut 23:4–7[3–6] on the one hand and Deut 7:1–3 on the other. Further, while the influence of 1 Kgs 11:1–11 is more implicit in Ezra 9–10, here Nehemiah himself quotes Solomon's bad example (Neh 13:26).

Neh 13:23 mentions intermarriages with Ashdodites, Ammonites and Moabites. It is generally assumed that the inclusion of Ammon and Moab are a later addition (i.e., to align the situation with Deut 23), since there is no conjunction after Ashdod in Hebrew and v.24 omits Ammon and Moab altogether.[109] The purpose of their inclusion is likely intended to evoke the prohibition of Deut 23:4–7[3–6]. It is perhaps worth noting that both Neh 13:1–3 and 23–31 only use the prohibition regarding Ammonites and Moabites from Deut 23 and stop short of listing Edom and Egypt.

Nehemiah, like Ezra in his prayer (Ezra 9:12), quotes Deut 7:3 and contends with the exiles to swear by it not to intermarry or let their children intermarry with these other peoples (Neh 13:26). From the way it is used in both books of EN it seems that it was a standard reference for banning intermarriage.

Nehemiah, as observed above, cites Solomon's sin in this respect, which connects Neh 13:23–31 not only with 1 Kgs 11:1–11 but also with Deut 23:4–9[3–8]. 1 Kgs 11:2 alludes to the prohibition of intermarriage in connection with Solomon's foreign wives: מן־הגוים אשר אמר־יהוה אל־בני ישראל לא־תבאו בהם והם לא־יבאו בכם. Generally this is translated as "from the nations of whom YHWH had said to the sons of Israel, 'You shall not associate with them [lit. go among them לא־תבאו בהם] and they shall not associate with you [lit. go among you לא־יבאו בכם].'" The idiomatic use of the Hebrew ...לא יבא ב in 1 Kgs 11:2 occurs in Deut 23:2–9[1–8] with its repeated prohibition for various groups to go into the assembly of YHWH (לא־יבא

---

[108] Fishbane notes the parallel (*Biblical Interpretation*, 126–27). Also Blenkinsopp, *Ezra-Nehemiah*, 351.
[109] Loring W. Batten, *A Critical and Exegetical Commentary on the Books of Ezra and Nehemiah* (ICC; Edinburgh: T&T Clark, 1913) 299; Fishbane, *Biblical Interpretation*, 124 fn. 51; Williamson, *Ezra, Nehemiah*, 397; Blenkinsopp, *Ezra-Nehemiah*, 362.

...בֿ).[110] The reference in Kings to a divine command using the same phrase as the one in Deut 23:2–9[1–8] and Solomon's marriages to wives from the four nations (Moab, Ammon, Egypt, Edom) listed in Deut 23 make the connection likely. If the above reasoning is correct then understanding Deut 23:2–9[1–8] as a reference to intermarriage has precedent already in the Deuteronomistic History.

The most obvious difference between Ezra 9–10 and Neh 13:23–30 is that Nehemiah does not mention divorce as a solution and it is unlikely that such measures were applied by him. First, the oath extracted has a preventative function; it does not deal with marriages already contracted. Cursing the laymen (v.25) and calling an imprecation on the guilty priests (v.29) seems to indicate that in Nehemiah's view the marriages could not be undone. This act of cursing may, however, be more significant than just being a sign of a temper tantrum that expressed displeasure or frustration. It may well communicate the principle that God's judgment will come on those who have broken the terms of the covenant, which finds an analogy in the curses pronounced in Deut 27:15–26 and 28:15–68. The specific issues the exiles committed themselves to in the covenant renewal of Neh 10:29–40[28–39] are precisely the ones that they disobeyed in Neh 13. Further, as mentioned in §3.1.1, the unusual expression of entering into a curse and an oath (ובאים באלה ובשבועה) in Neh 10:30[29] resonates with a similar expression of crossing over into God's covenant and oath/curse in Deut 29:11[12] (לעברך בברית יהוה אלהיך ובאלתו). This may provide further support for the theory above since it seems to have formed part of the conceptual world of the exilic community. Thus there may be a close link here between the breaking of the (renewed) covenant and the subsequent cursing of those whose action caused irremediable damage.

4.4.3 *The Reason for the Ban*

Unlike Ezra 9:1–2, Neh 13 does not mention "abominations" or "the holy seed" in connection with the intermarriages although ערב as referring to "mixture" in Neh 13:3 may have some resonances with the "holy seed." The scriptural associations of ערב from Exod 12:38 and Num 11:4 suggest a negative influence that weakens resolve for the allegiance of YHWH, while the specific reference to Deut 23:5–6[4–5] indicates that association with the Ammonites and Moabites (and their latter day equivalents) is destructive because of the actively hostile attitude of these nations.

Nehemiah in Neh 13:23 is primarily concerned that the descendants of mixed marriages were losing their ability to speak Hebrew. Although the text

---

[110] Fishbane, *Biblical Interpretation*, 125. BDB notes that בוא followed by the suffix ב has the sense "of associating with." E.g., Josh 23:7, 12 (והתחתנתם בהם ובאתם בהם והם בכם "and intermarry with them, so that you associate with them and they with you"— NASV); Gen 49:6 (בסדם אל־תבא נפשי בקהלם אל־תחד כבדי) "Let my soul not enter into their council; Let not my glory be united with their assembly"—NASV). BDB, 931 בוא §1.f.

does not spell out the implications of this, it may indicate an anxiety that these children will thereby have lost access to Torah. Similarly the citation of Deut 7:3 may signal a fear of idolatry/apostasy although again this is not spelt out. When Nehemiah refers to King Solomon in v.26, he merely states that "the foreign women caused even him to sin" (גם־אותו החטיאו הנשים הנכריות). 1 Kgs 11 defines Solomon's sin as idolatry and apostasy (vv.4–8) and a breaking of YHWH's covenant and his commandments (vv.9–11). Further, it highlights an issue that may have had relevance for the exiles; namely that Solomon did not abandon the worship of YHWH entirely, but "married" the worship of YHWH with those of other gods. The text stresses that "his heart was not *completely* with YHWH, his God" (ולא־היה לבבו **שלם** עם־יהוה אלהיו—v.4) and that "he did not follow YHWH *fully"* (ולא **מלא** אחרי יהוה—v.6). Similarly, Neh 13 illustrates this compromised attitude to YHWH: nepotism, not giving tithes for the Levites' needs, the breaking of the Sabbath and the ignorance of the Hebrew language among children from mixed marriages.

It is possible, of course, that Neh 13:23–31 understands Solomon's example differently from the way 1 Kgs 11:1–11 envisages it and which takes the significance of that passage in a different direction. We see this, for instance, in Sir 47:20, which reinterprets Solomon's sin in terms of defilement of the family line. One would expect, however, to have a more explicit indication of such a re-reading when the passage is otherwise so firmly associated with the problem of idolatry. Further, the overall perspective of Neh 13, which strongly reflects the thinking of both Deuteronomy and the Deuteronomistic History, makes this possibility less than convincing.

We see in the above passage then the same reticence about mentioning idolatry explicitly and the same cluster of associations surrounding those defined as non-Israelites as in the rest of EN, namely the negative influence which erodes faithfulness to YHWH. In fact, Nehemiah, like Ezra 9:1 refers to the sin of intermarriage as "unfaithfulness" (מעל). Although מעל may have the technical sense of sacrilege as Milgrom understands it in Ezra 9–10 it is also a word, as I shall argue, that can be used in a non-technical sense of breaking the covenant (see discussion in §7.2.1).

4.5 Conclusion

This chapter has examined the list of nations in Ezra 9:1, the pentateuchal basis for their inclusion, their connection with the term "abominations," the variant reading in 1 Esd 8:68, what foreignness might mean and why the text focuses especially on women but not men and finally a comparison with the intermarriage crisis in Neh 13. I argued that in the MT's version the basis for the list is to be found in Deut 7:1–3; Deut 23:4–7[3–6] and Lev 18:3 and that the "abominations" associated with them were idolatry and sexual immorality. The list included groups who were representative of these heinous sins rather than intended to specify the particular nations with whom intermarriage was unacceptable. The alternative reading in 1 Esdras, which replaced the Amorites with the Edomites was explained from the wider context of the book which stressed the negative role Edom played in the downfall of Israel. I also suggested that this alteration shifted the meaning of "abominations" toward an understanding which focused more strongly on the hostility of some of these nations to God's people and on their influence, which eroded allegiance and faithfulness to YHWH's covenant and commandments. I argued that foreignness referred to people who were not Israelites/Judahites by birth. If there were among them those who remained in the land after the Exile then they must have assimilated both by descent and by religion to such an extent that they had no legitimate reason to be called a part of Israel. The emphasis on women was shown to be part of a deliberate parallel between Israel's pre- and postexilic state highlighting the sin of the secular and religious leadership along the lines particularly reflected in the story of Solomon. The comparison with Neh 13 suggested a similar reason for the ban on intermarriage as in the case of Ezra 9–10 based on Deut 7:1–3, Deut 23:4–7[3–6] and using the narrative of 1 Kgs 11:1–11 although some aspects of Neh 13:23–31 will await further consideration in Chapter 7.

5

Ḥērem Law and Ezra 9–10

The key legal passage behind Ezra 9:1 is Deut 7:1–3 and we have seen so far that the exiles looked for justification for their actions in Torah. However, the *ḥērem* law of Deut 7 understood as the extermination of the local inhabitants of Canaan, plays little part in the story of the intermarriage crisis and the solution offered.[111] The only actual reference to the word חרם is in Ezra 10:8, but the practice there is applied to Israelites rather than to the local "foreign" inhabitants and has no apparent connection with Deut 7. Moreover, there is no obvious parallel for confiscation of property in the pentateuchal legislation—the closest text specifically relating to the *ḥērem* of property is Lev 27:21, 28. The context of Lev 27, however, deals with voluntary consecration of land, livestock, (and people?), whereas the *ḥērem* in Ezra is imposed by the assembly and refers to what is generally considered moveable property (רכוש).[112] This state of affairs is all the more noteworthy, since the postexilic community is so emphatic about obeying the law, yet in Ezra 9–10 the *ḥērem* of Deut 7 appears to be ignored, while the *ḥērem* that is practiced is seemingly without legal foundation.

In this chapter I propose to address two questions relating to *ḥērem* so as to understand the legal setting of Ezra 9–10. First, how can the missing component of *ḥērem* in the intermarriage crisis be explained: was it considered irrelevant, temporarily suspended or was it reinterpreted in the light of the postexilic situation? Secondly, how did the exiles arrive at their particular understanding of the law, in the verse where they do apply *ḥērem* (Ezra 10:8)? In order to answer these questions I will examine first the relevant legal material as well as other texts in the Old Testament to see how the concept of *ḥērem*

---

[111] In setting up the issues of Ezra 9–10 (§3.3) I mention Exod 34:11–16, which equally contains the prohibition against intermarriage but without the *ḥērem* law. However, as I explained there the verbal connections are much stronger with Deut 7.

[112] BDB, 7399 רכוש §1.

changed over time and to demonstrate the degree of flexibility and the various directions that the interpretation of the term took. Although my primary focus needs to be the legislative material and that of Deuteronomy in particular, the narratives and prophetic texts where the word occurs will provide a useful background of comparison for the various ways the concept has been interpreted and re-interpreted. This will then be followed by the consideration of the various strategies that the postexilic community might have used to interpret the law in their circumstances.

There are two aspects to *ḥērem* in the Old Testament which need to be tackled in order to answer the questions raised about Ezra 9–10; one relates to the *ḥērem* of people, which I shall refer to as "enemy *ḥērem*," and the other to that of property. When dealing with the former we need to ask first whether the command in Deuteronomy is to be taken at face value as extermination or understood metaphorically. Secondly, the scope of the *ḥērem* law demands closer consideration, that is, who the objects of *ḥērem* are to be and why? When handling the issue of property *ḥērem* the question is what becomes of the possessions made *ḥērem* and to what extent are such actions voluntary or mandatory.

5.1 Enemy *Ḥērem* in the OT

5.1.1 Metaphorical or "Literal?"

One of the key questions in trying to understand what Ezra and his circle have made of the *ḥērem* law is whether it is interpreted as destruction/death in the Pentateuch and especially in Deuteronomy, or if it has a metaphorical meaning already in these legislative materials.

Moberly in his essay on the implications of the *Shemaʿ* takes Deut 7 to present the *ḥērem* law as "a metaphor for religious fidelity" (p.135) with only two practical expressions: the prohibition of intermarriage and the destruction of heathen cultic objects.[113] This move kills two birds with one stone. It eliminates the perceived discrepancy between the command to exterminate the seven nations and the prohibition of intermarriage with the same people. Moreover, it explains the silence of Ezra 9–10 on the *ḥērem* of these nations, since then the prohibition to intermarry and/or ally oneself with the local population can be seen as the fulfillment of the deuteronomic command of *ḥērem*.

However, there are strong arguments for taking *ḥērem*, when its objects are people, to mean extermination or death, especially in Deuteronomy and the Deuteronomistic History. I start with the legal sections first, which tend to be

---

[113] Moberly, "Toward an Interpretation of the Shema" in *Theological Exegesis: Essays in Honor of Brevard S. Childs* (ed. C. Seitz & K. Greene-McCreight; Grand Rapids, MI: Eerdmans, 1999) 134–137.

economical in their wording and therefore more ambiguous at times. The narratives then can flesh out the meaning with some more detail.[114]

The first occurrence of *ḥērem* in the canon is Exod 22:19[20] which merely says that the idolatrous Israelite should be made *ḥērem* without giving any further detail as to what this might entail.[115] Alt takes *ḥērem* as synonymous in meaning with מות יומת ("he shall surely be put to death"). In his view, the original legislation ran like this: זבח לאלהים אחרים מות יומת ("whoever sacrifices to other gods shall surely be put to death." When יחרם ("shall be made *ḥērem*") came to replace אחרים ("other") then מות יומת dropped out. He notes that the alternative reading אחרים is found in the Samaritan Bible, Alexandrinus and some minuscules.[116] Alt's theory ignores the fact that מות יומת does not occur in any of the versions in conjunction with אחרים and is therefore too speculative. Nevertheless, granted that his reconstruction is correct, it still does not follow logically that the two terms are therefore synonymous. Others have objected that *ḥērem* could not mean death, since the previous law about sodomy (v.18) specifies the death penalty (מות יומת) and why would two texts, one after the other, use two different words for death?[117] This argument, however, is not conclusive either, since *ḥērem* could have an additional dimension (such as the sacrificial connotation noted in §5.1.3), while at the same time still be a form of the death penalty. Moreover, there are other texts where *ḥērem* clearly means extermination preceded by a similar offence punishable by the death penalty (Deut 13:2–12[1–11], cf. 13:13–16[12–15]). It is perhaps possible that *ḥērem* is a later addition to the early text of Exod 22 in order to align it with the later deuteronomic theory of *ḥērem*. As the text now stands, however, we must conclude that the meaning cannot be decided with certainty.

There is nothing ambiguous about the fate of the human being mentioned in Lev 27:29, however; "he cannot be ransomed, he shall surely be put to death" (לא יפדה מות יומת). More difficult are the circumstances that would lead to a *human being* made *ḥērem* considering that the rest of the chapter is dealing with the *ḥērem* of property, which assumes a peace-time context once Israel is settled in the land. Lohfink when discussing Lev 27:28 argues that

---

[114] I am aware that the interpretation of *ḥērem* in the individual books should not be collapsed into one, nevertheless tracing the meaning of חרם through the sources gives us a better appreciation of the term overall.

[115] I use the canonical order of the Protestant English Bible for convenience without making any assumptions as to the dating of these texts or the various stages of development that the concept of *ḥērem* has undergone.

[116] Albrecht Alt, "Die Ursprünge des israelitischen Rechts," *Berichte über die Verhandlungen der Sächsischen Akademie der Wissenschaften zu Leipzig Philologisch-historische Klasse*, Bd 86, Hft 1 (Leipzig: S. Hirzel, 1934) 45.

[117] Christa Schäfer-Lichtenberger, "Bedeutung und Funktion von Herem in biblisch-hebräischen Texten," *BZ* 38 (1994) 274. She suggests further that *ḥērem* must mean expulsion from the community; although she gives no reason for this interpretation other than her argument above, that *ḥērem* here cannot mean death. However, I fail to see why *ḥērem* would automatically mean expulsion if it is not death.

people dedicated in *ḥērem* remain alive probably as slaves, although there does not seem to be any basis in the text to assume so. Perhaps he deduces this from the vow to dedicate persons to YHWH in Lev 27:1–8, which Wenham argues is connected to the idea of slavery in that such persons may free themselves from the vow by paying the amount that they might fetch in the slave market.[118] Regarding v.29 Lohfink says,

> To distinguish this case [v.28] clearly from the killing of a person, v.29, referring to the ancient *ḥērem* punishment, was appended. The crucial point is that v.29 uses the hophal, which shows that we are dealing with a different and distinct case.[119]

One is hard-pressed to follow the logic of the argument. First, putting so much weight on the verb form to distinguish between two kinds of legislation seems to me misguided. The Hophal is employed only in two other cases (Exod 22:19[20]; Ezra 10:8); all other texts where the verb occurs use the Hiphil of חרם, including the war passages against the Canaanites and the punishment of the idolatrous Israelite city (Deut 13:13–18[12–17]). If Lohfink is thinking of Exod 22:19[20] here, then he is linking Lev 27:29 with a text that does not actually spell out what *ḥērem* involves. Thus it is difficult to identify it as referring to the same thing as Lev 27:29 purely on the strength of the verb form. More importantly, the Hebrew has no markers to suggest a break between v.28 and 29. If the text wanted to make it unambiguous that human beings are not to be killed, would it not have been easier to say in v.29 something like this: "But as to the *ḥērem* of people, they shall not be ransomed, they shall be slaves in the temple forever." The distinction, however, as the text now stands is far from clear. Rather, the emphasis is on the comparison with the ordinary dedication, highlighting the difference between the two forms of consecration. Thus, the person/thing dedicated in the ordinary way may in certain instances be redeemed, *whereas* (note the Hebrew אך at the beginning of v.28) what is *ḥērem* is irrevocable; once given it cannot be retrieved. The verse follows up the command with the added explanation that all *ḥērem* is most holy (קדש קדשים whereas the status of ordinary consecration is קדש in 27:9, 14). V.29 then underlines the seriousness of *ḥērem* by repeating its irredeemable character in the case of human beings, spelling out their fate in no uncertain terms ("they shall surely be put to death" מות יומת). Therefore in its context, v.29 stresses that not even in the case of human beings can exceptions be made regarding *ḥērem*. Thus Lohfink's argument that v.28 refers to a different kind of *ḥērem* from that of v.29 effectively falls down and with it the idea that the *ḥērem* of people can mean a fate other than death in the text.

More uncertain is the case of Num 18:14 where all *ḥērem* is assigned to the priests. Does this include human beings? The noun חרם could refer to both

---

[118] Gordon Wenham, *The Book of Leviticus* (NICOT; Grand Rapids MI: Eerdmans, 1979) 338.
[119] N. Lohfink, "חרם," *TDOT* 5:199.

people (e.g., Lev 27:28; Josh 6:17; 1 Kgs 20:42; Isa 34:5, etc.) and possessions (Lev 27:28; Deut 13:17–18[16–17]; Josh 6:18; 7:1; 1 Sam 15:21, etc.), although the context of the chapter makes it more likely that *ḥērem* means property here. An indication of how this command was understood in the Exilic-Postexilic Period is the use of this command in Ezek 44:29, where the context suggests produce and animals.

The deuteronomic legislation leaves little doubt that חרם is meant to be read as extermination or annihilation. Deut 7 does not mention death, yet the text elaborates on the meaning of חרם exhorting the Israelites to strike the Canaanite nations (הכיתם—v.2), to make the names of their kings perish "until you have destroyed them" (והאבדת את־השמם ... עד השמדך אתם—v.24). The fate of these nations is destruction, as it is repeatedly emphasized (עד אבד—v.20, עד השמדם—v.23).

One of the objections to reading חרם in Deut 7 as annihilation is the perceived tension between *ḥērem* as extermination and the following prohibition of intermarriage or covenant-making in vv.2–3. If the population is massacred, then no marriage or covenant is possible with them. The tension, however, can be resolved if one reads the prohibition of alliance and intermarriage as potential alternatives to total annihilation, which the Israelites might find attractive and which are nevertheless deemed wrong.[120] There is a similar structure evident at the end of the chapter regarding idols which are to be burned (vv.25–26). A number of alternatives follow, however, implying the possibility that this is not done. The Israelites might take the gold or silver (presumably before burning the rest) or bring the idol into the house instead of destroying it. Yet in this case no one seems to feel any tension even though by the same token the command to burn the idol should be interpreted merely as a prohibition not to appropriate any part of it or carry it into one's house.

The next text to examine is Deut 13:13–18[12–17], which commands the inhabitants of an idolatrous Israelite city to be struck with the edge of the sword (הכה תכה את־ישבי העיר ההוא לפי־חרב—v.16[15]), while the city and the booty is burned as a whole burnt offering (כליל ליהוה—v.17[16]). It is worth noting that in the previous section of chapter 13, the individual who entices others to idolatry, whether a false prophet or dreamer (v.6[5]) or a private individual (v.7[6]) is to be put to death (vv.10–11[9–10]), while over the city that becomes idolatrous as a result of such enticement *ḥērem* is to be exercised (v.16[15]). Thus the two phrases are used here for a similar offence, which makes one wonder if they are synonymous, even if the nuance of meaning is not identical. Schmitt theorizes that חרם signifies more than the death penalty and that it includes the children and the property of the criminal, which would fit

---

[120] Joel N. Lohr argues something similar (*Chosen and Unchosen: Conceptions of Election in the Pentateuch and Jewish-Christian Interpretation* [Sifrut 2; Winona Lake IN: Eisenbrauns, 2009] 167–72 esp. 168–9).

Deut 13:13–18[12–17] nicely (as well as the sin of Achan in Josh 7).[121] It could also explain why it is *ḥērem* and not מות יומת that is used in Exod 22:19[20], if the two terms are similar in meaning. On the other hand, the *ḥērem* law dealing with the Canaanites does not allow for this additional meaning, since there the booty belonged to Israel (see §5.1.2).

Finally, the last legislative piece relating to *ḥērem* in Deuteronomy makes it unambiguous that extermination is meant. Deut 20:16–18 gives instructions concerning wars against cities that are within Israel's inheritance and commands their annihilation including women and children. Israel should leave no one alive who breathes (לא תחיה כל־נשמה—v.16).

One other text that has some bearing on this question is Deut 21:10–14, which regulates the case of the captive woman whom an Israelite might wish to take as a wife. One might argue that this negates the *ḥērem* law in Deut 20:16–18 and is proof that not all human beings were meant to be killed in *ḥērem*. However, I believe that the explicit command regarding the extermination of all in the Canaanite cities is a stronger argument than the silence of Deut 20:16–18 regarding the origins of the captive woman.[122]

The narratives confirm the above picture. First, it is often emphasized when a city falls under *ḥērem*, that no survivor was left (לא השארנו שריד— Deut 2:34; 3:3; Josh 10:28, 37, 39), or nothing/no one that breathes (לא נותר כל־נשמה—Josh 11:11), or that Israel struck the inhabitants with the edge of the sword (ויכו אתה לפי־חרב—Josh 8:24, also Josh 10:28, 35, 37, 39; 11:11, 12, 14). Secondly, in some passages חרם is set in parallel with the unambiguous death penalty (מות יומת). So for instance Israel takes an oath to put to death anyone who did not come to the assembly in Judg 21:5, followed by the execution of *ḥērem* on the inhabitants of Jabesh-Gilead, who failed to appear at the meeting (v.11). Similarly, in 1 Sam 15:3, the *ḥērem* of all that Amalek has is linked with putting men, women, and children (as well as animals) to death (והמתה מאיש עד־אשה מעלל ועד־יונק).

5.1.2   The Scope of the Command

Another question that needs further consideration is the scope of the command for *ḥērem*. The law affected most obviously two groups in particular: idolatrous Israelites and the seven nations living in Canaan. In fact the

---

[121] Götz Schmitt, *Du sollst keinen Frieden schliessen mit den Bewohnern des Landes: Die Weisungen gegen die Kanaanäer in Israels Geschichte und Geschichtsschreibung* (BWANT 91; Stuttgart: Kohlhammer, 1970) 91.

[122] From a historical-critical perspective the discrepancy has been explained by the later addition of vv.16–18 into Deut 20, whereas no reference to the issue of *ḥērem* was made in the case of Deut 21:10–14. Nevertheless, whatever might have been the original shape of these commandments I take the final form as my point of reference. From this vantage point Deut 21 needs to be read in the light of what is clearly stated in Deut 20, which would imply that the context for the law about the captive woman is war against nations outside of Canaan.

legislation only mentions those two groups with a possible unspecified third in Lev 27:29 for which, as mentioned before, we do not have a context. On the other hand, the narratives testify to the gradual extension of the term to other groups and situations. The most notable of these is the use of *ḥērem* in the case of the Amalekites. Although Deuteronomy commands the extermination of the Amalekites (25:19) it does not call this חרם, while 1 Sam 15 does. Perhaps the avoidance of the word in Deuteronomy indicates that the original context of the law was the extermination of nations within the land of Israel and therefore Amalek did not qualify. Similarly, in 1 Chr 4:41 the Meunites are made *ḥērem* in the territory of Simeon during Hezekiah's time, but the raid on the Amalekites (v.43) is not called חרם. On the other hand in 1 Kgs 20:42, Ben-Hadad, the king of the Arameans and his people were supposed to have been annihilated (חרם) by King Ahab, who instead made peace with him. Thus not all of our sources use *ḥērem* in a precise way.

A further move is observable in the destruction of various nations not by Israel but by the Assyrian king Sennacherib described as a form of חרם (2 Kgs 19:11; 2 Chr 32:14; Isa 37:11). The verb is used similarly in 2 Chr 20:23 where Ammon and Moab fight Edom. In the prophets this trend continues with the verb gradually losing any of its previous fixed specific application and comes to mean simply extermination or destruction irrespective of who does it to whom and why. Thus it is used for Babylon's attack on Judah and other nations (Jer 25:9), other nations' destruction of Babylon (Jer 50:21, 26; 51:3), the King of the North's action against the King of the South (Dan 11:44), YHWH's move against the Sea of Egypt (Isa 11:15), the nations (Isa 34:2), Edom (Isa 34:5), and Israel (Isa 43:28).

5.1.3 The Intention of the Command

The object of the *ḥērem* law has largely to do with idolatry, and idolatry in the land at that, whether it is committed by an Israelite or by the Canaanites. In the former case, the command is punitive (Exod 22:19[20]), although it might be argued that the strict measures also serve to warn off potential offenders. In the case of the Canaanite nations the command is meant to prevent Israel from falling into temptation by eliminating its source (Deut 7:4; 20:18). Deuteronomy in particular stresses that Israel is not to interfere with nations outside the land (Edom—Deut 2:5; Moab—Deut 2:9; Ammon—Deut 2:19) and *ḥērem* only applies to the people within the territory YHWH has given them (Deut 2:31; 3:2). This is perhaps explicable by what has been considered the association of *ḥērem* with the sacred sphere.[123] McConville in his commentary on Deuteronomy gives a helpful description of this idea.

> The "devotion to destruction," in religious history, means putting to death every living creature [...] as a kind of sacrifice to Yahweh, on the ground

---

[123] Lohfink even goes as far as to suggest that the sacred is a counter-sphere to *ḥērem*. "חרם," *TDOT* 5:184.

that the land belongs to his "holy sphere," and is given only to those whom he has designated "holy." The underlying concept is that whatever is not "holy" cannot come into Yahweh's presence. Conversely, the killing, as in sacrifice, is a kind of assimilation into the holy sphere, a making "holy."[124]

In Deut 13:13–18[12–17] the procedure for dealing with the idolatrous Israelite city has the added character of a whole burnt offering (כליל ליהוה— v.17[16] cf. Deut 33:10; 1 Sam 7:9; Ps 51:19[17])), which is meant to appease YHWH's wrath (למען ישוב יהוה מחרון—v.18[17]). The command to destroy Jericho completely, including the spoil, may also have sacrificial connotations. The booty normally belonged to Israel (see §5.2), so the חרם of Jericho is unusual and Greenberg theorizes that it has the character of first fruits offerings: the giving of the first spoils of Canaan wholly to God.[125] Thus in the wars against Canaanites *ḥērem* is a destruction in devotion to God.

Outside the Pentateuch the reasoning for *ḥērem* sometimes diverges from idolatry. Thus in the case of the Israelites, Judg 21 (esp. vv.5, 10–11) recounts the massacre of Jabesh-Gilead for not coming to the assembly, which was called to deal with the sin of the Benjamites. With the extension of the practice to nations outside of Canaan the added reasoning for *ḥērem* may be hostility toward Israel; most notably in the case of the Amalekites, who attacked YHWH's people along the way from Egypt to the Promised Land (1 Sam 15:2–3 cf. Deut 25:19).[126] As the scope of *ḥērem* widens the reasons for its execution grow more opaque and, as noted earlier, it becomes merely a synonym for extermination and destruction. Only on the odd occasion does a text evoke the idea of sacrifice (Isa 34:6) and occasionally it even contrasts sacrifice and *ḥērem* as in 1 Sam 15.[127]

5.2 Property *Ḥērem* in the OT

The legal portions of the Pentateuch deal predominantly with people in connection with *ḥērem* and in most instances have no or only limited information on what happens to the property of those under *ḥērem*.

The two passages dealing with the *ḥērem* of the Canaanite nations do not refer to the spoil.[128] Deut 7:25–26 mentions the destruction of idols in order to eliminate the danger of idolatry, but apart from this has nothing to say about the property or possessions of those seven nations.[129] Deut 20:10–18 discusses

---

[124] J. G. McConville, *Deuteronomy* (AOTC 5; Leicester: Apollos / Downers Grove IL: IVP, 2002) 88.
[125] Moshe Greenberg, "Herem," in *Encyclopaedia Judaica* (16 vols.; ed. C. Roth; Jerusalem: Keter, 1971–72) 8:347–48.
[126] I am not making a historical observation here, merely a canonical one on the differing uses of *ḥērem* in different texts.
[127] Lohfink, in fact, argues that it is a deliberate polemic against seeing *ḥērem* in sacrificial terms ("חרם," *TDOT* 5:195).

wars against "cities very far from you" (הערים הרחקת ממך מאד—v.15) and those within Israel's inheritance (ערי העמים האלה אשר יהוה אלהיך נתן לך נחלה—v.16) only the latter of which is denoted as *ḥerem* (v.17). The single difference mentioned for the wars against the Canaanites is that not only the men but all the population is to be exterminated (v.16 cf. v.13). Since the fate of the booty is not referred to in this case one might reasonably infer that the same regulation applies as in the case of the cities "far from you," where the spoil was Israel's to keep (v.14). Thus the indirect evidence suggests that the people could have the booty in any war, including wars of *ḥerem*.

The two texts dealing with the *ḥerem* of idolatrous Israelites vary in the treatment of property. Exod 22:19[20] does not mention it, Deut 13:16–17[15–16] prescribes the burning of an idolatrous city including the livestock and all the booty.

The *ḥerem* of property in peace-time means its irrevocable consecration for the use of the priesthood/sanctuary (Lev 27:21, 28). V.28 does not specify the fate of the devoted item, but the general context of the chapter (devotion of property for the use of the priesthood/sanctuary) suggests that *ḥerem* here involves the same. This is further strengthened by the fact that the legislation points out two differences of *ḥerem* as opposed to simple consecration, namely that *ḥerem* is irrevocable (the item cannot be redeemed) and the consecration of people involves their death.

The narratives dealing with *ḥerem* against Israel's enemies in the Pentateuch (mostly Deuteronomy) and in the Deuteronomistic History reflect the same ambiguity and variety regarding the handling of property. It is often not mentioned specifically (Num 21:2–3; Josh 10:1, 28, 35–40; 11:21; Judg 1:17; 21:11; 1 Kgs 9:21; 20:42). In other instances the spoil goes to Israel (including the livestock—Deut 2:35; 3:7; 8:27; Josh 11:14). In Jericho, the livestock is destroyed and the spoil is burned except for the silver, the gold, and the articles of bronze and iron, which were put in the temple treasury (Josh 6:21, 24). In 1 Sam 15 Saul is condemned for not destroying the livestock in the *ḥerem* against the Amalekites and not even the possibility of using them as sacrificial offerings is acceptable as an alternative.

---

[128] I am using Canaanite in this section as a convenient shorthand for all the inhabitants listed in the land (i.e., Perizzites, Hivites, Jebusites, etc.).

[129] Greenberg infers from Deut 6:11 that the Israelites were meant to keep the spoil of the cities under *ḥerem*, but this does not seem to me very convincing from the above verse, although I agree with him that the legislation generally allowed for spoil to be kept ("Herem," 345). To be sure, Deut 6:11 speaks of houses with good things in it, which would indicate that they were not destroyed, nevertheless, the overall imagery has more of a rhetorical force to suggest that Israel is coming into an inheritance prepared and ready, a land that is cultivated (vineyards and olive trees) and established with cities, hewn cisterns, etc. The actual details are incidental; rather the emphasis is on the gift nature of the land, which should remind Israel of YHWH, the giver of it all, in order that she might not be enticed into idolatry (vv.12–15).

The only prophetic usage of the term which affects the question of property describes Israel's destruction of foreign nations and the *ḥērem* of their wealth (Mic 4:13). It is unclear whether the latter is destroyed or consigned for temple use.

5.3 Dedication and Destruction

Even though we cannot be sure of the exact stages of development that the concept of *ḥērem* has undergone, nevertheless this brief survey has highlighted some important aspects of the concept.[130] Within the pentateuchal legislation, the deuteronomic use of the term gives us the fullest and most specific picture of what *ḥērem* might entail. It essentially involves a destruction of the object (whether person or thing) and its ultimate purpose is to prevent or to deal with idolatry in the land. Thus, in Deuteronomy, it affects only Israelites and the local inhabitants of Canaan traditionally listed as the seven nations occupying the land. As the expression "*ḥērem* to YHWH" and the occasional sacrificial aspect testify, it is a form of dedication or devotion of the object to God.

There seem to be two lines of thought within this deuteronomic form of *ḥērem*, which surface in the other sources and take the concept in two different directions. Whether Deuteronomy pulled the two strands together or other sources picked up on one or other of those aspects evident in Deuteronomy is difficult to tell. Either way, it is a development worth noting. One strand emphasizes the element of destruction, which becomes the primary feature of the word in some narratives and in the prophetic writings until it lacks any of its specifically deuteronomic characteristics. Thus, beyond the Pentateuch, the use of the term becomes looser; it may affect nations outside Israel. In its most lax application *ḥērem* may be executed by any nation (or even by God) on any other nation. What remains a standard feature of the word, however, is the meaning of annihilation and complete destruction. In fact, when it comes to people, it is the single most consistent feature of *ḥērem* throughout all its occurrences with the only possible question mark around Exod 22:19[20], which does not spell out what *ḥērem* entails.

The second strand of thought highlights the dedicatory nature of *ḥērem* and this is particularly prevalent where booty/property is involved. Since the spoil of war belonged to Israel, its voluntary dedication to YHWH on occasion (as in the case of Jericho) is a war-time expression of the peace-time practice of property *ḥērem* as outlined in Lev 27:28–29. The devotion of the valuable items from the spoil of Jericho to the temple treasury finds its parallel in the voluntary offering of the Israelite's property for the use of the sanctuary/priesthood. Perhaps the poignant story of Achan's sin and the general association of *ḥērem*

---

[130] As mentioned earlier (see fn. 126 on p.64), I wish to emphasise here that I am not making a traditio-historical claim about the development of *ḥērem* but merely commenting on the diversity of usage within the OT canon.

with destruction, which has a finality about it, finds its echo in the most holy status assigned to the property *ḥērem* in Lev 27 and in the emphasis there of its irrevocable nature.

Finally, the purpose of the *ḥērem* law as demonstrated in Deuteronomy is both punitive when dealing with an idolatrous Israelite and preventative when it affects the Canaanites in that it eliminates for Israel the source of temptation to idolatry (and apostasy). Beyond the Pentateuch, the cause for *ḥērem* broadens to include hostility against Israel (1 Sam 15) and the failure of Israelites to turn up for an assembly in order to deal with communal sin (Judg 21). Thus as the scope of *ḥērem* widens, so the reason or need for it become less defined.

5.4 Enemy *Ḥērem* in Ezra 9–10

Although my main concern as a background for Ezra 9–10 is Deuteronomy, nevertheless, in the previous section I have evaluated all the other occurrences of חרם in the Old Testament to give a wider context for understanding how the term was used. That the *ḥērem* of people in Deuteronomy means extermination seems clear to me. In claiming such a meaning for *ḥērem*, however, there is one other objection, namely that it is difficult to envisage a *Sitz im Leben* for such a command. As Milgrom puts it, "why should a document [i.e., Deuteronomy] of the eighth or seventh century, a time when the Canaanites posed no threat whatsoever, demand their extinction?"[131] Milgrom's statement, however, implies several tacit assumptions. First, it takes for granted the idea that Deuteronomy has a secret agenda read back as a command into the age of the conquest to give it added authority. Secondly it presupposes that the action required will be identical to the one presented in the book. However, neither assumption is necessarily valid.

It is possible to see Deuteronomy as a document looking back on Israel's history and seeing impending doom (or already realized disaster, if one posits an exilic date for the book). In this situation the author(s) may simply be asking the question of what went wrong. The answer could then be the lack of commitment demonstrated by Israel in destroying the sources of temptation that eventually led to the nation's downfall. Such a context would still allow, even demand, action to be taken, yet may not necessarily imply the need for an exact imitation of the original command.

If we take the above proposal as the *Sitz im Leben* for the deuteronomic *ḥērem* law, the question still remains as to what the righteous Israelite is meant to do. Is he to apply the command literally and make up for the lack in the zeal of his ancestors? If there are no more Canaanites, can he extend the law to other nations, such as the ones inhabiting his land? Can the extermination be re-interpreted metaphorically to mean action other than killing? Can the reason or purpose for *ḥērem* be broadened? In other words, can one re-interpret the

---

[131] Jacob Milgrom, "Religious Conversion and the Revolt Model for the Formation of Israel," *JBL* 101/2 (1982) 172.

meaning, the scope and the purpose of *ḥērem*? The previous survey of the use of *ḥērem* suggests that this is precisely what has happened, although interestingly, the meaning of *ḥērem* as extermination is the most constant element in its application.

Thus we come to the question of how the exilic group understood the *ḥērem* law of Deut 7, the passage that played a key role in their argument against intermarriages. There are at least three possible alternatives. First, the postexilic community might have felt that the command was no longer relevant in their age. It was given for the time of the conquest only, when the tribes entered the land inhabited by other nations. Secondly, they might have considered the command to be suspended for the time being because it was impracticable when Judah (Yehud) was merely a Persian province without the freedom to make its own independent decisions or lead wars. Thirdly, if the commandment was seen as valid and not suspended then it must be reinterpreted in order to apply it to the new situation that arose after the exile. The question then becomes what aspects of the law need to be rethought.

5.4.1   No Longer Relevant?

If the command is interpreted by Ezra 9–10 to be locked in time and only applicable to the seven Canaanite nations, who were gone by the time of the exile, then there is no room for חרם in the Postexilic Period any more.[132] This would explain why the *ḥērem* law is not mentioned at the beginning of Ezra 9 even though it forms the backdrop of the deuteronomic command prohibiting intermarriage.

Thus Hoffman argues that the *raison d'être* for the Deuteronomistic descriptions of doing *ḥērem* in Joshua is to combat xenophobic tendencies in the Postexilic Period by making it clear that there are no more Canaanites in the land.[133] As Hoffman envisages the law's *Sitz im Leben* it is likely to be a polemic against Ezra and groups with similar xenophobic tendencies, who continue to apply the law. In Ezra's case this is done by calling people to avoid intermarriage, which Hoffman considers "anachronistic, groundless and null" (p.207).

However, there are several difficulties with Hoffman's case. First, he does not differentiate between *ḥērem* and the intermarriage ban even though the two are clearly not the same (unless, of course, one follows the metaphorical reading within Deuteronomy, in which case *ḥērem* effectively equals no intermarriage and no alliance). Secondly, the *Sitz im Leben* for the *ḥērem* law

---

[132] This is the classic rabbinic position. Cf. Moshe Greenberg, "On the Political Use of the Bible in Modern Israel: An Engaged Critique," in *Pomegranates and Golden Bells: Studies in Biblical, Jewish and Near Eastern Ritual Law and Literature*, ed. David P. Wright, David Noel Freedman and Avi Hurvitz (Winona Lake IN: Eisenbrauns, 1995) 469.

[133] Yair Hoffman, "The Deuteronomistic Concept of the Herem," *ZAW* 111 (1999) 204–207.

that Hoffman advocates is simply unconvincing when numerous texts in the Deuteronomistic History highlight precisely the neglect that characterized Israel in exterminating all the Canaanites. So, for instance, Josh 15:13; 16:10; 17:12 refer to the nations that Israel did not drive out and Josh 23:12–13 warns against intermarriage precisely because the local population has not been annihilated.[134] Judges gives reasons for the failure of carrying out *ḥērem* (Judg 2:1–3; 2:21–3:6) and in 2 Samuel there is further evidence of individual Canaanites living in the land (11:3; 24:16). Surely, if the aim is to make a point about the extinction of the Canaanites and the uselessness of following the *ḥērem* law it is done in a fairly unconvincing way. Rather, the careful reader is left with the impression that the problem is precisely the lack of total commitment to the *ḥērem* law and that there is a direct correlation between this laxity and Israel's sin. By leaving the sources of temptation alive, the nation was led astray into idolatry and apostasy.

Further, beyond Hoffman's theory, the more general problem with considering the *ḥērem* law irrelevant or invalid is that the reason which necessitates *ḥērem*, namely idolatry, allows the law to be broadened to include any other nation who may pose a similar threat to Israel's exclusive worship of YHWH. Thus the suggestion that the absence of Canaanites in Ezra's time makes the *ḥērem* law irrelevant is not a clinching argument.

Finally, it is unlikely that a group like Ezra's circle, depicted in Ezra 7–10 as intent on obeying the Law, would consider any aspect of it obsolete. To use a modern parallel, Ezra's *ḥārēdîm* are more likely to be like Orthodox Jews than Reform ones. The latter, are happy to make the Torah, in Levenson's words, "a contingent product of history" and thereby subordinate the law to the processes of history and its changing circumstances.[135] On the other hand, orthodox Jewry would want to uphold the validity of Torah even when certain aspects of it could not be practiced. Thus, we turn to the next option in dealing with the issue of *ḥērem*.

5.4.2 *Suspended?*

If the people of the *gôlâ* thought that the law of Deut 7:2 was still in force to be carried out on the present inhabitants of the land (i.e., "the people(s) of the land(s)"), the lack of political independence has made the command impossible to obey. In a way, the returned exiles faced a similar impasse as Jews after 70 C.E., who had to come to terms with the loss of the temple and the

---

[134] This incidentally is an example of how Deut 7:1–3 functions in practice. The command was to exterminate the Canaanite nations but since this has not been done during the conquest, therefore Joshua warns against the alternative danger of intermarriage. Clearly the two are differentiated: Israel did not obey the law of *ḥērem* and exterminate these nations; she must now do the next best thing and not intermarry.

[135] Jon D. Levenson, "The Eighth Principle of Judaism and the Literary Simultaneity of Scripture" in *The Hebrew Bible, the Old Testament, and Historical Criticism: Jews and Christians in Biblical Studies* (Louisville, KY: Westminster John Knox, 1993) 75–76.

impossibility of carrying out the prescribed sacrifices. In the case of the latter, orthodox Jewry has found alternative forms for obeying the command such as prayer, or the study of Torah, which do not ultimately replace the former, but provide a way of bridging the gap in the present age. On this reading, the expulsion of the foreign wives may be seen as a temporary measure, even a symbolic form of *ḥērem*, purging the community from foreign influence because it is in no position to purge the land itself.

The question of the basic principle, however, remains. If circumstances change and make the execution of a law impossible how is one to decide whether the measures in their place are meant to be permanent or temporary? In the case of the *ḥērem* law there are at least two reasons why one might see the solution in Ezra 9–10 as a permanent re-interpretation of the command in Deut 7. First, the Ezra narrative gives no indication that what is being done in the case of the mixed marriages is only second best, but only that the situation is dealt with entirely in accordance with the Law. Secondly, there is no hint in the history of the kings at the time of spiritual renewals and reforms that Israel is expected to massacre its non-Jewish population in obedience to *ḥērem* law. There are only two isolated occurrences of *ḥērem* beyond the conquest; one dealing with the Amalekites in 1 Sam 15, and the other with the Meunites during Hezekiah's reign (1 Chr 4:41).[136]

Overall, however, after Israel is settled in the land, the emphasis shifts away from the need to do *ḥērem* though the worship of other gods continues to be a central concern, and intermarriage, feared in Deut 7:3–4, is indicated as one of its causes as seen in the examples of Solomon and Ahab (p. 51). Thus the motivating force for both *ḥērem* and the ban on intermarriage is the same: it is meant to deal with the problem of apostasy. The purpose remains unaltered, merely the way of handling the matter changes.

---

[136] The case of the Amalekites in 1 Sam 15 is exceptional in more ways than one. I have already noted that it applies the term to a nation outside the boundaries of Israel, the cause for its destruction is not idolatry, but hostility to God's people, it contrasts *ḥērem* with sacrifice and includes the destruction of the spoil as well. Thus it is divested of its deuteronomic associations entirely. The theme of the need to exterminate Amalek is a recurring one, yet it nowhere else refers to this as *ḥērem*. It surfaces in the book of Esther, where the wicked Haman is portrayed as a descendant of the Amalekite king, Agag (Esth 3:1) and who is destroyed along with his family (Esth 7:10; 9:6–10, 14) through the services of another Benjamite, Mordecai, a descendant of Kish, like Saul. The raid and extermination of the Amalekites are also mentioned in 1 Chr 4:43, but again without the label of *ḥērem*.

5.4.3 Reinterpreted: Ḥērem Violation

A slightly different approach is advocated by Milgrom regarding the place of *ḥērem* in the story of Ezra 9–10.[137] He argues that if Ezra only forced the divorce of local non-Israelite wives then he effectively applied the *ḥērem* law of Deut 7:1–3 to the local inhabitants of his day. This explanation depends on the distinction between עמי הארץ (local non-Israelite inhabitants) and עמי הארצות (foreigners). The intermarriages are then to be seen as tampering with what is dedicated as *ḥērem*, which is a form of trespass upon *sancta*. Such a transgression constitutes a מעל ("unfaithfulness") for which an אשם ("guilt offering") must be brought (Lev 5:14–16).

Milgrom's theory falls down, I believe, primarily because there does not seem to be a clear distinction in the story between עמי הארץ ("peoples of the land") and עמי הארצות ("peoples of the lands"). Ezra 9:1, 2 and 11 use the latter, Ezra 10:2, 11 the former. Milgrom assumes that the occurrence of עמי הארצות in Ezra 9 is erroneous but this is hard to believe. Moreover, if the narrative is making a sharp distinction between local inhabitants and foreigners, then the inclusion of foreign nations like Ammon and Moab in Ezra 9:1 is confusing and lends itself to misunderstanding.

There are also further difficulties with Milgrom's proposed view above. The notion of *ḥērem* violation rests on the idea that if a person takes something from things dedicated as *ḥērem*; it profanes the objects of *ḥērem*, because as things devoted to God they have holy status. The idea that one should not take anything which is assigned as *ḥērem* only occurs five times in the Old Testament, twice in Deuteronomy (7:26; 13:18[17]), twice in Joshua in connection with the Achan story (6:18; 7:12) and once in the context of Saul's disobedience (1 Sam 15:21). However, the point emphasized in all instances is not what happens to the status of the desecrated object of *ḥērem*, but how the act affects the thief. Thus, Deut 7:26 warns against taking an idol into one's house lest the thief becomes *ḥērem* himself. It is possible to see in this verse the profanation of the object by *ḥērem* violation, nevertheless, the warning may merely mean that the person becomes trapped by idolatry and therefore comes under *ḥērem* himself (cf. Deut 13:13–18[12–17]). Alternatively, it might mean that the same fate awaits those who steal from what is *ḥērem*, namely death and destruction. However, the idols are not considered holy and there is no mention of their desecration or any consideration that the idols "belong" to YHWH and he is robbed of his "due." Deuteronomy 7, as a whole, does not present intermarriage as wrong because it constitutes *ḥērem* violation but because it leads to idolatry and apostasy. The warning to avoid idolatry in v.4 is followed up by the emphasis on the status of God's people as holy, which implies that the intermarriage and ultimately its consequences (idolatry, apostasy) jeopardize this

---

[137] Jacob Milgrom, *Leviticus 1–16: A New Translation with Introduction and Commentary* (AB 3; New York: Doubleday, 1991) 360. This is an alternative theory to his more often quoted one, which I shall discuss in detail in Chaps. 6 and 7.

holiness. In Deut 13:18[17], the command not to take anything that is *ḥērem* is connected with turning God's anger away. The idea seems to be collective responsibility; if Israel takes from the things that YHWH ordered to be destroyed then it is as though she became a party to the sin of the idolatrous city. Her disobedience in dealing with sin according to God's command would identify her with those who worshiped other gods. Again, there is no indication that the concern is with profanation of consecrated things.

Although the booty was Israel's even when a city was made *ḥērem*; in the case of Jericho Joshua orders the entire spoil to be devoted to YHWH as well. However, only the gold, silver, and the articles of bronze and iron, which were assigned to the temple treasury are mentioned as holy (Josh 6:19); nothing is said of the status of anything else among the *ḥērem*. Achan's sin constitutes breach of the covenant as well as theft and deceit (7:11) without any reference to profanation. It is interesting to note that the text stresses the impact of *ḥērem* violation on the camp of Israel; they supposedly come under *ḥērem* themselves (Josh 6:18; 7:12). However, restoring the stolen *ḥērem* (v.13) and presumably dealing with the sinner in their midst apparently resolves the problem. Thus we see that the term is not always applied very precisely, since clearly the Israelite camp does not fall under the same judgment as Achan, who actually committed the act, yet the same expression is used to describe them as the actual perpetrator of such a crime (Deut 7:26).

One other text may be drawn into the discussion which has some bearing on this question of profanation. Lev 27:28 specifically mentions that everything dedicated as *ḥērem* is most holy and cannot be redeemed, which would imply that taking something back that was already dedicated as *ḥērem* would profane it. Note, however, the relative laxity of usage again. Whereas Josh 6:19 calls some *ḥērem* items holy, Lev 27:28 describes them as most holy. In any case, the issue of profanation is not spelt out and the regulation refers to voluntary dedication of one's own property in a peace-time context, which differs considerably from the other references mentioned above. In conclusion, profanation seems to play little or no part in the *ḥērem* texts.

Even if one accepts the theory of profanation, a further objection raised by Hayes is that "it assumes that the prohibited non-Israelites are the objects of desecration (as devoted *ḥērem* that has been violated). Yet in Ezra 9:1–2 at least, it is clear that the Israelites themselves are the objects of desecration (as holy seed that has been profaned)."[138]

Nevertheless, she concedes that it is not impossible that *ḥērem* forms part of the background to the issue in Ezra 9–10, particularly because of her findings regarding the use of Deut 7:26 as it is interpreted in some postexilic literature such as 4QMMT and *Jub.* 30.[139] Deut 7:26 states that anyone who takes an abomination (תועבה) into his house, that is, an idol (cf. v.25), will

---

[138] Christine E. Hayes, "Intermarriage and Impurity in Ancient Jewish Sources," *HTR* 92/1 (1999) 12–13.
[139] Ibid., 31.

become *ḥērem* like it (והייתה חרם כמהו). Hayes notes that in 4QMMT line C6 identifies the idol of Deut 7:26 as the idolater/non-Israelite, whom one should not bring into one's house, that is, marry. She further observes that a similar identification between idol and idolater is made in *Jub.* 30, where the Levitical prohibition to give one's seed to Molech (Lev 18:3), originally referring to child sacrifice, is understood as a ban on giving one's child in marriage to an idolater/non-Israelite. This identification of idolater and idol makes the view of taking intermarriage as a form of *ḥērem* violation more plausible.

The application of Deut 7:26 as part of the argument for the ban on intermarriage is an attractive idea and may well form the background used in Ezra 9–10. It is a concept, however, which if used, is not fully worked out in the mixed marriage crisis. As noted above, Deut 7:26 states that the person bringing an idol into the house becomes *ḥērem* himself. It would thus logically follow that if the wives are under *ḥērem* and are excluded from the community of Israel by being sent away, then so should their husbands be. However, in Ezra 9–10 it is only those who do not comply with the community's decision in dealing with the crisis, who are excluded (10:8). To use a parallel situation, it is as if Achan only had to relinquish what he had stolen and otherwise could escape unharmed. Thus, on several grounds it is unlikely that the intermarriage crisis is to be seen as *ḥērem* violation in the sense Milgrom advocates it here.

5.4.4 Reinterpreted: Divorce as Ḥērem

It follows from the above that if Ezra and his circle consider Deut 7 and the *ḥērem* law both relevant and in operation then this is only possible if they understand the command metaphorically. In a way, this solution has some affinities with the first option: *ḥērem* as extermination only applies to the Canaanites at the conquest. Nevertheless, because the Law is valid, therefore it must apply even if in a different way than before.

If the above reasoning is right at all from the logic of how the narrative presents Ezra and his circle, then how is *ḥērem* interpreted? We have noted that the standard understanding of *ḥērem* involves death. In Ezra 9–10, instead of *ḥērem*, we find the repeatedly used term בדל (Niphal). The women are not destroyed physically as in the instances of *ḥērem* noted elsewhere, nevertheless their exclusion from the community that is seen to represent life is a form of death; they are effectively put away as if they did not exist. Thus, if my contention is right that the solution to the intermarriage crisis is a form of *ḥērem*, then this is a new development, which has no precedent in the literature we know of before Ezra.

The choice of words used in the story may well highlight the specific perspective of the narrative. Thus, it is worth considering the significance of the expressions used for marriage and divorce respectively, neither of which are the usual terms although there can be little question as to their substance.[140] The Hiphil יצא (Ezra 10:3) means literally "to cause to go out" as opposed to the wives' previous married status as "to cause to dwell" (Ezra 10:2—Hiphil ישב). The word pair evokes YHWH's act of causing Israel to go out of Egypt (Exod 20:2; Deut 5:6; 6:12, etc.—Hiphil יצא) and to dwell in her own land (Deut 11:31; 12:10, 29; 30:20, etc.—Qal ישב). In fact, she is specifically admonished to drive out the local inhabitants so that they do not dwell there (Exod 23:33—Qal ישב). Is it possible that these marriages were seen as giving legitimacy to foreign people to dwell in the land and consider it theirs, while their sending out would signify that they had no place among God's people and on their land?[141] Such a view would tie in with the concern for taking hold of and keeping the land, which is a prominent feature in both Neh 9 and in Ezra's prayer (esp. Ezra 9:12; see my discussion in §3.1.1).

5.4.5 "Let It Be Done According to the Law"

The re-interpretation and metaphorical usage of *ḥērem* for understanding the divorces would account for the otherwise curious fact that the exiles claim the law as the source of their authority ("let it be done according to the law" וכתורה יעשה—Ezra 10:3) even though the command in Deut 7:3–6 does not tackle the problem of what happens once such intermarriages have occurred. Neither is there any precedent elsewhere in the Torah for such an action. In fact, Fishbane argues that the exiles' statement that they aim to "act according to the law" is presumptuous, since there is no clear basis for their decision in the Law. Thus, they can only act on a particular interpretation of the Law, not the Law itself.[142]

Williamson suggests that the reference is possibly to Deut 24:1–4, which gives a provision for divorce if there is "something shameful" (lit. "a

---

[140] The word used for marrying in Ezra 9:2 is נשא, which, as observed earlier (see fn. 66) is late in origin but is undoubtedly referring to marriage. So does התחתן in 9:14, which sometimes has the connotation of political alliance strengthened through marriage (cf. Gen 34:9; 2 Chr 18:1). While the sending away is generally assumed to be divorce, Epstein, argues that the wives were merely sent away without a proper divorce. In his view the procedure could not have been annulment because the idea that marriage between a Jew and a heathen was invalid was only introduced in the era of the tannaim. Louis M. Epstein, *Marriage Laws in the Bible and the Talmud* (Cambridge MA: Harvard University Press, 1942) 167, 174.

[141] Alternative suggestions include H. G. M. Williamson's who explains the unusual word pair by saying that they express a pejorative attitude to these marriages (*Ezra, Nehemiah* [WBC 16; Nashville TN: Nelson, 1985] 150–51), while T. Witton Davies goes as far as to say that the unions were not considered proper marriages (*Ezra, Nehemiah and Esther* [Edinburgh: Jack / London: Caxton, 1909] 144–45).

[142] Michael Fishbane, *Biblical Interpretation in Ancient Israel* (Oxford: Clarendon, 1985) 117.

naked thing" ערות דבר) in the wife.[143] Lipton in her stimulating article on Ezra 9–10 observes certain verbal links between the divorce legislation in Deut 24:1–4 and Ezra 9–10.[144] First, she notes that although Deut 24 uses שלח (Qal) not יצא for sending the wife away (cf. Ezra 10:3 יצא Hiphil), the wife in Deut 24:2 leaves (יצא Qal) and this parallels the husband sending her away (v.1). The second link she sees is that the exiles got together "to seek the matter" (לדריוש הדבר) in Ezra 10:16 (i.e., investigate) while Deut 24:1 gives the complementary element of the pair (seek-find) and equally has "matter": "the husband has *found* the nakedness of the *matter.*" Thirdly, Ezra 10:19 reads "they gave their hand to expel their wives" (ויתנו ידם להוציא נשיהם), generally interpreted as "pledged" or "vowed." This Lipton connects to the writing of the bill of divorce in Deut 24:1, 3, which the husband "gives into her hand" (ונתן בידה). She observes the awkward formulation in Deut 24, which in both verses leaves out the "it" (the bill of divorce) from the phrase. She theorizes that this may be a fixed formula for divorce and assumes that the same is meant in Ezra 10:19. She further observes that Deut 24:4 also uses הטמאה and תועבה, words that are central in Ezra's prayer in describing what is wrong with such marriages (9:10–12).

I agree with Lipton that the proceedings described in Ezra 10 refer to divorce and that the request for time to investigate the matter in Ezra 10:13 also indicates this.[145] Her verbal links, however, are tenuous, particularly her third one concerning Ezra 10:19, which would be the clinching argument if it worked. However, Deut 24:1, 3 have "gives *into her* hand" (ונתן בידה), whereas the exiles give *their own* hands (ויתנו ידם) without the prefix ב and with the masculine plural pronominal suffix on יד, which unambiguously indicates that the reference is not to the wives' hands. Other versions do not throw any more light on Ezra 10:19 either. The LXX mirror translates the Hebrew using the same expression of "giving their hands to expel" (καὶ ἔδωκαν χεῖρα αὐτῶν τοῦ ἐξενέγκαι γυναῖκας αὐτῶν) and Josephus has "immediately cast out" (Whiston's translation) εὐθὺς ἐξέβαλον in *Ant.* 11.5.4 in his recounting of the relevant verse.

Thus the reference to Deut 24:1–4 may explain what legal rulings the exiles followed in their divorce proceedings but it throws no light on how "foreignness" was a legitimate reason for divorce. Perhaps it might be argued that the stereotypical connotation of sexual immorality associated with "foreign women" may be equated with ערות דבר. However, none of the distinctive key words of the legislation such as ערות דבר ("naked matter") or ספר כריתת ("bill of divorce") or the Piel of שלח ("to send away") feature in Ezra 9–10, which would indicate that the legal background for the exiles' action needs to be found elsewhere.

---

[143] Williamson, *Ezra, Nehemiah*, 151.
[144] Lipton, "The Furnace of Desire: Forging Identities in Foreign Bedrooms," in *Longing for Egypt and Other Unexpected Biblical Tales* (HBM 15; Sheffield: Sheffield Phoenix, 2008) 221–225.
[145] Ibid., 221.

Another alternative for explaining the reason behind the divorces other than seeing it as a metaphorical interpretation of *ḥērem* is possibly Deut 23:4–9[3–8]. If those of mixed descent were meant to be excluded from the community then the divorces may be seen as part of such exclusion. Using Deut 23 rather than the *ḥērem* idea may better explain why the husbands who contracted such marriages are not excluded from the community. On the other hand, Deut 23 does not deal with foreign wives, only with the descendants of such mixed marriages. Also, it regulates access to the assembly of YHWH (לא־יבא... בקהל יהוה), which one would expect, meant worship in the temple rather than the kind of total exclusion from the life of the community that the divorces imply in Ezra 9–10. As a comparison, Neh 13:1–3 excludes all foreigners from Israel on the basis of Deut 23:4–7[3–6], but here again it is not clear what this implies (see discussion in §4.4).

If we understand the divorces as a form of *ḥērem* in a metaphorical sense, however, then the already established links with Deut 7:1–3 form an adequate legal background for explaining the exiles' action. Although the deuteronomic command only refers to the local inhabitants of Canaan, we have seen in the development of the *ḥērem* idea that the original scope is often widened outside of the Pentateuch to include other nations. Furthermore, if the ultimate objective, following the deuteronomic understanding of *ḥērem*, is the avoidance of idolatry and concomitant sins, then this could mean the extension of the law's scope, which is what the list in Ezra 9:1 with its inclusion of non-Canaanite nations indicates.

5.5 Ḥērem of Property in Ezra 10:8

As already mentioned in the introduction of this chapter, the only time the word חרם occurs in Ezra–Nehemiah is in Ezra 10:8. The context is the oath of the leadership to do according to the proposal laid out by Shecaniah and to send the "foreign" wives away. An assembly is called and those who do not appear in Jerusalem within three days are threatened with their property (רכוש) becoming *ḥērem* and they themselves being excluded (בדל) from the assembly of the exiles (מקהל הגולה).

It is not clear from the MT text what happens to the property that becomes *ḥērem*, although commentators generally agree that it is most likely confiscated and made use of in the temple and/or by the priesthood.[146] 1 Esd 9:4 and Josephus (*Ant*.11.148) both remove the ambiguity by stating clearly that the possessions which are made *ḥērem* become temple property. There is precedent for this in the story of Jericho, where some valuables are put into the temple treasury and in the regulations of Lev 27:21, 28; Num 18:14, and Ezek 44:29

---

[146] Joseph Blenkinsopp, *Ezra-Nehemiah: A Commentary* (London: SCM, 1988) 190; Loring W. Batten, *A Critical and Exegetical Commentary on the Books of Ezra and Nehemiah*, (ICC; Edinburgh: T&T Clark, 1913) 342; C. F. Keil, *The Books of Ezra, Nehemiah, and Esther* (trans. Sophia Taylor; Edinburgh: T&T Clark, 1873) 128, etc.

although in the case of the latter three instances it is not spelt out whether objects of ḥērem are voluntarily devoted or confiscated. Thus, there is no explicit precedent for the kind of confiscation that we encounter in Ezra 10.

There are two narratives which show certain parallels with the situation depicted in Ezra 9–10 and may shed light on the source for this action of the exiles. In Judg 21 the community takes an oath to put to death all those who do not appear at the assembly in order to deal with the Benjamites. Jabesh-Gilead fails to turn up and is duly made ḥērem (vv.10–11). However, the penalty for non-compliance and non-appearance is only death without any reference to the fate of possessions. Another similar incident, this time without the mention of ḥērem is 2 Chr 15:13.[147] Again the community assembles in Jerusalem after king Asa's restoration of the altar in the Jerusalem Temple. The people enter into covenant to seek YHWH (ויבאו בברית לדרוש את־יהוה—v.12) and swear an oath to him (וישבעו ליהוה—v.14). Whoever does not comply with this communal decision is to be put to death. Again property is not mentioned, nevertheless the communal decision and oath in a certain matter as well as the death penalty for non-compliance is present.

In comparison, the death penalty is replaced by the double measure of exclusion and the confiscation of property in Ezra 10:8. Schneider traces the exclusion back to the Mosaic command "to be cut off" (Exod 12:15, etc.), which originally meant the death penalty. He argues that once Israel lost her independent statehood, the concept "to be cut off" meant exclusion from the civil and religious community.[148] In Ezra's case, however, it can be objected that he was empowered to authorize the death penalty (Ezra 7:26), so the loss of the monarchy in itself does not explain the decision of the exiles in this matter. Williamson also notes that banishment was not envisaged in the Pentateuch, but the death penalty came to be interpreted this way and Horbury traces the development of this transformation from the meager evidence of biblical sources and the Jewish literature of the Second Temple Period to the later rabbinic writings.[149]

The above, however, still does not quite explain the sudden appearance of property confiscation. If we consider the significance of ḥērem as death and destruction, then there is a certain logic to its replacement not only by exclusion but by exclusion *and* the confiscation of property. If death means that the person does not exist in the estimate of a community then the confiscation of property underlines this loss of status. The word רכוש generally means moveable property and a person's wealth may indicate his substance and standing in the community. Thus the loss of property may mean the disenfranchisement of the person involved. One difficulty with this way of understanding Ezra 10:8 is that

---

[147] Blenkinsopp notes the similarity (*Ezra-Nehemiah*, 190).
[148] Heinrich Schneider, *Die Bücher Esra und Nehemia* (Bonn: Peter Hanstein, 1959) 154.
[149] Williamson, *Ezra, Nehemiah*, 155; William Horbury, "Extirpation and Excommunication," *VT* 35/1 (1985) 13–38.

רכוש does not include land, and would thus go against the thrust of this argument.

An alternative source could be Deuteronomy 13:13–18[12–17], where the idolatrous Israelite city is destroyed including people, livestock and possessions. Here both exclusion and confiscation of possession find their parallel measure. The deuteronomic command is particularly appropriate to Ezra 9–10 in that it affects Israelites who have sinned, it describes moveable wealth (livestock and booty—vv.16–17) and by referring to the sacrificial aspect of *ḥērem* (כליל ליהוה) it provides a bridge from destruction to devotion for temple use.

Ultimately we do not know the exact background to Ezra 10:8, since there is no specific explanation of the *ḥērem* of property. This absence of justification makes one wonder if by this time it was standard practice without the need for further explanation.

5.6 Conclusion

In this chapter I have sought to answer the question what role the *ḥērem* law of Deut 7:1–3 played in the understanding of the intermarriage crisis and its solution. In reviewing *ḥērem* in the OT, I concluded that enemy *ḥērem* consistently meant extermination and death throughout, although its scope and intention showed more variety outside the Pentateuch. In the case of property *ḥērem* the legislation called for the destruction of possessions when dealing with the idolatrous Israelite city, but did not demand the booty of the Canaanite cities under *ḥērem*. In peace-time *ḥērem* meant the voluntary and irrevocable dedication of any possession (livestock, land, etc.) for the use of the temple/priesthood. I suggested that the two strands of overarching characteristics for *ḥērem* were devotion/dedication on the one hand and destruction on the other. These two aspects, where separate, took the concept in two different directions, the former on its own expressing the peace-time dedication of property for temple use, the latter the indiscriminate extermination of any enemy.

Next I evaluated the various hermeneutical strategies that the exiles may have used in their interpretation of Deut 7:1–3. I argued that the most likely move for Ezra and his circle in the story was to opt for a metaphorical reinterpretation of the deuteronomic legislation, which involved separation rather than death. This seemed to me a more convincing basis for the exiles' insistence that the divorces were "according to the law" than Deut 24:1–4 or 23:4–9[3–8]. The extended scope of the exiles' action, which may have included women who were not local inhabitants, was indicated by the list of nations which incorporated peoples other than the original seven nations of Canaan. This tendency found its parallel in the way the *ḥērem* law was understood more broadly in the non-pentateuchal material. It may also have been justified on the basis that the intention of Deut 7:1–3 was to protect from idolatry and such a threat was not limited to local inhabitants as the story of the kings of Israel and Judah demonstrated (e.g., 1 Kgs 11:1–11).

As far as Ezra 10:8 and the confiscation of property I argued that the Ezran story had affinities with Judg 21 and 2 Chr 15:13. In both of these cases Israel was making a community decision, taking an oath and threatening non-compliance with the death penalty. I suggested that in Ezra 10:8 the death penalty was replaced by the double measure of exclusion and confiscation of property, the latter of which may have also expressed the loss of status and standing in the community. This twin penalty also found some parallel in Deut 13:13–18[12–17], although the measures there were stricter: the people were killed and the possessions destroyed.

In conclusion then, I have argued that the divorce proceedings were a kind of *ḥērem*, but instead of the law taking the form of extermination in Ezra 9–10, it was re-interpreted metaphorically as separation from the "foreign" wives and possible separation as well as confiscation of property for any Israelite who did not comply with the community's decision to deal with the crisis.

6

Holy Seed and Intermingling

So far I have examined various questions relating to the first argument brought by the exiles against intermarriages in Ezra 9:1. We have seen that the deuteronomic command not to intermarry with the local Canaanites lest Israel learns their idolatrous practices and turns away from her God (Deut 7:1–3) is extended with a list of other foreign nations (Deut 23:4–7[3–6], Lev 18:3) near and further afield. The common denominator in all of them is their association with the stereotypical sins of idolatry and sexual immorality summed up in the term "abominations" (תועבות).

Ezra 9:2 introduces another explanation into the crisis, namely that through the intermarriages the "holy seed has intermingled with the peoples of the lands" (והתערבו זרע הקדש בעמי הארצות). The inherently holy status of Israel as a nation is a deuteronomic concept evident in the chapter prohibiting intermarriage (עם קדוש—Deut 7:6). Also, the word "abominations" (תועבות), which in Deut 7:25–26 denotes idols, occurs in Ezra 9:1, 11 and 14. Thus it may seem at first glance that the danger anticipated by such intermarriages is no different from that implied by Deut 7, which is the result of the worship of foreign gods or idols.

There are, however, at least two reasons to think that we are dealing here with a reasoning distinct from the one laid out in Deut 7. First, the replacement of עם ("people") with זרע ("seed") may be significant. Secondly, the indiscriminate divorce of all the "foreign" wives irrespective of their religious commitment suggests an inherent quality in the women which is unacceptable. This is further reinforced by the sending away of their children with them, which implies that the effects are irreversible for the descendants. Thus we encounter here a new motif which emerges with Ezra in the Postexilic Period.

This chapter will therefore examine "the holy seed" rationale more closely as an argument why intermarriages are unacceptable which is distinct from the one in Ezra 9:1. I shall first expand on the above statement by considering the use of "seed" (זרע) and on the tension between this reason for the ban on mixed marriages and the standard one warning against the danger of idolatry in Deut 7:1–3. Next I shall consider the possible source(s) and legal background which may have contributed to this new rationale against intermarriage and will compare similar developments in the Jewish literature of the Second Temple Period.

6.1 "Holy Seed": A Distinct Rationale

	Ezra 9:2a	
כי־נשאו מבנתיה להם ולבניהם והתערבו זרע הקדש בעמי הארצות.	Ezra 9:2a	For they have taken some of their daughters as wives for themselves and for their sons, so that the holy seed has intermingled with the peoples of the land (NASV)

6.1.1 The Significance of זרע

The noun זרע literally means "seed" of a plant (Gen 1:11; 47:23) or more infrequently "semen" (Lev 15:16; 22:4). The latter use often takes on a more figurative sense of "descendants," a term particularly prominent in the Abraham narrative (Gen 12:7; 13:15–16; 15:3–5; 16:10; 17:7–10, etc.). In the priestly material the "seed of Aaron" refers to those descended from the priestly clan (זרע אהרן—Lev 21:21; 22:4; Num 17:5[16:40]). Similarly, the "seed of David" denotes the royal lineage of King David (זרע דוד—2 Sam 22:51; 1 Kgs 2:33; 11:39). In all these instances, physical descent is the defining aspect of the term. In Deuteronomy, a major source of background for EN, the word זרע is less prominent, used only in the context of the promises given to the patriarchs (e.g., Deut 1:8; 4:37; 10:15; 11:9, etc.), while Israel is mostly referred to as the "people," the "children /sons of Israel" (עם, בני־ישראל).[150] Since the concept of Israel's holy status in Ezra 9:2 is most likely derived from Deut 7:6, it is all the more conspicuous and surely not co-incidental that זרע replaces עם. There is precedent for using זרע in connection with the whole nation elsewhere in Scripture; Israel is called the "seed of Abraham" (זרע אברהם—2Chr 20:7, Ps 105:6), sometimes the "seed of Israel" (זרע ישראל—1Chr 16:13; Neh 9:2) or the "seed of Jacob" (זרע יעקב—Ps 22:24[23]) emphasizing thereby the descent from the patriarchs.

The linking of Israel's holy status with the notion of "seed," however, is new and carries with it the sense that holiness is conferred by physical descent as in the case of the priests. The context of EN, its preoccupation with genealogical lists (Ezra 2; 7:1–5; 8:1–14; Neh 7; 12:1–26) further underlines the importance of physical descent. Moreover, the need for the exiles to prove their ancestry in order to be considered "Israel" (note the use of זרע for

---

[150] עם—Deut 2:4; 4:6; 7:6; 9:12–13, 26; 10:11; 14:2; 17:16; 18:3, etc.; בני־ישראל—Deut 1:3; 4:44, 45, 46; 23:18[17]; 24:7; 31:19, 22, 23, etc.

"descendant"—Ezra 2:59) reinforces the idea that ancestry determines status and that this status is compromised by mixed descent. There is also precedent for the idea of desecration caused by a possibly questionable lineage: the priests of Ezra 2:62 cannot prove their priestly descent and are therefore considered "desecrated/defiled [and excluded] from the priesthood" (ויגאלו מן־הכהנה). Further, the priests who intermarried with the "peoples of the land" are specifically described as the desecrators/defilers of the priesthood in Neh 13:29 (גאלי הכהנה).[151]

6.1.2   Indiscriminate Expulsion

If intermarriage with those not defined as part of "Israel" affects "the holy seed permanently because of an inherent quality in them, then this requires an absolute ban without exceptions and without alternatives. This is in some tension with the prohibition of intermarriage based on the fear of idolatry/apostasy in Deut 7:1–3 since such a reason does not denote an innate defect. In Deuteronomy the severity of the prohibition to intermarry is in direct proportion to the likelihood of religious threat. Thus the ban is absolute regarding the Canaanites, but allows for some exceptions in other cases. So, for instance, as mentioned in §4.1 the law of the beautiful captive woman (Deut 21:10–14) permits marriage with such a woman presumably because without a family she is less likely to lead the Israelite husband to apostasy. Deut 23:4–9[3–8], which lists the various groups excluded from the assembly of YHWH (קהל יהוה), also allows for some variation in the attitude toward the nations involved. Thus Egypt and Edom are treated more leniently than Ammon and Moab and with the former two the effect on the offspring seems to diminish after a few generations when the descendants are no longer excluded from the קהל. Although in Deut 23 the decisive factor seems to be the particular sinful actions of these nations in the past toward Israel rather than their potential influence detrimental to her future, the past is perhaps indicative of their general attitude. In any case, these regulations demonstrate that the ban on intermarriage with non-Israelites is not absolute and rigidly inflexible, at least not in Deuteronomy.

If the issue in Ezra is only the threat of idolatry and the fear of apostasy, then one would expect some distinction between wives who were following other gods and influencing their husbands in that direction and other wives who had committed themselves to abandoning their old ways and following YHWH. The exiles may have also looked for a different solution to the problem and demanded that the wives follow the religion of their Israelite husbands. It might be argued that Deut 7 does not envisage exceptions either, but we have already noted that this absolute ban is relativized somewhat by the varying degrees of permission for intermarriage in other cases (Deut 21:10–14; 23:4–9[3–8]). By contrast, all the "foreign" women not defined as part of "Israel," the "sons of the exile" (בני־הגולה) are expelled in Ezra 9–10.

---

[151] For a further discussion on the meaning of גאל as desecration or defilement see §7.2.1.

Also, it has to be remembered that the "inflexibility" of Deut 7 may stem from gaps within the legislation. It is well-known that the pentateuchal law does not cover all potentialities or deal with each individual case; rather it provides some guiding principles for decision-making.[152] Thus Deut 7 leaves a number of questions unanswered such as what is to be done in the case of already contracted marriages or what happens to women who are willing to part with their idolatrous way. Narrative on the other hand deals with individual instances and concrete situations, as we see in Ezra 9–10, where such practical questions cannot be avoided. Thus the inflexibility in Ezra 9–10 is of a different nature from the one evidenced in the Torah.

A further alternative for explaining the absolute ban on intermarriage in Ezra 9–10 is Kaufmann's view, who contends that the phenomenon of religious conversion was not known in EN's time and hence this solution could not be contemplated by the exiles. Although the story of Ruth may spring to one's mind as a possible counter-example, Kaufmann argues that hers is not a case of religious conversion but that of territorial proselytism; the association of a foreigner in the covenant of Israel.[153] Whatever the fine points of definition may be, it is hard to deny that Ruth's devotion as expressed in her verbal vow involves a commitment to Israel's God (Ruth 1:16). Even if this does not exactly match the procedure for later Judaism's understanding of conversion, a similar demand toward the "foreign" wives should have sufficed for the exiles as a way of ensuring protection from the dangers of apostasy.

Therefore the cumulative evidence of the way זרע is understood and the indiscriminate expulsion of all foreign women may give sufficient support to the theory that Ezra 9:2 introduces a rationale distinct from the one reflected in Deut 7:1–3.

6.2 The Background for the Holy Seed Rationale

6.2.1 Resonances in Isa 6:13; Mal 2:14; Ps 106

The only other occurrence for the expression "holy seed" (זרע קדש) is in Isa 6:13, where it denotes the remnant purified through judgment. It is generally assumed that Isa 6:13 is post-Isaianic at least and most argue that it is actually postexilic.[154] Williamson in particular is an advocate of it being a

---

[152] Judaism, aware of the hiatus between principles and practice, bridges the gap through the interpretative process as evidenced in the oral Torah.

[153] Yehezkel Kaufmann, *History of the Religion of Israel, Vol. IV., From the Babylonian Captivity to the End of Prophecy* (New York: Ktav, 1977) 343 fn. 50. (For a more detailed description of the various categories he uses see Ibid., Chap. 4.)

[154] E.g., H. G. M. Williamson, *Ezra, Nehemiah* (WBC 16; Nashville TN: Nelson Publishers, 1985) 132; Hans Wildberger, *Isaiah 1–12* (trans. Thomas H. Trapp; Minneapolis MN: Fortress, 1991) 258; G. B. Gray, *A Critical and Exegetical Commentary on the Book of Isaiah 1–39* (ICC; Edinburgh: T&T Clark, 1912) 111; Brevard S. Childs, *Isaiah* (Louisville KY: Westminster John Knox Press, 2001) 58. For a

postexilic addition on the basis that the "holy seed" in Ezra 9:2 is a sophisticated piece of hermeneutic that brings together several biblical texts and is firmly embedded in its context while Isa 6:12–13 when compared to v.11 show a change of speaker (v.12), a change of meter (v.13) and adds an element of "hope" (v.13) into a passage otherwise concerned with judgment.[155]

The expression in Isa 6:13 stands in opposition with "seed of evildoers" (זרע מרעים) in Isa 1:4, both groups being part of Israel, which seems to make the inherent holiness of all Israel unlikely. Rather it may be the result of purging. Moberly on the other hand argues for the inherent holiness of the "seed." He suggests that the verse is not about the stump which remains after the rest has been burned. Rather, the stump itself receives the burning after the tree has been felled. That is, after the initial devastation of the land (the falling of the tree) there is more to come to those who survived (the burning of the stump). Thus the purifying action of God is an ongoing and potentially unceasing process because God is holy and his people, though inherently holy in status, are in constant need of purification in practice.[156]

It is interesting to note, that while the MT has the indefinite זרע קדש, the Isaiah Scroll from Qumran (1QIsa^a) is using the definite זרע הקדש that we find in Ezra 9:2. Quell supposes on this basis "that the scribe was following a usage current in his group and that Ezra 9:2 had not been without influence."[157] Quell also observes the emendation in the LXX (and Vulgate) translations of Isa 1:9. The MT reads, "Unless the LORD of hosts has left us a *few survivors* (שריד כמעט), we would be like Sodom, we would be like Gomorrah" (NASV), while the LXX replaces שריד כמעט with σπέρμα ("seed"). Quell assumes that the translations owe this change to the ideology of Israel as the "holy seed" (Ezra 9:2, Isa 6:13).[158]

Mal 2:14 speaks of a "godly seed" (זרע אלהים), which those Israelites not living in intermarriage with foreigners seek. The passage earlier condemns marriages with foreign women who are described as "the daughter of a foreign god" (בת־אל נכר—v.11). The crime is called an "abomination" (תועבה), by which Judah has profaned the sanctuary (כי חלל יהודה קדש יהוה). It is not entirely clear whether the profanation of the sanctuary is the result of mixing the seeds or the threat of apostasy/idolatry. Thus the text may well stay within the conceptual world of Deut 7. In any case, the passage is too ambiguous to allow very far-reaching conclusions.

---

list of scholars who consider vv.12–13 original to Isa 6 (e.g., Delitzsch, Bredenkamp, Kittel) see Otto Kaiser, *Isaiah 1–12* (trans. R.A. Wilson; London: SCM, 1972) 84 fn. b.
[155] Williamson, *Isaiah*, 35.
[156] Moberly, "'Holy, Holy, Holy:' Isaiah's vision of God" in *Holiness Past and Present* (ed. Stephen C. Barton; London: T&T Clark / New York: Continuum, 2003) 134–136.
[157] G. Quell, "σπέρμα," *TDNT* 7:542. John D. W. Watts adopts the Isaiah Scroll's reading (זרע הקדש) and translates is as "the seed of the holy" (*Isaiah 1–33* [WBC 24; 2nd ed.; Nelson, 2005] 101, 103).
[158] Quell, *TDNT* 7:542.

The vocabulary of Ezra 9:2 also occurs in Ps 106, which reflects on Israel's past history and YHWH's dealings with his people. On closer inspection, however, it too keeps to the pattern of thought set out in Deut 7. Thus the psalmist laments that God punishes Israel by casting their seed among the nations (ולהפיל זרעם בגוים— v.27) and in enumerating her sins, mentions that they did not destroy the peoples but mingled with them and learnt their practices (לא השמידו את־העמים... ויתערבו בגוים וילמדו מעשיהם—v.34). Although the psalm does not refer to intermarriage or *ḥērem*, the progression of thought in vv.34–36 follows the sequence of Deut 7. The command to destroy the nations on entering the land as set out in Deut 7:1–2 is ignored (Ps 106:34). Israel mingles with them and succumbs to idolatry (Deut 7:2–4 cf. Ps 106:35–36) so that it becomes a snare to her (פן תוקש בו—Deut 7:25 cf. ויהיו להם למוקש—Ps 106:36). Notably, the two key words of Ezra 9:2 (זרע and התערב) are not combined in the psalm but occur in separate verses and the issue of holiness is not raised.

6.2.2 Milgrom: Deut 7 & Jer 2:3

| קדש ישראל ליהוה ראשית תבואתה כל־אכליו יאשמו רעה תבא אליהם נאם־יהוה. | Jer 2:3 | Israel was holy to the LORD, The first of His harvest. All who ate of it became guilty; Evil came upon them," declares the LORD. (NASV) |

Where among the pentateuchal commands would one find the source for Ezra's way of thinking? One possible solution is Milgrom's suggestion that Ezra and his circle has spun a legal midrash using the theological concept of Israel's holiness as set out in Deut 7:6 and fusing it with the prophetic image of Jer 2:3 where Israel is God's holy crop eaten by her enemies.[159] While in Jeremiah it is the nations who do the desecration, in Ezra 9 the exiles themselves are responsible for allowing it through intermarriage. Milgrom argues that this is essentially a deuteronomic view of holiness (Deut 7:6; 14:2, 21), which sees Israel and not only the priests and nazirites as being inherently holy (cf. Lev 21:6; Num 6:5), whereas "For P, holiness [of the people] is a desideratum not a fact, an ideal not a status."[160] This idea of Israel's inherent holiness, which is desecrated by the marriages with foreign women, is described by Ezra 9:2 as a מעל ("unfaithfulness"), a term that indicates the sin of desecration or oath violation.[161] The theory is further reinforced by the action of the priests who

---

[159] Jacob Migrom, *Cult and Conscience: The Asham and the Priestly Doctrine of Repentance* (Leiden: Brill, 1976) 71–73.
[160] Ibid., 72.
[161] Jacob Milgrom, "The Concept of *Ma'al* in the Bible and the Ancient Near East," *JAOS* 96/2 (1976) 236–247.

bring a guilt offering (אשם) in Ezra 10:19, the prescribed sacrifice for the "trespass upon *sancta*" (Lev 5:14–16).[162]

On the whole, Milgrom's solution to the background of Ezra 9:2 is an appealing and elegant one and he seems right in his assumption that the issue here is *sancta* desecration. The imagery of Jeremiah utilizes the concept of holy food eaten by those who are profane. Although Milgrom does not mention this, the concept would have been readily graspable for the exiles, who themselves excluded those priests of uncertain genealogy from eating of the most holy things (Ezra 2:62–63) because they were considered "profaned/defiled" (גאל). Nevertheless, using Jeremiah's holy food analogy would not explain why intermarriage itself with any non-Israelite would constitute desecration. There is precedent for the defiling effect of certain foods, there is none for intermarriage itself. In Deut 7 it is idolatry and apostasy which is the decisive factor and elsewhere in the Deuteronomistic History, the condemnation of intermarriage is grounded similarly in its effects of leading people into foreign worship (e.g., 1 Kgs 11:1–8).

We have seen so far that Deut 7:6 plays an important part in the exiles' understanding of Israel's holiness as a people, but neither it, nor Jer 2:3 can fully account for the way the intermarriages in themselves have a profaning effect on God's holy seed. So we turn to our next possible option.

6.2.3 Lev 19:19 & Deut 22:9–11

Both Lev 19:19 and Deut 22:9–11 prohibit sowing (לא־תזרע) with seeds of two kinds (כלאים) and there is reason to assume that this legislation formed the background of thought for the "holy seed" rationale in Ezra 9:2.

בהמתך לא־תרביע כלאים שדך לא־תזרע כלאים ובגד כלאים שעטנז לא יעלה עליך.	Lev 19:19	You shall not breed together two kinds of your cattle; you shall not sow your field with two kinds of seed, nor wear a garment upon you of two kinds of material mixed together. (NASV)

---

[162] C. F. Keil argues that guilt offerings were brought not only for the priests but also for the people even though the text does not state this explicitly, but it is evident from the context (*The Books of Ezra, Nehemiah, and Esther* [trans. Sophia Taylor; Edinburgh: T&T Clark, 1873] 133). Similarly, Milgrom thinks that it would not make sense that all Israel was guilty of מעל (Ezra 9:2, 4; 10:2, 6, 10) but only the priests brought an אשם. The alternative that only the priests needed to bring such an offering would mean that Ezra followed the stricter school of Ezekiel which prescribed an אשם for carcass contamination in the case of the priests but not for the layman (*Cult and Conscience*, 73, fn. 262).

לֹא־תִזְרַע כַּרְמְךָ כִּלְאָיִם פֶּן־תִּקְדַּשׁ הַמְלֵאָה הַזֶּרַע אֲשֶׁר תִּזְרָע וּתְבוּאַת הַכָּרֶם. לֹא־תַחֲרֹשׁ בְּשׁוֹר־וּבַחֲמֹר יַחְדָּו. לֹא תִלְבַּשׁ שַׁעַטְנֵז צֶמֶר וּפִשְׁתִּים יַחְדָּו.	Deut 22:9–11	You shall not sow your vineyard with two kinds of seed, or all the produce of the seed which you have sown and the increase of the vineyard will become defiled. You shall not plow with an ox and a donkey together. You shall not wear a material mixed of wool and linen together. (NASV)

Both regulations deal with forbidden mixtures although there is some variation in the commands. Deuteronomy replaces field with vineyard, gives an explanation for the command, changes interbreeding two kinds of cattle to ploughing with two kinds of animals and specifies what garment mixture is prohibited (wool and linen).

The obvious connection between these injunctions and Ezra 9:2 is the use of "seed" and the prohibition of mixing. Another link is the reference to a vineyard (כרם) in Deut 22, which, along with vine (גפן—Ps 80:8–11[7–10]), was probably a well-known symbol for Israel (e.g., Isa 5:7; Jer 12:10) by the time the exiles returned and it endured at least into the first century C.E. (e.g., Matt 21:33). Also the use of גדר as fence/hedge around a vineyard in Ezra's prayer (9:9) may be read as a metaphorical expression of God's protection over his vineyard, Israel (Ezek 13:5; 22:30).[163]

Deut 22:9 makes it clear that sowing seed between the vine rows changes the status of both the produce of the seed sown (הזרע אשר תזרע) and the fruit of the vine (תבואת הכרם). What is somewhat obscure, however, is the exact status the author has in mind. The Hebrew literally means "lest it be consecrated" (פן־תקדש—Qal 3rd fem. sing).[164] The confusion of what this signifies is illustrated by translations both Jewish and Christian, ancient and modern.

---

[163] Several English translations simply use "wall" (e.g., KJV, NRSV, NASV), which is misleading in that it could be taken to mean the city wall around Jerusalem (NIV, NLT use "a wall of protection," RSV "protection" and JSP "fence"). The usual word for city wall, however, is חומה rather than גדר (cf. Neh 1:3; 3:33[4:1]; 4:1[4:7]; 7:1, etc.). Moreover, the גדר in v.9 is in (around) Judah and Jerusalem (ביהודה ובירושלם) *not* around Jerusalem only. גדר is most often used for a hedge or fence around a vineyard, or along a road (cf. Num 22:24; Ps 80:13[12]; Isa 5:5) and thus in Ezra 9 it is more likely to have a metaphorical meaning. See also Williamson, *Ezra, Nehemiah*, 136–37.

[164] The Syriac version has the Hithpael with the same meaning and the Samaritan Pentateuch the Hiphil (תקדיש—2nd masc sing: "lest you consecrate").

ἵνα μὴ ἁγιασθῇ	lest it be consecrated	LXX
דלא תאבדון	lest you destroy	Tg. Neof.
דילמא תתחייב יקידתא	lest it will be condemned to be burned	Tg. Ps.-J.
דילמא תסתאב	lest it will become defiled	Tg. Onq.
lest it be forfeited		NRSV, JPS [1917]
lest it be forfeited to the sanctuary		RSV
lest it becomes defiled		KJV, NKJV, NIV, NASV
may not be used		JPS Tanakh [1985]
forbidden to use		NLT

The above evidence suggests that the regulation was understood in two different ways; one assumed that the MT's wording meant the holy nature of anything thus mixed, which was therefore devoted to the temple and not to be used by the owner for his own purposes; while the other saw the mixing of seeds as defilement or profanation, which rendered the produce utterly useless for any purpose and ultimately to be destroyed. The LXX follows the MT using the Greek equivalent for the Hebrew קדש; the Targums along with other Jewish sources (*Sipre Deut* par. 230:1 and *b. Ked* 56b) mostly emphasize that no benefit is to be derived from the produce for the owner. Modern translations equally alternate between the two viewpoints of sanctification and defilement.

These two explanations correspond to two major views regarding כלאים. The most frequently adopted one is that such mixing goes against the divinely ordered separation of distinct species and creates chaos in the world (Gen 1; 6:1–6, etc.).[165] Strictly speaking, separation is actually a wider principle, which includes aspects other than mating practices between species. Thus the idea involves the separation of the elements as demonstrated in the creation account (darkness-light, waters above-below, waters and dry land, etc.), the separation of the holy and profane, the clean and unclean as expressed in the walls surrounding the temple (Ezek 42:20), in the prohibition for the priesthood to drink wine when coming into the sanctuary (Lev 10:10), and in the injunction to distinguish between clean and unclean meat (Lev 11:47). This latter command is a mark of Israel's holiness, an expression of her separation from other peoples (Lev 20:24–26). It is this idea of Israel's, or if we draw a narrower circle, the priesthood's separate status, which is the key. This principle is then applied and worked out systematically in other aspects of creation not obviously related to holiness. Thus, in my estimate, the trigger is not some "ancient taboo against

---

[165] E.g., S. R. Driver, *A Critical and Exegetical Commentary on Deuteronomy* (ICC; Edinburgh: T&T Clark, 1902) 252; Mary Douglas, *Purity and Danger: An Analysis of Concepts of Pollution and Taboo* (London: Routledge and Keegan Paul, 1966; repr., London: Routledge Classics, 2002) 67.

unnatural or abnormal combinations"¹⁶⁶ but this issue of holiness, which is applied to what God's holy people eat, wear, breed, how they sow and plough.

Although the ban on various activities relating to כלאים does not include human "seed," yet it is easy to see that the command lends itself to a metaphorical application of banning intermarriage with other nations. McConville notes the possible sexual connotations (vineyard, Song 8:11–12; ploughing, Sir 25:8) in the imagery used.¹⁶⁷ Carmichael goes even further in arguing that the laws of mixtures is a commentary and critique on the exogamous marriages in the patriarchal narratives and are not to be taken literally, but are symbolically referring to sexual matters.¹⁶⁸ Although his main theory is imaginative, it is rather far-fetched in the application of its details (e.g., Shechem the son of an ass (Hamor), sexually ploughed Dinah, the daughter of the ox (Jacob/Israel—Gen 49:6). More importantly, as Milgrom puts it with some exasperation, if the lawgiver wanted to condemn exogamous marriages would it not have been simpler to prohibit these in the law on sexual relations in Lev 18 or 20, for instance, rather than sending cryptic and rather obscure messages?¹⁶⁹ It is more likely that the laws were meant to be taken at face value, even though they also have a wider symbolic significance and thus lend themselves to the justification of endogamy.

If we follow the explanation of Deut 22:9 and understand the reason for the prohibition to be the defilement/profanation of the mixed seed then the logic of the prohibition is easily transferable to the situation in Ezra 9. In §3.2.2 I have noted the connection between Ezra 9 and 8 reflected in the key word בדל (8:24; 9:2), which describes the priests' separation when they carried the vessels back from Babylon and deposited them in the temple and the need for the people to separate from their "foreign" wives. This separation is connected to holiness in each case (8:28; 9:2). As the priests needed to be holy to deposit the consecrated vessels in the temple, so Israel could not appear before God's holy presence (cf. Ezra 9:15) unless she separated from the "foreign" women.

The second possible reason for the *kil'ayim* laws is proposed by Milgrom, according to whom "mixtures belong to the divine realm, on which the human being (except for divinely designated persons, the priests) may not encroach."¹⁷⁰ Thus he argues that the cherubim are hybrid creatures (Ezek 1:5–

---

[166] J. G. McConville, *Deuteronomy* (AOTC 5; Leicester: Apollos / Downers Grove IL: IVP, 2002) 338.

[167] Ibid., 338. See also Michael Fishbane, who thinks that ploughing is a *double entendre* referring to sexual matters (*Biblical Interpretation in Ancient Israel* [Oxford: Clarendon, 1985] 59, fn.38).

[168] Calum M. Carmichael, "Forbidden Mixtures in Deuteronomy XXII 9–11 and Leviticus XIX 19," *VT* 45 (1995) 433–448.

[169] Jacob Milgrom "Law and Narrative and the Exegesis of Leviticus XIX 19," *VT* 46/4 (1996) 547.

[170] Jacob Milgrom, *Leviticus 17–22: A New Translation with Introduction and Commentary* (AB 3A; New York: Doubleday, 2000) 1659.

11), the curtain of the tabernacle and the veil is made of a combination of wool and linen and so is the high priest's ephod, breastplate and belt (Exod 28:6, 15; 39:29).[171] Milgrom also observes a certain gradation of holy status evident in that the high priest has several clothes items made of this mixture, while the ordinary priest is only allowed a belt made of wool and linen (Exod 39:29), and the tassel of the lay Israelite contains merely one violet wool thread.[172] This latter is not indicative of Israel's holy status, but is a reminder that the ordinary people also need to aspire to holiness.

Milgrom's explanation would fit in with Deut 22:9 if the crucial Hebrew word תקדש is understood as "sanctified." Then mixing the seeds would result in their acquiring holy status to be forfeited to the sanctuary. If he is right then Deut 22 cannot be the source for the holy seed rationale in Ezra 9:2, which is more in line with the separation view mentioned first. On the other hand, his theory does not wholly account for the prohibition of interbreeding animals or ploughing together with them. On Milgrom's reasoning we might expect that the priests would be allowed to interbreed animals and use such animals in the temple. Also, it is questionable whether the cherubim can be called hybrid creatures. What Ezekiel describes is imagery using human categories, which is surely not equivalent to saying that these creatures are the *result* of such interbreeding. Milgrom's main and most convincing argument rests on the use of the mixture of wool and linen, where one might readily grant that he has a point, but he is weak on explaining the other laws relating to *kil'ayim*. Milgrom's main objection against the "separation of species" view is that it has no relevance for the mixed seeds, which are not "mated" in the ground, but are kept apart.[173] Clearly, in the case of the mixed seeds the analogy with intermarriage breaks down; nevertheless, even if the two kinds of seed do not "mate" in the ground the point of the prohibition is that they occupy the same ground. In any case, the overall cluster of *kil'ayim* laws carry ideas of interbreeding and as examples from the Second Temple Period show, there were those who saw in the prohibition of mixed seeds an analogy for banning intermarriage (see §6.2.4). Finally, the separation theory makes better sense of the *kil'ayim* law overall and accounts for all the various forms of separation, which Milgrom's theory does not do.

6.2.4   Lev 21:7–15

A final source which may contribute to our understanding of the background of the holy seed rationale is Lev 21:7–15 regulating the marriages of priests, particularly v.14, where the high priest is only allowed to marry a virgin

---

[171] Ibid., 1659–61.
[172] Although the text does not explicitly mention wool, it is generally assumed, since it was the only known material to be dyed. Thus it is argued that the otherwise linen tassel demonstrates the same mixture as certain garments of the priesthood.
[173] Milgrom, *Leviticus 17–22*, 1659.

of his own people (v.14b). V.15 goes on to explain that this is necessary, so that the high priest may not profane his seed (ולא־יחלל זרעו). Thus we see precedent here for considering prohibited marriages as profaning the offspring of such unions. The priestly status of holiness is applied to the people in Ezra 9:2 (as is the case in Deut 7:6) and it would be logical to transfer to them the priestly requirements for preserving their holy status.

Although according to Torah the ordinary priest was not barred from marrying a foreigner, only a harlot (Lev 21:7); the prohibition may have become part of the legal basis for condemning intermarriages, since in early Jewish Literature (e.g., *Jub.* 30:7–8; *T. Levi* 9.9–10) marrying a Gentile came to be seen as "harlotry" (*zĕnût*). I have already argued in §4.2 that the word "abominations" (תועבות) in Ezra characterizing the nations listed has connotations not only of idolatry (Deut 7:25–26) but of sexual immorality (Lev 18:26–30). In light of these observations it is possible that the priestly prohibitions of Lev 21:7–15 contribute to the background for condemning mixed marriages in Ezra 9–10.

6.3 Similar Developments in Jewish Literature

In the period of the Second Temple the question of intermarriage is a central one and it is instructive to see how the Jewish literature of the period handles the issue. Tobit recommends endogamy and observes that "their seed shall inherit the land" (Tob 4:12), although we do not find any indication that this seed is seen as holy. *The Testament of Levi*, as mentioned before, specifically condemns priestly marriages to foreigners (*T. Levi* 9.9–10).

> Beware of the spirit of fornication; for this shall continue and shall by thy seed pollute the holy place. Take, therefore to thyself a wife without blemish or pollution, while yet thou art young, and not of the race of strange nations. [Charles' transl.]

4QMMT (B75–82) uses a combination of the laws of *kil'ayim* from Lev 19:19 and Deut 22:9–11 to guard against intermarriage (understood to be between priests and laypeople or between Israelite and non-Israelite).[174] MMT C6 bans intermarriage on the basis of Deut 7:26, which prohibits one to bring an idol into one's house. Thus the Qumran document reinterprets the idol of Deut 7:26 metaphorically as the idol-worshiper.

---

[174] The text is fragmentary and it depends on one's reconstruction of who the supposed parties of the prohibited intermarriages are. In any case, the point I wish to make here is simply that there is precedent for the kind of argument implied in the reasoning of Ezra 9:2. For the more widely accepted view that the prohibition refers to intermarriages between priesthood and laity see Elisha Qimron and John Strugnell, eds., *Miqsat Ma'ase Ha-Torah*, (vol. 5 of *Qumran Cave 4*; DJD 10; Oxford: Clarendon, 1994) 5:55 n.75. Also Milgrom, *Leviticus 17–22*, 1659–60. For the view that the intermarriages in question are between Israelites and non-Israelites see the insightful article of Christine E. Hayes, "Intermarriage and Impurity in Ancient Jewish Sources," *HTR* 92/1 (1999) 25–35.

Another command frequently used as a justification against intermarriage with foreigners is the injunction not to give one's seed to Molech (Lev 18:21 & 20:2–3), where seed refers to an Israelite woman given in marriage to an idol-worshiper. *Jub.* 30:10 uses Lev 18:21 to condemn the sexual relationship between Shechem and Dinah and possibly also makes reference to Lev 21:9 in v.7. Significantly, the book omits the suggestion of circumcision as a way for foreigners to join the community of Israel mentioned in the biblical story of Gen 34. The polluting nature of foreignness is not to be eliminated by the act of circumcision. The book of Judith alludes to the same incident of Gen 34 describing the rape of Dinah as not only shameful for her but as polluting her womb (9:2).

6.4 New Rationale: Why Needed?

Ezra 9:1–2 condemns intermarriage on two grounds. The first, based on Deut 7, argues that it will lead Israel into apostasy with all its dire consequences. This is the standard reason for guarding against intermarriage. Why then is there need for another rationale, one that is unknown before the exile? Why is the argument which was acceptable before not sufficient any more? We have already seen the trend in the early Jewish literature of the era that the holy seed rationale in Ezra 9:2 is not an isolated phenomenon.

Perhaps the key to this question is that the holy seed rationale gives legal justification for an absolute ban on intermarriage without "ifs" or "buts," unlike the deuteronomic command. Thus it provides a watertight argument for complete abstention from such marriages.

That there was a perceived need for the returned exiles to tighten their defenses can hardly be doubted. The thought that Israel's downfall was caused by the worship of foreign gods was deeply ingrained in the Postexilic Period. It is also clear that this danger took on more subtle forms than the blatant veneration of foreign deities of which there is not one incident mentioned in such postexilic books as Haggai, Malachi or EN. Instead, Haggai admonishes the people because they neglect the building of the temple and concentrate on their own material advancement (1:2–4). He pronounces them as unclean as if they had touched a corpse (2:13–14). Malachi complains that the people bring faulty animals, show contempt to God and are tired of his service (1:8, 13–14). They withhold their tithes (3:8–9), divorce their Israelite wives and marry foreign women (2:11, 14) and are even too blind to recognize how they have sinned. EN, too, condemns intermarriages (Ezra 9–10; Neh 13:23–29), mentions such sins as usury exacted by Jews from their brothers (Neh 5:1–5), the encroachment of a foreigner on temple grounds (Neh 13:4–5), tithes withheld (Neh 13:10) and the Sabbath broken (Neh 13:15–16). The picture that emerges from these witnesses is of a people whose resolve to follow God has weakened and who are therefore more prone to fall prey to evil influences. Under such circumstances it becomes high priority that such influences be minimized.

Later rabbinic Judaism has, on the whole, returned to the deuteronomic reasoning for the ban on intermarriage and the holy seed rationale gradually receded into the background. Thus for instance, *m. Meg.* 4.9 metes out a rebuke for anyone who translates Lev 18:21 as meaning the impregnation of an Aramean woman.[175]

האומר "ומזרעך לא תיתן, להעביר למולך" (ויקרא יח,כא), מן זרעך לא תיתן לאעברא בארמיתא—משתקין אותו בנזיפה.	If one translates [lit. "says"], "And you shall not give of your seed to pass over to Molech" (Lev 18:21) as "And you shall not give of your seed to impregnate an Aramean [i.e. foreign] woman," they shall silence him with a rebuke. (translation mine)

The forbidden translation plays on the Hebrew להעביר (Hiphil עבר—"to cause to pass") and takes it as a Piel ("to impregnate"). The Palestinian Talmud elaborates on this interpretation (*y. Meg.* 4.10) adding R. Ishmael's teaching which explains that the sons of such a marriage will be raised as enemies of God.[176]

תני רבי ישמעאל זה שהוא נושא ארמית ומעמיד ממנה בנים מעמיד אויבים למקום.	R. Ishmael teaches: This is the one who marries an Aramean woman and raises sons by her, he raises enemies for God. (translation mine)

Similarly, *Tg. Ps.-J.*'s translation of Lev 18:21 focuses on the consequence of idolatry that will be the fate of the offspring.[177]

ומן זרעך לא תיתן בתשמישתה לציד בת עממין למעברא לפולחנא נוכראה.	Of your seed you shall not give in marital intercourse to a daughter of the nations to pass over to foreign worship. (translation mine)

Thus the danger is seen in the religious influence of the foreign spouse which will ultimately lead to foreign worship. Conversion to Judaism eliminates the danger of apostasy and allows the ban on intermarriage to be lifted.

---

[175] *Mishnah* (Hebrew), n.p. [cited 20 April 2012]. Online: http://www.mechon-mamre.org/b/h/h2a.htm

[176] *Palestinian Talmud* (Hebrew), n.p. [cited 20 April 2012]. Online: http://www.mechon-mamre.org/b/r/r2a04.htm

[177] *Targum Pseudo-Jonathan* (Aramaic), n.p. [cited 20 April 2012]. Online: http://cal1.cn.huc.edu

At the time of the return from exile and the turbulent period of religious clashes and political wars the desire for justifying a more rigid separation was understandable. Once the emerging rabbinic Judaism has grown strong and established and has settled down to a life without homeland and temple it was able to draw a less inflexible line between itself and outsiders.

6.5 Conclusion

In this chapter I have examined the "holy seed" rationale condemning intermarriage with foreigners in Ezra 9:2, which I argued to be distinct from the deuteronomic reasoning of "moral defilement" based on the use of the "seed" in Ezra 9:2 and the absolute nature of the ban. I noted similar vocabulary and resonances in Isa 6:13; Mal 2:14; Ps 106:27, 35 and sought to locate the source for the "holy seed" rationale. Milgrom's theory was evaluated first, namely that Ezra 9:2 is using Jeremiah's prophetic imagery (Jer 2:3) and merges it with the legislation in Deut 7 to create the notion of *sancta* desecration through intermarriage. The laws of *kil'ayim* in Lev 19:19 and Deut 22:9–11 were examined next followed by the priestly regulation for marriage in Lev 21:7–15. The latter two options were found more persuasive than Milgrom's suggestion. I observed that there were similar lines of thought evident in some other Jewish Literature of the Second Temple Period (notably 4QMMT and *Jub.* 30), which made the ban absolute irrespective of the foreign spouse's attitude and did not allow conversion and/or circumcision as a route for integration into the community of Israel. Finally, I sought to answer the question why the "holy seed" rationale was needed at all when Deut 7 (& 23) could have given adequate support for the ban on intermarriage. It was argued that the weakened spiritual state of the returned exiles may have given rise to the need to place an absolute ban on intermarriage in the hopes of protecting a religiously less resistant people from the threat of foreign influences. The "holy seed" rationale provided the legal basis for precisely this kind of prohibition without exceptions.

7

Profanation and Impurity

So far, I have looked at the legal background of "the holy seed" rationale as an argument distinct from the usual deuteronomic prohibition in Deut 7:1–3 based on the threat of idolatry as well as some roughly contemporary sources that seem to use a similar line of thought from the Second Temple Period. In this chapter I will examine the logic of "the holy seed" rationale and evaluate in particular Milgrom's influential theory that the holy seed is desecrated by marriages with non-holy/profane "foreign" women.[178] As

---

[178] It is generally assumed that the "foreign" women adversely affect the "holy seed" even if it is unclear if the issue is profanation or defilement. It is worth mentioning here Diana Lipton's unusual view that it is the profane seed which becomes holy and threatens to seize the land. She uses the analogy of Gen 6:1–6 where the interbreeding results in mighty progeny ("The Furnace of Desire: Forging Identities in Foreign Bedrooms," in *Longing for Egypt and Other Unexpected Biblical Tales* [HBM 15; Sheffield: Sheffield Phoenix, 2008] 230–238). "In addition to the problem of the violence that filled the earth (Gen. 6.11–12), the sons of gods have cohabited with daughters of men to produce a super-race of mighty men possessed of (until God addressed it) the attribute of immortality. By means of the flood, God removed both the violence (6.13) and all traces of these quasi-immortal people (6.7) and started afresh. Here, then, is a biblical text where the offspring of a union involving males identified with divinity, the sons of gods, and females that are manifestly human, the daughters of men, produces offspring that, even if they are not divine, have the primary attribute of divinity, immortality. Further, the narrative in its present form suggests that the progeny of this union will seize or fill the land, hence the need for a flood to remove them from it." Ibid., 231. This is an interesting theory although it seems to me ultimately counter-intuitive. The intertextual links between the two texts are somewhat forced but even more importantly the issue in Ezra 9:2 is holiness, not divinity/immortality. Throughout the OT holiness is affected by the profane or the defiled, rather than the other way around. As Jacob Milgrom argues, where *sancta* is seen as contagious, it is lethal (e.g., Exod 19:12–13; Num 4:15; 2 Sam 6:6–7;

discussed in §6.2.2, Milgrom argues that the desecration is further indicated by the אשם sacrifice (guilt/reparation offering for sacrilege—Lev 5:14–16; Ezra 10:19) and the repeated use of מעל "unfaithfulness" in the text (Ezra 9:2, 4; 10:2, 6), which is the technical term for "trespasses against *sancta*" and oath-violation.

This is a rather attractive solution yet a closer inspection of the text raises a number of questions. While מעל can be used in a technical sense, it can also mean simply unfaithfulness by breaking the covenant. The אשם sacrifice can indeed be for the sin of desecration; at the same time, it is conspicuous that the 20% compensation as specified in Lev 5:14–16 is absent from the text. Further, Milgrom assumes that Israel is the holy seed, but the precedents in the *kil'ayim* laws (especially Deut 22:9) and Lev 21:7–15 point to the offspring rather than the Israelite husbands as the desecrated ones. Finally, the leaders' complaint that the "holy seed intermingled with the peoples of the lands" leaves the status of the "foreign wives" and their effect tantalizingly open: are they profane or impure and consequently do they desecrate or defile? Ezra in his prayer alludes to Lev 18:24–30 and states that the Canaanites have made the land unclean with their abominations and filled it with impurity; a repetition of which he fears in his own day. This suggests that the women are impure, which immediately raises the question what the nature of their impurity is.

The structure of this chapter will work its way through the questions arising from Ezra 9–10 relating to "the holy seed" as set out above. In the process I shall bring in possible analogies as well as similar texts (specifically Neh 13:23–31) in order to bridge the gaps left in the passage. A short introduction into purity terminology in the scholarly literature will be followed by a discussion of Milgrom's theory of sancta desecration. I will particularly examine the two textual arguments that Milgrom brings: the use of מעל and אשם. The question will then be raised about the identity of the "holy seed"; in other words, who is affected by the foreign wives: the husbands and/or the offspring of these unions. Next I will consider Lev 21:7–15, which text, I argue, provides a suitable analogy for understanding "the holy seed" rationale. Finally, I shall look into the nature of impurity attributed to the Canaanite nations and, by extension, to the "foreign wives" in Ezra's time.

7.1   Purity Terminology

Scholarly literature is divided on the terminology it uses for describing biblical impurities, yet there is a certain consensus about two main types of impurity which are best described by Klawans in his monograph, *Impurity and*

Leviticus 1–16: A New Translation with Introduction and Commentary [AB 3; New York: Doubleday, 1991] 443–456).

Sin in Ancient Judaism. His own terms for them are "ritual" and "moral" impurity respectively.[179]

Although these names are probably the most widespread and common ones to describe impurities in the scholarly literature, it is generally recognized that they are problematic on several counts. For one thing, they are anachronistic and one must be careful not to impose them onto an ancient system of thought that does not entirely fit the modern distinctions or distinguish clearly between them. For another, the word pair may reinforce a stance of anti-ritualism and the superiority of "morality" over ritual and set up the prophets with their denunciations of the cult over against a priesthood engaged in seemingly meaningless ceremonies. Further, the word "moral" may evoke the idea of a narrow morality or moralizing. In any case, the source of "moral" impurities such as idolatry do not comfortably fit into a straightforward "moral" category. Other similar possibilities are "levitical," "priestly," "cultic" versus "spiritual," "religious."[180] Wright suggests "permitted" or "tolerated" versus "prohibited" impurities, while Frymer-Kensky takes yet a different approach, highlighting the contagion element in what Klawans calls "ritual impurity" and the danger that ensues from pollutions that involve wrongdoing and which she calls "danger-beliefs."[181]

Despite the difficulty with Klawans' terminology I wish to retain it simply because as a shorthand it captures the essence of these two types of impurity better than some of the other ones listed above. One of the hallmarks of "ritual impurity," as Klawans points out, is that it is mostly the result of natural processes that are often unavoidable such as birth (Lev 12:1–8), death (human corpses and carcasses of impure animals—Lev 11:1–47; Num 19:10–22), bodily flows (e.g., Lev 15:1–33), scale diseases (Lev 13:1–14:32) and the by-product of purificatory procedures (e.g., Lev 16:28; Num 19:8). This kind of impurity is generally not sin, although can become sinful if the impure persons refuse to

---

[179] For ritual impurity see Jonathan Klawans, *Impurity and Sin in Ancient Judaism* (New York: Oxford University Press, 2000) 23–25; for moral impurity see Ibid., 26–30; for a briefer version of the main differences see Idem., *Purity, Sacrifice, and the Temple: Symbolism and Supersessionism in the Study of Ancient Judaism* (New York: Oxford University Press, 2006) 55–56.

[180] For a short critique of some of these see David P. Wright, "The Spectrum of Priestly Impurity," in *Priesthood and Cult in Ancient Israel* (ed. Gary A. Anderson & Saul M. Olyan; JSOT SS 125; Sheffield: Sheffield Academic, 1991) 151–52. fn. 3. and Klawans, *Impurity and Sin*, 22–23.

[181] David P. Wright, "Unclean and Clean (OT)," in *Anchor Bible Dictionary* (vols. 1–6; ed. David Noel Freedman; New York: Doubleday, 1992) 6:729–30; Idem., "The Spectrum of Priestly Impurity," 151–2. He uses "permitted" in the first article and "tolerated" in the second for the category that Klawans terms "ritual impurity." Tikva Frymer-Kensky, "Pollution, Purification, and Purgation in Biblical Israel," in *The Word of the Lord Shall Go Forth: Essays in Honor of David Noel Freedman in Celebration of His Sixtieth Birthday* (ed. Carol L. Meyers and M. O'Connor; Winona Lake IN: Eisenbrauns, 1983) 403–404.

purify themselves or if they come into contact with the holy (hence impure persons are excluded from the sanctuary). Thus the adjective "ritual" is apt "because this kind of impurity affects the ritual status of persons stricken by it" and purity is achieved in part by rituals (washing, bathing, sacrifice and often including a period of waiting).[182] Ritual impurities spread through direct or indirect contact with impure persons, objects or substances, normally by touch or physical proximity.

Klawans' "moral impurity" on the other hand is the result of grave sins: sexual immorality (e.g., Lev 18:24–30), idolatry (e.g., Lev 19:31; 20:1–3) and bloodshed (e.g., Num 35:33–34). The single most distinguishing feature of this type of impurity is that its source is serious wrongdoing that can only be purged by the removal of the sinner from life, or in some cases from the land, or by sacrificial atonement. Thus the attribute "moral" has to be understood this way as encompassing sins that are moral-religious in nature. This is the sense in which, for want of a better word, I wish to use the term. "Moral" impurity is not contagious by contact and does not jeopardize the "ritual purity" of others. It nevertheless affects the land of Israel and the sanctuary from afar, that is, without the sinner entering the temple, although the sin still has to be committed in Israel for the land and the sanctuary to be defiled.

The particular difficulty that the Ezran narrative poses is that according to the above classification the women have a "moral impurity" which, however, is not contagious, yet the effects of these wives on the holy seed seem to be communicated in a way that is akin to the contact-contagion of "ritual impurity." This issue also feeds into the larger question posed by scholars whether Gentiles were considered "ritually impure," a view that is based on the influential work of Emil Schürer and Gedalyahu Alon.[183] This debate is especially prominent in discussions of Jewish-Gentile table fellowship and interaction in New Testament studies in general and with reference to Acts 10 and Gal 2:11–14 in particular.

The reason for asking this question is in part to understand the logic of the argument; namely why intermarriages are unacceptable with these "foreign women" and also to probe into the kind of value judgment that is made about

---

[182] See Klawans, *Impurity and Sin*, 22–23.

[183] Emil Schürer argues for the ritual impurity of Gentiles on the basis that they do not keep the ritual purity laws and are therefore ritually impure themselves and ritually defile those who come into contact with them (*Geschichte des jüdischen Volkes im Zeitalter Jesu Christi* (2 vols.; Leipzig: J. C. Hinrich, 1911) 2:48. Gedalyahu Alon does not explicitly state though seems to assume that the ritual impurity of Gentiles is rooted in what he believes is the biblical notion that idols are ritually defiling. He assigns the concept of Gentile ritual impurity in the form of Halakah to the beginning of the Second Temple Period ("The Levitical Uncleanness of Gentiles," in *Jews, Judaism and the Classical World: Studies in Jewish History in the Times of the Second Temple and Talmud* [trans. Israel Abrahams; Jerusalem: Magnes, 1977] 187–88). For a refutation of Alon's idea that idols and idolatry are ritually defiling see Christine E. Hayes, *Gentile Impurities and Jewish Identities: Intermarriage and Conversion from the Bible and the Talmud* (New York: Oxford University Press, 2002) 215–221.

them. Profane is clearly a more neutral category which in some instances can have perfectly legitimate contact with the holy: thus the priests who are holy can marry Israelites (Lev 21:7 cf. v.14) who are profane by default though at the same time the latter are called to aspire to holiness themselves.

7.2   Sacrilege in Ezra 9–10?

7.2.1   The Use of מעל in Ezra 9–10

As already indicated, Milgrom proposes that the word מעל in the cultic legislation of the Old Testament is used in the context of *sancta* desecration and oath violation. In the case of the latter he observes that God's covenant with Israel involved an oath and not surprisingly therefore, מעל is often applied when speaking of Israel's idolatry/apostasy in non-cultic contexts as well (2 Chr 12:1–2; 33:19; Num. 31:16; 2 Chr 28:22–25).[184] In Ezra–Nehemiah the term occurs five times in connection with intermarriage (Ezra 9:2, 4; 10:2, 6; Neh 13:27) and once, in Nehemiah's prayer the word מעל denotes disobedience to God's commandments and is blamed for the Exile (Neh 1:8 cf. Lev 26:40). Similarly, in Ezra's prayer the primary issue seems to be the forsaking (9:10) and breaking (v.14) of the commandment not to intermarry with the Canaanites (Deut 7:1–3). Already once the violation of YHWH's covenant resulted in exile (v.7) and the further breach of it may lead to total destruction (v.14). Beyond the holy seed mentioned by the leaders in v.2 there is no further repetition or allusion to desecration. Thus it may well be that מעל does not refer to sacrilege of the "holy seed" but to the unfaithfulness in breaking God's covenant through apostasy and idolatry. Indeed this is the sin that the Deuteronomistic History considers the prime reason for the Exile which is reflected in Ezra's prayer and which chimes in with Lev 26:14, 32–33, 40 as well. As Milgrom observes, the latter is the only pentateuchal passage that explicitly connects the מעל of covenant breaking with the punishment of the Exile.[185]

7.2.2   The Meaning of אשם in Ezra 9–10

Milgrom's second support for his theory of sancta desecration (מעל) comes from the אשם sacrifice that is offered in Ezra 10:19. However, there are still several questions connected to it that need addressing. First, the regulation for the אשם sacrifice in Lev 5 prescribes a ram or its monetary equivalent and 20% compensation in the case of unintentional sacrilege (vv.14–16) whilst any mention of reparation is omitted in Ezra 10:19. Secondly, it is not unambiguously clear if the reference to the אשם sacrifice is meant to encompass an offering only for the high priestly family, the priests in general or lay Israelites as well.

---

[184] Jacob Milgrom, "The Concept of *Ma'al* in the Bible and the Ancient Near East," *JAOS* 96/2 (1976) 238.
[185] Ibid., 239.

Unfortunately Milgrom does not address the issue of compensation, although one way of explaining the lack of it is to say that the desecration of people rather than objects is a novelty and it may be that the implications of this new form of sacrilege have not been properly worked out, that is the issue of compensation. It may also have been difficult to judge its measure since we are not dealing here with sacred objects, whose monetary value is more easily assessed, but with people. On the other hand, the valuations of people who make a difficult vow (Lev 27:1–8) may give an indication how such compensation in the case of desecration of people may be calculated if that is indeed the issue in Ezra 9–10. Further, if one takes the holy seed to mean the Israelite spouses who are desecrated by their foreign wives then it is possible to argue that these men are both victims/objects as well as perpetrators/subjects of desecration in that they allow it to happen by marrying foreign women. In this case, compensation may be omitted for the obvious reason that both the cause and the recipient of compensation are the same people. At the same time, it is still possible to say that the compensation is to be given to God because the holy people belong to him and by desecrating themselves they have offended YHWH.

A further question which has some bearing on the אשם sacrifice is whether it is actually the Israelite spouses or their offspring who are desecrated. If the latter then an אשם should only be required of those who had children from these marriages. To this question of the "holy seed" I shall return in the next section.

There are only two cases in the Pentateuch where a ram is offered as an אשם without compensation. One immediately follows the regulation on unintentional sacrilege in Lev 5:14–16 and deals with unintentional, unknowing disobedience to some negative commandment (vv.17–19). Milgrom understands the latter to mean sacrilege in which the perpetrator is not aware that he or she had committed it but has nevertheless guilt feelings which lead him or her to suspect the worst: "he has affronted the deity; he has committed sacrilege against the sancta."[186] Thus, the difference between the first and the second scenario is that in the former desecration is unintended but it eventually comes to light, while in the latter it is merely suspected but not known (והוא לא־ידע— v.18) even at the time the אשם is offered. Logically, only a ram is brought without compensation since the crime is only suspected,[187] and we might add, the object of desecration is unknown. If Milgrom is right in the interpretation of this passage then it cannot form the background to the Ezran case of no compensation, since the exiles are well aware of their guilt and not merely suspect that they have committed a sin.[188]

---

[186] Milgrom, *Leviticus* 1–16, 333.

[187] Ibid., 335.

[188] As Milgrom himself notes, his interpretation of vv.17–19 accords with the rabbinic view (e.g., *Sipra*, Ḥobah, par. 12:1; *m. Ker.* 5:2–8; *Ker.* 22b [baraita]) but goes against the majority scholarly opinion, which sees the section as a "displaced *ḥaṭṭā't* passage" and understandably so, since it replicates the language of Lev 4:2, 13, 22, 27 and sacrilege

The second example of a ram offered as an אשם without monetary compensation is in Lev 19:20–22.[189] The offence is the violation of a slave girl who has been betrothed to another man (lit. "acquired for a man" נחרפת לאיש— v.20), but has not been set free yet. On the one hand, Milgrom argues, her betrothal makes this a case of adultery; on the other as a slave she is not a legal person, therefore the death penalty for adultery cannot be applied (v.20).[190]

The question is what this marginal case law is doing in the chapter on issues of holiness? And why is the necessary sacrifice an אשם? Milgrom submits that the real offence is sacrilege against God's name and the desecration of the oath taken at Sinai for which the appropriate offering is the אשם. The adultery in this marginal case cannot be classified as such and punished accordingly. Nevertheless, it remains an offence against God which is indicated by the necessity of bringing the אשם.

> In sum, the resolution of the crux of the 'āšām brought by the paramour or seducer of a slave-woman rests on the assumption that in Israel adultery was considered a violation of the Sinaitic covenant. In the ancient Near East, although adultery was considered a sin against the gods, it had no juridical impact, whereas in Israel its inclusion in the covenant guaranteed legal consequences. The death penalty for clear-cut adultery could never be commuted. However, in the case of Lev 19:20–22, where investigation shows that the betrothed slave-woman had not been emancipated, her paramour or seducer could not be punished. He is not an adulterer because she is not a legal person. Nevertheless, he has offended God by desecrating the Sinaitic oath and must bring his 'āšām expiation.[191]

(מעל) is not mentioned in it. Nevertheless Milgrom's argument makes sense since in its present place and form the section is subsumed under the default case of the inadvertent sacrilege introduced by כי (v.14) while the section in vv.17–19 is affixed with the particle ואם, the standard indicator of a subordinate case and is followed by the prescription of an אשם sacrifice. The phrase in v.17 is awkward, however, since it contains both ואם and כי (ואם־נפש כי). This leads Milgrom to concede that 5:17 may have been an independent law originally, which was copied verbatim, prefixed by ואם and incorporated into the law against sacrilege. Ibid., 331–32.

[189] Gordon Wenham reads בקרת as "compensation" (*The Book of Leviticus* [NICOT; Grand Rapids MI: Eerdmans, 1979] 270–71) rather than "punishment" (BDB, 1244 בקרת) or "inquest" (Jacob Milgrom, *Leviticus 17–22: A New Translation with Introduction and Commentary*, [AB 3A; New York: Doubleday, 2000] 1669–70) but Milgrom convincingly shows that "investigation" is to be preferred mainly because in a case that is potentially a capital offence establishing the girl's exact status (half-slave, half-free) is essential to giving the correct verdict (Ibid, 1669–70). For an evaluation of the various interpretive possibilities of בקרת see Ibid., 1668–71. Milgrom argues that compensation is not given because the girl's betrothal means that her master is only her partial owner (Ibid., 1665). In any case, if Wenham were right we would expect the text to specify the measure and recipient of such compensation.

[190] For the argument summarised here see Milgrom, *Leviticus 17–22*, 1665–1677.

[191] Ibid., 1675.

One of the things that Milgrom notes about the אשם sacrifice is that in most cases it is possible to offer a monetary equivalent rather than an actual ram but he stresses that in Lev 19:20–22 a monetary exchange is not in view; the offender has to go to the trouble of getting the right unblemished animal.[192] If Milgrom's overall interpretation is along the right lines, namely that the offence atoned for by the אשם is a desecration of the covenant oath at Sinai, then we may speculate that the lack of compensation on the one hand and the insistence on an actual sacrificial animal on the other are an indication of a direct offence against God and his name, which cannot be measured in terms of monetary value.

Thus the case relating to the violation of the betrothed slave girl may shed light on the issue in Ezra 9–10, as in both instances there is no compensation offered and the אשם is an actual ram.[193] If these two aspects of the אשם sacrifice indeed indicate that the offence in question is a more direct one against YHWH then it is possible to read the Ezran story as one of covenant breaking and sacrilege in the sense of desecrating God's name. Although Milgrom himself refers to the covenant at Sinai for the oath violation in Lev 19:20–22, for the story of Ezra 9–10 a better candidate would be the covenant and oath entered into in Moab (Deut 29:11[12]). Particularly noteworthy is the indication there that the covenant and oath are not merely with those who are present there that day but with those who are not there (vv.13–14[14–15]); presumably indicating the covenant's binding nature to the generations who come later. It also closely links the abominations (תועבות) of the nations and the sin of idolatry with the breaking of the covenant (v.16[17]). Understanding the אשם sacrifice as intended for covenant violation and oath breaking would also be in line with the way מעל is used in the chapter. Further the possible link between Deut 29:11[12] and Neh 10:30[29] (see §3.1.1) and the deuteronomic curses which may form the background for Nehemiah's cursing of those who intermarried (Neh 13:25—see §4.4.2) both point to similar notions within the wider context of EN.

Overall, it is noteworthy that אשמה as Israel's "guilt" is mentioned more often in Ezra 9–10 than any other term for sin (9:6, 7, 13, 15; 10:10, 19). Synonymous expressions include מעל ("unfaithfulness"—9:2, 4; 10:2, 6) as already mentioned, עון ("iniquity, sin"—9:6, 7, 13), probably one of the most generic terms for sin;[194] מעשינו הרעים ("our evil deeds"—9:13) and פשע ("to rebel, cast off allegiance"—10:13); a term that is used both for rebellion against secular rulers (e.g., 1 Kgs 12:19; 2 Kgs 3:5; 2 Chr 36:13, Ezek 17:15) and by extension against God and his covenant (e.g., Isa 1:28; Jer 3:13; Ezek 2:3; Hos

---

[192] Ibid., 1675.
[193] The Talmud connects Lev 21:19–22 with Ezra 10:19 in *b. Ker.* 11a on the basis that in both instances an אשם is offered, although the rabbinic conclusion seems a forced one, namely, "that they all had intercourse with designated handmaids."
[194] It is striking that חטאת which is perhaps even more a general term for sin is entirely missing in these chapters.

7:13, 8:1). While עון and מעשינו הרעים are too general to be of any help in establishing the nuance of the sin in question, both פשע and מעל indicate unfaithfulness to God and his covenant through disobedience. This is borne out by Ezra's prayer which repeatedly refers to Israel's past sin that led to the Exile and the present repetition of the same sin with an emphasis on breaking God's commandment. How does אשמה fit in with this overall picture? The word can denote the act of wrongdoing, the feelings of guilt that ensue, the punishment or consequence of sin. It does not necessarily have a technical meaning of the sin or guilt of sacrilege in the same way as מעל does not. In the light of this, it seems to me that the overall tenor of the mixed marriage crisis is the breaking of the covenant by the disobedience to the commandments and particularly the threat of idolatry and apostasy.

In contrast, the chapter has little to say about desecration of the "seed" apart from the one reference to "holy seed." If one adds to that the fact that an actual ram and no compensation is required and offered in Ezra 10:19, then an אשם for the desecration of the offspring or the Israelite spouses seems an unlikely interpretation when the rest of the chapter uses both אשמה and מעל in a more general sense of covenant-breaking and disobedience. This is not to negate that sacrilege of a kind is an issue in the passage and that the holy seed rationale plays a supportive role in the argument against mixed marriages. Nevertheless, I would want to suggest that an אשם brought for desecrating the covenant and the oath entered into in Moab (Deut 29:11[12]) would give a more coherent account of Ezra 9–10 than Milgrom's theory.

The second question to examine with regard to the אשם sacrifice is for whom it is brought. Ezra 10:19 only mentions the high priestly family (the sons of Jeshua, son of Jozadak and his brothers) to have offered it. If this is how the text should be read then it would suggest that a distinction is made between priests and laymen in which case the אשם is indeed brought for the sin of profaning the high-priestly offspring as described in Lev 21:15. A similar interpretive option is offered by Maccoby who keeps the distinction between priests and laymen but suggests that the אשם is brought by all the priests who mistook their wives to be Jews and allowed them to eat the holy portions.[195]

On the other hand, Milgrom assumes that even though the text is silent about a lay אשם offering, it must be implied, while Hayes similarly takes for granted that an אשם is required from and offered by all.[196] This seems to be a

---

[195] Hyam Maccoby, "Holiness and Purity: The Holy People in Leviticus and Ezra-Nehemiah" in *Reading Leviticus: A Conversation with Mary Douglas* (ed. John F.A. Sawyer; Sheffield: Sheffield Academic, 1996) 167.

[196] Jacob Milgrom, *Cult and Conscience: The Asham and the Priestly Doctrine of Repentance* (Leiden: Brill, 1976) 73. Hayes, *Gentile Impurities*, 29. Contra Saul M. Olyan who distinguishes between the Ezra memoir which treats both lay and priestly intermarriages as sacrilege and the Ezra third person narrative which only requires an אשם from the priests. He criticises Hayes for understanding the אשם as if it related to lay

logical conclusion given that there is no distinction made between laymen and priests elsewhere in the text in terms of their sin. Whatever the "guilt" these people had, it applied to all equally. Moreover, when the intermingling of the holy seed is mentioned in Ezra 9:2, the exiles specifically highlight the sin of the princes and rulers, who have been "foremost in this unfaithfulness" (היתה במעל הזה ראשונה), which again indicates the guilt of all, not only of the high-priestly family. Further, the sentence about pledging to send the wives away followed by the offering of the אשם in Ezra 10:19 is general enough to be a kind of summary introductory phrase even though it comes inserted after the listing of the first few names in the priestly list. Moreover, if one insists on reading the verse rigidly to apply only to those just listed in v.18 then one would also have to assume that the first part of the sentence in v.19 (the pledge to send the wives away) only applied to those few mentioned in v.18. This is untenable and therefore we may safely conclude that in the light of all these arguments the אשם sacrifice is brought for all those involved in intermarriages with foreigners, laymen and priests alike.

In conclusion I submit that the אשם offering is for the sin of breaking the covenant and the oath entered into in Moab atoned for by sacrificing an actual ram without monetary compensation and offered by priests as well as the laity. This constitutes an "unfaithfulness" (מעל). I would want to maintain that sacrilege in the sense of profaning the holy seed is at issue in Ezra 9–10. However, its role should not be overstated. The text is largely and more prominently concerned with covenant violation by disobedience to the deuteronomic commandment not to intermarry with the Caananites (Deut 7:1–3) which is extended to apply to all foreigners.

7.2.3 Who Are the Holy Seed?

The next question to examine is who the exiles thought the "holy seed" was: the Israelites who were in some way affected by their foreign wives or their children who were of mixed descent? Milgrom's theory of sancta desecration implies the former: it is the Israelites who lose their sanctity by contact with these women. However, it is not clear in Milgrom's theory how the desecration happens: is it by physical/sexual contact akin to the way ritual desecration of holy objects might occur or by the adverse influence of these women by virtue of the close marriage relationship? If one reads the intermingling of the "holy seed" in the spirit of Deut 7 then the spouses are influenced by the idolatrous practices of the wives that lead them in turn into idolatry and apostasy from the one true God.

On the other hand, as discussed in §6.1.1, the replacement of "people/nation" (עם) by "seed" (זרע) may indicate a shift in emphasis to physical descent and the concern might become the mixed descent of any

---

Israelites ("Purity Ideology in Ezra-Nehemiah as a Tool to Reconstitute the Community," *JSJ* 35/1 [2004] 7–8. fn. 22).

offspring from such unions. Further, the use of זרע links Ezra 9 to the *kil'ayim* laws (Lev 19:19/Deut 22:9–11) and the profanation of the high priestly offspring (Lev 21:14–15); the two pentateuchal "forerunners" of the desecration by intermarriage idea both of which point to the offspring as the focus of attention. In Deut 22:9 specifically, it is both the produce of the seed and the increase of the vine; that is, the fruit of both plants that are affected (though it is not entirely clear whether one should speak of defilement or desecration). Again, in the case of Lev 21:14 it is the "seed," that is, the offspring of illegitimate marriages which is profaned; there is no indication that the priest who intermarried is affected. These analogies seem to indicate that the mixed descent of the children is a serious issue in Ezra 9–10.

The argument one might raise against seeing the descendants as the seed is that Ezra 9:2 speaks of the intermingling of the holy seed and clearly it is not the children who do the mixing. One might think of the seed in the sense of "semen" which became mixed, but there are two possible difficulties with this. First, the Hithpael of ערב ("to mix") is a reflexive verb, which seems to indicate intentionality: "the holy seed has mixed itself with." Therefore seed may more accurately refer to the Israelites who intermarried. Secondly, the ancient understanding of conception did not envisage the male sperm fertilizing the female egg and thus any imagery of the mixing of seeds in this sense breaks down. Against the latter it may be argued that the *kil'ayim* laws as an analogy to intermarriage do not quite work either, nevertheless it remains a fact that they were used in the Second Temple Period for just that purpose. It is harder to counter the argument from the meaning of the Hithpael and thus it is safer to assume that "seed" means the adult Israelites.

Nevertheless, this interpretive decision does not invalidate the point made above that there is a strong emphasis on descent and on the impact such marriages have on the offspring. It is also worth noting in this respect that the effect of the foreign wives on the Israelite spouses and on the children is different. The Israelite husbands only needed to separate from their foreign wives (והבדלו...ומן־הנשים הנכריות—10:11) whereas the children were permanently removed from Israel by being sent away with the women (להוציא כל־נשים והנולד מהם—10:3 see also 1 Esd 9:36). The separation of the husbands from the foreign wives may well have been a necessary step to avoid producing offspring that is "compromised" in its lineage rather than as an act motivated by the fear of being personally affected by the wives.

7.2.4 The Precedent in Lev 21:7–15

In order to understand the intermarriages in Ezra 9–10 further I shall consider here the possible precedent in the priestly and high priestly marriage regulations of Lev 21. Three questions are particularly pertinent here. First, what is the force of חלל in Lev 21:15 in the verse that gives the reason for the restrictions "so that he does not יחלל his seed?" Is the meaning sacrilege or defilement? Secondly, what is the rationale behind the categories of women excluded from priestly and high-priestly marriages? Uncovering the logic underlying this list may shed light on how the foreign women were viewed in Ezra 9–10. Thirdly, how is the profanation/defilement communicated?

The technical meaning of the Piel verb חלל in the priestly legislation is desecration or profanation, that is, the illegitimate contact of the holy with the common/profane (חל).[197] However, Lev 21 is not so precise in its application of the term. For instance, v.4 states that the priest is required not to defile (יטמא) himself with the dead of any relatives by marriage (an issue of ritual purity) and "so חלל himself." Milgrom explains the choice of this word as follows.

> Normally, we would have expected the word lĕhiṭṭamĕ'ô, since contact with the dead results in defilement, pollution. The verb ḥillēl 'desecrate' was chosen deliberately to emphasize the effect of the pollution on the person of the priest: he is desanctified and, hence, disqualified to handle or be in the presence of sanctums—in other words, to serve as a priest.[198]

It is clear from this example that the term here is used in a more fluid way and Milgrom notes further examples where the distinction between טמא and חלל is gradually dissolved not only in the Holiness Code but also in Ezekiel. Thus idolatry in Lev 20:3 defiles (טמא) the sanctuary while in Ezek 23:39 it profanes (חלל). Conversely, the name of God is profaned in Lev 20:3 but defiled in Ezek 43:7–8.[199] Milgrom's explanation that the use of חלל focuses on the effects of the act on holiness is plausible and further supported by two other examples he notes in Lev 21:12 and Lev 22:9.[200] Both of these deal with corpse defiled priests coming into contact with the holy yet use the Piel verb חלל. One might wonder how it is possible to distinguish between defilement and sacrilege but the problem is not insolvable. In all three cases (Lev 21:4, 12; 22:9) טמא is used in conjunction with חלל which clearly indicates that the writer is aware of the distinction. The juxtaposition of חלל and holiness in all three cases (21:6, 12; 22:9) confirms Milgrom's theory that the writer/editor of these chapters is concerned with holiness whatever might be the cause that compromises it. In the case of Lev 21:7, 15 there is no mention of defilement (טמא), only profanation (חלל) and so we may assume that the issue is the loss or diminishment of holiness without the added implications of (ritual) defilement.

In order to understand the reason for the marriage restrictions it is worth probing further into the reason for the choice of women listed as unacceptable for priestly or high priestly marriages. The marriage regulation for an ordinary priest forbids marriage with a harlot, a woman who was raped (חללה),[201] or a divorcee (v.7) to which list the widow is added in the case of the

---

[197] For the five variations on most sacred, sacred, common and impure see Milgrom, *Leviticus 1–16*, 977–78.
[198] Milgrom, *Leviticus 17–22*, 1800–1801.
[199] Ibid., 1801.
[200] Ibid., 1327.
[201] Although most English translations translate זנה וחללה as a hendyadis (NRSV; NIV; BDB, 2491 חללה), I follow Milgrom here who understands חללה as a woman who was

high priest, who is obliged to marry a virgin of his own people (v.14 cf. v.10). Ezek 44:22 extends the high priestly requirements to all priests,[202] and Neh 13 seems to follow the same line of thought, while Ezra 9–10 goes even further by applying it to all Israel.

What holds these categories of prohibited women together? The obvious common element in the harlot, the raped woman (חללה), the divorcee and the widow is their lack of virginity. Yet, why does the high priest or the priests in general need to be protected from getting wives who had sexual experience (legitimate or illegitimate)? Moreover, how does the foreigner fit into this list?

Sexual intercourse whether in marriage or outside it is considered ritually defiling although this is one of the minor impurities that only requires bathing and waiting until evening as a form of purification (Lev 15:18). In trying to establish the overarching reasons for ritual impurities Wright and Frymer-Kensky among others suggest that all of them are connected to death and sex both of which are incompatible with God's nature.[203] Abstaining from any contact with these is absolutely essential for maintaining purity in a ritual context. Clearly, there is no issue of ritual defilement connected with sexual *experience* per se although as noted above the sexual *act* itself leads to a minor and temporary ritual impurity. Yet the marriage restrictions on the priests and the high priest are perhaps a symbolic expression of their higher status as ministers of a holy God who are themselves consecrated to his service. Evidently, it would not be feasible for the hereditary priesthood to be celibate but the closest approximation to the marriage ideal is preferred.

Thus the priestly marriage restrictions cannot be explained on the basis of ritual purity; nevertheless they are connected to the sexual act and involve a certain gradation. Harlotry is a sin and a deliberate one at that, which is even used as a picture of Israel's unfaithfulness to God (e.g., Jer 3:6–10; Ezek 16, etc.). On the other hand, rape is by definition unintentional on the part of the victim, although it too involves a stigma.[204]

---

raped, based on the combination of חלל I "profane, desecrate" and חלל II "pierce." Thus a חללה is a "desecrated, pierced one," that is, raped. He argues that the hendyadis is unacceptable because זנה is a clear and specific enough term that needs no further qualification and the order of זנה וחללה is reversed in v.14 thereby providing an ascending list to v.7's descending one in terms of severity of offence. His argument is convincing and his interpretation of חללה fits logically into the progression. Ibid., 1806–8. For חללה as a deflowered woman see also *HALOT* 1:320.

[202] However, the regulation in Ezekiel allows a priest's widow to marry another priest.

[203] Wright, "Clean and Unclean," 739; Frymer-Kensky, "Pollution," 401. Maccoby similarly argues that the two sources for ritual impurity are connected to sex and death. Maccoby, *Ritual and Morality*, ix. Milgrom also connects God's nature and his incompatibility with the human condition although he derives all ritual impurities from the notion of death. Milgrom, *Leviticus 1–16*, 1002.

[204] Milgrom argues that there is no stigma attached to rape in Israel and quotes Deut 22:28–29 (*Leviticus 17–22*, 1807). This is hard to believe, however, as 2 Sam 13:13

Divorce is not an offence in the OT; Deut 24:1–4 permits it if the husband detects "a naked thing" (ערות דבר) in the wife. Although the expression's meaning is uncertain, later the Shammaites understood it as sexual misconduct while the Hillelites broadened the term to include "any matter" in which the husband was displeased with the wife (*b.Giṭ.* 90a).

Milgrom argues that both with respect to the harlot and the divorcee there may be practical reasons for their inclusion among the prohibited women. In the case of the former the priest may not be sure that the offspring is really his if the woman is promiscuous, while in the latter she may be suspected of pregnancy, barrenness or unfaithfulness.[205] While such considerations may have a role to play in the argument, the particular issue, it seems to me, is ultimately a theology of holiness that is capable of expressing in these commandments a certain kind of symbolic significance.

Thus I submit that the reason for excluding the divorcee from a priestly marriage is that she falls short of the marriage ideal as set forth in Gen 2:24. As Jesus points out, the allowances made for divorce are the result of a hardness of heart and not the way things should be since in the beginning it was not so (Matt 19:8) and "what God has joined together let no man separate" (v.6). From a modern perspective one might question whether it was indeed the divorced wife who was at fault, and it is even possible to argue on the level of the text that she is not entirely to blame. The order in which prohibited classes of women are listed in Lev 21:7 suggests that a raped woman is less desirable than a divorcee even though the former is a victim and clearly innocent of any crime. If a divorcee is less seriously a problem then this may be because sexual misconduct is merely suspected not proven or perhaps the only issue is that she had a previous marriage.

When we move from the marriage restrictions of the ordinary priests to that of the high priest widows are added to the list of undesirable connections. Milgrom cites Isa 54:4 where God speaks to Israel ("For you will forget the shame of your youth, And the reproach of your widowhood you will remember no more.") to show that widows carried a stigma and uses the story of Naomi and Ruth to argue that widows generally had low self-esteem (Ruth 1:13, 20).[206] His conclusions, however, are surely unconvincing. Isaiah does not speak of widows in general, only of Israel as a widow in humiliation. If widowhood is generally shameful then by the same token so is youth. Similarly, Naomi is a specific example of a widow in whose case there is a hint of judgment in the loss of her husband and son-in-laws, which may not be generalized. On the contrary, the provision of Levirate marriage (Deut 25:5–10) and the repeated appeal to

---

demonstrates the opposite. Here Tamar pleads with her half brother Amnon not to rape her and asks "As for me, [if you do this] how can I remove my reproach?" (ואני אנה אוליך את־חרפתי).

[205] Milgrom, *Leviticus 17–22*, 1805, 1808.
[206] Ibid., 1819.

care for the orphan and the widow (Deut 24:17–21) suggest a concern for the vulnerable rather than a condemnation of her condition.

Rather than an automatic indication of reproach and judgment, widowhood brings in another aspect alien to the divine: death. It is precisely the introduction of death into human existence—no ideal condition—that creates the kind of scenario where a woman has legitimate sexual experience before her (second) marriage and yet, or rather, precisely thereby falls short of the ideal of marriage: sexual innocence before marriage (Gen 2:25), honorable behavior within the union (Deut 24:1; Gen 38:9–10) that was not intended to end either by divorce or death.

The command for the high-priest to marry a virgin (lit. "a maiden") of his own people (אִם־בְּתוּלָה מֵעַמָּיו יִקַּח אִשָּׁה—Lev 21:14) may mean either an Israelite girl (which is how Ezek 44:22 takes it) or a priestly daughter (Josephus, *Ag. Ap.* 1:31; *Keter Torah*).[207] In either case a foreigner is implicitly excluded. At first glance, it may be less obvious how this fits into the preceding explanation about the concern for upholding an ideal of marriage without prior sexual experience (legitimate or illegitimate, deliberate or unintended). After all, if virginity alone is the issue, a foreign virgin need not be excluded. On the other hand, the ultimate concern with holiness sets the foreign women apart in another sense: their status with regard to holiness.

If one tries to put the different categories of people on a continuum from not holy to most holy then foreigners are furthest away from God as people who are common/profane (חֹל) with regard to holiness and cannot attain holiness *qua* foreigners. Israelites are one step closer as people who are set apart to God as his, who in the priestly legislation are expected to aim for holiness though their holy status is not inherent like the priesthood's.

Thus the command to marry Israelite girls or girls from priestly families is again a likely indication of the priests' closeness to a holy God, of their special elevated status.

It is perhaps no accident either that the regulations concerning priests follow on from a long list of sexual malpractices associated with the Canaanites in Lev 18 and 20. Although a foreign virgin would by definition be untainted in this respect, her overall status as not set apart to YHWH would still remove her further from qualifying as a priest's wife. It is interesting in this respect that the rabbinic writings, which allow converts to intermarry with lay Israelites and see in conversion a transformation of Gentile seed into Israelite seed, nevertheless maintain some distinction between a priest and a lay Israelite regarding the requirements for marriage. The priest may not marry a convert, only the daughter of a convert and there is much discussion on whether a daughter of two converts should be permitted to do so or not. Yet another view allows even a

---

[207] Ibid., 1819. Milgrom notes that the text does not explicitly state the girl's virginity normally indicated by the phrase לֹא־יָדְעָה אִישׁ (e.g., Judg 11:39; 21:12). Nevertheless it is to be assumed. See Ibid., 1818.

convert to marry a priest if her conversion occurred before the age of three.[208] As it is clear from the above, there is dispute about the details; nevertheless, the obligations of a priest are higher than the lay Israelite's.

We see then that despite the broader category of being "common" which applies to any lay Israelite and even to foreigners there are certain subgroups which are unacceptable in relation to the holy despite the fact that these may not be sinful in themselves. We may conclude then that for the protection of their offspring's holiness it is necessary for the priests to keep away from anything that is deficient in the sense that it falls short of the ideal whether this is the result of an individual's sin or merely caused indirectly by sin that cannot be blamed on the particular person in question. Thus lurking behind these regulations is a "moral" ideal even though groups who are excluded may not be sinful in individual terms.

We then come to our final question on Lev 21:7–9, 13–15: how does desecration happen? Generally when holy objects are profaned this is done either by ingesting (e.g., the holy portions of sacrifices—Lev 22:14–15) or by touch (Uzzah touches the Ark—2 Sam 6:6–7, the sons of Kohath should not touch sanctuary furnishings while transporting them—Num 4:15) and sometimes even by gaze (the Beth-Shemeshites look into the Ark—1 Sam 6:19). This kind of sacrilege is akin to the way "ritual impurity" is communicated.

As noted above, the priestly marriage restrictions in Lev 21 have an underlying reasoning that reflects a "moral-religious" ideal, which overlaps with what one might expect in terms of "moral purity." When it comes to the influence on the priestly spouse the text does not specify the exact effects of marriage with a harlot, a raped woman, a divorcee or a widow. Yet the emphasis on the priest's consecration suggests that marriage with these classes of women is irreconcilable with holiness and the priestly calling even though profanation of the priests themselves is not mentioned. What is explicitly stated is the desecration of the high-priestly offspring (v.15), but presumably priestly intermarriages with the prohibited groups of women listed in v.7 are equally profaning for the "seed."

Regarding moral impurity, the general consensus is that it does not defile anyone but the sinner and is not communicated by physical contact or proximity. Nevertheless, there is precedent for moral impurity to impact the wider environment and particularly what is holy. For instance, bloodshed (Num 35:33–34) and prohibited sexual acts (Lev 18:24–30) defile the land and child sacrifice to Molech (Lev 20:1–3) does the same to the sanctuary. Further, in some instances it seems to affect holiness, that is, to profane, without defiling. Thus Lev 21:9 suggests that a promiscuous priestly daughter profanes her father while the high priest who marries one of the prohibited classes of women profanes his offspring (vv.14–15). Milgrom notes the parallel and summarizes it thus:

---

[208] See Hayes' discussion of rabbinic sources on intermarriage between priests and female converts (*Gentile Impurities*, 171–184).

> V.15 is speaking of the high priest's desecration of his offspring *by means of prohibited sexual activity*; just as its twin verse (v.9) clearly refers to the intergenerational effect of *prohibited sexual activity*.[209]

Milgrom interprets the two types of profanation differently following here the rabbinic view. Namely, he thinks of the profanation of the father as metaphorical (see *b. Sanh.* 52a) which does not lead to the suspension of his priestly function but affects his reputation nevertheless.

> To be sure, *hll*, indeed, is metaphoric regarding the priest, since in no way does it disqualify the father from officiating in the sanctuary. However, as the rabbis well recognize, her action casts a stigma on her father. In all likelihood, he has no desire to be seen in the company of his fellow priests; it is *as though* he were disqualified.[210]

On the other hand, he takes the profanation of the offspring as genuinely affecting the status of the children with regard to their priestly descent. Thus in agreement with the rabbis he suggests that daughters from prohibited marriages cannot eat sacred food (*m. Ter.* 8:1; *Sipre Zuta* on Num 18:11) and sons cannot officiate in the sanctuary (*Sipra Nedaba* par. 4:6).[211]

Apart from the weight of tradition, it is not immediately obvious from the text why there should be a differentiation between the two profanations in the way Milgrom and the rabbis suggest. One difference between the two instances is that the cause of profanation (the daughter) is burned in v.9 and thus the evil is purged, as it were. Rather than treating the profanation of the priest (father) as metaphorical we might speculate that the cause of moral defilement is removed by the punishment of the sinner (the daughter) and therefore the issue does not affect the father further.

From an anthropological point of view the long-lasting impact of profanation on the offspring perhaps reflects the recognition that the consequences of sin may have an effect on the following generation (cf. Ezek 18:2) rather than work backwards from the children to the parents. It also expresses the concern that children whose views are still being shaped in the process of growing up are more vulnerable to the influence of their parents. Granted the text in Lev 21:15 does not speak about influence; nevertheless the loss of the children's holy status graphically illustrates the less tangible effects that an unacceptable parental alliance might have on the children. Their effective exclusion from the priestly class as indicated by their profaned status ensures that any adverse influence on the children are contained and not perpetuated to the next generation.

---

[209] Milgrom, *Leviticus 17–22*, 1836.
[210] Ibid., 1810.
[211] Ibid., 1820.

7.3 The Status of the "Foreign" Wives: Profane or Impure?

As noted earlier, Ezra 9:2 does not state what the intermingling of the holy seed results in: desecration or impurity. I have argued in §§7.2.1 and 7.2.2 that מעל is not necessarily used in a technical sense of *sancta* desecration, and that it is possible to interpret the אשם sacrifice as offered for something other than "trespass against *sancta.*" Nevertheless, I agree with Milgrom that profanation does occur although I see this process affecting the children and argue for a strong connection between the Ezran "holy seed" rationale and the priestly marriage restrictions in Lev 21:7–15.

There are some obvious similarities between the two texts. First, whatever goes wrong in both cases happens by way of marriage with a prohibited class of women and it affects the children, who are excluded from the community of Israel in Ezra 9-10 and explicitly described as profane in Lev 21:15. Secondly, holiness in both has to do with a "moral-religious" ideal (see §7.2.4 for Lev 21:7-15). In Ezra 9–10 the foreign women are characterized by "abominations" (תועבות), the standard vocabulary used to describe idolatry and sexual immorality (e.g., Deut 7:25–26; 17:3–4; Jer 44:4; Lev 18:22; Ezek 22:11). Further, Ezra's prayer connects the abominations of the Canaanite nations with the impurity (טמא) which defiled the land of Israel in v.11. The verse is an oblique reference to Lev 18:24–30 and the language is an echo of Lev 18 and 20, where the sexual immorality of the Canaanites (Lev 18:6–23 cf. v.24), child sacrifice to Molech (18:21) and necromancy (20:6) are blamed on both the defilement of the land and the expulsion of the previous inhabitants. Moreover, Israel is threatened of the same consequences if she imitated their practices. By analogy, the peoples of the lands in Ezra's day are associated with these abominations. Thus the language overall speaks of "moral impurity" in Ezra 9–10.

A possibly ambiguous term is the designation of the defiled land as ארץ נדה, a word more often associated with "ritual" than "moral" impurity. Milgrom derives the nominative נדה from the root נדד or נדה both of which carry the meaning "chase away, expel"; hence its use for menstrual impurity (Lev 15:20) on the one hand, since the blood is "expelled" from the body and also for its opposite in the expression מי נדה, the water for removing/expelling certain ritual impurities (Num 19:13, 20).[212] Despite the more common association of נדה with "ritual" impurity, Lev 20:21 is a clear example of the sexual sin of incest and shows that the word can equally be used in the sense of "moral" impurity. The noun נדה is also used of idols, which are carried out of the temple during Hezekiah's reform (2 Chr 29:5) and Zion is described as a נדה (an unclean thing) who went after her lovers (Lam 1:8–9, 17, 19): a graphic picture of "spiritual adultery" and rebellion against YHWH. It is notable that many postexilic sources use imagery from ritual defilement and purification to depict "moral impurity." Thus Ezek 36:17 compares the sin of Israel (bloodshed and

---

[212] Milgrom, *Leviticus* 1–16, 745.

idolatry cf. v.18) with the impurity of a menstruous woman (כתמאת הנדה) and uses the ritual language of purification by water to describe YHWH's act of cleansing from sin in v.25. Similarly, Zech 13:1 speaks of a fountain that will be opened for sin and for "impurity" (לחטאת ולנדה). Surely, the fountain is symbolic of "moral-religious" cleansing akin to the language of Ezek 36:25 and is to be understood metaphorically, since no actual water can simultaneously cleanse from sin and from "ritual impurity." On the basis of the above, it is safe to conclude that ארץ נדה is an apt term for Ezra to use in order to express the "moral" defilement of the land by idolatry and prohibited sexual practices as detailed in Lev 18 and 20 in particular.[213]

At the same time there is also a shift in emphasis as we move from the priestly regulations of Lev 21 to Ezra 9–10. The requirements of high priestly marriage are phrased in positive terms focusing on sexual purity expressed in virginity and only imply the rejection of a non-Israelite (or non-priestly) spouse. In contrast, Ezra 9–10 is concerned with the explicit problem of foreignness which is closely associated with "moral" impurity caused by prohibited sexual practices and idolatry.[214]

Another difference compared to Lev 21:14–15 is that the "moral-religious" ideal behind the restrictions on the priesthood is more explicit in Ezra 9–10. In the case of the former some of the women cannot be considered sinful (such as the raped woman or the widow) even if their particular status reflects the effects of sin. In the case of the latter the foreign women are unambiguously characterized by "moral impurity," which on the analogy of Lev 21:9, 15, affects the children in the form of desecration: the changing of their holy status to profane.

---

[213] Because of the association of נדה with ritual impurity, Alon in particular has argued that idols in the Bible were considered ritually impure and this is strongly connected in his reasoning with the cause of inherent Gentile impurity. Alon, "Levitical Uncleanness," 146–189. On the other hand, Hayes refutes Alon's claim and convincingly shows that both the ritual impurity of idols and of Gentiles is a rabbinic innovation which served to reinforce the ban on intermarriage. For a detailed discussion see Hayes, *Gentile Impurities*, 40–43, 53–54, 215–221.

[214] Although idolatry is not mentioned explicitly anywhere in EN or specifically in Ezra 9–10 it should be clear by now that the text is best read as clearly alluding to it. It is, of course, possible to construe such references as תועבות or ארץ נדה as a merely stereotyped depiction of Gentiles, yet there might be reasons for speaking of idolatry cautiously. As Maccoby points out, the hint of syncretism in Ezra 4:1–2 is obvious for anyone who is familiar with Israelite history. He maintains that the "coded" way in which the real issue is indicated is due to the fact that the exiles lived in the Persian empire, which itself practiced "a tolerant syncretism" and it may not have been too pleased to hear of tension as a result of an exclusivist, intolerant monotheism. Maccoby, "Holiness and Purity," 165–166. I do not agree with Maccoby that the holy seed rationale is mere "aristocratic language" which the empire would have understood but which played no decisive role in the exiles' reasoning. Nevertheless he makes a shrewd observation regarding the covert nature of the central issue; namely idolatry and syncretism.

7.4 *Ma'al* and Purity Language in Neh 13:23–31

7.4.1 מעל *in Neh 13:26*

In §4.4 I have already argued for a strong deuteronomic influence in Neh 13:23–31. As I have shown there the legal basis for the ban is Deut 7:1–3 and Deut 23:4–7[3–6] and is further reinforced by the narrative example of King Solomon (1 Kgs 11:1–11). Although there are possible alternative readings of the latter story (cf. Sir 47:20), Neh 13:23–31 does not make it clear that the disapproval of Solomon's foreign marriages is based on something other than disobedience to God's covenant and commandments and the sin of idolatry and apostasy. Further Nehemiah's reaction to the sin of intermarriage is to make the Israelites swear an oath not to intermarry and to curse those who already have. I suggested that this again is in line with the deuteronomic thinking of curses reserved for those who disobey the commandments and pointed out the similarity of vocabulary between the exiles, who entered into an oath and a curse at the covenant renewal in Neh 10:30[29] committing themselves among other things that they would not intermarry (10:31[30]), which echoed the crossing over into God's covenant and oath/curse in Deut 29:11[12]. What may alter this overall picture is the use of מעל in Neh 13:27 and some other words related to purity language and to the examination of these I turn now.

Based on Milgrom's idea of מעל indicating sacrilege, Hayes concludes that Neh 13:23–30 considers lay intermarriages as profaning (because מעל is used in v.27 in connection with lay people) and priestly ones as defiling based on Neh 13:29, which refers to the "defilers" of the priesthood (גאלי הכהנה) and on v.30, which states that Nehemiah "purified them" (טהרתם) from everything foreign.[215] As in the case of Ezra 9–10, מעל may not have the technical priestly sense of desecration here and the fact that holiness is not mentioned at all but that other aspects of the text point to covenant breaking may add support to the position that the issue is covenant breaking. Further, the smooth transition with a simple *waw* from the lay people to a priestly example of the same problem may go against Hayes' distinction between the laity and the priesthood in this respect. Also, as I shall argue below, the statement in v.30 may refer to all intermarriages, not merely to priestly ones. Moreover, it is difficult to see how foreign women of the same status can have a different impact on the lay people and the priests. In order to unravel the puzzle I shall examine the meaning of the two terms relating to purity: גאל and טהר.

7.4.2 גאל *II in Neh 13:29*

The word גאל II is used in a number of contexts in the Old Testament. It could be connected to the "moral" impurity of shedding blood (Isa 59:3) and oddly, be combined with characteristics of "ritual" impurity as in Lam 4:14 where those defiled by blood (i.e., by committing murder cf. v.13) cry out

---

[215] Hayes, *Gentile Impurities*, 27–28.

warning others not to touch their garments. It is as if their "moral" impurity were contagious by physical contact. The word גאל may also refer to the defilement derived from eating potentially unclean food (Dan 1:8); to lame, blind and otherwise defective sacrificial animals which are considered "defiled food" (לחם מגאל—Mal 1:7) and which defile the table of the Lord (Mal 1:12) and to the sin of general disobedience to God (Zeph 3:1). It may even characterize YHWH's garments "stained" by the lifeblood of the nations on the day of vengeance (Isa 63:3). The above list shows that the word is used in a whole spectrum of contexts without any clearly delineated technical sense of either "moral" or "ritual" defilement. The dictionaries are not even entirely clear whether the issue is always defilement or if the term might refer to desecration. For instance, BDB considers the Pual verb form in Ezra 2:62 to mean desecration (see table below). The reference is to the priests of uncertain genealogy who are "excluded from the priesthood" (lit. "desecrated/defiled out of"—ויגאלו מן־הכהנה) and not allowed to eat the most holy things. It is not obvious from the context, however, whether doubtful lineage involves defilement or sacrilege. The table below illustrates the various views represented in the dictionaries.[216]

	de-secrate	desecrate or defile	defile be defiled defile self	Ezra 2:62	Neh 13:29
BDB	Pual	Piel	Niphal, Hiphil	desecrated	–
NIDOTTE	–	Piel	Niphal, Pual	defiled	ritually defiled
HALOT	Piel	–	Niphal, Pual (ritual) Hithpael	ritually defiled	–
DCH			Niphal, Pual Hithpael Piel Hiphil	"they were defiled away, i.e., disqualified from, the priesthood"	"defilement(s) of the priesthood"

As shown above, the majority treats גאל as defilement and where mentioned at all, the dictionaries opt for that meaning in Neh 13:29. Further, the balance seems to be tipped toward ritual defilement within that classification. This is understandable given that the purity and holiness of the priests is

---

[216] BDB 1351 גאל II.; Richard E. Averbeck, "גאל," *NIDOTTE* 1:794–5; *HALOT* 1:169–170; *DCH* 2:295–96. Unfortunately *TDOT* does not treat גאל II; it merely notes that it is a by-form of געל. (Helmer Ringgren, "גאל," *TDOT* 1:351).

primarily associated with their ritual role performed in the sanctuary and certainly Ezra 2:62, where the word also occurs, is dealing with an issue of ritual holiness/purity. On the other hand, we have seen that the context of Neh 13:23–27 is largely Deuteronomistic in outlook with an emphasis on covenant breaking and the hint of idolatry/apostasy: an issue of "moral" defilement.[217]

What then is the background for vv.28–31? It is worth noting that Nehemiah's complaint is not that the priests were defiled by foreign women but that *they* (the priests) became "the defilers of the priestly office and the covenant of the priesthood and the Levites" (גאלי הכהנה וברית הכהנה והלוים). The expression "covenant of the priesthood" (ברית הכהנה) evokes the incident of Baal Peor (Num 25) where Israel "began to play the harlot" (ויחל העם לזנות).[218] The episode combines the sexual immorality of Israelite men with Moabite women (v.1) and the predictable consequences of apostasy and the worship of their gods (v.2). Phinehas receives the "covenant of perpetual priesthood" (ברית כהנת עולם—v.13) as a result of his zeal in executing the couple who flagrantly disobeyed YHWH in a high-handed manner. Thereby he averts YHWH's wrath (השיב את־חמתי מעל בני־ישראל—v.11) and makes atonement for Israel (ויכפר על־בני ישראל—v.13): an obviously priestly duty.

In Neh 13 the priests not only do not stop the lay people from intermarriage and covenant breaking but they themselves engage in it, including even the high priestly family. This is a striking reversal of the priestly role the ancestor Phinehas played and a corruption of the office that the priests were called to fulfill. Thus the issue for priests and for laymen alike seems to be the same in Nehemiah: the "moral" defilement associated with disobedience to YHWH's covenant and commandments specifically relating to intermarriage and apostasy. The effects of such sins are different for priests than for laymen only in degree, not in kind. Since the priests hold a leadership position the

---

[217] A slightly altered meaning is given to גאלי in some Greek manuscripts, which render the word as ἀγχιστεία (the duty/right/responsibility to act as a kinsman), suggesting that the sin of these foreigners is that they seek kinship with the priesthood (see Loring W. Batten, *A Critical and Exegetical Commentary on the Books of Ezra and Nehemiah* [ICC; Edinburgh: T&T Clark, 1913] 302.

[218] The verb חלל in the Hiphil can mean "to desecrate" or "to begin." The LXX takes Num 25:1 as desecration (καὶ ἐβεβηλώθη ὁ λαὸς ἐκπορνεῦσαι εἰς τὰς θυγατέρας Μωάβ) and this is certainly possible with the Hebrew although the large majority of English translations go with "to begin" (e.g., RVS, NRSV, KJV, NKJV, NASV; New Jerusalem Bible, Darby; JPS 1917; NIV. Exceptions are JPS Tanakh 1985: "the people profaned themselves by whoring"; NAB: "the people degraded themselves by having illicit relations"; NLT: "some of the men defiled themselves by sleeping with the local Moabite women"). In any case, even if חלל is to be read as desecration, it cannot have the technical priestly meaning of "sacrilege" since Israel is not obviously designated as holy in the way the priests or the holy objects in the Temple are. The context suggests that Israel's sin is to be understood as a kind of degradation or "moral" defilement along the lines suggested in Lev 18.

consequences are more serious in that their disobedience makes a mockery of their calling and disqualifies them from holding such an office.

In comparison, we may note the similarity of approach in the book of Malachi, which brings together a comparable cluster of ideas evident in Neh 13:23–31 and in Num 25. Although Mal 1:7–12 looks on the surface to be about a ritual purity issue yet the underlying concern is "moral-religious": the complacent and contemptuous attitude of the priesthood toward the worship of their God, followed by Mal 2 which rebukes the priests for the falsity of their instruction that has led many to stumble (vv.8–9). It is worth noting the importance of instruction in Neh 8:2, 8, 13 and Ezra 7:10, 25 and the tacit assumption in Ezra 9–10 that the mixed marriage crisis was the result of inadequate instruction on intermarriages before Ezra's arrival. In Mal 2 we also encounter the combined sin of illicit sexual activity/intermarriage and apostasy ("Judah [...] has married the daughter of a foreign god" יהודה... ובעל בת־אל נכר—2:11). The chapter mentions "My covenant with Levi" (בריתי את־לוי—v.4), similarly to Neh 13:29, and the specific reference to this covenant being of life and peace (בריתי היתה אתו החיים והשלום—v.5) echoes "My covenant of peace" (בריתי שלום—Num 25:12) in the incident at Baal Peor. We see then that the issue of mixed marriages, the lack of adequate Torah teaching on the matter and the fear of apostasy or at least complacency toward the worship of YHWH because of foreign influence is a recurring concern already in the early Postexilic Period.

7.4.3 טהר in Neh 13:30

One last aspect to consider in Neh 13:28–31 is the word טהר ("to purify") in v.30 in which Nehemiah ostensibly purifies "them" (טהרתים) from "everything foreign" (כל־נכר). As noted earlier, the majority of scholars see in the priestly intermarriages of Nehemiah 13 an issue of ritual purity, in which case the purification from all things foreign is of a ritual nature and the object of purification are the priests. I shall address these questions in turn.

First, as to the question whether purification is "ritual" in nature, *TDOT* lists three possible meanings for טהר: "cultic purity" and two "figurative occurrences" where the word can either mean "moral purity" or "pure, unadulterated."[219] This makes a non-ritual understanding of purification a legitimate option to consider. Further, the wider context and background of both vv.28–31 and vv.23–27, as we have seen, consistently point toward a concern for "moral purity" in the face of the stereotypical sins of apostasy and idolatry and the concomitant dangers of disobedience to Torah. Moreover, the agent of purification is Nehemiah himself, which makes it unlikely that the issue is ritual purity. After all, Nehemiah is no priest and has no authority or business executing any purification rite. In contrast, where the issue seems to be "ritual

---

[219] Helmer Ringgren, "טהר," *TDOT* 5:287–296 (esp. 291). Similarly, Richard Averbeck, "טהר," *NIDOTTE* 2:338–353.

impurity" or desecration, he gives orders to the priests to deal with the matter. Thus he "commanded" (ואמרה) the room Tobiah had occupied in the temple to be purified (טהר Piel—v.9) earlier in the chapter and again "commanded" (ואמרה) the Levites to purify themselves (טהר Hithpael) and come as gatekeepers to sanctify the Sabbath day (v.22).

Secondly, are the objects of purification the priests only or also the lay people? If the former then there might be justification for assuming that defilement only affects the priests. The way in which v.30 is embedded between verses discussing the priesthood and Levitical duties suggests at first glance a reference to the priests and it directly corresponds to the defilement of the priesthood in v.29. The clause "I purified them" (וטהרתים—v.30) is followed by "and appointed duties for the priests and the Levites, each in his task." If "them" refers to the same group, that is, to the Levites and the priests, then the explicit naming of these in the next clause is unnecessary. The sentence would make perfect sense if it simply ran "I purified them from everything foreign and appointed *them* (להם) their duties, each in his task." It would thus be logical to assume that the object of purification is a wider group since the sentence then specifies a subgroup (Levites and priests) in the next clause.

If the issue is not the ritual purification of the priesthood alone then we might consider the option that v.30 is a kind of summary statement either of the section on intermarriage or even of the whole chapter. If so, then either vv.23–29 or Neh 13 in its entirety may provide the clues for what the content of such purification is. If we opt for the former, then Nehemiah's measures in the mixed marriage crisis are the acts of purification meant here. His actions have two aspects to them: judgment and prevention. On the one hand, the cursing of the lay culprits may indicate his conviction that divine judgment is coming on those who break the covenant in this way. On the other, the oath that the laity swears is meant to prevent further such marriages. Similarly, the banishment of the high priest's grandson is both an act of judgment divesting him of priestly office and a preventative measure to protect the laity from priests who may lead Israel astray. We may also speculate on the basis of Neh 13:3 that the children of such intermarriages were excluded from the assembly and that the overall approach more than likely excluded divorce (see §4.4.2).

If v.30 is a summary statement for the whole chapter then the content of purification and what "everything foreign" might mean, can be defined even more widely. Hardly any commentators actually raise the question of what כל־נכר may mean. The rare few that do make no connection between these words and the chapter preceding them and are simply guessing. Batten, for instance, notes that "everything foreign" must involve more than the mixed marriages, although he does not elaborate what else might be included and what makes him think so.[220] Keil is more definite in claiming that כל־נכר probably

---

[220] Batten, *A Critical and Exegetical Commentary*, 302.

refers to heathen customs as well.[221] However, if we understand v.30 as a summary statement (along with v.31) then the meaning of what "everything foreign" is and what kind of purification is at issue is given content by the whole chapter. Thus it would include the "purification" of Israel from mixed descendants (v.3), the cleansing of the temple premises from the foreigner Tobiah (v.9), the restoration of the Sabbath from being profaned by buying and selling at the influence of foreigners (v.18), and the purification of Israel and the priesthood from foreign marriages (vv.23–29). In other words, טהר would have the non-technical sense of cleansing from all foreign influence no matter in what form it came and Nehemiah would simply be the orchestrator of all these changes, not the one who necessarily executes all the acts of purification.

This meaning would fit well with the third sense of טהר listed in *TDOT* of "being/making pure or unadulterated." Although this is primarily a meaning that describes various cultic utensils made of gold (e.g., Exod 25:11, 17, 29, 31, etc.) one might speculate that the word in Neh 13:30 may carry the same association of cleansing Israel, her laity, Levites and priests from the influence resulting from the mixing/associating with foreigners.[222] Such a summary statement of the whole chapter would fit well with the rest of v.30 and v.31, in which Nehemiah appoints the Levites and priests their tasks (e.g., vv.11, 13, 22) and organizes wood supplies and finally prays to God to be remembered.

7.5 Conclusion

The "intermingling of the holy seed" in Ezra 9:2 raises questions relating to purity and holiness. Milgrom is right to suggest that the issue is the desecration of the holy seed; nevertheless I have argued from the context that מעל in EN is used in the sense of covenant breaking and oath violation rather than that of "trespass against *sancta.*" I have also speculated based on the violation of the slave girl in Lev 19:20–22 that the lack of compensation and the actual offering of a ram as an אשם (rather than its monetary equivalent) may similarly indicate a direct offence against YHWH, specifically against the covenant oath taken perhaps at Moab (Deut 29:11[12]).

The upshot of these observations is that the primary concern of the exiles is covenant breaking and foreign influence which is characterized by idolatry and sexual immorality. The "holy seed" rationale is only a secondary argument that supports and strengthens the ban on intermarriage. An examination of Lev 21:7, 14–15 has shown that the priestly restrictions on intermarriage uphold a "moral-religious" ideal and the transgression against these jeopardizes the holiness of the children. "Moral impurity" is not

---

[221] C. F. Keil, *The Books of Ezra, Nehemiah, and Esther* (trans. Sophia Taylor; Edinburgh: T&T Clark, 1873) 296.

[222] Hayes understands the purification in a sense of separating Israel from foreign "admixture," although my interpretation is considerably wider than hers and implies not only intermarriages but other forms of foreign influence (*Gentile Impurities*, 71).

contagious by contact and does not defile anyone except the sinner, yet it can affect the holy such as the sanctuary and the land. Further, Lev 21:9, 15 provide precedence for intergenerational profanation as a result of "moral impurity" or of unions that somehow fall short of the "moral-religious" ideal. On the same analogy, I argued that the foreign women in Ezra 9–10 are considered "morally impure" and their effect is profanation without [ritual?] defilement affecting irrevocably the children of such mixed marriages.

Further, I suggested that a comparison with Neh 13:23–31 shows a similar picture. The word מעל is more likely to refer to covenant breaking and oath violation, while the defilement of the priesthood shows verbal and conceptual links to the story of Num 25, where Israel gave in to idolatry and sexual immorality and where Phinehas' zeal earned him "the covenant of eternal priesthood." I argued that by their negative example and possibly lack of faithful Torah teaching, priests who intermarried with foreigners degraded (in this sense "defiled") their office and hence were no longer worthy to continue in it. Finally, Nehemiah's concluding statement of purifying them from everything foreign is, in my view, best read as a summary statement of either the intermarriage crisis (vv.23–29) or the whole chapter and it has the non-technical sense of simply getting rid of any foreign influence that led Israel into disobedience away from her commitment to her God.

8

Conclusion to Part I

I opened the first part of this book with a description of the old Lutheran dichotomy of law versus grace and explored ways in which Christians attempt to integrate the Law into their understanding. In Chapter 2 I observed that the most common practices were found to be the framing of the Law with covenant and "theologizing." I suggested that the first allowed Christians to think of obedience to God's commandments as a grateful response to his salvation, while the second could overcome the difficulty of what to do about laws that seem irrelevant or not directly applicable for Christian use. I then juxtaposed these with two Jewish responses, which were meant to show that Jews are also trying to articulate their own positions in ways that can be meaningful in a Christian context and that their contributions are a far cry from the old caricature of Jewish legalism. The two particular aspects I highlighted through Levenson's and Lipton's input were the recognition that the laws of God are not only rooted in redemption but in creation as well and that blind obedience to his commandments may be counter-productive when it does not involve active engagement with the God who commands.

In Chapter 3 I turned to the context of Ezra 9–10, first to the wider background of Neh 9 and then to the more immediate chapters preceding the Ezran intermarriage crisis. In Neh 9 I traced some of the ideas raised in Chapter 2. I argued that the prayer looks back on Israel's history as a record of God's gracious dealings within the covenant made with Abraham to make him a great nation and give him the land. I observed at the same time the centrality of the Law, obedience to which was the benchmark of Israel's faithfulness to YHWH. The creational aspects of the prayer were also noted and the need for recognizing the inherent goodness of God's laws, which was a consideration I raised in my discussion of Jewish responses to the Law. I suggested that the linkage of the Law with God's Spirit indicated a dynamic aspect to the "instruction" (torah), which again resonated with notions of constant and fresh engagement discussed in Lipton's re-evaluation of the Law. Ezra 7–8 further reinforced this picture of the importance of Torah as well as the need for holiness and separation for the priests who carried the holy vessels. This latter principle was then seen to be extended to the laity in the question of intermarriages in Ezra 9–10. Ezra 9:1–2 set the scene for the crisis with two legal reasons for the ban on intermarriage: the threat of idolatry as expressed in Deut 7 on the one hand and the intermingling of the "holy seed" on the other.

The rest of this first part of the book then concerned itself with questions relating to these two reasons. Chapters 4 and 5 discussed issues relating to the first reason for prohibiting intermarriage focusing specifically on the list of nations in Ezra 9:1 (Chapter 4) and on the question of the ḥērem law (Chapter 5). Chapters 6 and 7 then explored matters connected with the second reason concentrating on the possible legal background for this new and distinct rationale as well as analogous developments in other Jewish literature of the time on the one hand (6), and on the logic and meaning of the argument on the other (7).

Chapter 4 suggested that the three sources for the nations list was Deut 7:1–3, Deut 23:4–7[3–6] and Lev 18:3 and the common denominator that held the list together was the "abominations" associated with them. I argued that these were primarily the stereotypical sins of idolatry/apostasy (Deut 7:1–13) as well as sexual immorality (Lev 18) and to some extent hostility toward God's people. I have also suggested on the analogy of later Jewish usage that these ideas did not mean necessarily that idolatrous and sexually immoral practices were attributed to every single "foreigner" but that these notions summed up in the term "abominations" became a convenient shorthand for characterizing those outside of Israel. A comparison with the issues in Neh 13:1–3 and Neh 13:23–31 showed that again Deut 7:1–3 and Deut 23:4–7[3–6] played a part in the argument against mixed marriages coupled with an explicit use of 1 Kgs 11:1–11, a narrative passage that only surfaced implicitly in Ezra 9:1–2 through the emphasis on the leadership's sin and on marriages with "foreign" *women*.

Chapter 5 considered the question what role the original ḥērem law of Deut 7 may have played in Ezra 9–10. I argued that the divorces in Ezra 9–10 may be understood as a form of ḥērem coupled with the exclusion of those Israelites who did not go along with the communal decision and the confiscation of their properties. My assessment of the development of the concept in the Pentateuch and the Old Testament more broadly and the parallel trends I found there supported these notions. This chapter also demonstrated the exiles' remarkable amount of flexibility in applying old laws to a new situation.

Chapter 6 claimed that the exiles' reason for wanting separation from the foreign wives, which was expressed in the notion of the "holy seed" was a distinct rationale. It very likely originated in a cluster of ideas, most probably in Lev 19:19/Deut 22:9–11 and the priestly marriage restrictions of Lev 21:7–15. The arguments from "the holy seed" in 4QMMT and *Jub.* 30 also showed a similar array of passages with the addition of Lev 18:21. The sudden appearance of this rationale in the same time period and its later gradual disappearance prompted the question why Deut 7 with its ban on intermarriage did not suffice for those who subscribed to this new notion. I suggested that this may have been due to the level of perceived threat to the community's life by outsiders. The "holy seed" rationale made the ban on intermarriage absolute without exceptions and thus was perhaps seen to be a more effective tool of defense than Deut 7.

Finally, Chapter 7 examined more closely the way the "holy seed" rationale was to be understood. I particularly assessed Milgrom's theory of *sancta* desecration based on the use of מעל and אשם in Ezra 9–10. I concluded that the idea of the "holy seed" should not be overplayed in the text and that these two Hebrew terms are used in Ezra 9–10 in the context of covenant breaking and oath violation. On the analogy of intergenerational profanation as a result of "moral impurity" in Lev 21:9 and 15, I argued that the foreign women were considered "morally impure" and thus profaned the holy status of the children. A comparison with Neh 13:23–31 suggested that מעל there was also more likely used in the sense of covenant breaking and that the purity language in vv.29–30 had a non-technical sense of degradation of the priestly office on the one hand, and cleansing of the community from foreign influences on the other.

Having considered in detail some of the exegetical questions relating to the interpretation of pentateuchal regulations in Ezra 9–10 in the second part of this book I now turn to the issue of how a Christian reader may benefit from this story of the Ezran intermarriage crisis.

PART II

9

Introduction to a Christian Reading of Ezra 9–10

The story of Ezra 9–10 is a challenging case for interpretation of the OT as Christian Scripture since the expulsion of the foreign wives and their divorce en masse by the exiles is often seen in suspicious readings of the text as a case of outright racism with a possible land-grabbing power-play behind the scenes masquerading as religious righteousness. Even more shocking is the fact that the text does not merely describe the incident as an account of what has happened with a suspended judgment or leaving the reader to draw his own conclusions. Rather, the way the narrative is set out, it invites approval of such an act of religious fervor and commitment to the God of Israel. It is presented as following on from Ezra's mission to teach Torah (Ezra 7:10, 25) and it affirms the action taken by the exiles to be "according to Torah" (כתורה—Ezra 10:3).

What are we to make of such a story and how can it be part of Scripture? In order to answer that question I will first look at Christian interpretations of the narrative to see the particular tensions and trouble spots that commentators encounter and to understand how they read this difficult text. I will also consider Jewish interpretations of Ezra 9–10 in order to cast in high relief the different concerns and premises that the two traditions bring to the text. I will then think further about the reasons for such differences.

Secondly I will look at how the wider Christian canon deals with this story and will particularly focus on the way biblical tradition constrains controversial solutions such as the one found in Ezra 9–10 while it retains them within Scripture. I will also reflect on the benefits of having such a story in the canon. As a further example of how tradition works and provides checks on contentious issues, I shall follow the history of the "holy seed" rationale in postbiblical rabbinic tradition and show that the exiles' reasoning did not stand the test of time.

Next I will examine at greater length the main NT counterpart to the Ezran intermarriage crisis: 1 Cor 7:12–16, its background, solution and the principle behind it. Although the meaning and authorship of 2 Cor 6:14–7:1 is debated, for the sake of completeness I will also briefly discuss this passage.

Finally I will draw on Mary Douglas' anthropological insights on purity to explore the motivation behind the "holy seed" rationale as well as its effects and the unforeseen ramifications of the exiles' reasoning. My purpose is to see what can be learnt from the story more positively beyond enumerating the constraints that the canon and tradition place on it and limiting its applicability. This will then be followed by a comparison with the contemporary solution to intermarriages given by the Roman Catholic Church. The reason for choosing the RC position as a kind of "case study" is simply because Protestant denominations are more informal in their disapproval of mixed (i.e., Christian— non-Christian) marriages and do not have any means of officially enforcing compliance with their principles. Thus for practical purposes the RC solution to the problem of intermarriage and the underlying convictions driving it are more easily traceable and comparable with Ezra 9–10.

Owing to the nature of the discussion the length of the following chapters will vary considerably depending on the amount of material there is available and on the degree of difficulty or importance a certain question has in the overall framework I am building up. Thus for instance there is more to engage with, say, in the Christian tradition on Ezra 9–10 than in the Jewish, and a more detailed analysis needed in comparing a NT perspective with Ezra than in considering the relatively uncontroversial question of canonical constraints on the story.

10

Ezra 9–10 in Christian Interpretation

First I turn to Christian assessments of Ezra 9–10 both as they occur in OT theologies and in commentaries on EN. Although references to the intermarriage crisis are scant in OT theologies I shall include them here for the sake of completeness. They will also help set the scene for the more detailed discussions in EN commentaries. In my overview of OT theologies I have chosen three "representative" cases: Eichrodt's from among an older-style scholarship and Goldingay's and Rendtorff's as two more recent examples. However, I shall also refer to some other OT theologies that reflect something of the trend within OT scholarship with regards to EN.

From among the commentaries I have selected the work of scholars who attempt to combine scholarship and the world of the academy with a Christian faith perspective. Despite the broad similarities, the points I have found interesting or worthy of mention are scattered among them and for this reason I will not present just one or two examples but will compare a wider range in order to show a broader spectrum of opinions with varying shades of approval, understanding or disapproval of Ezra 9–10. There is very little pre-modern Christian discussion of EN, at least that I can find, hence most of my conversation partners are contemporary scholars. As a comparison, however, I shall occasionally cite Matthew Henry (1662–1714) and Thomas Scott's (1747–1821) commentary as a contrast to the specifically contemporary modern/postmodern concerns. In examining the commentaries I shall group my review around three themes which run through all Christian commentaries dealing with the intermarriage crisis: exclusivism, divorce and application. The observations made will then provide material for further reflection.

10.1 OT Theologies

Searching through Old Testament theologies for a significant mention of Ezra–Nehemiah in general and the intermarriage crisis in particular are like looking for a needle in a haystack. The indexes normally show a handful of references relating to EN, which are little more than passing comments on incidental details, accounts of the historical situation in the Postexilic Period or issues of authorship.[223] The two topics that recur in the theologies which touch on EN in more significant ways are the charge of legalism and the issue of intermarriages normally seen as problematic because of the seemingly ethnic/racial rather than religious definition of Israel's identity. There is also some evidence of the struggle to take into account Jewish perspectives while presenting a Christian understanding of the Law and EN.

10.1.1 Eichrodt

The negative view of the Law in the Postexilic Period which was characteristic of much OT scholarship since Wellhausen is illustrated in the works of Eichrodt and von Rad. I have chosen Eichrodt as a representative example mainly because von Rad has nothing to say about the intermarriage and separation issue. He merely recounts the history in EN and makes some comments about the general postexilic situation in which he argues, following Noth, that the Law became absolute, detached from history (i.e., salvation history) leading to legalism with all its negative aspects.[224]

Eichrodt in his *Theology of the Old Testament* sees in the period after the Exile a welcome development at first where "the demands of morality became wider in scope and more profound in insight," which in turn meant that every area of life including "the cultic statutes also are brought within the sphere of ethical obligation."[225] Here he even refers to "Ezra's life-work" in positive

---

[223] E.g., Claus Westermann, *Elements of Old Testament Theology* (trans. Douglas W. Stott; Atlanta: John Knox, 1982) 76 (an excursus on the רוח יהוה), 156, 164, 169 (about the confessions and prayers in EN); Walther Zimmerli, *Old Testament Theology in Outline* (trans. David E. Green; Edinburgh: T&T Clark, 1978) 95 (illustrating the tension between priests and Levites in Ezra 2:40 (=Neh 7:43); Ezra 8:15), 96 (about the custom of casting lots in Ezra 2), 180–81 (EN as the Chronicler's work); Hans Walter Wolff, *The Old Testament: A Guide to Its Writings* (trans. Keith R. Crim; London: SPCK, 1974) 56–57 (EN as the work of the Chronicler; pinpoints the opposition to the Samaritan community as the background of the book); Ludwig Koehler, *Old Testament Theology* (trans. A.S. Todd; London: Lutterworth Press, 1957), endnote for p.56 (a translation issue in Ezra 10:3), 174 (notes the various words used for sin in Neh 9:2); Ronald E. Clements, *Old Testament Theology: A Fresh Approach* (London: Marshall, Morgan & Scott, 1978) 91 (reference to the Temple building), 168 (Ezra 4:2–3 as the possible beginnings of the Samaritan schism), 169 (Neh 13:23–27 as an episode reflecting the concern for the importance of Hebrew).

[224] Martin Noth, "The Laws in the Pentateuch: Their Assumptions and Meaning' in *The Laws in the Pentateuch and Other Studies* (trans. D.R.AP-Thomas; Edinburgh: Oliver & Boyd, 1966), 1–107. Gerhard von Rad, *Old Testament Theology: The Theology of Israel's Historical Traditions* (2 vols.; trans. D.M.G. Stalker; London: SCM, 1975) 1:85–92.

[225] Walther Eichrodt, *Theology of the Old Testament*, (2 vols.; trans. J.A. Baker; London: SCM Press, 1967) 2:340.

terms, which in Eichrodt's understanding set the cultic law alongside the moral but without disregarding "the majesty of the moral demand."[226] Eichrodt sees the first threat to this moral understanding in the shift from a dependence on God to an attitude of self-sufficiency in which "the ideal of the holy congregation" is "the condition to be established by men, with the help of the legal system."[227] Here we meet the language frequently used of the Law in the Postexilic Period associated with "anxiety-ridden subservience to formula," lack of firm moral orientation in a maze of external rules, "hair-splitting casuistry" and hypocrisy.[228]

Alongside this shift, so Eichrodt argues, Israel's nationalist and particularistic hopes for the future narrow down the validity of the legal system so that there are no moral obligations toward the heathens: they are treated with contempt, cruelty and violence (Esther; Jdt 8:35; 9:2–4; 10:12–13; 1 Macc 5, etc.).[229] It is in this context that he refers to Ezra 9 and Neh 13 in passing as he explains the motivation for the tendency of strict separation in the Postexilic Period.

> Two reasons made relentless segregation from the heathen environment seem the natural thing in ethical matters also: first, a community intent on holiness was bound to be anxiety-ridden about contamination by anything heathen, because their whole future depended on perfect fulfilment of the Law; secondly, God's consummation was restricted to the community of the Law, while the nations were primarily objects of judgment [fn. Ezra 9f; Neh 13:1–3; 28f]. It is true that in an earlier part of the period voices were raised in support of a freer and more understanding attitude toward the heathen. The beautiful stories of Ruth and Jonah mirror the universalist approach of the prophets and of the circles influenced by them; and an evaluation of pagan worship such as that expressed in Mal. 1.11 succeeds in formulating the universality of God's kingdom in the very cult-terminology of the priesthood in a way that cannot be surpassed. The apocalypse of Isa. 24–27, too, can proclaim judgment and salvation as embracing the whole world.[230]

Eichrodt's general thesis as well as similar formulations by von Rad, Noth and others operate with an a priori assumption that Israel has moved from a relationship of "grace" and dependence on God into one based on "works" and self-sufficiency. This Lutheran "grace versus works" paradigm has by now been seriously called into question mainly from the NT side.[231] It is true that

---

[226] Ibid., 341.
[227] Ibid., 342.
[228] Ibid., 346–48.
[229] Ibid., 343–44.
[230] Ibid., 343–44.
[231] Many works could be cited here by the representatives of the "New Perspective" (e.g., J. D. G. Dunn, R. Hays, N. T. Wright) but I merely wish to point to E. P. Sanders**Error! Bookmark not defined.**' groundbreaking study on the Jewish literature of the Second

"relentless segregation" is driven by anxiety but it is not about the perfect fulfillment of the Law. The evidence in Ezra 9 and in the wider context of EN is not that YHWH is an unrelenting deity, a stern taskmaster who misses and excuses nothing. Ezra's prayer suggests that YHWH has been gracious, not dealing with Israel according to what she deserved but showing her mercy in partial restoration (Ezra 9:8–9, 13). It is precisely in the face of God's grace that Israel's sin is all the more shocking and it is portrayed as being the very sin that drew the judgment of exile on her head. Yet, when the sin is recognized, hope is expressed that all is not lost (Ezra 10:21). Confession and doing YHWH's will (which in this instance is understood as sending the foreign wives away) is seen as the way forward (Ezra 10:11). Moreover, the public prayer in Neh 9 is a prime expression of the understanding that YHWH is gracious and covenant-keeping despite Israel's continued wickedness and sin. The exiles' approach to a relationship with YHWH is still based on his חסד ("grace" or "covenant faithfulness"), only there is a deeper awareness etched into consciousness by the Exile that his patience and mercy are not endlessly inexhaustible and that sin cannot continue indefinitely without consequences. EN demonstrates that what is expected and required is not perfect obedience without sin but a steady disposition of commitment and faithfulness to YHWH and his Torah in which there is room for mistakes and error, as well as a way provided for cleansing and restoration.

Although the alleged "legalism" of the Postexilic Period is dismissed as an unfair charge today, Eichrodt's second point contrasting the "narrow-minded" approach of Ezra 9 and Neh 13, with the more "universalist" approach in the stories of Ruth and Jonah is very much a live issue. A little earlier in his OT theology Eichrodt footnotes Ezra 6:21 and Neh 10:29–30[28–29] to exemplify a more universalist tendency which accepts proselytes from "heathenism" as long as they are willing "to be incorporated into the community built on the Law."[232] The comparison with Ruth and the arguably varying attitudes within EN are recurring observations in scholarly interpretations of EN. To these I shall return in more detail when discussing the commentaries. Here I merely want to make two brief comments, one on Ruth, the other on the supposed "universalism" in Jonah.

While Ruth is held up as a positive example of openness in Christian commentaries, it is interesting to note the rather different Jewish perspective, which is somewhat embarrassed by the story of Ruth precisely because it makes David a descendant of a Moabitess (Ruth 4:18–22) and casts doubt on his status as an Israelite (cf. Deut 23:4[3]). The Talmud exempts David from blame by claiming that the implied ban on intermarriage in Deut 23:4–7[3–6] only refers to men not women (*b.Yebam.* 77a). Approaching the question from a historical-critical perspective, the Jewish commentator Milgrom suspects in the command

---

Temple period and beyond in *Paul and Palestinian Judaism: A Comparison of Patterns of Religion* (London: SCM, 1977).
[232] Ibid., 255.

of Deut 23:4[3] an anti-Davidide polemic of the Northern Kingdom.[233] Thus we see that depending on one's particular concerns the story of Ruth may be cast in a very different light.

Although Nineveh was delivered from immediate judgment in the narrative because it repented at the preaching of Jonah this is not a story of "universal salvation" in any sense. Nineveh is not incorporated into Israel and there is no indication in the book that it has a share in, what might be termed, Israel's "eschatological" future. In fact, the exaggerated repentance of the Ninevites (prescribing mourning and fasting even for the beasts—Jonah 3:7–8), the use of *Elohim*, the generic term for God (Jonah 3:5–9), instead of YHWH, the name by which God is known in Israel, and the final sentence of the book suggest a certain amount of ignorance and limitations to the "relationship." Neither does the book speak of this aversion of judgment as the ultimate "saving" of Nineveh; rather this is an episode exploring divine justice and compassion and the tension between the two. The choice of the Ninevites functions in a similar way the Good Samaritan does in Jesus' parable. It raises the shock value of the story and brings into sharper focus the difficulty in seeing grace given rather than justice done to a cruel and ruthless enemy of Israel.

Although Eichrodt and von Rad represent the strand of OT scholarship which considers the Postexilic Period hopelessly legalistic, even among their contemporaries and increasingly in recent decades there are voices which try to "rescue" EN from the charge of legalism. Thus Westermann, for instance, remarks that the religion of the Law emerges in the Postexilic Period and becomes increasingly inflexible, nevertheless, he recognizes that the work of the Chronicler (to which he assigns EN) "contains a true vital piety" as "indicated by the many prayers that have been inserted in it over and over again."[234] Similarly, Anderson mentions Neh 8 in connection with Torah piety and contrasts the possible negative Christian reaction to the law as a burden with the Psalms' outlook on obedience to God as the source of joy.[235] In his *Living World of the Old Testament* he goes even further in giving an apologetic for the Law perceived in the Old Testament as a gift behind which stands the gracious Lawgiver who redeemed Israel; an idea well expressed in Neh 9.[236] The trend to defend the place of the Law in the Postexilic Period through framing it by the covenant and prevenient grace apparent here is evident in other OT theologies. In his *Theology of the Old Testament* Brueggemann follows this same pattern when he emphasizes the context of the covenant for the commandments, and

---

[233] Jacob Milgrom, "Religious Conversion and the Revolt Model for the Formation of Israel," *JBL* 101/2 (1982) 174.

[234] Claus Westermann, *Handbook to the Old Testament* (ed. and trans. Robert H. Boyd; London: SPCK, 1969) 261.

[235] Bernhard W. Anderson and Steven Bishop, *Contours of Old Testament Theology* (Minneapolis MN: Fortress, 1999) 254.

[236] Bernhard W. Anderson, *The Living World of the Old Testament* (2nd ed.; London: Longman, 1966), 455–459.

insists that EN does not represent a legalistic attitude.[237] A recent German Roman Catholic OT theology equally stresses Israel's faithful commitment to the covenant of YHWH expressed in the focus on Torah in EN.[238]

An approach that diverges somewhat from the above is Childs' who attempts to prove that EN is not legalistic by using the canonical shape of the book. He argues that the public reading of the Law placed as it is in Neh 8 rather than after Ezra 8 demonstrates that "the law does not function to evoke a confession of guilt" (i.e., "to dictate religious behavior by rules") but as "part of the liturgical celebration" of "the restored and forgiven community."[239] Childs is right to observe the repeated entreaty of the Levites to the people not to mourn or weep (Neh 8:9–11) but he overstates his case. First, in Neh 8 the issue is mainly that on this particular occasion Israel was meant to celebrate, not to mourn and in Neh 9:1, 3 mourning and confession duly follow. Similarly the recognition of sin in Ezra 9:1–2; 10:2 and a confession of guilt in Ezra 9:5–15; 10:1 are preceded by Ezra's commission to teach the law (Ezra 7:3, 10). The linkage between the two is surely implied. In any case, the recognition of sin as a result of understanding and hearing the Law may not be very different from the Christian approach of reading Scripture and responding to its instruction with repentance. Thus there is no reason to equate such a sequence with legalism.

10.1.2 Goldingay

Goldingay takes a slightly different tack when discussing EN. He, like many recent commentators, remarks that EN is not legalistic but his approach focuses mainly on the interpretation of Torah in EN and on what he considers a

---

[237] Walter Brueggemann, *Theology of the Old Testament: Testimony, Dispute, Advocacy* (Minneapolis MN: Fortress, 1997) 198–201, 446. Unfortunately Brueggemann has no succinct formulation of this and does not actually mention covenant with reference to EN, although he compares "the reconstitution of postexilic Judaism" with the Sinai event and then notes: "In a Christian discernment of the Old Testament and of emerging Judaism, what most needs to be resisted is the conventional Christian stereotype of legalism. In any serious commitment to obedience, to be sure, zeal may spill over into legalism. But in any attempt to set as antithesis "Christian grace" and "Jewish law," Israel's sense of itself will be distorted and caricatured. Israel, in these interpretive maneuvers and acts of self-discernment led by Ezra, is with considerable daring seeking to order its life in a way that is commensurate with the God who creates, saves, and commands." (Ibid., 446.)

[238] "Die Torazentrierung ist kein Ausdruck eines total verrechtlichten Gottesverhältnisses, sondern Israels Weg der Treue zum Bund mit JHWH." (The focussing on Torah is not an expression of a totally Law-based relationship with God but Israel's way of faithfulness to the covenant with YHWH.—translation mine) Erich Zenger et al., *Einleitung in das Alte Testament* (6th ed.; Stuttgart: Kohlhammer, 2006) 277.

[239] Brevard S. Childs, *Introduction to the Old Testament as Scripture* (London: SCM, 1979) 636.

flexible way of re-interpreting ancient laws.[240] Goldingay rightly perceives the importance of hermeneutics in showing that EN is not a legalistic book, even if his particular phraseology is sometimes less than felicitous.[241]

Regarding Ezra 9–10 he, like commentators in general, is concerned about the "racial"/ethnic issue, but defends the exiles' action based on the need for religious distinctiveness.

> The references to holiness and mixing are framed by references to abomination and trespass, again making clear that any ethnic separation that is required to safeguard holiness is secondary to the call to maintain a religious distinctiveness in the form of an exclusive reliance on Yhwh.[242]

There is a certain tension in the intermarriage crisis between reasoning and resolution and the two perspectives evident in them are difficult to reconcile. On the one hand the reasoning in Ezra 9:1; 14 seemingly operates with the "moral defilement" concept as it is understood by Deut 7; on the other the separation is done along ethnic lines irrespective of religious status (i.e., all "foreign" wives are divorced without any examination whether they have religious commitments to YHWH or some other god(s)). This discrepancy comes to expression in Goldingay's comments and is evident, as we shall see, in the arguments of other scholars as well. In §6.1 I have suggested that alongside the "moral defilement" theory of Deut 7 there is a secondary argument based on the notion of "holy seed" which would mean the automatic profanation of the descendants of mixed marriages by way of the "foreign" and therefore profane spouses. Holiness in this argument is not an ethical category in the same way priestly holiness or the default profane status of lay Israelites in the priestly material is not about morality.

Goldingay does not define in what sense he uses holiness, but it seems that on the whole he operates with a moral understanding. Thus a few pages earlier he uses Ezra 6:21 and Neh 10:29[28] as examples for the inclusion of peoples who are willing to join the exilic community and commit themselves to YHWH followed by the statement that

> Israel's holiness does not imply an ethnic principle. A "mixed group" came out of Egypt with the "holy nation" (Exod 12:38; 19:6) without there being any sense of impropriety. It would have been easy to attribute the unfaithfulness of the people in the wilderness to the influence of this group, but the story never does so. The community's distinctiveness in relation to other peoples relates to recognition of Yhwh, not to questions of ethnicity in themselves (see, e.g., Lev 20:7; Deut 7:6; 14:2, 21 in their

---

[240] John Goldingay, *Old Testament Theology* (3 vols.; Downers Grove, IL: IVP Academic, 2003–2009) 1:738–40.

[241] I have noted in the general introduction of this book the problematic nature of such expressions as "a relaxed attitude regarding the fixedness of the scriptural text" and the sentence "Serious commitment to the authority of Moses' Teaching goes along with a freedom in rewriting that Teaching." Ibid., 740.

[242] Ibid., 748.

context). Conversely, although Ezra 2 and Nehemiah 7 imply that the community basically comprises people who have come back from exile, such people can forfeit their membership in the community (Ezra 10:7–8).[243]

First, the immediate objection one might raise is that Goldingay fails to address the obvious counter-argument from Ezra 9–10; namely that the foreign wives are divorced without distinction, which suggests that Israel's holiness does imply "an ethnic principle" even though the former cannot be *equated* with the latter. Secondly, it is doubtful if the mixed multitude (ערב רב) in Exodus is as neutral a description as he makes it out to be (see my discussion in §4.4.1).

The point to be emphasized then in the exodus context is not that no blame is attached to the mixed multitude (which we have seen is not entirely the case) but that the blame is still a moral-religious one similar to the theory of Deut 7. The issue with the "rabble" element in Num 11:4 is not their foreignness per se but their evil influence. Granted, the latter is indirectly connected to the former in the sense that foreign nations in general do not know YHWH or follow his Law and are therefore seen as idolatrous and often immoral. The linkage of foreignness, idolatry and immorality is intrinsically connected with the concept of holiness. Moberly highlights this feature in his *Old Testament of the Old Testament* when comparing Mosaic Yahwism with the patriarchal religion and summarizes the difference thus.

> Finally, we have seen the difference between patriarchal and Mosaic religion is perhaps most conveniently epitomized by the notion of holiness, as expressed by *qds*. The concept of holiness, from Exod. 3:5 onward, focuses the exclusive, demanding, regulated, mediated, and sanctuary-centered relationship between YHWH and Israel, while the absence of holiness in patriarchal religion equally epitomizes its open, unstructured, and nonlocated unaggressive nature, its "ecumenical bonhomie."[244]

There are of course individual foreigners in Israel's narrated history (Jethro, Rahab, Ruth, Naaman, etc.) who to varying degrees recognize something of YHWH's purposes or who show themselves "righteous" or God-fearing, but these are more the exceptions that prove the rule. It must also be noted that the Deuteronomistic History shows on occasion a tenor not dissimilar to that of the Genesis narratives (such as the friendly relations with and help received from Hiram king of Tyre in 1 Kgs 5:15–26[1–12]). Nevertheless, where holiness is a central concern, as in the priestly legislation or in parts of Deuteronomy, foreignness is strongly associated with wickedness and "moral" evil.

---

[243] Ibid., 744–45.
[244] R. W. L. Moberly, *The Old Testament of the Old Testament: Patriarchal Narratives and Mosaic Yahwism* (Minneapolis MN: Fortress, 1992) 104. For a detailed comparison from a theological perspective see Ibid., Chap. 3.

Returning to Goldingay's argument that holiness does not imply an ethnic principle, I suggest that his own examples show a combination of concern with the religious-moral issue *and* physical descent and can only prove that holiness cannot be *equated* with an ethnic principle. He is right that the latter is not the final arbiter, at least not in the examples he lists, but it is certainly a consideration. It is the tantalizing nature of holiness as both a "moral" and a "non-moral" category which makes the issue a confusing one.

10.1.3 Rendtorff

Rendtorff is a scholar who has actively contributed to Jewish-Christian dialogue and, as such, one would assume that he handles the sensitive and difficult story of Ezra 9–10 in a way that takes into account Jewish perspectives. In his general work he urges Christian scholars to look at rabbinic interpretations although notes the difficulties, namely the lack of accessibility for Christians to study rabbinic Hebrew at university and to get hold of books that might help their introduction into this specialized area.[245]

Unfortunately, his recently published OT theology (*The Canonical Hebrew Bible: A Theology of the Old Testament*) is disappointing in several respects. Although he, like Goldingay, is sensitive to Jewish concerns and tries to dissociate the "Law" from the negative connotations of an earlier scholarship, there is no real engagement with the substantive issues of the Law in general and Ezra–Nehemiah in particular.

His OT theology falls into three parts; the first gives an overview of the biblical books following the order of the Hebrew canon (Torah, Prophets and Writings), the second examines various themes and concepts (such as creation, covenant and election, Torah, Moses, David, Zion, etc.) linking them through cross-references to the first part. The third section deals with issues of hermeneutics. His approach is consistent with the program he sets out in his essay "Old Testament Theology: Some Ideas," although there he does not envisage the chapter on hermeneutics.[246]

In his handling of the general theme of Torah ("The Center of Israel's Life: the Torah"—pp. 478–508) in the second part of his OT theology Rendtorff introduces the Torah as God-given with a short explanation into the various meanings of the word. This is followed by a more detailed treatment of the Decalogue and some observations on the Book of the Covenant. Admittedly the chapter pulls in biblical passages other than Exodus, yet overall, this is little more than a re-telling in sequential order of the ten central commandments that were spoken directly by God rather than through the mediation of Moses.

---

[245] Rolf Rendtorff, "Rabbinic Exegesis and the Modern Christian Bible Scholar," in *Canon and Theology: Overtures to an Old Testament Theology* (trans. Margaret Kohl; Edinburgh: T&T Clark, 1993) 17–24.

[246] Rolf Rendtorff, "Old Testament Theology: Some Ideas for a New Approach," in *Canon and Theology: Overtures to an Old Testament Theology* (trans. Margaret Kohl; Edinburgh: T&T Clark, 1993) 10–13.

Rendtorff considers the rest of the commandments to be elaborations on these central themes (p.481), and therefore does not address them in any detail. However, he treats the so-called "cultic" aspects of life (sanctuary, sacrifices, festivals) separately in his following chapter (pp.509–544). Granted that the Decalogue has a central place in the Torah on any reckoning, it is disappointing that beyond repeating the biblical injunctions there is no discussion of wider issues involving the place of Torah in a Christian reading of the Old Testament.

Rendtorff's treatment of Torah in Ezra–Nehemiah is equally lacking in analysis and it seems to be again a mere recounting of the events in the book including the mixed-marriage crisis, Ezra's mission, as well as the public reading of the Torah. There is a brief section at the end noting that beside the Jerusalem Temple, the Torah comes in as "a new element," "which from now on becomes the essential basis of Israel's self-understanding" (p.401). Yet, there is practically no particular recognition that, for instance, the resolution or proposed resolution of the matter of the "foreign" wives is in any way difficult or problematic, neither is there any further discussion on matters of interpretation or in what way Torah is "new" or why it gains so much in importance after the Exile.

What accounts for such a lack of engagement with the biblical texts? The answer seems to be in Rendtorff's understanding of how an Old Testament theology is supposed to be constructed and in the various issues relating to Jewish-Christian dialogue as it is laid out in his *Canon and Theology*. In the essay encouraging a common Jewish-Christian reading of the Hebrew Bible he suggests that

> Theological interpretation of the Hebrew Bible is not dependent on the theological system of the religious tradition to which the particular interpreter belongs: the Hebrew Bible is a theological book in its own right, which can be, and must be interpreted theologically from the inside.[247]

He is right in wanting to allow the Old Testament to "speak for itself," as it were, yet what he advocates sounds like a historical theology of ancient Israel, which lacks the frame of reference to break out of the past and speak in any meaningful way to a Christian or Jewish faith community.[248] His effort to avoid the kind of "doctrinal bias" that gave, for instance, "the Law" such a negative connotation among Christians, leads him into a neutrality that is neither here, nor there, and is therefore detached from present concerns. It is hardly surprising, therefore, that his Old Testament theology is somewhat sterile, since

---

[247] Rolf Rendtorff, "Toward a Common Jewish-Christian Reading of the Hebrew Bible," in *Canon and Theology: Overtures to an Old Testament Theology* (trans. Margaret Kohl; Edinburgh: T&T Clark, 1993) 40.

[248] This is a point that Jon D. Levenson makes very poignantly in his "Theological Consensus or Historicist Evasion? Jews and Christians in Biblical Studies" in *The Hebrew Bible, the Old Testament, and Historical Criticism: Jews and Christians in Biblical Studies* (Louisville, KY: Westminster John Knox, 1993), 82–105.

all interpretive traditions whether Christian or Jewish are banned from it. One might ask then, what the purpose of such a historicizing exercise is, particularly in the area of theology, which is so closely linked with the life of faith and the understanding of believers in the present.

Even as a history of religion approach, it is sadly lacking, since studying history is ultimately based on a realization that its patterns have something to teach us, that what happened then affects how we think, act, or live now. In any case, neutrality is impossible and as the above suggests, not even necessarily helpful.

In one sense, Rendtorff himself recognizes that his Old Testament theology is not objective or neutral in its method or its terms and admits that his own systematizing, the categories and organizational principles that he uses to construct his theology has to do with particular and, in many respects, Christian perspectives and interests.[249] Thus, stopping short of connecting the two Testaments on the basis that thereby the New Testament will override the Old gives his book a truncated feel. The neat separation of Old and New Testament message that he envisages, is reminiscent of the classic division formulated by Stendhal into "what the text meant" and "what it means now,"[250] which is valuable, but has only limited usefulness. For as Lash says in his critique of this widely held concept,

> If the questions to which ancient authors sought to respond in terms available to them within their cultural horizons are to be "heard" today with something like their original force and urgency, they have first to be "heard" as questions that challenge us with comparable seriousness.[251]

Since the enterprise is already a Christian one and is meant to enhance the understanding of Christians with regards to their Old Testament Scriptures then it is odd that Rendtorff should insist on keeping the OT message independent of Jewish or Christian traditions as if these were only window-dressing that could be added to the application later without disturbing the essential part of interpretation. A Christian reading need not mean a biased hermeneutic that collapses the Old Testament's message into the New.

In conclusion, we may note that while many OT theologies have little or nothing to say about EN, the topic edges into consciousness via the discussion of the Law in the Postexilic Period. The recent trend is increasingly to defend EN against an earlier charge of legalism in the Postexilic Period evident in the writings of such theologians as Eichrodt, Noth and von Rad. The strategy of those rejecting the alleged legalism in EN most often conceive of the Law as

---

[249] Rolf Rendtorff, *The Canonical Hebrew Bible: A Theology of the Old Testament* (trans. David E. Orton; Leiden: Deo, 2005) 750.

[250] Krister Stendhal, "Biblical Theology, Contemporary," in *Reading the Bible in the Global Village* (ed. H. Räisänen et al., Helsinki: SBL, 2000) 70.

[251] Nicholas Lash, "What Might Martyrdom Mean?" in *Theology on the Way to Emmaus* (London: SCM, 1986) 81.

being in the context of the covenant following on from God's gracious deliverance of his people. Some point to specific aspects in EN such as the joy accompanied by the public reading of the Law in Neh 8, the canonical shape of the book which does not conceive of the Law as a legalistic system dictating religious behavior by rules and the lively interpretive tradition which flexibly re-applies ancient laws to new situations. With regard to the matter of separation in EN and especially the intermarriage crisis in Ezra 9–10 Goldingay's evaluation highlights the struggle with the charge of a racial/ethnic principle at work. Rendtorff's approach, on the other hand, exemplifies some of the practical difficulties of integrating Jewish perspectives while at the same time providing a meaningful Christian reading of the Law and EN.

10.2 EN Commentaries

Having given a birds-eye view of EN in OT theologies, from the mid-twentieth century and some more recent works, I shall now turn to a closer inspection of commentaries on EN. The discussion and evaluation of Ezra 9–10 in the commentaries circle around two interrelated matters, which a modern Christian reader would, as it is frequently pointed out, find difficult. One is the issue of exclusivism and the possible charge of "racism"; the other is the ethically questionable divorce of the foreign wives. These two topics and the further question of "application" for the Christian reader provide the three sections around which my own assessment of Christian interpretation in the commentaries will take place.

10.2.1 Exclusivism and Purity of Religion

The topic of separation in various forms permeates the whole book of EN, but none is quite as difficult as Ezra 9–10, which view is well reflected in the scholarly comments. Williamson in his EN commentary calls Ezra 9–10 "the least attractive parts of Ezra–Nehemiah if not of the whole OT."[252] This is perhaps a slight exaggeration, though the sentiment is understandable and indeed shared and echoed by others. In *The New Interpreter's Bible* which has as its general aim "to bring the best in contemporary biblical scholarship into the service of the church to enhance preaching, teaching, and study of the Scriptures" Ralph W. Klein's reflections on Ezra 10 start with the caveat that "It is difficult to find redeeming theological value in this chapter."[253] Likewise Smith-Christopher in the recently published *Theological Bible Commentary* (2009) calls the final two chapters of Ezra "the most controversial passages in

---

[252] H. G. M. Williamson, *Ezra, Nehemiah* (WBC 16; Nashville TN: Nelson, 1985) 159.
[253] Choon-Leong Seow et. al., eds. *The New Interpreter's Bible: A Commentary in Twelve Volumes*, (Nashville TN: Abingdon, 1999) 3:xvii. Ralph W. Klein, "The Books of Ezra and Nehemiah," in *The New Interpreter's Bible: A Commentary in Twelve Volumes* (ed. Choon-Leong Seow et. al., Nashville TN: Abingdon, 1999), 3:746.

postexilic biblical literature."[254] It is interesting in this respect that a series like the *The Bible Speaks Today*, which attempts to produce commentaries for a specifically Christian audience on possibly all books of the Bible, has so far not brought out a commentary on EN, or more precisely, on Ezra. Nehemiah, who is often seen as more accessible for Christian consumption and is frequently singled out as a model for godly leadership and praised for his "managerial" skills, has a commentary all to himself. One wonders if perhaps this is an indication of the difficulty-cum-unease with the book of Ezra with its temple building, exclusivism and the particularly offending episode of the foreign wives.

Nevertheless, Christian commentators who write about it make an effort to give the story a fair hearing and help the lay reader understand the narrative on its own terms. In the defense of the exiles' action the prime argument is that despite the harshness of the measures and the suspicion of racism it was first and foremost a matter of preserving the purity of religion or religious identity. Thus Williamson speaks of the danger of the faith becoming watered down, Kidner of the concern for religious purity, McConville similarly of the underlying issue of the purity of religion.[255]

To what extent the racial charge is acknowledged or admitted to have played a part varies. Most Christian commentators place the emphasis on the religious dimension although the same uneasy tension between religious identity and ethnicity is evident as in Goldingay's discussion. On the one hand, Fensham denies the racial charge altogether; others like Kidner do not address it directly, while the majority of scholars tacitly or explicitly accept it to varying degrees, although with caveats.[256] Thus Williamson argues that the concept of Israel as a holy people in Deut 7:6–7 "has now been twisted by the misapplication of a quite separate law [he refers to Lev 19:19] into an idea of racial, as distinct from religious, separation."[257] Nevertheless he affirms that the underlying concern for religious separation was "absolutely right."[258] Likewise Clines argues that despite the "racialist" motive evident in the reasoning in Ezra 9:2 "the defense

---

[254] Daniel L. Smith-Christopher, "Ezra and Nehemiah," in *Theological Bible Commentary* (ed. Gail R. O'Day and David L. Petersen; Louisville KY: Westminster John Knox, 2009) 158.

[255] Williamson, *Ezra, Nehemiah*, 159–60. Derek Kidner, *Ezra and Nehemiah: An Introduction and Commentary* (TOTC; Leicester: IVP, 1979) 22. J. G. McConville, *Ezra, Nehemiah and Esther* (DSB; Edinburgh: St Andrew Press, 1985) 61. David J. A. Clines, *Ezra, Nehemiah, Esther* (NCB; Grand Rapids MI: Eerdmans / London: Marshall, Morgan & Scott, 1984) 117–18.

[256] F. C. Fensham, *The Books of Ezra and Nehemiah* (Grand Rapids MI: Eerdmans, 1982) 124. At the same time he acknowledges that "Sometimes this purity of religion seems to have been confused with purity of blood among the Jewish descendants" (Ibid., 18). However, it is unclear from the context if Fensham thinks of a specific incident within EN or makes a general statement regarding the Postexilic Period.

[257] Williamson, *Ezra, Nehemiah*, 132.

[258] Ibid., 162.

of the 'holy race' is engaged in more strictly on religious grounds than has been the case with most so-called 'religious' persecutions and wars."[259] Similarly, Allen states that racial purity is pursued on religious grounds, namely the fear of being led astray into worshiping other gods.[260]

"Election for Mission"

Two particular arguments recur in the course of the discussion regarding the exiles' action in Ezra 9–10. First, the harsh measures for the protection of religious identity are justified on the basis of what I would term as the "election for mission" argument.

Fensham, for instance, negates the racial charge altogether and sees in the separation purely an expression of the "election for mission" principle.

> The term "holy" shows that the term "seed" has nothing to do with racial prejudice. It is the people whom God had elected as his people (Exod. 19:6) to carry his revelation, to be a light to the nations (Isa. 42:6). It was a question of the living relation between the Lord and his people, and not of who one's ancestors might be. When the living relation is broken, they are no longer the people of God (Hos. 1:9). By intermingling with foreign nations and being contaminated with their idol worship, the true religion was in danger of losing its pure character.[261]

Williamson on the other hand condemns what he sees as the exiles' reasoning, which in his view combines the notion of religious separation with racial distinctiveness.

> The concept of the seed of Abraham, elect by God as a "holy people" not because of any superiority but in order to be his servant for the blessing of the nations (e.g. Gen 12:1–3, 7; Deut 7:6–7) has now been twisted by the misapplication of a quite separate law into an idea of racial, as distinct from religious separation.[262]

At the same time, however, he also emphasizes the need for separation using the same "election for mission" argument.

> Israel's election was not merely for her own comfort, but so she might shine as a witness to the nations for God and his standards (see Gen 26:4). This could not be achieved without the maintenance of her distinctive self-identity, and this was thought to be threatened by mixed marriages.[263]

And a couple of pages later:

---

[259] Clines, *Ezra, Nehemiah*, 117–18.
[260] Leslie C. Allen and Timothy S. Laniak, *Ezra, Nehemiah, Esther* (NIBCOT 9; Peabody MA: Hendrickson, 2003) 73.
[261] Fensham, *The Books of Ezra and Nehemiah*, 125.
[262] Williamson, *Ezra, Nehemiah*, 132.
[263] Ibid., 160.

Israel's mission could only make headway if she maintained the servant identity that separated her from the nations to whom she should mediate the revelation of God.[264]

One might readily acknowledge from a Christian perspective that these scholars have a point. Christianity builds on Jewish foundations: Jesus' teaching, his understanding of himself and his mission appeal to Israel's Scriptures; his first followers are Jews and god-fearing proselytes; the early missionaries of the church, as Acts portrays them, seek out the synagogue and the Jews for the good news first. It is only gradually with the latter's increasing resistance that the Christian mission takes a different direction. It is perhaps also of importance that the church's first significant theologian and the one who attempted to work out a theology of the Gentile mission is the thoroughly well-educated Pharisee Paul rather than the undoubtedly great but in rabbinic matters untrained Peter (Acts 4:13). Had Israel accepted a syncretistic mode of existence it could well have lost its distinctiveness and failed to have provided the springboard both for Jesus' ministry and the church's mission. Admittedly, one can find examples where it is precisely learned Pharisees like Nicodemus who are puzzled by Jesus and "syncretistic" and theologically "misguided" people like the Samaritan woman of John 4 who accept him wholeheartedly. Nevertheless, the overall shape of Jesus' and the church's mission unquestionably needed that Jewish religious basis which provided the context for it.

In this respect, McConville, who expresses similar ideas, puts it better when he says that separation is of benefit in the long term.

> If we are tempted to think of the Books of Ezra and Nehemiah as unattractively exclusivist, we may reflect that the separation of Judah *from* the peoples was part of a plan of God which was ultimately *for* the peoples.[265]

The language, however, is still somewhat controversial insofar as the people who are affected by the exiles' actions, most notably the "foreign" wives, are not the ones who will ultimately benefit from these measures and which makes the argument less than satisfactory from the perspective of the suffering party. Nevertheless, at least in McConville's formulation the explanation does not demand the exiles to be aware of a plan on God's part; it is merely a legitimate retrospective argument for justifying the need for religious distinctiveness.

More problematic, I believe, is the way Williamson and Fensham connect the notion of election with the idea of "mission." Israel in this context is seen as the servant elected for the purposes of witnessing and mediating the revelation of God to the nations.

Fensham uses Exod 19:6 as his proof text together with Isa 42:6. He is right in linking Exod 19:6 with Ezra 9, since holiness (and election, the category

---

[264] Ibid., 162.
[265] McConville, *Ezra, Nehemiah*, 131.

which underlies it) is a key theme in both. Yet the connection of Exod 19:6 with the Isaianic servant is tenuous and such a view of election and holiness is not at all envisaged within the categories of the EN narrative. Again, it can readily be granted that for the Christian church the Deutero-Isaianic texts became crucial in the light of Jesus' mission as the servant who was despised and rejected (Isa 53) and as the one who became the "light to the nations" (Isa 49:6). By extension the church's mission to the Gentiles could make sense in this light. Yet the texts in themselves are not as clear; it is only with Christian hindsight that they could be understood the way these are used in this instance by Fensham.

Within their own Isaianic contexts Israel's role in this "mission to the Gentiles" is unclear. The various categories such as the "servant," the "anointed one," the "light to the nations" can have more than one referent. Sometimes to be sure, it is possible to read them as the nation Israel (Isa 42:6), at other times it is hard to understand the servant without thinking of an individual who will act also *for* Israel's benefit (49:6). Yet in other contexts the anointed is identified with a historic and non-Israelite person, Cyrus (Isa 45:1), and in one instance the light to the nations is specifically equated with YHWH's law and justice (Isa 51:4).

There are some references to the nations acknowledging YHWH (e.g., Isa 45:14) although the context envisages the inversion of Israel/Judah's subjugation under foreign powers (cf. Isa 61:5–6). Since the focus of these passages is not on the fate of the nations per se, it does not actually clarify what such an acknowledgement might entail: recognition of YHWH's power as supreme and his person as the only God or more? Isa 56:6–8 speak of foreigners who will join themselves to YHWH, keep his Sabbaths and covenant, and their sacrifices will be accepted in the temple; a statement unparalleled elsewhere in the Hebrew Scriptures. Nevertheless, there is no indication in all of these texts as to what role Israel plays in all this.

For the notion of election for mission Williamson uses as his prime text the blessing given to Abraham and then reiterated to Isaac. Gen 12:3 receives here a particular Christian re-reading derived perhaps from the Pauline understanding of Abraham (e.g., Rom 4, Gal 3–4) and from a Christian re-evaluation of Israel's role and fate in salvation history. Looking back from the NT it is possible to interpret Abraham's role as ultimately leading to the blessing of the Gentiles, but the understanding that the sole purpose of Israel's election is the blessing derived from it by the nations is not the point that Gen 12 makes. This is further underlined by the ambiguous nature of the Hebrew נברכו בך (v.3). The Niphal of ברך allows either the passive "and all the families of the earth *will be blessed in you*" or the reflexive "and all the families of the earth *will bless themselves by you*" (i.e., Abraham's blessing will be the measure by which other nations will evaluate their own blessings).[266] The blessing promised

---

[266] In a recent detailed study that considers the Niphal and Hithpael of ברך in parallel texts to Gen 12:3b, Keith N. Grüneberg argues for the passive sense for the Niphal in Gen 12:3b ("and in you all the families of the earth will be blessed") on grammatical grounds.

to Abraham overflows to the lives of others who are in contact with him and his descendants (e.g., Lot—13:5–6; Ishmael—17:20; Laban—30:27; Potiphar—39:5), but in Genesis the focus is firmly on Abraham and his seed.

Similarly, Williamson also uses Gen 26:4 (והתברכו בזרעך כל גויי הארץ—"and in your seed all the nations of the earth will be blessed/will bless themselves"). It is not clear what motivates this choice of quoting the blessing reiterated to Isaac rather than the original one given to Abraham in Gen 12:3 and reconfirmed in Gen 22:18 (verbatim the same as Gen 26:4). Perhaps Williamson wanted to use a text which mentioned specifically the "nations" (גוים) rather than the "families" (משפחות) of the earth or one which referred to the "seed" (זרע) of Abraham, although in either case Gen 22:18 would have been equally appropriate. Perhaps also Gen 26 where Isaac is admonished not to go down to Egypt but to stay in the land gives the issue of separation a sharper focus. However, Williamson's emphasis is on being a witness for God's standards while the wider story of Gen 26 is eminently unsuitable for such a purpose. Isaac, like Abraham earlier, lies shamefully about his wife in order to safeguard his life and it is the Philistine Abimelech who proves himself upright in protecting both him and his wife. Moreover, the divine blessing and its material manifestations of wealth only stir up jealousy in the Philistines (26:14).

The other standard text which is equally common in this argument and which Williamson uses is Deut 7:6–7. It is meant to illustrate the point that election and holiness gives Israel no ground for thinking herself superior. Although Williamson sees in the Ezran story a racist distinction, the narrative shows none of the racial superiority associated with the concept. Ezra's prayer (Ezra 9:6–15) expresses shock and horror at Israel's continuing sin and recognizes her lowly status ("we are slaves"—v.9) in the same way that Neh 9:5–37 speaks of God's faithfulness in his choice of Israel despite her continuing disobedience and wickedness.[267] Although ideas of holiness which encourage separation can potentially lead to a sense of superiority it may not be a foregone conclusion that this will inevitably be the case. In fact, as the above examples from EN illustrate, the narrative does not seem to bear out such an assumption.

At the same time, he acknowledges that "while this promise does result from Yhwh's concern for all humanity, in context its primary force is to stress Abraham's greatness as the one through whom this momentous divine purpose will be achieved" (*Abraham, Blessing and the Nations: A Philological and Exegetical Study of Genesis 12:3 in its Narrative Context* (BZAW 332; Berlin: Walter de Gruyter, 2003) 243. On the other hand, Moberly argues that Gen 12:3b within its Genesis context is to be understood in the sense that Abraham will become a great nation *not for the sake of* the nations but rather *in spite of* them. In his view the Niphal here is reflexive and is interchangeable in meaning with parallel texts where the Hithpael is employed (Gen 22:18; 26:4). R. W. L. Moberly, *The Theology of the Book of Genesis* (Cambridge: Cambridge University Press, 2009) 141–161 (see esp. 149, 151).

[267] Clines also observes the lack of racial superiority in Ezra's prayer and the absence of any expressions for foreign racial inferiority (*Ezra, Nehemiah*, 118).

Deut 7:6–7 as an illustration of the "election for mission" is problematic mainly because the election and holiness of Israel is in the context of the *ḥērem* law.[268] Whatever may have been intended by this command, the language used speaks of destruction and death for the inhabitants of Canaan. Israel, chosen and holy, does not serve here the better future of the nations; rather, it is the nations who are "sacrificed" for the purposes of keeping Israel intact from their harmful and idolatrous influences.

Further, in the wider perspective of the OT, the nations are on the periphery of Israel's vision, graciously allowed to join in her blessing under some circumstances (e.g., Rahab, Ruth, etc.) but their inclusion is generally individual, occasional and incidental. The prophetic vision of the nations flocking to share Israel's blessing (Zech 8:20–23) seems to underline the abundant goodness of God's restoration of her rather than an interest in the fate of the nations per se. Similarly, the acknowledgement and worship of the one true God by the nations, whether done freely (Isa 2:3) or under compulsion (Isa 45:14), is merely a sign demonstrating the glory and power of Israel's God whom even the nations will have to honor.

Admittedly, both Williamson and Fensham are careful with their expressions using words that express relatively "stative" acts.[269] Israel in their words (see previous quotes by them) is to "*shine* like a witness," "*mediate* the revelation of God" to the nations or "*carry* his revelation." Perhaps the one instance which may speak of Israel's role as the faithful nation giving an example to other peoples with her commitment to YHWH and his laws is Deut 4:6 and significantly this is situated within the Torah. Here Israel's obedience to the commandments is her wisdom in the sight of the nations, who in turn recognize her greatness and understanding. Yet even in this example there is no recognition of YHWH by the nations at the same time. Thus we may conclude that there is no explicit mandate for mission in the OT analogous to the NT's, not even in a passive sense. While Deutero-Isaiah is full of possible hints, it would be unfair to expect Israel to have (without benefit of Christian hindsight) the kind of understanding of her role that Williamson and Fensham see.

---

[268] For a discussion on some contemporary issues relating to election and violence see R. W. L. Moberly's study, which also deals with the interpretation of *ḥērem* in Deut 7 ("Is Election Bad for You?" in *The Centre and the Periphery : A European Tribute to Walter Brueggemann* [ed. Jill Middlemas, David J. A. Clines and Else Holt; Sheffield: Sheffield Phoenix, 2010], 95–111). Scholars who justify the *ḥērem* law in Deut 7 on the basis of the "election for mission" idea are for instance Christopher Wright, *Deuteronomy*, (NIBCOT 4; Peabody MA: Hendrickson, 1996) 11; John Goldingay, "Justice and Salvation for Israel and Canaan," in *Reading the Hebrew Bible for a New Millennium: Form, Concept, and Theological Perspective* (ed. Wonil Kim et al., Studies in Antiquity & Christianity I; Harrisburg PA: Trinity Press International, 2000) 186; J. G. McConville, "The Shadow of the Curse: A Key to Old Testament Theology," *Evangel* 3/1 (1985), 3.

[269] I am grateful to Walter Moberly for suggesting this term borrowed from grammar where stative verbs express a state or condition.

In Ezra and indeed in Mosaic Yahwism, election is connected not with mission but with holiness. Election and holiness are presented as two sides of the same coin, two expressions of the same concept.[270] Israel is chosen so that she may fully belong to her God and she is holy, separate to indicate her elected status for being the exclusive and precious possession of YHWH. The focus is the vertical dimension rather than the horizontal; indeed the horizontal ties if they are deemed destructive to this vertical relationship are severed without mercy.

Ruth and Conversion

So far, I have examined one of the arguments ("election for mission"), which is used as justification for the need of preserving religious identity in Ezra 9–10. The other observation regularly made by scholars concerns Ruth and the concept of "conversion" which we have already seen in one example in Eichrodt's OT theology.

Since the exclusivism in EN is particularly difficult to swallow some commentators try to show that the narrative is not what it seems, that is, despite the separatism conversion for foreigners and non-exiled Judeans is a genuine possibility, hence the citing of Ezra 6:21 and the acceptance of Ruth as examples within the EN narrative and in the wider canon of the OT respectively. This view is well-expressed in McConville's comments on Neh 13:1–3:

> [P]resumably, neither the measure of Ezra nor this of Nehemiah was intended to foreclose the possibility of becoming "Israelite" by conversion. Cf. again Ezra 6:21, and the conversion and acceptance of Ruth the Moabitess (Ruth 1:16–17).[271]

If one turns to pre-modern commentators (although not many have written on EN), the emphasis is similarly on the possibility of conversion. The commentary of Matthew Henry and Thomas Scott assume this as an option even for the wives of Ezra 9–10 and likewise think that those who separated themselves from the peoples of the lands in Neh 10:29[28] were proselytes from the nations.[272]

Some others are less explicit about conversion as an option in Ezra 9–10, but still see the possibility for it expressed within EN, especially in Ezra 6:21. Thus Kidner defends the separatism of the exiles which is "balanced and

---

[270] Admittedly, Genesis provides a different paradigm focusing on election but without the element of separation and holiness characteristic of Mosaic Yahwism. It might be noted, however, that mission is not a part of either perspective despite scholarly arguments to the contrary.

[271] McConville, *Ezra, Nehemiah*, 144.

[272] Matthew Henry and Thomas Scott, *A Commentary upon the Holy Bible from Henry and Scott: With Occasional Observations and Notes from Other Writers* (2 vols.; London: The Religious Tract Society, 1834) 2:418, 433.

illuminated by the welcome given to genuine converts."[273] In commenting on Neh 13:1–3 he notes the reference to the deuteronomic law (23:4–6[3–5]) and continues:

> True to the Old Testament's style, the prohibition is stark and unqualified, to make the most powerful impact, but the reader knows that elsewhere there are balancing considerations. It is the Ammonite or Moabite in his native capacity as the embodiment of Israel's inveterate enemy and corrupter who is in view: the son or 'daughter of a foreign god' (Mal 2:11), burrowing into the life and even the language of Israel (verses 23ff.). But let him come as a convert, like Ruth the Moabitess, and he will be entitled to a very different reception.[274]

Williamson argues similarly in pointing out that the exiles "were willing to receive individuals who wished to join with them in sincerity; cf. Ezr. 6:21."[275]

Slightly more misgivings are expressed by Klein in *The New Interpreter's Bible*, which notes the varying attitudes within EN and the wider canon but is less inclined to smooth over the differences. The *NIB* observes positive (Ruth, Exod 22:21), ambivalent (Gen 34, Jacob versus Simeon and Levi) and (by implication) negative (Ezra 10) voices, while admitting that Ezra 6:21 shows a less hostile attitude.[276] The *NIB* also expresses more suspicion regarding the designation "foreigner" and wonders if those so described are truly alien people (such as the Ammonites, Moabites) or non-exiled Jews as well.[277] It also speculates about the reason for such antagonism to foreigners in connection with Ezra 4 and even wonders whether the events described in terms of psychological warfare and intimidation were real happenings or merely "paranoid justifications" for the *gôlâ* to reject the offers of help.[278]

Among the Christian commentators I have chosen for comparison, Allen goes possibly the furthest in seeing a contrast and tension between the openness in the book of Ruth and the "liberal stand" of Isa 56:3–8 on the one hand and the separatism of EN on the other. Nevertheless, he, too, comments on Ezra 6:21, which he also understands as a modification of the exiles' exclusivism.[279] At the same time he tentatively attempts to harmonize Ezra 6:21 and Ezra 9 by suggesting that the former describes the acceptance of non-exiled Judeans who wanted to join the *gôlâ* rather than all foreigners, since Ezra 9 does not envision conversion and pursues racial purity.[280] If understood this way, so Allen argues, then there is no racial line to be crossed in either instance.

---

[273] Kidner, *Ezra and Nehemiah*, 22.
[274] Ibid., 128.
[275] H. G. M. Williamson, "Ezra and Nehemiah," in *New Bible Commentary: 21st Century Edition* (ed. D. A. Carson, D.A. et al.; Leicester: IVP, 1994) 424.
[276] Klein, "Ezra and Nehemiah," 747.
[277] Ibid., 850.
[278] Ibid., 700.
[279] Allen, *Ezra, Nehemiah*, 37.
[280] Ibid., 73.

Effectively, his view makes the racial/ethnic boundary decisive in determining who can have any chance of being "in."

Some further comments are in order here. First, the difficulty with the evaluation of these views is that we simply do not know precisely who the enigmatic "people(s) of the land(s)" were and in some instances what exactly separation entailed. The first option I have considered takes Ezra 6:21 and the story of Ruth as normative and harmonizes Ezra 9–10 and other examples of separation in EN assuming implicitly the possibility of conversion. The last option sees Ezra 9–10 as decisive within EN and harmonizes Ezra 6:21 accordingly making physical descent the final arbiter. However, maintaining the difference between the approaches of Ezra 6:21 and Ezra 9–10 is equally possible, all the more so, since from a historical-critical perspective Ezra 1–6 is a separate unit with some distinctive traits of its own in other respects. Although it is difficult to prove or disprove the conversion theory, I would argue that both in the light of EN overall and of the specific argument regarding the "holy seed" in Ezra 9:2 conversion is simply not in view in Ezra 9–10.

Secondly, if one stays with the other possibility of rigid separation from all "foreigners" without any other option then the difficulty still remains as to what a Christian reader should make of such an episode. How is one to resolve the possible tension within EN itself and also between EN and the wider OT canon? Further, NT verses are frequently quoted to give guidance to the Christian reader regarding the issues in Ezra 9–10 (divorce, intermarriage, etc.), but the wider frames of reference for Christians and Jews respectively are often assumed even though spelling it out might help clarify the issues.

10.2.2 *Divorce*

So far, I have explored the commentaries regarding the exclusivism in Ezra 9–10 as well as the two issues connected with it ("election for mission" and "conversion"). I now turn to the question of divorce, the unique solution found by the exiles to deal with the intermarriage crisis.

The argument regarding divorce follows a similar pattern in Christian commentaries on EN. First, it is generally acknowledged that the measures seem harsh or even that it is cruel to the women (Klein).[281] Perhaps the only exception to this rule is the Puritans Henry and Scott who applaud the exiles' determination and who incidentally emphasize more the cost to the exiles than the effects on the wives.

> The case is plain; what has been done amiss, must be undone again as far as possible; nothing less than that is true repentance. To us now it is certain that sin must be put away, with a resolution never to have any thing more to do with it, though it be dear as the wife of thy bosom, nay, as a

---

[281] E.g., McConville, *Ezra, Nehemiah*, 69. Fensham, *The Books of Ezra and Nehemiah*, 135. Klein, "Ezra and Nehemiah," 746.

right eye, or a right hand; otherwise there is no pardon, no peace. What has been unjustly got, cannot be justly kept, but must be restored.[282]

Practically all scholars then point out that the OT permitted divorce and refer to Deut 24:1–4 but add the caveat that Mal 2:16 nevertheless condemns it.[283] This is followed by an outline of the NT's position with or without Jesus' estimate (in Matt 5:31–32 or Matt 19:9 and parallels) but definitely including Paul's admonition that a believer should not divorce his or her unbelieving spouse (1 Cor 7:10–16); a situation considered analogous to that of Ezra 9–10.[284]

As to the evaluation of the incident there are various efforts to defend the exiles' measures among the Christian commentators. Fensham's is perhaps the least nuanced in assuming that there is a clear legal basis for such divorces without recognizing the ambiguity of the legislation both in terms of intermarriages and how one is to deal with them. He says that

> Foreign women were married contrary to the law of God. The marriages were illegal from the outset. The sending away of the women is to guard the exiles against the continuation of an illegal act. With their foreign wives they lived in sin. Thus it is clear from v.4 that there is a strong legal background against which Shecaniah has formulated his proposal.[285]

Clines and Williamson mention a similar argument as one possible rationale specifically for the divorces; namely that the wives may have been seen as "unclean" which might qualify as an "indecency" (ערות דבר) in Deut 24:1–4 although they merely present this as the exiles' possible viewpoint and do not endorse it as Fensham seems to do.[286]

McConville also draws attention to the difference between the social consequences of a divorce today and in EN, where the wives were sent back to their non-Jewish extended families rather than left to struggle with children as single parents.[287]

Another possibly mitigating circumstance for the divorces which recurs in the commentaries is the similar situation mentioned in Mal 2:10–16 where Jewish wives had been divorced in order to make room for new foreign wives. If the people in Ezra 9–10 are similarly guilty of such double transgression then, so goes the argument, this would considerably reduce sympathy for them.[288] It is of course difficult to argue against this view from silence, although it is hard to

---

[282] Henry and Scott, A *Commentary upon the Holy Bible*, 2:418.
[283] E.g., Kidner, *Ezra and Nehemiah*, 71; McConville, *Ezra, Nehemiah*, 69; Klein, "Ezra and Nehemiah," 746.
[284] E.g., Williamson, *Ezra, Nehemiah*, 161; Klein, "Ezra and Nehemiah," 746; McConville, *Ezra, Nehemiah*, 69.; Henry and Scott, *A Commentary upon the Holy Bible*, 418.
[285] Fensham, *The Books of Ezra and Nehemiah*, 135.
[286] Clines, *Ezra, Nehemiah*, 126–27; Williamson, *Ezra, Nehemiah*, 151.
[287] McConville, *Ezra, Nehemiah*, 70.
[288] Williamson, *Ezra, Nehemiah*, 160; McConville, *Ezra, Nehemiah*, 70; Kidner, *Ezra and Nehemiah*, 71., Allen, *Ezra, Nehemiah*, 73.

imagine that the exiles of Ezra 9–10 would labor the legally more ambiguous and difficult point of intermarriage without even a sideways mention of the more obvious sin of divorcing Jewish wives for no better reason than to marry foreign women.

A fascinating though speculative question is Shecaniah's own position in this issue. He is identified as the son of Jehiel, one of the sons of Elam (Ezra 10:2) whose father is among those who married foreign women but agreed to divorce them (10:26). Goldingay takes Shecaniah to be the son of such a mixed marriage who is nevertheless accepted as a true Israelite because of his obvious commitment to YHWH.[289] Goldingay thus thinks that conversion is a possibility for the adult children of those from mixed marriages and that therefore the story is not so different from that of Ruth. However, it is equally possible that Shecaniah is the son of a Jewish mother and that either his mother died and his father remarried or, if one accepts the Mal 2:10–16 scenario, that his mother was divorced for the sake of a foreign wife.

Although such speculation may seem entirely fruitless and the questions it raises certainly cannot be answered with any degree of certainty the benefit of pondering the various possibilities is the awareness that the heart of the story lies elsewhere. The obscurity and the somewhat frustrating lack of detail in the direction where scholarly interests often lie is an indicator that we are examining the blurry edges of an image which focuses elsewhere. The story is interested neither in the connection between Shecaniah and his father, nor in defending the divorces.

At the other end of the Christian scholarly spectrum are more suspicious voices such as the *NIB* which wonders about the covert reasons for the divorces such as wanting to ensure political control or the fear of losing land through exogamous marriages.[290] It is interesting in this respect that those more sympathetic to the exiles' actions see them as the ones in a weaker position tempted perhaps to intermarry with the local population in order to climb higher in the social hierarchy or acquire land.[291] Those more dubious of the exiles' good intentions such as the *NIB* assume that they are guarding their existing power and land and dealing with any threat to these under cover of pious religious talk. This is not the place to prove or disprove either view and since we know so little of the historic circumstances outside of what the text in EN tells us the question can hardly be answered beyond any reasonable doubt. My own focus in any case stays within the categories of the text. I merely wish to note here how our general approach to the text may influence our assumptions.

Among those who stay within the theological categories of the text yet offer scathing criticism of the divorces is Robert North, who wrote the section on Ezra–Nehemiah in *The New Jerome Bible Commentary*.

---

[289] Goldingay, *OT Theology*, 1:749.
[290] Klein, "Ezra and Nehemiah," 746–7.
[291] E.g., Kidner, *Ezra and Nehemiah*, 115.

> Natural law obligations of justice and decency toward spouses in good faith and utterly innocent children seem never to have entered into the heads of these reformers, excited by a kind of mob psychosis for which Ezra cannot escape blame [...]. The dangerous and casual claim that "God's rights outweigh all human considerations" can only be called fanaticism. Still less does "maximum enforceableness for existing religious authorities" take precedence over profoundly human obligations of commutative justice. On the other hand, the need of safeguarding religious truth and duty is also a natural law obligation; but the fact that the conduct of those influenced by Ezra is presented in the Bible as praiseworthy and normative does not mean that it is impeccable or inerrant.[292]

The issue the *NJBC* raises is a pressing one: how is one to handle a text which presents an ethically doubtful or difficult issue in a positive light? This is a question I will return to when discussing the constraints that the canon places on Ezra 9–10.

A further observation worth noting with regard to the divorce issue is that despite the obvious ethical difficulty this problem is tackled in the commentaries a lot more straightforwardly than the question of exclusivism and the charge of racism. This may be the case partly because there are clearer guidelines in the NT regarding divorce which seem to apply directly to the issue at hand. Also, within the OT divorce is both permitted but at the same time recognized as not ideal (Gen 2:24 cf. Matt 19:8 "but from the beginning it has not been this way") and in some instances downright wrong (Mal 2:16). Thus the implicitly positive portrayal of this act in Ezra 10 is counterbalanced by other considerations within the wider canon. Secondly, our own increasing familiarity with divorce breeds if not contempt, at least a certain amount of indifference or acceptance. The unease with divorce is less with divorce per se and more with the aspect of exclusivism implicit in it. Divorce *en masse* and particularly for religious reasons is more suspect, but divorce as such is becoming more commonplace and less shocking.

10.2.3 *Application*

The Christian applications and evaluations of Ezra 9–10 take two directions; one is concerned with Christian distinctiveness, the other with the role of Scripture, though the first is a more obvious and prominent concern for the interpreters.

Commentators are at pains to safeguard the Christian reader from imitating the exiles' approach to mixed marriages. Williamson, for instance, points out in the "Explanation" section for Ezra 9–10 that the story is descriptive

---

[292] Robert North, "Ezra and Nehemiah," in *The New Jerome Biblical Commentary* (ed. Raymond E. Brown, Joseph A. Fitzmyer, and Roland E. Murphy; London: Geoffrey Chapman, 1989), 391.

and not prescriptive.²⁹³ He also makes his own position clear in arguing that Ezra 9–10 misinterprets the deuteronomic prohibition along racist lines even though the ban on intermarriage in Deuteronomy is on religious grounds (see also p.132). He further observes that the NT reinforces the OT's rejection of this racial standpoint (e.g., Acts 17:26; Gal 3:28; etc.). Williamson sees an analogous situation for the scenario of Ezra 9–10 in the Christian marrying an unbeliever,²⁹⁴ although he adds the usual caveats about divorce being ruled out for the Christian (1 Cor 7:12–13). As a final point for application, Williamson draws a parallel between Israel's efforts for distinctiveness and the Christian church's need to be salt and light.

> Finally if we may overlook for the moment the details of how Ezra worked out the principle of Jewish distinctiveness, his underlying concern was absolutely right. Israel's mission could only make headway if she maintained the servant identity that separated her from the nations to whom she should mediate the revelation of God. In just the same way, Christians individually and collectively as the Church are called to be "light" and "salt," elements that function effectively precisely because of their difference from the setting in which they are placed; "But if the salt has lost its savor..." (cf. Matt 5:13–16).'²⁹⁵

McConville tackles this question by making a useful distinction between Israel's situation and the church's and how their different positions affect the way the underlying issue of purity of religion is worked out.

> In a day when marriage between people of different nationalities is a perfectly acceptable commonplace Ezra's dismay can seem like a gross overreaction. Yet in reality, the need for the purity of the race was simply a logical extension of the fact that the people of God, in those days, took the form of a nation. It was a nation, not a church, that manifested the possibilities of life with God.²⁹⁶

This is an important insight and necessary when one is trying to draw parallels between Ezra 9 and the Christian church today. At the same time it is somewhat arguable how "logical" this extension of "racial purity" is from the self-definition of the people of God as a nation. After all, rabbinic Judaism was able to maintain the self-understanding of Israel as a nation, yet found ways to incorporate foreigners through conversion. I suggest that there is an added

---

²⁹³ Williamson, *Ezra, Nehemiah*, 161–2.
²⁹⁴ Somewhat surprisingly in the *New Bible Commentary* he thinks it unwise to look for a direct parallel in a Christian's marriage with a non-Christian. Perhaps what he means is that one should not aim to imitate the exiles' action of divorce or that the issue is wider than merely intermarriage and that the Christian should avoid all situations where his faith may be weakened. Williamson, "Ezra and Nehemiah," 432.
²⁹⁵ Williamson, *Ezra, Nehemiah*, 162.
²⁹⁶ McConville, *Ezra, Nehemiah*, 61.

element, namely a particular understanding of holiness which makes the extension an understandable one.

In his application McConville emphasizes the issue of intermarriage less, rather, his point is that

> For Christians, therefore the implication of this false trail of the exiles [i.e. their intermarriage with foreigners] is in terms of basic commitments which run counter to the commitment to Christ. This can happen where whole churches seek to "marry" Christian belief with current philosophies, and the Gospel is reduced to a code of decent behavior, rather than the word of life. [...] In its relationship with Hinduism, for example, which is by its nature omni-tolerant, a Christianity which seeks a middle way, or tries to establish a *tertium quid*, has actually become Hindu and is no longer Christian. [...] On a personal level, the pursuit of goals and interests which are in themselves neutral is reprehensible if it has taken the place of a zeal for God and for the holiness of his people.[297]

Thus McConville extends the application for the Christian much more widely than the marriage issue precisely because Israel is a nation and therefore concerned with "racial purity," to use his term, whereas the church is not. Nevertheless, he recognizes that the marriage of two partners who are not equally committed to Christ can also be a challenge in discipleship.[298]

The *NIB* follows a similar pattern of application focusing on the wider issues beyond marriage. At the same time it is more ambivalent about Ezra 9–10 as an example and uses the moral tension the modern reader feels when encountering the story juxtaposed with the social pressure of today for inclusion to highlight the essential difficulty in maintaining religious distinctiveness today.

> Almost all contemporary Christians would agree that moving toward gender and ethnic diversity is a radical imperative for the church. But how should we to [sic] respond to the difficult interfaith questions facing us today? What is the Christian response to other religions? What is the boundary between witness and dialogue? The biblical ambivalence toward outsiders and the excesses recounted in Ezra 10 call us to serious reflection on these questions today. Ignoring interfaith questions is irresponsible. But in addressing these issues we should not be surprised by different approaches at [sic] different people, or even by conflict within ourselves. How do we maintain the integrity of the faith without excluding others?[299]

The *NIB*, as mentioned earlier, also notes the different "voices" of the canon regarding attitudes to "foreigners," which helps to distance the reader from the story at hand as a model for imitation.

Commentators at times get rather "desperate" in their attempts to find a suitable application to the point where the actual narrative loses almost all

---

[297] Ibid., 61.
[298] Ibid., 71.
[299] Klein, "Ezra and Nehemiah," 747.

connection with the posited application. So, for instance, after a cursory nod toward the question of identity and debates of who is "in" and "out," Smith-Christopher juxtaposes the need for stability with that of openness to change concluding his application thus.

> Modern sympathies with the preservationist or traditionalist concerns of an Ezra certainly have a point in an age when churches are often called upon to abandon their traditions wholesale in the name of a simplistic "relevance." Tradition, however, must never shut out a Ruth, a Moabite, nor be allowed to silence the voices of appropriate change in the modern world.[300]

Although the general argument that different circumstances require different approaches is not unusual in these reflections on Ezra 9–10, Allen is more specific about the kind of circumstances such an attitude indicates.

> In our own age it is difficult to sympathize with parts of Ezra–Nehemiah. The work offends modern Christian readers as exclusive and even racist. Yet most of us have religious roots in denominations that began as sects. Such sects broke away from the larger religious community, steering a separatist course and flying from the mast the colors of neglected and necessary truths. Different times require different responses, and it was the judgment of Ezra and Nehemiah and their supporters that a rigorous stand was necessary in times aggravated by political and economic stress. The survival of the weakened community was at stake. Truth had to be zealously guarded and worked out in strict policies, to prevent the community from being swallowed up among the nations. Whenever the church faces threat and persecution, Ezra–Nehemiah is available as an inspiring source exemplifying the conviction and courage the church needs to face its own trials.[301]

Allen's self-searching admission about the origins of one's own religious community brings the issue closer to home for many Protestants, although he completely ignores Catholicism and his use of "sect," though sociologically descriptive, is problematic because of its pejorative associations.[302] At the same time his comments highlight the fact that such strict separatism is the sign and attitude of an internally weak and threatened group. Openness is always easier from a position of strength—or indifference.

To these points Williamson adds another in the *New Bible Commentary* in which he wrote the section on EN. In his general introduction there he

---

[300] Smith-Christopher, "Ezra and Nehemiah," in *Theological Bible Commentary* (ed. Gail R. O'Day and David L. Petersen; Louisville KY: Westminster John Knox, 2009) 159.

[301] Allen, *Ezra, Nehemiah*, 11.

[302] Mary Douglas, for instance, replaces "sect" with "enclave" as she explains in the Introduction to the 1996 edition of her book *Natural Symbols* because of the negative connotations the word has in the church (*Natural Symbols* [2nd ed.; London: Routledge Classics, 2007) xx.

observes the use of the Pentateuch, which, as he notes, was written under different circumstances from EN's day.

> Perhaps for that very reason many had come to regard it as a dead letter. It was Ezra's particular contribution, as we shall see, to develop methods of interpretation which taught them to draw out the underlying principles of Scripture so that they could be applied anew in their own later day, something which is necessary for us as it was for them. Adherence to the teachings of this book (which of course is as much about God's grace and salvation and the nature of faith as it is about "law" strictly defined) gave them, as it does us, the major means of access to the knowledge of God.[303]

Williamson then draws special attention to this feature of EN with regard to the incident in Ezra 9, where fresh interpretation of pentateuchal material allowed the exiles "to appreciate that marriage with an unbelieving foreigner was no different in principle from marriage with the local inhabitants of Canaan."[304] In a sharp observation but equally relating to interpretation Clines comments on the paradox that a more "literalist" reading of Deut 7 would have resulted in a laxer policy on intermarriage since the nations with whom intermarriage is prohibited in Deut 7 were extinct by EN's time.[305] Thus it was precisely a more flexible/metaphorical reading and interpretation of the law, which led to a stricter segregationist policy.

10.3 Conclusion

In this section I sketched the outlines of the way Ezra 9–10 is interpreted and the kind of moves commentators make to explain the story and its implications for the Christian reader. Recent OT theologies have taken on more sympathetic approaches to the Postexilic Period and to the Law but continue to struggle with the issue of exclusivism and alleged racism in the story as well as with presenting a Christian understanding of the Law and EN. The commentaries similarly reflect the tension between wanting to affirm the need for religious distinctiveness while recognizing the problematic nature of the Ezran solution.

There are two possible dimensions I find missing from the above interpretations. First, commentators use some implicit guidelines to constrain the direct emulation of the story but they tend not to spell out the larger framework and underlying principles which may guide the reader in the way they deal with tensions between various perspectives in Scripture. Secondly, Christian scholars obviously struggle with the question of how such a story may be "applied" or what one can learn from it. There is an uneasy tension between the broad affirmation made by scholars that religious distinctiveness is important and the objectionable solution advocated by the exiles. If religious distinctiveness is

---

[303] Williamson, "Ezra and Nehemiah," 423.
[304] Ibid., 431.
[305] Clines, *Ezra, Nehemiah*, 134.

important, in what way does the Ezran story contribute to an understanding of how it is (not) to be maintained? In order to answer these questions it is necessary to appreciate our own presuppositions and map out a larger framework for interpretation as I set these out in my introduction (Chapter 9). To these I shall turn next.

11

Ezra 9–10 in Jewish Understanding

Considering Jewish perspectives in our interpretation of Ezra 9–10 is an appropriate avenue to pursue as Christian scholarship increasingly recognizes and appreciates the other postbiblical interpretative tradition and what it has to contribute to understanding. Jewish-Christian dialogue does not mean giving up one's own faith position or a blurring of the differences. Rather it may be a fruitful way to clarify where each tradition stands in comparison to the other while at the same time gaining insights from that other perspective as well as becoming aware of one's own assumptions.

11.1 Jewish Perspectives

11.1.1 Ancient Texts

The first thing one might note about Jewish perspectives is the relatively small number of sources one can turn to when it comes to an interpretation of Ezra 9–10. Among the ancients I was able to find only two: Josephus' *Antiquities* (11.5.3–4 [139–153]) and 1 Esdras (8:68–9:36), the latter of which is an almost identical rendering of the MT and thus has little additional perspective to offer.[306] Josephus recounts the story in paraphrased form but in

---

[306] I noted in §4.1.5 that the one significant difference between the MT's version of the intermarriage crisis and that of 1 Esdras is the replacement of the Amorites with Edomites in the list of nations with whom intermarriage is unacceptable (Ezra 9:2 cf. 1 Esd 8:69). As I have argued there, this is of a piece with the book's general grudge against the Edomites. Otherwise, the only other noteworthy divergence in 1 Esdras is that it makes the MT's sometimes ambiguous statements explicit. E.g., Ezra 10:8 mentions the property ḥērem of those who do not comply with the community decision to divorce the foreign wives while 1 Esd 9:4 makes it clear that this means the use of their livestock as Temple sacrifices. Similarly, Ezra 10:44 merely mentions that some of the foreign wives

language similar to the MT. The only point worth highlighting is the historian's unabashed and wholehearted approval of the divorces, which he sees in terms of the tension between human interest and faithfulness to God.

> [Those that divorced their foreign wives] had a greater regard to the observation of the law than to their natural affection, and immediately cast out their wives, and the children which were born of them [...].[307]

This, however, is not a specifically Jewish point of view but a pre-modern one. One may compare the translator of Josephus, William Whiston (1667–1752), who adds the following footnote to Josephus at this point.

> This procedure of Esdras, and of the best part of the Jewish nation, after their return from the Babylonish captivity, of reducing the Jewish marriages, once for all, to the strictness of the law of Moses, without any regard to the greatness of those who had broken it, and without regard to that natural affection or compassion for their heathen wives, and their children by them, which made it so hard for Esdras to correct it, deserves greatly to be observed and imitated in all attempts for reformation among Christians, the contrary conduct having ever been the bane of true religion, both among Jews and Christians, while political views, or human passions, or prudential motives, are suffered to take place instead of the divine laws, and so the blessing of God is forfeited, and the church still suffered to continue corrupt from one generation to another.

Similarly, the commentary of Matthew Henry and Thomas Scott on Ezra endorses the action as an expression of true repentance (see §10.2.2 on p.151), although they point out elsewhere that divorce is not an option for Christians (1 Cor 7:12–13).

Beyond the above two sources the Ezran story of intermarriage does not feature in the ancient texts of the Second Temple Period. Although the figure of Ezra looms large in the literature of the era, the accounts given of him have no connection to the biblical Ezra narratives (see 4 Ezra, 5 Ezra, 6 Ezra—also known collectively as 2 Esdras).[308] In these works Ezra appears as a second Moses and lawgiver (e.g., in 2 Esd 2:33 Ezra receives a command on Mount Horeb; in 2 Esd 14:1–3 he is commissioned from a bush by the voice of God like Moses). At the same time, beyond the genealogy of Ezra (2 Esd 1:1–3), which largely though not entirely corresponds with the one given in Ezra 7:1–5, there is no other link between the biblical Ezra who arrives in Judah after the Exile (historically often estimated to be around 458 B.C.E.) and the Ezra who prays to God in the 30th year after the destruction of Jerusalem (2 Esd 3:1). In

---

had children as well without actually saying that the exiles have divorced them, whereas 1 Esd 9:36 unambiguously states the sending away of the wives with the children.
[307] Josephus, *Ant.* 11.5.4 (152).
[308] It is interesting in this respect that Sirach omits the figure of Ezra from his list of worthies entirely even though he mentions Zerubbabel and Jeshua (Sir 49:11–12) as the Temple builders and Nehemiah (Sir 49:13) as the rebuilder of the walls of Jerusalem.

fact, despite the period's intense concern with issues of mixing and intermarriage, other texts do not tend to refer to the solution offered in Ezra 9–10.

11.1.2 Rabbinic Discussions

Similarly, later Jewish sources, mainly rabbinic literature, are again sporadic with their comments and have little to say about the story. Rashi's commentary on Ezra has mostly insignificant textual points to make that do not address the bigger issues of the account. The incident of Ezra 9–10 occasionally gets a mention sideways via discussions of pentateuchal laws (e.g., *Gen. Rab.* 7.2; *b. Ker.* 11a).

As a typical example of what Jewish interpreters considered important in the story it is worth looking at *Gen.Rab* 7.2.

> Jacob of Ḳefar Nibburaya ruled in Tyre: It is permitted to circumcise the infant son of a Gentile woman on the Sabbath. When R. Haggai heard this he said to him, "Come and be flagellated." "Shall he who states a Scriptural ruling be punished!" exclaimed he. "And how is this Scriptural?" "Because it is written, *And they declared their pedigrees after their families, by their fathers' houses*" (Num. I, 18), he answered. "You have not ruled well," said he to him. "And whence can you prove this to me?" "Lie down and I will prove it to you," he retorted. "It is written, *Now therefore let us make a covenant with our God to put away all the wives, and such as are born of them*" (Ezra x, 3). "And will you actually punish me on the strength of tradition!" he protested. *"And let it be done according to the* Torah" (*ib.*), quoted he. Said he: "Hammer away thy hammering [i.e. strike me], for it is well taught."

The original question circles around the problem whether a Gentile woman's son born of a Jewish father is a Jew or not. If he is, then he can be circumcised on the Sabbath like any other Jewish boy whose circumcision falls on a Sabbath. Jacob of Ḳefar Nibburaya argues for patrilineal descent with an appeal to Num 1:18 and answers the circumcision question in the affirmative. Rabbi Haggai cites Ezra 10:3 and reasons that since the children are sent away with the foreign wives there, this must mean that they follow the status of their mother and are to be considered Gentiles, in which case circumcision is out of the question for them. The story of intermarriages is not a material for discussion or interpretation in its own right; rather it is used as a mine for information on a legal question.

However, it is worth noting here that its authority is only valid insofar as it is seen to be in line with the Pentateuch. Thus Jacob of Ḳefar Nibburaya (advocating patrilineal descent) is incensed at the use of the Hagiographa for determining a legal question rather than appealing to the Pentateuch, hence his exclamation, "And will you actually punish me on the strength of tradition!" To this the rebuff is a further citation of Ezra 10:3 "And let it be done according to the Torah," which presumably indicates as the Soncino edition of the Midrash helpfully notes, that the Ezran ruling is seen to be pentateuchal in origin, possibly referring to Deut 7:4 as it is interpreted in *b. Qidd.* 68b. The rabbinic argument there is that although the prohibition speaks of intermarriage both with foreign men and women (Deut 7:3), v.4 only describes the consequences of such a marriage if the father is a Gentile ("he will turn away your son from following me") calling "your son" only the offspring of a mixed marriage where the mother is a Jew. The implication for the rabbis is that if the son of a Gentile woman is not called "your son" then he must be a Gentile too following the status of his mother; hence matrilineal descent.

A second example for rabbinic interpretation I wish to consider is from *b. Ker.* 11a, which discusses the violation of the betrothed slave girl in Lev 21:20–22 and connects it to the intermarriage crisis in Ezra 9–10 on the basis that the same אשם sacrifice is offered in both texts. The citation of Ezra 10:19 comes in the middle of a section on liability answering the question when the man is obligated to offer an אשם.

> R. Isaac said: One is liable only in the case of a possessed handmaid, as it is written, *"That is a bondmaid, designated for a man."* And where do we find that the term *"designated"* [neḥerefeth] implies that a change has taken place?—It is written, *And strewed groats* [harifoth] *thereon.* [2 Sam 17:19] Or as it is written, *Though thou shouldest bray a fool in a mortar with a pestle among groats* [harifoth]. [Prov 27:22]
>
> *And they gave their hand that they would put away their wives; and being guilty, they offered a ram of the flock for their guilt* [Ezra 10:19]; said R. Ḥisda: This teaches that they had all had intercourse with designated handmaids.

Rabbi Isaac argues that the אשם sacrifice is only to be brought if the slave girl has been "possessed," that is, if the sexual contact has been consummated.[309] Rabbi Isaac explains his reason by pointing to the unusual word "designated" (*neḥerefeth*) [generally taken to mean betrothed], which he understands to imply the loss of virginity by pointing to two other passages where the same root refers to the changed status of grain. This argument is then followed by a comparison with Ezra 10:19, where the same type of sacrifice (an אשם) is offered for the offence. The resemblance between the two is more striking when we consider that, as the Mishnah for this *gemara* points out, this is the only instance of "forbidden [sexual] connection" where the sacrifice required is not a sin-offering (חטאת). Based on this similarity, Rabbi Ḥisda claims that the exiles' case in Ezra 9–10 must be like the one described in Lev 19:20–22 and therefore the women that are divorced should be seen as betrothed slaves who have been violated.

---

[309] Cf. the Mishnaic text on which this *gemara* comments, which states that in other cases of sexual misconduct sexual contacts are punishable as well as consummated connection. In the instance of the betrothed slave girl in Lev 19:20–22, however, it is only the latter that is subject to the law.

164 "According to the Law"

This halakic example demonstrates an interest in Pentateuch laws where other texts, such as Ezra 9–10 may be pulled in to be used as illustrations to a particular law based on some similarity between the legal regulation and a narrative. However, there is no attempt to study the story of Ezra and the intermarriage crisis for its own sake, nor to reflect that on its own terms, the narrative does not support the kind of interpretation that Rabbi Ḥisda suggests.

11.1.3 Recent Jewish Scholarship

Although there are recent Jewish scholars who comment on EN, the perspective is often not explicitly Jewish but "modern." For instance, Eskenazi's study on EN (*In an Age of Prose*) follows a literary-narrative approach and Japhet's several articles on EN are interested in historical-critical questions (such as authorship, chronology and composition).[310] Kaufmann's *History of the Religion of Israel*, which also deals with the intermarriage crisis in Ezra, is primarily an attempt at historical reconstruction of Israel's religion with a sharp polemic aimed at liberal Protestant views.[311] Yet another approach is reflected in a joint article by Eskenazi and Judd (a biblical scholar and a sociologist respectively) who consider inner-Jewish religious tension within modern Israel using the insights of sociology and the analogous situation in Ezra 9–10.[312] This perhaps comes closest to being paralleled by a Christian concern for religious distinctiveness although here again the Jewish perspective is primarily "historical" in its interest rather than "applicational." In addition to the above the rabbinic tradition of discussing Ezra 9–10 via pentateuchal laws also continues (e.g., Epstein, *Marriage Laws*, 162–67; Milgrom, *Lev 1–16*, 359–361).

Among the moderns, the only explicitly Jewish engagement with Ezra that I have found which might be comparable to the Christian faith perspective was in the *Jewish Study Bible*, the self-confessed aim of which is to combine academic scholarship with Jewish exegesis. As the Introduction states in describing the contributors to the volume

> They employ state-of-the-art scholarship and a wide range of modern approaches; at the same time, they are sensitive to Jewish readings of the

---

[310] Sara Japhet, "The Composition and Chronology in the Book of Ezra–Nehemiah" in *Second Temple Studies: 1. Persian Period*, (ed. Philip R. Davies; JSOT SS 117; Sheffield: JSOT Press, 1991), 189–216; Idem., "Sheshbazzar and Zerubbabel. Against the Background of the Historical and Religious Tendencies of Ezra–Nehemiah," *ZAW* 94 (1982), 66–98; Idem., "The Supposed Common Authorship of Chronicles and Ezra–Nehemiah Investigated Anew," *VT* 18 (1968), 330–371.
[311] Kaufmann, *History of the Religion of Israel, Vol. IV., From the Babylonian Captivity to the End of Prophecy* (New York: Ktav, 1977) 4:325–358.
[312] Tamara C. Eskenazi & Eleanore P. Judd, "Marriage to a Stranger in Ezra 9–10," in *Second Temple Studies: 2. Temple Community in the Persian Period*, (ed. Tamara C. Eskenazi & Kent H. Richards; JSOT SS 175; Sheffield: JSOT Press, 1994) 266–285.

Bible, to classical Jewish interpretation, and to the place of the Bible in Jewish life.[313]

The introduction and brief commentary of Hindy Najman to the books of EN in it (pp.1666–1670) discusses the history, date and composition of these two books, which is in conformity with modern biblical studies. This is followed by a description of Ezra listing his various accomplishments attributed to him by tradition (pp.1669–70). The focus on the figure of Ezra as a second Moses is also in keeping with the general Jewish trend we have noted so far that concentrated on the person more than on the story itself. Najman quotes the rabbis' opinion that "Ezra was sufficiently worthy that the Torah could have been given through him if Moses had not preceded him" (*t. Sanh.* 4.4).

The incident in Ezra 9–10 is labeled as a "legal crisis" (p.1669) and Najman further remarks that

> His [Ezra's] legal innovations are not seen as such, but are depicted as proper interpretation of eternally binding Mosaic law (see Ezra 7.10; Neh 8.1). This principle is at the heart of rabbinic interpretation, and his authenticity is never called into question within rabbinic Judaism. (p.1670)

Commenting on Ezra 10:3 and the exiles' injunction "let it be done according to the Law" she notes the presupposition in the text that "Mosaic authority should be ascribed not only to the law explicitly stated in Deut 7.3, but also to its interpretation or elaboration." (p.1684) and in the same place compares it with a similar assumption in 1 Kgs 11:1–2 where Solomon's foreign marriages are seen as an offence against the Law.

Najman further observes parallels between Ezra's complete fast (no food or water—Ezra 10:6) and Moses' after the golden calf incident (Exod 34:28; Deut 9:18). She discerns an influence of "torah narratives" in Ezra 10:12–14 (presumably referring to Exod 19:8 in particular although she does not specify) "involving the Israelites' willingness to accept the authority of Moses and to agree to obey particular laws." (p.1686). These comments again highlight the analogy between Moses as the first and Ezra as the second lawgiver.

11.2 Accounting for the Difference

11.2.1 *Torah versus Writings*

We are now in a position to summarize our findings in the light of the meager evidence. First, the Jewish perspective is primarily concerned with the figure of Ezra as the second Moses and is interested in the intermarriage narrative insofar as it deals with the interpretation of pentateuchal laws; the focus of the story being its "legal" aspect. That there is so little written on Ezra is not surprising given the nature of Jewish interpretation and its primary interest

---

[313] Adele Berlin and Mark Zvi Brettler, *The Jewish Study Bible* (Oxford: Oxford University Press, 1999) x.

in Torah and its concern with how the commandments may be understood and applied for the practicing Jew.

Secondly and following on from the above, the intermarriage crisis in Ezra 9–10 is of lesser significance as part of Jewish Scripture known as the "Writings." We have already seen an illustration of this in *Gen. Rab.* 7.2. The interpretation in Ezra 10:3 is only accepted as authoritative because it is seen to be aligned with the pentateuchal regulation in Deut 7:4 as outlined in *Qidd.* 68b. The outrage at quoting "tradition" (i.e., from the "Writings" here) rather than Torah (i.e., the Pentateuch) well demonstrates the unacceptability of non-pentateuchal portions of Scripture to argue a legal case.

Thus the legal interpretations of Ezra 9–10 are not problematic for Jews despite some aspects that do not readily fit with the Pentateuch (such as the "holy seed" rationale and the ruling to divorce foreign wives irrespective of conversion) because they are not authoritative as a pattern to follow. Jewish tradition seems happy to record debates with contradictory views without embarrassment and in this respect the solution presented in the narrative of Ezra 9–10 may be one option in an ongoing debate on intermarriage.

The lesser authority of the "Writings" in determining legal matters is further underlined by the earlier observation that Second Temple texts do not refer to Ezra 9–10 in their justification of the ban on intermarriage. Writings such as *Jub.* 30 or 4QMMT cite the Pentateuch: its legal material for validation (Deut 7:3; Lev 19:19) and its narratives as instances of exemplary behavior (Gen 34—the zeal of Simeon and Levi in the story of Shechem and Dinah).

11.2.2 *Halakah & Haggadah*

A further difference underlying the relative scarcity of Jewish commentary and reflection on Ezra and the intermarriage crisis there is the distinction between Haggadah and Halakah in terms of their authority. The latter refers to legally binding rulings or interpretations of such, while the former are stories which are illustrative or explicative in nature and cannot be appealed to as a final arbiter in a legal dispute. Heschel notes this particularity of Jewish thinking although he argues for a reappraisal of the importance of Haggadah.

> Halacha, the rationalization of living, is not only forced to employ elements which are themselves unreasoned; its ultimate authority depends upon agada. For what is the basis of halacha? The statement "Moses received the Torah from Sinai." Yet this statement does not express a halachic idea. [...] The event at Sinai, the mystery of revelation, belongs to the sphere of agada. Thus while the content of halacha is subject to its own reasoning, its authority is derived from agada.[314]

---

[314] Abraham J. Heschel, *God in Search of Man: A Philosophy of Judaism* (New York: Farrar, Straus & Giroux, 1955) 338. For an insightful reflection on the interrelationship between deeds and faith, Halakah and Haggadah see Ibid., 281–360 (esp. 336–347). A recent example of this prioritising of narrative over norm is evident in John Goldingay's

In contrast, a Christian approach is more likely to place an emphasis on the narrative further reinforced by postmodernity's interest in the "story." As Jenson puts it,

> The message of Jesus' resurrection, the gospel, is a message about an event and so itself has the form of a narrative. Therefore, when the church sets out to read Scripture as a whole, the kind of unity by which she construes this whole is narrative unity. The church reads her Scripture as a single plotted succession of events, stretching from creation to consummation plotted around exodus and resurrection.
>
> *[After some intervening paragraphs on rabbinic Judaism and its focus on Torah where the narrative provides the supporting role, he continues.]*
>
> The church reads Israel's Scripture as what comes, and must come, before the gospels and so reads the whole of her Scripture as fundamentally narrative; here Torah plays the supporting role, providing the moral structure that any narrative must have to be intelligible.[315]

Apart from the instinctive Christian orientation toward narrative as guidance based on the centrality of the gospel as narrative, there is also precedent in both Old and New Testament for "narrative" overruling "norm" (i.e., legal regulation). In Jer 3:1–3 God appeals to the regulation in Deut 24:1–4 to show that Israel, the faithless wife who has been divorced (Jer 3:8) cannot return to her first "husband," YHWH. Nevertheless, he again calls to her to return in repentance and he will be gracious to her (v.12). Likewise Hos 11:1–7 portrays Israel in terms reminiscent of the rebellious son in Deut 21:18–21 who is to be stoned. Yet God exclaims "How can I give you up, O Ephraim? How can I surrender you, O Israel? [...] My heart is turned over within Me, All My compassions are kindled." (v.8)[316]

One might argue that these examples are only analogies and metaphors since the commandments apply to human relationships. On the other hand, the debates Jesus was involved in with the Pharisees are more obviously legal cases with one interpretation set against another. In the divorce debate (Matt 19:4–5) Jesus uses the creation story (Gen 2:24) to argue against the Hillelite interpretation of Deut 24:1–4 which allowed divorce for "any matter" (*b. Giṭ.* 90a). That this is a subversion of the halakic method of interpretation is illustrated by Rivkin's comment on this incident (he is using Mark 10:2–12).

> Jesus, in this instance, is not attacking the *paradosis*, "the Tradition," but the very command of Moses. The Pharisees stand guard in this instance over the integrity of the Written Law, the Pentateuch. For this reason, they

---

OT Theology with its threefold division of "narrative, faith, and ethics." See discussion in §2.1.1.

[315] Robert W. Jenson, "Scripture's Authority in the Church," in *The Art of Reading Scripture* (ed. Ellen F. Davis and Richard B. Hays; Grand Rapids MI: Eerdmans, 2003) 29.

[316] I am grateful to Walter Moberly for pointing to the example in Hosea.

test Jesus; they are seeking to determine whether he is undermining the Law. And his answer could leave little doubt that he set himself up as an independent authority, *pitting a nonlegal passage in Genesis against a legal passage in Deuteronomy.*[317] [italics mine]

Similarly, when challenged that his disciples break the Sabbath by picking grain Jesus cites the story of David and his companions eating consecrated bread in 1 Sam 21:6 using a non-pentateuchal narrative precedent to underline his point.

The Handling of Ruth

It is instructive to compare here the Christian approach to the story of Ruth with the Jewish one. For the latter there is no difficulty with Ezra and a comparison with the narrative of Ruth does not even come into the picture because narrative cannot overrule halakic interpretation. In this respect, Ezra and his circle fit into this same tradition in that narrative exceptions such as Moses' Cushite wife or Ruth do not enter into their arguments.

In discussing Christian perspectives on Ezra 9–10 I have already remarked on the difficulty some Jewish interpretation has with Ruth (see p.134), which has nothing to do with Ezra. Rather it is problematic because, on the face of it, it is an exception to the halakic rule in Deut 23:4[3], which does not allow the descendants of Moabites and Ammonites to enter the assembly (קהל) of YHWH to the tenth generation thereby implying the prohibition of intermarriage with these nations. This is indeed an embarrassment, since Israel's most distinguished king and the ancestor of the awaited Messiah should thus be subject to exclusion from the assembly of God, since Ruth was King David's great-grandmother.

Although David's ancestry for Jewish interpretation is disconcerting in light of Deut 23:4[3] the law is not thereby made void. *B.Yebam.*77a states that two bonds were fastened on David, that is, on his dynasty: Ruth the Moabitess and Naamah the Ammonitess (Solomon's wife and Rehoboam's mother). These were loosened when it was declared that the exclusion of the Moabites and Ammonites only refers to males (*m. Yebam.* 8:3, see also *b. Ketub.* 7b). Rashi similarly takes the prohibition in Deut 23:4[3] as a ban for Ammonite and Moabite men to marry an Israelite woman. Likewise *Sipre Deut* par. 249:1 explains that the grammatical form in Deut 23:4[3] is male and adds as further justification that the culprits against Israel were Ammonite/Moabite men, since it is generally men, not women, who greet guests.

The Jewish concern then is to align her story and David's ancestry with the deuteronomic command. The case of Ruth, however, in Jewish interpretation is somewhat exceptional because here the norm is reinterpreted in order to vindicate David's lineage. Nevertheless, it is true in general terms that the reference point for Jewish interpretation is Halakah and it is noteworthy that the

---

[317] Ellis Rivkin, *A Hidden Revolution* (Nashville TN: Abingdon, 1978) 91.

story of Ruth does not therefore annul the deuteronomic command; it merely modifies its understanding.

At the same time, the effort to absolve David of guilt sets the interpretation of Deut 23:4[3] in some tension with Ezra 9–10 because the problematic intermarriages are all with women and if the deuteronomic command has only males in view then there could have been no objection to these women in the first place provided they made a commitment to Israel's God. Significantly, there is no discussion in the rabbinic literature about the discrepancy and no effort to harmonize the law with this particular narrative. Rabbinic writings often report alternative views on legal matters without embarrassment and thus Ezra 9–10 may be seen as one such on the question of intermarriage.

On the other hand, for Christians the primary emphasis tends to be on story. Thus tension between various narratives is disconcerting because the basic principles for faithful living are more likely to be derived from these. Typically, the "openness" of the book of Ruth is used as a "corrective" to the exclusiveness of Ezra 9–10. Narrative for Christians is thus the main reference point with "norm" providing certain limits on what is considered acceptable behavior. Thus, as we have seen, Jesus' sayings on divorce (Matt 19:1–9 and parallels) and Paul's advice in 1 Cor 7:12–16 constrain the straightforward imitation of the exiles' action in Ezra 9–10.

11.3 Conclusion

Considering Jewish perspectives on Ezra 9–10 I have noted that there is very little actual discussion on the story in ancient, rabbinic or modern sources; rather Jewish interpretation is interested in the legal aspects of the narrative and this is understandable in the light of its overwhelming emphasis on interpreting and doing "torah." Moreover, due to the particular nature of classic Jewish interpretation which gives primary authority to the Pentateuch as opposed to the "Writings" and prioritises Halakah (norm) over Haggadah (narrative), the tension spots lie elsewhere than in the corresponding Christian interpretation of the story. The above analysis does not remove the difficulty for Christian interpretation but makes one aware to some extent of the reasons for it. Thus it may be a useful tool to show that some of the Christian unease with Ezra is conditioned on the particular priorities that Christians hold and the controlling function they give to narrative.

12

Constraints from Canon and Tradition

12.1 Ezra 9–10 in the Christian Canon

One of the obvious questions that a Christian reader needs to address when considering the intermarriage crisis in Ezra 9–10 is what the specific Christian constraints are on the story. This is a topic that most commentators quickly address if only to make sure that the ethically doubtful aspects of the narrative are not imitated. Since the question is dealt with in a fairly standard and uncontested way, it can easily be summarized.[318] Ezra 9–10 in effect is treated as a rather exceptional case that is not to be followed in its solution of divorce although the aim of preserving religious distinctiveness is seen as praiseworthy. Christians are then pointed first to the OT counter-examples such as Ruth, who though a foreigner is accepted because of her commitment to Israel's God. With regard to divorce Mal 2:16 is mentioned to show God's attitude to it ("I hate divorce"),[319] coupled with the divorce sayings of Jesus (Matt 5:31–35; 19:1–9; Mark 10:2–12) as well as the admonition of Paul in 1 Cor 7:12–16 advising Christians not to divorce their unbelieving spouse if he or she is willing to stay within the marriage.

---

[318] For specific examples see Chap. 10 reviewing Christian interpreters.

[319] I personally question the wisdom of using Mal 2:16 as a kind of prooftext because the verse in its immediate context does not condemn divorce out of hand; rather it disapproves of the specific scenario where Jews divorced their Jewish wives in order to marry foreign women who worshiped other gods. Nevertheless, Jesus' teaching on divorce in general makes it clear that divorce is not what God envisaged for humankind and in that sense the condemnation of divorce is right even if that perspective is not so unambiguously obvious from within the OT.

12.1.1 Selective Reading (Brettler)

This is a useful framework but at the same time it leaves the Christian reader with a general concern for maintaining religious identity while the particulars leave one disconcerted over the story's implications for the foreign wives involved in the drama. The upshot of this is that the controversial elements outweigh the benefits of such a narrative and the temptation is largely to ignore it as an incident that has little new to teach and is mainly an embarrassment as an episode of racism and exclusion. Brettler, a Jewish scholar reflecting on the authority of Scripture, puts it well.

> I suggest that, whether people realise it or not, by ignoring certain passages and highlighting others they create a textbook Bible out of the sourcebook Bible. Most people do not go about "whiting out" large sections of the text. Instead, they *effectively* white out passages by treating them as if they were written in a miniscule, impossible-to-read 3-point font while others are written in a large, 36-point bold type. Thus, nothing is excised from the sourcebook—it is still all there, since the Bible cannot be changed—but only certain parts are readable, and thus intelligible and truly authoritative.[320]

What Brettler means by the process of creating a textbook Bible out of the sourcebook Bible is that Scripture is more like an anthology with many different perspectives. Such a work, however, is difficult to credit with authority, says Brettler, when it voices views that are not entirely compatible with each other. Interpretation, evaluation and selection produce a textbook Bible that speaks with one voice and can therefore be ascribed authority. This is certainly one way of dealing with the tensions in Scripture and Brettler himself affirms such a move as necessary.[321]

Brettler's view is attractive at first glance although he is less than clear on the criteria by which the selection process takes place and he admits himself that there are no obvious guidelines. Among other things he mentions the primacy of Torah (i.e., pentateuchal) texts, the relative importance of passages based on the number of times they are mentioned in Scripture or the number of biblical authors who do so and the frequency with which they occur in the liturgy or are quoted by the rabbis.[322]

---

[320] M. Z. Brettler, "Biblical Authority: A Jewish Pluralistic View," in *Engaging Biblical Authority: Perspectives on the Bible as Scripture* (ed. William P. Brown; Louisville KY: Westminster John Knox, 2007), 5.

[321] Ibid., 4–5. "According to my view of biblical authority, it is within my rights to "select" particular biblical texts as more important than others. To paraphrase American jurisprudence, not all texts are created equal. I perform this selection out of an awareness that the Bible is a contradictory anthology, and thus speaks in many voices, and if I want it to be authoritative for me (within my community), I must decide which voice is authoritative."

[322] Ibid., 6.

There is undoubtedly value in recognizing the relative importance of a particular matter by the frequency with which it occurs in various biblical texts. It is also a useful tool to consider the history of interpretation (in Brettler's case this is rabbinic tradition) and the role a particular thought plays in the life of the community (Brettler's example is liturgy), which is an expression of how crucial an idea was seen to be over a longer period. At the same time, Brettler's criteria are loose to the extent that they allow one to pick and choose to a certain extent according to personal preference. His own formulation when discussing the concrete example of the tension between Exod 20:5–6 (intergenerational punishment) on the one hand and Deut 7:9–10 and Ezek 18 (personal responsibility) on the other is revealing.

> *I would prefer* to see Deuteronomy 7 and Ezekiel 18 as the more authoritative texts, in part because they comport better with the God in which *I would like to believe* and in part because postbiblical rabbinic tradition has deemed those texts as by and large the "winners," with the idea of personal responsibility "trumping" intergenerational punishment.[323] [italics mine]

Moreover, such a selection process that Brettler advocates effectively silences certain texts as non-authoritative even though he himself talks of some texts being more authoritative than others. In fact, he is trying to have his cake and eat it. He takes it as axiomatic that the "Bible cannot be changed" (see earlier quote on p.171 of this book), presumably because Jewish tradition affirms its authority. Yet, by virtually eliminating certain texts from the canon he unwittingly creates the question why tradition saw it fit to bestow authority on these texts at all. If the differences between what he sees in the Bible as contradictory texts came about possibly as a result of historical development, as he suggests (p.7), with certain views "trumping" others, then why retain the "losers" at all? Brettler simply does not address the issue of why the *whole* Bible should have authority, even the "loser" texts, and what benefit there is derived from keeping them.

What Brettler fails to consider is that evaluation and assessment does not start with postbiblical readers and interpreters of the text but within the biblical tradition itself. Michael Fishbane develops the idea of what he calls "inner-biblical exegesis," the practice of biblical writers to re-evaluate earlier traditions, and he traces the re-interpretation and re-appropriation of both halakic and haggadic material within Scripture.[324] To this concept we might add that the overall shape of the canon also throws a different light on its individual

---

[323] Ibid., 7.
[324] Michael Fishbane, *Biblical Interpretation in Ancient Israel* (Oxford: Clarendon, 1985). For a shorter version of some of his ideas see his "Inner-Biblical Exegesis: Types and Strategies of Interpretation in Ancient Israel" in *The Garments of Torah: Essays in Biblical Hermeneutics* (Bloomington & Indianapolis: Indiana University Press, 1989), 3–18.

Constraints from Canon and Tradition 173

parts; an approach that has become particularly associated with the works of Brevard Childs and also of James Sanders.[325]

12.1.2 "Critical Traditioning" (Davis)

To the question of "inner-biblical exegesis" with regard to Ezra 9–10 I shall return shortly. First, however, I wish to consider how the canon influences the way the story is to be understood. When one reads Ezra 9–10 in its immediate context, it is set out as an example of Torah faithfulness which, it is hoped, may avert God's wrath (Ezra 10:2–3 cf. 9:14).

In Ezra 9:1–2 the elders' complaint that the people did not separate themselves but intermarried follows directly on the story of Ezra's return to Jerusalem (Ezra 8) with the purpose of teaching Torah (Ezra 7:10). Placing the intermarriage crisis immediately after this sequence indirectly implies a connection between teaching and understanding Torah and recognition of sin. This is further reinforced by Shecaniah's suggestion in Ezra 10:3 to divorce the "foreign" wives referring to Ezra's (presumably) earlier advice ("according to the counsel of my lord" בעצת אדני)[326] and to the law. Ezra himself, a positive character in the story with an impressive priestly genealogy (Ezra 7:1–5), is appalled at the mixed marriages (9:3) and in his prayer indirectly blames such intermarriages for the Exile (9:12). Moreover, as Najman points out in her marginal notes of the *Jewish Study Bible* there are echoes in the story of the first giving of the Law and the figure of Ezra as a second Moses (see §11.1.3 on p.165). All these features indicate that the narrator presents the separations as commendable, which is endorsed both by the community's respected leaders and by the majority of the people, as well as backed by the authority of Torah (or rather, by the exiles' reading of it).

---

[325] Brevard S. Childs' first tentative suggestion for a new approach was introduced in *Biblical Theology in Crisis* (Philadelphia: Westminster, 1970) followed by his *Introduction to the Old Testament as Scripture* (London: SCM, 1979) and *The New Testament as Canon: An Introduction* (Philadelphia: Fortress, 1985), where he further developed his "canonical approach." For a later refined proposal see his *Biblical Theology of the Old and New Testaments: Theological Reflection on the Christian Bible* (Philadelphia: Fortress, 1993). Similarly James Sanders in *Torah and Canon* (Philadelphia: Fortress, 1972) and in *Canon and Community* (Philadelphia: Fortress, 1984) argued for "canon(ical) criticism," a phrase that originates with him. R. W. L. Moberly adopted Childs' canonical approach and applied it in his *The Bible, Theology and Faith* (Cambridge: Cambridge University Press, 2000) although Childs did not recognise the approach as his ("Critique of Recent Intertextual Canonical Interpretation," *ZAW* 115 [2003], 173–184).

[326] The Masoretic pointing makes this "the counsel of *the Lord*" (אֲדֹנָי), that is, God, rather than "my lord" (אֲדֹנִי). The former is improbable as H. G. M. Williamson shows (*Ezra, Nehemiah* [WBC 16; Nashville TN: Nelson, 1985] 143). Cf. also LXX, 1 Esdras—ὡς ἂν βούλῃ ("as you advise" or NRSV "as it seems good to you").

If one widens the scope to the whole book of EN, it is noticeable that separation is a central theme of these two books in general, even though the Hebrew root of the word "to separate" (בדל) and its derivatives do not occur in every instance. The concept features in the course of the building projects of both the temple (Ezra 4:1–4) and the Jerusalem wall (Neh 2:20), is present in the celebration of the Passover feast (Ezra 6:21), required in marriages (Ezra 9–10; Neh 10:31[30]; 13:28) and in the assembly of YHWH (Neh 13:1–3), and symbolized in the closing of the city gates for the Sabbath. Thus in most aspects of life: family, work of a sacred nature and/or of national significance, rest and worship, separation is seen as necessary. No blame or disapproval is attached to these actions; rather they are shown in a positive light as a sign and characteristic of those committed to YHWH (Neh 9:2; 10:29[28]). In Neh 13:1–3 separation is portrayed as the direct consequence of understanding and following the Law while profaning the Sabbath (not separating it from normal work days) is seen as one of the sins which led to the Exile (Neh 13:17–18).

At the same time, as I have shown in my exegesis (see §§4.4 and 7.4), the intermarriage crises are treated somewhat differently in Ezra 9–10 and Neh 13:23–31. In the latter case, seemingly no divorces are enforced and I have argued that the references to defilement and purification are not connected to the holy seed rationale as they are in Ezra 9–10. Why did Nehemiah's solution in Neh 13 diverge from Ezra's in Ezra 9–10? There have been several explanations suggested. It is sometimes assumed that Nehemiah has seen the failure of the Ezran way (e.g., Rudolph), which, if it was carried out at all, did not solve the problem of intermarriages.[327] Williamson, based on Nehemiah's "rough and ready response," thinks that the incident was localized and on a small scale and wonders if Nehemiah would have had the authority to force the men to divorce their wives.[328] Blenkinsopp, on the other hand, argues that the difference in his solution to that of Ezra's is deliberate and is indicated by the fact that divorce is passed over both here and in the covenant stipulations of Neh 10.[329] It is difficult to draw any hard and fast conclusions since the narrative is to a large extent open-ended.

Similarly, I have already referred earlier to the distinction drawn between the rigid approach in Ezra 9–10 and the arguably more flexible one in Ezra 6:21. In all these instances it is doubtful whether the variations are significant; the accounts lend themselves both to a certain amount of harmonization and to the maintenance of the differences. In any case the events are not presented in such a way as to assume a deliberate effort on the narrator/editor's part to highlight these differences or even to show a particular

---

[327] E.g., Wilhelm Rudolph, *Esra und Nehemia mit 3.Esra* (HAT 20; Tübingen: Mohr Siebeck, 1949) 209. Ezra 10 ends abruptly and the Hebrew of v.44 is ambiguous. The MT is generally understood to mean that some of the foreign wives even had children, while 1 Esdras makes the meaning unambiguous by stating that the wives were put away.

[328] Williamson, *Ezra, Nehemiah*, 398–99.

[329] Joseph Blenkinsopp, *Ezra–Nehemiah: A Commentary* (London: SCM, 1988) 352.

preference for any of these.³³⁰ Nevertheless, the careful reader can notice these variations and draw the conclusion that even on EN's reckoning the question is not so straightforward, whether the narrator intended to portray this or not.

The position in Ezra 9–10 is further relativized by the wider canon. As noted before, commentators often point to Deut 7, which bans intermarriage on the basis of "moral defilement" (i.e., the threat of idolatry) without recourse to the "holy seed" argument or to the example of Ruth who was accepted due to her commitment to YHWH. Ultimately, the NT's approach to divorce finally "trumps" the solution in Ezra 9–10. This, however, still leaves open the question I noted in connection with Brettler's approach; namely why such a text as Ezra 9–10 was included in the canon at all.

Here the perspective of Ellen Davis on the authority of Scripture is most helpful and her idea, which she terms "critical traditioning," is worth quoting at length.

> It is sometimes implied that the biblical writers' propensity for retention, evident especially in the Hebrew Bible, was a mindless reflex. The tradents were so burdened by the tradition that it made them clumsy; they did not care (nor perhaps even notice) that the juxtaposition of conflicting views makes for labored reading. Or maybe they were afraid to throw anything away; thus the canon evidences something akin to the neurotic compulsion to stuff the basement with old junk. But it seems to me more likely that the preference for retention reflects the author-scribes' understanding that simply throwing away old ideas, even bad ones, is not the most effective way of handling them. For it is easy enough to discard one ideology and replace it with another one, a new idea system devoid of any history. But what distinguishes a tradition from an ideology is just this sense of history. A tradition earns its authority through long rumination on the past. A living tradition is a potentially courageous form of shared consciousness, because a tradition, in contrast to an ideology, preserves (in some form) our mistakes and atrocities as well as our insights and moral victories. Moreover, with its habit of retention, a tradition preserves side by side the disagreements that are still unresolved in the present. So the price that must be paid by those who are (from a biblical perspective) privileged to live within a tradition is accepting a high degree of inherent tension. The possibility open to them, which is not open to committed

---

³³⁰ Contra Blenkinsopp who argues that the omission of divorces in Neh 13:23–27 confirms the failure of the Ezran measures in Ezra 9–10 (*Ezra-Nehemiah*, 352). There are, however, a number of other interpretations possible, such as L. H. Brockington's who sees in the differences proof that Ezra came after Nehemiah historically (*Ezra, Nehemiah and Esther* [CB; London: Nelson, 1969] 19–20), or Williamson's who suggests that Nehemiah's spontaneous reaction and his different treatment of the intermarriage crisis indicate the localised and restricted nature of the problem rather than the fact that Nehemiah's mission preceded Ezra's (Williamson, *Ezra, Nehemiah*, 398). The variety of ways in understanding the differences between the solutions to intermarriage in Ezra 9–10 and Neh 13:23–27 demonstrate my point that the narrator/editor does not portray the differences in order to highlight one preferred solution and critique others.

ideologues, is repentance, the kind of radical reorientation of thinking that the New Testament writers term *metanoia*, literally, "a change of mind."[331]

Davis' juxtaposition of how tradition operates as opposed to ideology is a helpful way of understanding the way the authority of Scripture works. Retaining a tradition such as Ezra 9–10 even if it does not cohere with later conclusions and practices may, as Davis suggests, be a way of preserving unresolved disagreements. The preservation of "dead ends" or "mistakes" within Scripture may also be a safeguard against committing the same errors. As is well known among students of history, those who forget it, tend to repeat its mistakes.

Despite the helpful framework Davis sets, I am hesitant to go as far as calling certain intervening stages in the unfolding of an idea a mistake unless Scripture itself does so. There are aspects that are ambiguous in the Ezran intermarriage solution and certainly the long-term view in Scripture and tradition makes it questionable as a viable option. Perhaps though we should be slow in reaching a final judgment and recognize that with any issue as big as guarding religious commitment and identity there is usually more than one side to the question. Having the opportunity to reflect on different solutions makes one aware that such issues are often not straightforward and each answer to the question may carry its own dilemmas and implications.

As far as Fishbane's inner-biblical exegesis, it is worth noting that while other parts of Scripture exercise a certain amount of indirect critique on Ezra 9–10 and offer solutions other than the one presented there, it is noteworthy that there is no direct reference and re-appropriation of the Ezran material, nor a direct polemic against it. Perhaps this is an indication that the story did not play a crucial role for later readers (due perhaps in part to its position among the "Writings"), and its solution is not addressed elsewhere. It is truly a "dead end" in that respect. At the same time, Ezra 9–10 engages in its own inner-biblical exegesis regarding some pentateuchal texts in the canon. As I argued when discussing Ezra and *ḥērem*, the Ezran solution may be understood as a reinterpretation of the *ḥērem* law where extermination is replaced by divorce (of the women) and expulsion and the confiscation of property (of those Israelites who do not comply with the community's decision—Ezra 10:8). Thus what is often seen as a completely cruel and heartless action may actually be a "softer" option to the harshness of the deuteronomic command if the latter is taken at face value.[332] On the other hand, the re-appropriation of the priestly idea of

---

[331] Ellen F. Davis, "Critical Traditioning: Seeking an Inner Biblical Hermeneutic," in *The Art of Reading Scripture* (ed. Ellen F. Davis & Richard B. Hays; Grand Rapids MI: Eerdmans, 2003) 168–69.

[332] Implied in the above statement is of course the notion that the deuteronomic command in its own context is to be taken at face value rather than understood metaphorically from the start. For the various viewpoints see my exegesis on *ḥērem*. Further, the fact that the extermination of foreign peoples was utterly impracticable as well as impossible to carry out when Judah was a province of Persia is beside the point here, since the narrative does

"holy seed" which is defiled by intermarriage with non-Israelites as set out in Lev 21:15 is not one that endured the test of time.

Although the solution in Ezra 9–10 may have had its own problems, it may also be the case that under certain circumstances such a story opens up and teaches new lessons in unexpected ways. Although in the present climate of inclusivism the benefits of Ezra 9–10 may seem unlikely, yet it is worth considering that for the editors of Mosaic Yahwism the patriarchal religion may have looked similarly problematic and incompatible with their own tradition. Nevertheless, they preserved the narrative and allowed some of the differences to stand.[333] What seemed like a temporary and, from the perspective of the Yahwist, in many respects a superseded form of faithful adherence to God, became in some aspects a model and example for Christianity which in turn reconstrued Mosaic Yahwism as an interlude (Gal 3:15–18). Conversely, Christianity has allowed the material reflecting Mosaic Yahwism to stand recognizing the benefits in that tradition. This is not to say that Christians one day might think that divorcing spouses in a mixed marriage (i.e., the marriage of a Christian and a non-Christian) is the right thing to do, in the same way that adherents of Mosaic Yahwism (or for that matter Christians) did not (do not) think that sacrificing on various altars outside of Jerusalem (e.g., Gen 12:7–8; 13:18; 26:25; 33:20) or setting up a pillar to worship God (Gen 28:18) are practices to be imitated. In all such cases of re-appropriating earlier material, there is a certain amount of abstraction, metaphorical and analogical reading involved. It does mean, however, that the uncompromising faithfulness demonstrated by the exiles at a moment of crisis and accomplished at great personal cost is one that is indeed praiseworthy even if their specific solution is not to be imitated and ethically questionable. Likewise, the effort of the exiles and Ezra to reinterpret the legal tradition in a way that makes the laws of God relevant and applicable to their own time is a principle well worth adopting even if the particular interpretation they favor is not.

To the question of what one can learn positively from the intermarriage crisis of Ezra 9–10 I shall return later. Suffice it to say here in conclusion that Scripture's way of dealing with texts reflects the kind of evaluation necessary for the postbiblical reader and thus it provides an example of how it is to be done. As Ellen Davis puts it, the disagreements within Scripture foster a "critical consciousness."

> The canon offers us a model for how established religious convictions, even those established by authoritative texts, may be challenged and debated within the community of faith. Every biblical writer who departs from the tradition does so by highlighting other neglected elements of the

---

not present the divorces as a "second best" option or a compromise but as the only reasonable and right course to take.

[333] For a fascinating study on this see R. W. L. Moberly, *The Old Testament of the Old Testament: Patriarchal Narratives and Mosaic Yahwism* (Minneapolis MN: Fortress, 1992).

tradition; every innovation is established on an older foundation. From this precedent I take the principle that if we disagree with a certain text on a given point, then it must be in obedience to what we, in community with other Christians, discern to be the larger or more fundamental message of the Scriptures. In other words, disagreement represents a critical judgment, based on keen awareness of the complexity of Scripture and reached in the context of the church's ongoing worship, prayer, and study.[334]

To this question of tradition I shall turn next.

12.2 Lessons from Tradition

Beyond the constraint that the canon places on the interpretation of a difficult passage another way to evaluate a difficult concept within a biblical text is to see what later tradition made of it. Since the "holy seed" rationale is the most controversial aspect of the Ezran intermarriage narrative it is worth considering how it was evaluated beyond the confines of the Bible. Due to its specifically Jewish aspect this notion can only be traced within the Jewish tradition. Nevertheless it may be instructive to see whether the idea stood the test of time and if it did not (as the "holy seed" rationale did not) why this might be so.

12.2.1 The Holy Seed in Rabbinic Tradition

In §6.2.4 I have already indicated something of the history of the "holy seed" rationale, which became prominent in the Second Temple Period in some Jewish literature as a way of combating intermarriage and assimilation. In comparison, it is practically expunged from later rabbinic tradition to the point where Najman can confidently claim that Ezra's interpretation of the pentateuchal laws on intermarriage are authoritative and have not been called into question (see p.165). She is right insofar as rabbinic tradition has not directly associated the holy seed rationale with Ezra 9–10 and therefore had no argument with the story and the person of Ezra. Nevertheless, indirectly the Jewish interpretative tradition has brought its silent judgment to bear in that the ban on intermarriage today is firmly based on Deut 7:3 (*b. 'Abod. Zar.* 36b) and defines the boundary around Israel in ways that are permeable via the route of conversion.

The only trace of the holy seed rationale is evident, according to Hayes, in *b. Yebam.* 76a–77b which discusses whether a blemished priest (i.e., one with crushed testicles) is allowed to marry a female convert.[335] Generally, rabbinic

---

[334] Ellen F. Davis, "The Soil That Is Scripture," in *Engaging Biblical Authority: Perspectives on the Bible as Scripture* (ed. William P. Brown, Louisville KY: Westminster John Knox Press, 2007) 39.

[335] See Christine E. Hayes' illuminating discussion on this (*Gentile Impurities and Jewish Identities: Intermarriage and Conversion from the Bible and the Talmud* [New York: Oxford University Press, 2002] 178–184).

texts prohibit the marriage of a priest with a Gentile even if converted, citing Ezek 44:22, which commands priests to marry virgins of the seed of the house of Israel (e.g., *m. Qidd.* 4:6–7; *m. Bik.* 1:5; *p. Qidd.* 4:6, 66a). However, at the beginning of the discussion in *b. Yebam.* 76a–77b, an Aramaic gloss, which Hayes thinks may not have been original to the question, poses the issue differently.[336] "Does he [the priest] remain in his state of holiness and is he consequently forbidden [to marry a convert] or does he not remain in his state of holiness and is he consequently permitted?" In other words, the ban on a priest's marriage with a Gentile or convert is made contingent here on his state of sanctity rather than on his status as priest. If the genital blemish profanes the priest, then he is no longer holy and therefore can marry a convert. If, on the other hand, he remains holy despite the blemish, then the prohibition continues to stand. Hayes sees in this a resurrection of the Ezran "holy seed" rationale, which she considers to be a fourth century Babylonian amoraim insertion.[337] She theorizes further that the argument may owe something to Ezra's reputation in Babylon and to the emphasis on genealogical purity in Persia.[338]

Hayes is right that the view on which the above rabbinic argument is based is different from the "moral-religious" reason generally associated with Deut 7:3 (the danger of an idolatrous offspring) and clearly distinguished from it.[339] However, it is not obvious that the issue of holiness/profaneness has anything to do with the "holy seed" rationale of Ezra. For one thing, "seed" or any other word for offspring is not mentioned at all in connection with holiness in the argument. For another, the priest with such a blemish may not even be able to procreate, in which case his disputed status of holiness or profaneness is irrelevant from the point of view of the offspring.

Reasons for Its Disappearance

Despite this isolated case, which as we have seen may be disputed as an example of the holy seed rationale anyway, there is considerable leniency in the rabbinic laws on intermarriage.[340] Hayes attributes this to the shift from the importance of lineage to a merit oriented society especially in Palestine, where Torah learning is ranked higher than pure genealogy (e.g., *m. Hor.* 3:8, where a *mamzer* scholar takes precedence over an *am haaretz* [ignoramus] priest).[341]

Beyond the shift that Hayes notes toward merit, it is instructive to consider what else may have led to the elimination of the holy seed rationale

---

[336] Ibid., 179.
[337] Ibid., 184.
[338] Ibid., 184.
[339] *B. Yebam.* 76a compares the case of the genitally blemished priest and the issue of holiness and profaneness with the command in Deut 7:3 and says, "Is the law there [in Deut 7:3] due at all to holiness or profaneness? [It is merely due to] the possibility that he might beget a child who would worship idols."
[340] For a detailed discussion, see Hayes, *Gentile Impurities*, 145–192.
[341] Ibid., 188–191.

from the ban on intermarriage. Reflecting on the sexual interpretation of Lev 18:21, which was often used as an argument against intermarriage, Vermes suggests that the late tannaitic rabbis' disapproval stemmed from an anti-zealot attitude.[342] The Mishnah gave zealots the license to kill those who cohabited with Gentile women ("Whoever... has intercourse with a Gentile woman [lit. Aramean], zealots may attack him" *m. Sanh.* 9:6). However, the Palestinian Talmud explicitly states the sages' disapproval of the above statement as well as Phinehas' deed (*y. Sanh.* 9:11, 27b). Hayes further notes the similar attitude expressed in *b. Sanh.* 82a, which counsels against instructing a zealot to punish a Jew who cohabits with a Gentile woman and which expresses some ambivalence toward Phinehas.[343]

The history of Jewish answers to the dilemma of assimilation in religious and cultural terms from postexilic times onwards shows that the "holy seed" rationale was overall a minority view which gradually disappeared and was overruled by the rabbinic solution that prohibited intermarriage with foreigners, yet allowed for their individual integration by way of conversion. The enduring consensus achieved by Judaism in this respect is a mark of its viability and validity. One may point to a comparably difficult issue that the early church faced regarding the interaction of Gentile and Jewish Christians, where the compromise accepted by the Jerusalem council in Acts 15 is effectively a half-way house between a Jewish and a later Christian view. Standing on an established Christian position in this respect, Acts 15 cannot be seen in isolation from later developments and neither can Ezra 9–10.

12.3 Conclusion

In this chapter I revisited one of the prime concerns of Christian commentators, namely how the emulation of the exiles' action might be limited. Beyond pointing to NT texts in order to achieve this end I aimed to construct a broader understanding of how the relationship between biblical texts and the wider canon works. I built here on the concept of "critical traditioning" introduced by Davis (the idea that already within Scripture existing traditions are re-assessed, transformed and re-appropriated) and examined the interrelationship between Ezra 9–10 and the Christian canon. This then created a model for the way postbiblical traditions continued the evaluating process and I considered specifically how rabbinic tradition handled the controversial "holy seed" rationale.

---

[342] Vermes, "Leviticus 18:21 in Ancient Jewish Bible Exegesis" in *Studies in Aggadah, Targum, and Jewish Liturgy in Memory of Joseph Heinemann* (ed. Jacob J. Petuchowski and Ezra Fleischer; Jerusalem: Magnes, 1981) 122.

[343] Hayes, *Gentile Impurities*, 155. "What is more, had Zimri forsaken his mistress and Phinehas slain him, Phinehas would have been executed on his account; and had Zimri turned upon Phinehas and slain him, he would not have been executed, since Phinehas was a pursuer [and Zimri acted in defense of his life]." (*b. Sanh.* 82a)

We have seen that both the canon and tradition move away from the kind of exegesis and understanding that the Ezran story demonstrates. This may teach us that there are ways that seem right under certain circumstances but prove to have serious implications, which the original participants may not have anticipated; implications that make the solution a dead end that needs to be abandoned.

13

NT Perspective: 1 Cor 7:12–16

So far I have considered Christian and Jewish interpretations of the Ezran intermarriage crisis, as well as the constraints that the Christian canon places on Ezra 9–10. Here I wish to think further about 1 Cor 7:12–16, which is the main counterpart to Ezra 9–10 and practically the only text in the New Testament that speaks explicitly of intermarriage.[344]

It may be argued that the Corinthian example is a different scenario and it is. The exiles have always been a part of God's people and made a decision to intermarry as such, whereas the Corinthian Christians found themselves in their present dilemma because they became Christians at some point *after* their marriage. However, the two situations are not that different if the exiles were not aware at the time of their marriage that this was wrong. The ban on intermarriage in the form it is advocated with all foreigners is without precedent elsewhere in the OT and the sin may have been committed in ignorance. If so, the exiles could not have averted the disaster and in this sense, the story has parallels with the Corinthian Christians' plight. Both groups face a *fait accompli* and it is instructive to see how it is handled in each case. To be sure the differences in the treatment of the problem arise from the differences in the two situations. Nevertheless, there are sufficient parallels between the two accounts to make a comparison a worthwhile enterprise.

The question behind such an investigation is to reflect on the way religious distinctiveness and intermarriage are approached in the NT and what the continuities and discontinuities are between the Ezran account and 1 Cor 7:12–16. It is hoped that such a comparison will further enrich an understanding

---

[344] To the interpretation of 2 Cor 6:14–7:1, which is often used as justification against Christian—non-Christian marriages I shall return later. Although I will argue that the "unequal yoke" may be applied to mixed marriages as a general principle, the text itself is not explicit about its referent. In fact, it may allude to a number of different partnerships not necessarily to do with marriage and is contextually more likely to refer to partnerships other than marriage (see further in §13.6).

of Ezra 9–10 and give a broader Christian perspective than a simple enumeration of constraints might do.

The overall meaning of 1 Cor 7:12–16 is fairly clear and is undisputed by commentators. Paul is giving instruction regarding mixed marriages where one partner is a "brother" or "sister" (ἀδελφός/ἀδελφή—v.15), that is, a Christian and the other an "unbeliever" (ἄπιστος—v.12), that is, a non-Christian. In light of his later statement to widows that if they remarry they should do so "only in the Lord" (μόνον ἐν κυρίῳ—v.39), it is safe to assume that the marriages in question here were contracted when both partners were still "unbelievers," one of which in the course of time has become a Christian.[345] Paul's ruling for this case in 1 Cor 7:12–13 is that a Christian should not seek divorce, but if the unbelieving spouse wants to initiate the procedure he or she should be allowed to do so (v.15).

The key verse which gives the reason for allowing the mixed marriage to continue comes in v.14.

ἡγίασται γὰρ ὁ ἀνὴρ ὁ ἄπιστος ἐν τῇ γυναικί καὶ ἡγίασται ἡ ἄπιστος ἐν τῷ ἀδελφῷ· ἐπεὶ ἄπα τὰ τέκνα ὑμῶν ἀκάθαρτά ἐστιν, νῦν δὲ ἅγιά ἐστιν.	For the unbelieving husband is sanctified through his wife, and the unbelieving wife is sanctified through her believing husband; for otherwise your children are unclean, but now they are holy. (NASV)

Paul's explanation why divorce is not necessary in such a case has some striking parallels with the arguments derived from the "holy seed" in Ezra 9:2, although the apostle seems to turn the categories of Ezra 9–10 on their head. Both texts deal with exogamy (though defined differently), both are concerned with issues of pollution and holiness, both recognize that intermarriage affects the status of the offspring. However, in Ezra 9:2 the implication is that the "foreign" women "defile/profane the holy seed," whereas in 1 Corinthians the believing spouse "sanctifies" (ἁγιάζω) the unbelieving partner so that the children are not unclean (ἀκάθαρτα) but holy (ἅγια—v.14). In other words, in Ezra 9:2 it is the "outsider" partner who has an adverse effect on the descendants especially, whereas in 1 Cor 7:14 it is the "insider" spouse whose beneficial influence overcomes that of the "outsider" the result of which is the holy status of the children.

The scholarly discussion centers on two questions in particular: the nature of "sanctification" and how it is communicated to the unbeliever. Paul's statement is seen as peculiar for two reasons. First, it is generally thought that the way he employs sanctification here is markedly different from the way he

---

[345] This is indeed the majority view of scholars based more on the overall content of the chapter than on the specific Greek expression. For a discussion of views see Antony C. Thiselton, *The First Epistle to the Corinthians: A Commentary on the Greek Text* (Grand Rapids MI: Eerdmans / Carlisle: Paternoster, 2000) 604.

views the concept elsewhere.[346] Namely, it is assumed that his use in this verse has closer affinities with a "ritual" understanding in that "sanctification" is passed on seemingly through physical (or rather sexual) contact and it is sometimes thought as "contagious."[347] Elsewhere, Paul speaks of holiness and sanctification in "relational" terms, that is, in the sense of belonging to God as his people (e.g., Rom 1:7; 1 Cor 1:2) or in a "moral" sense calling Christians to an ethical way of living (e.g., Rom 6:19; 12:1–21; 2 Cor 1:12; 1 Thess 3:13; 4:3–5). Secondly, this "ritual" view, if it is indeed that, departs significantly from the priestly legislation of the OT which does not allow for the extension of holiness in this way.[348] Rather, it is the impure and the profane which affects the pure and the holy (e.g., Hag 2:11–13).

Beyond the unusual view of sanctification there is a further noteworthy feature of 1 Cor 7:12–16. Paul's tone in discussing the issue is surprisingly placid and conciliatory compared to his passionate rhetoric addressing matters of grave concern in the Corinthian church, such as sexual immorality (e.g., 1 Cor 5:1–5; 6:12–20) or his defense of his own conduct in Corinth (1 Cor 9:1–14). Further, his instruction in 7:39 "only in the Lord" is almost like an afterthought, which, along with the smooth flow of the argument, leads Webb to conclude that intermarriage was not "an area of intense personal conflict between Paul and the Corinthians."[349]

Christians, like the returned exiles in Ezra, were a minority in a sea of alien cultures, and the threat to religious commitment in a mixed marriage would have seemed an obvious one. The fact that Paul's instruction to marry "only in the Lord" (v.39) is not more emphatic as well as the overall tone of his

---

[346] E.g., Gordon D. Fee, *The First Epistle to the Corinthians* (Grand Rapids MI: Eerdmans, 1987) 299; C. K. Barrett, *A Commentary on the First Epistle to the Corinthians* (2nd ed.; London: Adam & Charles Black, 1971) 164, Alistair S. May, *"The Body for the Lord:" Sex and Identity in 1 Corinthians 5–7* (London: T&T Clark International, 2004) 227, Yonder M. Gillihan, "Jewish Laws on Illicit Marriage, the Defilement of Offspring, and the Holiness of the Temple: A New Halakic Interpretation of 1 Corinthians 7:14," *JBL* 121/4 (2002) 715.

[347] Not all agree with this view but it is nevertheless the most striking aspect of the passage on a first reading. For a detailed review and critique of the various scholarly views see §§13.2 and 13.3.

[348] There is some debate whether there is precedent for holiness to be "contagious" in the way Paul uses it here to which I shall return in §13.4. Jacob Milgrom argues that originally *sancta* was seen to be contagious to persons as well as things (although for the former such contagion meant death—e.g., 2 Sam 6:6–7; Exod 19:13, etc.). This tradition is retained in Ezek (e.g., 46:20; 44:19 cf. 42:14) but revised in the priestly legislation so that, Milgrom contends, קדשׁ in Exod 29:37; 30:26–29 and Lev 6:11, 20 refers to things, not people (cf. also Hag 2:11–13). See his excursus "Sancta Contagion" (*Leviticus 1–16: A New Translation with Introduction and Commentary* [AB 3; New York: Doubleday, 1991] 443–456.

[349] William J. Webb, *Returning Home: New Covenant and Second Exodus as the Context for 2 Corinthians 6.14–7.1* (JSNT SS 85; Sheffield: JSOT Press, 1993) 208.

argument may simply indicate that the Corinthians required no convincing on the dangers of intermarriage; rather they may have needed to be persuaded that in this exceptional case intermarriage was acceptable.

Another factor that may have contributed to the mild tone and conciliatory solution is the innocence of those involved in the dilemma since it is the conversion of one spouse that creates this impossible situation. At the same time, it should make us ponder what Paul's priorities were in taking great pains to provide a theory that held marriage partners together, innocent or not, despite what might be thought of as a risk to religious allegiance. Moreover, it is worth noting that Paul does not merely argue that the believer remains immune to the negative influence of the unbeliever but assigns the believer a more strongly active role of influencing the unbeliever. If Ezra and his group created a rationale that inexorably led to separation with all foreigners then Paul aimed at achieving the opposite by reversing a similar argument.

In order to think further about the above questions I shall first look at the Jewish and Hellenistic background for intermarriages, examine the possible meaning of "sanctification" and how it works, what might be Paul's precedent for such thinking and consider what prompted Paul to take such a view in the first place.

13.1 Jewish and Hellenistic Background

The concern over exogamy and its association with defilement was widespread at the time, both from a Jewish and a Hellenistic perspective. The former became a matter of considerable importance from postexilic times onwards using often similar reasoning to Ezra 9–10 and the "holy seed" rationale there (see *Jub.* 30, 4QMMT (B75–82), *T. Levi* 9:9–10). Beyond the Jewish objection against intermarriage which we see in the literature referred to above (see also *b. Qidd.* 68b; *b. Yebam.* 45a), there were also Hellenistic voices, (Jewish and non-Jewish) which similarly deplored mixed marriages (religiously, ethnically, socially defined) and linked it with the idea of pollution. Here Deming proves particularly helpful in painting a picture of the social-ideological background of 1 Corinthians and providing analogies for the dislike of exogamy and the use of defilement in connection with it.[350] He mentions in passing the Roman polemic against new religions which are considered to destroy marriages (pp.136–37), although he finds closer parallels with 1 Cor 7 in the wisdom tradition of Ben Sira and the Stoic writings of Philo, as well as other non-Jewish Stoics. Deming shows, for instance, the similarities of language between Sir 13 and 2 Cor 6:14–7:1 (p.137).

> Whoever touches (ὁ ἁπτόμενος) pitch will be defiled, and whoever associates (κοινωνῶν) with a proud man will become like him. (13:1) (RSV)

---

[350] Will Deming, *Paul on Marriage and Celibacy: The Hellenistic Background of 1 Corinthians 7* (2nd ed.; Grand Rapids MI: Eerdmans, 2004) 136–144.

> Will a wolf have fellowship with a lamb?—so also a sinner with a pious man.
>
> What peace does a hyena have with a dog?—and what peace does a rich man have with a poor? (13:17–18) (NRSV)

Admittedly, there is no talk of intermarriage here, rather, the idea of association with the "wrong sort" and consequent defilement. On the other hand Sir 25:16–26 specifically discusses the evils of having a wicked wife concluding with the advice to separate from her "if she does not go as you direct" (NRSV v.26). Similarly, as Deming points out (p.138), the expression "being unequally yoked" (ἑτεροζυγοῦντες) in 2 Cor 6:14 is reminiscent of Sir 26:7 which speaks of the evil wife as a "rolling ox-yoke" (βοοζύγιον σαλευόμενον) evoking the image of two mismatched oxen with the yoke bobbing painfully up and down. In discussing the holy seed rationale in §6.2.3 I have already referred to Sir 25:8, which again uses the image of a yoke and ploughing with an ox and an ass to depict a "mismatched" marriage. This is clearly biblical language from Deut 22:10 which is re-used for supporting the argument against "mixed" marriage.

Equally, non-Jewish Stoic writers are concerned with the topic of association with outsiders in social interaction, friendship and in marriage. For instance, Deming refers to Musonius, who similarly describes marriage as a "yoke" (ζεῦγος) and says that if the marriage partners lack a common goal and one spouse refuses to "pull together with his or her yoke-partner" (ὁμόζυγος), then the couple ends up separating completely.[351] It is also noteworthy, as Deming himself points out on the same page (fn. 153), that Musonius' use of (ὁμόζυγος) ("one of like-yoke") chimes in with 2 Cor 6:14's use of ἑτεροζυγοῦντες ("being yoked differently").

As far as the idea of defilement and sanctification, Deming quotes Stoic philosophers such as Epictetus to show that social interaction with "outsiders" was considered to be defiling (Diatr. 3.16.1–6).

> We ought to enter cautiously into such social intercourse with laymen, remembering that it is impossible for the man who brushes up against the person who is covered with soot to keep from getting some soot on himself.[352]

Deming also refers to Philo's application of the term "unclean" to laymen as opposed to the wise and concludes that this is done under Stoic influence.[353]

---

[351] Musonius, frag. 13A.88.15, 24–29 L. (68.2, 13–19 H.) cited in Deming, *Paul on Marriage*, 144.

[352] *Epictetus: The Discourses as Reported by Arrian, the Manual, and Fragments* (ed. and trans. W. A. Oldfather; 2 vols.; LCL; Cambridge/London: Harvard University Press/Heinemann, 1959) 2:105, 107 cited in Deming, *Paul on Marriage*, 139.

[353] "[The wise have] opened up a new pathway, in which the outside world can never tread, ... and have brought to light the ideal forms which none of the unclean may touch." Philo, *Prob.* 3–4 (*Philo* [trans and ed. F. H. Colson; 9 vols; LCL; Cambridge/London:

Although Deming primarily assumes Hellenistic thought from philosophy to form the background of 1 Cor 7 we have also seen that Jewish texts of the Second Temple Period are similarly concerned with avoiding exogamy and connect intermarriage with defilement; texts which have a strong rooting in biblical notions of intermarriage and purity laws as well. Thus these ideas had common currency in both a Jewish and a Hellenistic setting.[354]

Moreover, Paul as a Roman citizen and diaspora Jew himself, in addition to being a well-educated Pharisee who studied "at the feet of Gamaliel" (Acts 22:3) in Jerusalem, could very likely move between Hellenistic philosophies and his own Jewish faith seamlessly. No doubt he was able to incorporate into his own explanations any concepts that might be helpful for his readers whether Jewish or Gentile.

Although the composition of the Corinthian congregation is debated,[355] it is reasonable to assume that even if one group dominated in Corinth, the church was not homogeneous. Thus whether the Corinthian concern was feeding on Jewish and biblical or Hellenistic and philosophical ideas, the fact that the concepts and the language were known in both contexts could make Paul's answer intelligible and meaningful for both groups of people.

We see then that intermarriage as well as other close contacts between outsiders and insiders (however defined) was seen as dangerous expressed in the idea of defilement. This background underlines the contrast between the general suspicion against mixed marriages and Paul's peaceable tone in the specific case explained in 1 Cor 7:12–16.

It is worth noting that there is an obvious difference between Hellenistic (Greek and Jewish) and non-Hellenistic Jewish examples in the mode of defilement envisaged. The former seem to use defilement (see earlier examples of dirt or soot) as a metaphor or symbol of negative "moral" influence through close association. What is at issue is social interaction, not physical contact per se. Put another way, the Hellenistic perspective emphasizes the "mental/religious/philosophical" incompatibility of "insiders" and "outsiders" whether in casual contact, friendship or marriage, and the image of soot or dirt one gathers by "rubbing up against the wrong person," as it were, is just that: an image or illustration of an abstract reality. In contrast, non-Hellenistic (and

---

Harvard University Press/Heinemann, 1929) 9:11, 13 cited in Deming, *Paul on Marriage*, 140.

[354] Martin Hengel in particular shows that Judaism and Hellenism are not two neatly distinguishable lines of tradition in the NT period despite the fact that NT scholars have often over-polarised the two. His book makes it clear that all Judaism was also Hellenistic (*Judaism and Hellenism: Studies in their Encounter in Palestine during the Early Hellenistic Period* [2 vols.; trans. John Bowden; London: SCM, 1974).

[355] E.g., Gillihan argues for a substantial Jewish contingent in Corinth ("Jewish Laws," 712–13, fn.6). Thiselton on the other hand concludes that "to assume a significant Jewish population in Corinth goes beyond the evidence" (*The First Epistle to the Corinthians*, 527).

largely sectarian) Jewish literature, such as *Jubilees*, 4QMMT or Ezra, conceives of the foreign influence as communicated specifically by physical or rather sexual contact. As mentioned before, 1 Cor 7:14 reverses the process of defilement into a process of sanctification but the question how this is transmitted to or bestowed on the unbeliever remains. To this I shall now turn, looking at both the issue of how sanctification is to be understood and also how it is communicated.

13.2 The Nature of Sanctification

The scholarly literature on the interpretation of sanctification in 1 Cor 7:14 is vast and without any consensus. Although the explanations commentators give are often difficult to classify combining several aspects, for the sake of simplicity and in order to gain an overview I shall group them around four categories: sanctification in a ritual (1), moral (2), or relational sense (3), or denoting a licit union (4).

13.2.1 Ritual?

The sanctification of the unbeliever is often understood as a ritual category described variously as "ceremonial," "ritualistic," or "cultic" and this is mainly deduced from the impression that holiness is "contagious" through physical contact, proximity or the sexual union and affects entrance into and/or participation in the believing community's life. One of the clearest expressions of this is by Collins.

> Were the children of the Corinthian neophytes not to participate in the holy condition of their parents they would be "unclean," that is, ritually impure. Use of this term implies that Paul's idea of the holiness of mixed marriage retains the cultic overtones of holiness language that has been present in his letter since 1:2. Holiness means belonging to God. It describes what is according to God's plan and design.[356]

And again later,

> The contrast with "holy," a cultic term, is "unclean," *akatharta*, a word that occurs elsewhere in the Pauline corpus only in a quotation of Isa 52:11 (2 Cor 6:17). Paul's notion of "holiness" is cultic rather than ethical.[357]

Similarly, Morris speaks of ceremonial uncleanness with reference to ἀκάθαρτα as something that cannot be brought into contact with God.[358]

---

[356] Raymond F. Collins, *First Corinthians* (Sacra Pagina 7; Collegeville MN: The Liturgical Press, 1999) 267.
[357] Ibid., 271.
[358] Leon Morris, *The First Epistle of Paul to the Corinthians: An Introduction and Commentary* (2nd ed; TNTC; Leicester: IVP / Grand Rapids MI: Eerdmans, 1985), 107.

Likewise, Evans comments on the meaning of the word thus: "Unclean, ἀκάθαρτα, in the ritual sense of profane, unsanctified or ritually defiled so as to be incapable of entering the sanctuary."[359] Grosheide also observes that "Unclean reminds us of ceremonial impurity among the people of Israel. It is the opposite of 'holy' and refers to people who are not connected with the church of God."[360]

Apart from these more obvious examples most commentators do not address specifically the issue whether the holiness discussed in v.14 is "ritual" or not. The only clues that might hint at a ritual or ritualistic understanding are the comments that speak of the way in which holiness or impurity is communicated as a "contagion" through physical contact (see §13.3 for details).

Despite the similarities, there are several reasons why ritual purity is unlikely to be the issue in 1 Cor 7:14. First, as Klawans argues, at this time ritual impurity of Gentiles is a questionable concept in its own right.[361] Attributing it to a non-Christian is even more doubtful. Secondly, Paul is nowhere else concerned with ritual purity; in 1 Cor 6:13–19, where the Christian's body is compared to the temple, the issue is clearly (sexual) immorality (πορνεία). The only other passage which might be conceived as discussing "ritual impurity" is 2 Cor 6:14–7:1 because of its reference to Isa 52:11 and the call to "purify ourselves from all defilement of flesh and spirit" (καθαρίσωμεν ἑαυτοὺς ἀπὸ παντὸς μολυσμοῦ σαρκὸς καὶ πνεύματος—7:1). However, the rhetorical questions in 2 Cor 6:14–16 with the word pair of δικαιοσύνη and ἀνομία ("righteousness" and "lawlessness") place the context in the "moral-religious" realm. Although the other word pair ναός θεοῦ and εἴδωλα ("the temple of God" and "idols") may be read as "ritual" categories, again the ritual impurity of idols is a debated concept which is again a later rabbinic innovation.[362]

Finally, and perhaps most importantly, the logic of ritual impurity simply does not work for the text. Had the unbeliever not been sanctified, the children would be ἀκάθαρτά, "unclean." What then is the status of the unbeliever before he or she is "sanctified?" The status of the children would indicate that he or she is "unclean." But if the unbeliever is ritually unclean, which is passed on to the children, how is it possible that the believing spouse is not affected by the uncleanness? Moreover, how can the unbeliever move from

---

[359] Ernest Evans, *The Epistles of Paul the Apostle to the Corinthians in the Revised Version with Introduction and Commentary* (The Clarendon Bible; Oxford: Clarendon, 1930) 96.

[360] F. W. Grosheide, *Commentary on the First Epistle to the Corinthians: The English Text with Introduction, Exposition and Notes* (NICNT; Grand Rapids MI: Eerdmans, 1953) 165.

[361] Jonathan Klawans, "Notions of Gentile Impurity in Ancient Judaism," *AJS Review* 20/2 (1995) 285–312.

[362] For a detailed discussion on the topic see Christine E. Hayes, *Gentile Impurities and Jewish Identities: Intermarriage and Conversion from the Bible and the Talmud* (New York: Oxford University Press, 2002) 215–221.

ritually impure to sanctified status? Purification is necessary before sanctification. Further, the ritual theory collapses entirely when we consider that ritual impurity calls for rites of purification and nothing of the kind is mentioned in 1 Cor 7:14. In any case, ritual impurity is a temporary condition which can be remedied unless, of course, it is understood to be *inherent*, on the analogy of the supposed inherent ritual impurity of Gentiles. If, however, Paul sees the impurity of the unbeliever as inherent then there is no remedy for it and hence purification and/or sanctification from the condition is a contradiction in terms.

13.2.2 Moral?

The second alternative for understanding sanctification in v.14 is one which attributes moral-ethical content to the term although it is taken in two directions. The first represented uniquely by Murphy-O'Connor ascribes to the unbeliever a certain measure of moral-ethical attitude demonstrated by the person's willingness to remain in the marriage, which is in accordance with God's will and divine plan (Gen 2:24 "one flesh" and the Lord's command not to divorce).[363] This qualifies him to be recognized as sanctified even as an ἄπιστος and the children are equally considered to be "holy" because presumably they "assimilate the behavior pattern of their parents."[364]

Murphy-O'Connor's solution is attractive because it lines up the meaning of sanctification here with Paul's usage elsewhere. The main objection one might raise against his view is that it locates the reason for sanctification entirely in the unbeliever, whereas the text uses the verb ἁγιάζω in the passive and the agent of the sanctification (if ἐν is instrumental) or the reason for it ("on account of," "united with," "in association with") is the believer.[365] If Paul had wanted to say that the unbeliever's attitude to marriage allowed for his sanctification he could have said something like "If the unbeliever agrees to remain in the marriage, then he is sanctified..."

Equally questionable is his assumption that the children's "holy" status is justified on the assumption that they imitate their parents' good moral behavior, since experience suggests that children's attitude may vary considerably from that of their parents despite good models seen at home.

The second sub-case under the "moral" heading shifts the emphasis away from the behavior of the unbeliever and on to the "moral" influence of the Christian spouse, which affects both the unbeliever and the children.[366] While the assumption that the believer's attitude will affect his or her family is a reasonable one, the effects of such influence are uncertain. Paul's statement on

---

[363] Jerome Murphy-O'Connor, "Works without Faith in I Cor., VII, 14," *RB* 84 (1977), 356.
[364] Ibid., 361.
[365] BAGD, 260, III, 3a.
[366] E.g., Thiselton, *The First Epistle to the Corinthians*, 530; Gregory J. Lockwood, *1 Corinthians* (Concordia Commentary; Saint Louis MO: Concordia, 2000) 242; Craig S. Keener, *1–2 Corinthians* (NCBC; Cambridge: Cambridge University Press, 2005) 65.

the other hand leaves no doubt about the sanctified/holy status of the non-Christian and the children. Thus a "moral-ethical" understanding of sanctification does not seem to fit the passage particularly well either.

13.2.3 Relational?

The third strand of interpretation sees the unbelieving spouse's sanctification as a "relational" category. The unbeliever is somehow "counted" with the believer and this concept is often traced to the notion of corporate solidarity. The clearest example of this view is Thrall's, who even translates "is sanctified" (ἡγίασται) in v.14 as "belongs to,"[367] and explains her choice to do so thus:

> The non-Christian partner himself (or herself) belongs to God's people by virtue of the marriage relationship. "*For the heathen husband now belongs to God through his Christian wife, and the heathen wife through her Christian husband.*" This is probably based on the idea which we find in the Old Testament that the family as a whole is like a single personality. What happens to one member of the family happens to all the other members as well, and what one member does he does representatively on behalf of the whole family, so that they are all involved in the consequences, whether good of bad.[368]

What might such belonging entail when it is not accompanied by salvation? Parry makes a useful distinction here between God's prior claim and possible call and the person's subsequent response, which still allows for a negative human response despite God's initiative (see v.16 "For how do you know, O wife, whether you will save your husband?").[369] The added advantage of such a relational view is that there is some precedent for this in Paul's usage of "holiness" in Rom 11:16 where he designates all (unsaved) Israel as holy on the basis of the "firstfruits" (Jewish Christians) with the expectation and hope of salvation in the long term.[370] There is a similar distinction latent in the notion of children's baptism, namely that God has set apart/has a prior claim on the offspring of Christian parents and therefore they can be baptized (Acts 16:34) despite the lack of personal profession of faith (cf. Acts 8:37).[371]

---

[367] Margaret E. Thrall, *The First and Second Letters of Paul to the Corinthians* (CBC; Cambridge: Cambridge University Press, 1965) 51.
[368] Ibid., 53.
[369] John Parry, *The First Epistle of Paul the Apostle to the Corinthians in the Revised Version with Introduction and Notes* (Cambridge: Cambridge University Press, 1916) 73.
[370] Noted also by Fee, *The First Epistle to the Corinthians*, 300–301.
[371] Although the earliest manuscripts do not contain this verse, which underlines the need for faith and gives a formulaic confession of faith, it is clear from the context that the Ethiopian official understands and affirms the gospel. Moreover, Philip's action of baptising him is an answer to the rhetorical question in v.36 ("What prevents me from being baptised?").

This is a more convincing solution to the interpretative crux in 1 Cor 7:14 than either the "ritual" or "moral" option, although there is one possible difficulty. Namely, if the unbeliever is counted with the believer on the basis of "representation" or "corporate solidarity" what makes the Christian partner the decisive member? If it is the automatic result of the Christian spouse being a Christian then would the same principle apply when a marriage is contracted between a Christian and a non-Christian? This would diminish an argument against marrying a non-Christian and would clash with the notion in 2 Cor 6:14–7:1 that close alliance with an ἄπιστος inevitably affects a Christian adversely.[372]

13.2.4 Licit union?

A fourth trend related and overlapping with the third sees sanctification of the spouse as a way of saying that the marriage is a licit one. Calvin, for instance, argues for sanctification in this sense, that is, that it shows the lawful nature of the marriage and guarantees the protection of the Christian spouse from contamination.

> While this *sanctification* is taken in various senses, I refer it simply to marriage, in this sense—It might seem (judging from appearance) as if a believing wife contracted infection from an unbelieving husband, so as to make the connection unlawful; but it is otherwise, for the piety of the one has more effect in sanctifying marriage than the impiety of the other in polluting it. Hence a believer may, with a pure conscience, live with an unbeliever, for in respect of the use and intercourse of the marriage bed, and of life generally, he is sanctified, so as not to infect the believing party with his impurity. Meanwhile this *sanctification* is of no benefit to the unbelieving party; it only serves thus far, that the believing party is not contaminated by intercourse with him, and marriage itself is not profaned.[373]

---

[372] This argument does not depend on the exact meaning of ἄπιστος or ἑτεροζυγοῦντες although I shall argue below that the former refers to unbelievers and the latter in its present context possibly to partnerships other than marriage (see §13.6). The point is that 2 Cor 6:14–7:1 demonstrates a direction of influence predominant in the OT from the "unholy/unclean" toward the "holy/clean."

[373] John Calvin, *Commentary on the Epistles of Paul the Apostle to the Corinthians* (trans. John Pringle; Grand Rapids MI: Baker, 2005) 241–42. A similar view is expressed by Goudge, who equally interprets ἡγίασται as a reference to the marriage, although his understanding is based more on the corporate solidarity of the family and does not explicitly deal with contamination. "The consecration spoken of is not personal consecration, but consecration for the purpose of the marriage union, so that there remains nothing in it contrary to Christian holiness. This is just what the Christian partner would need to know. God looks on the family as a corporate whole, and it takes its character in His sight from the Christian member of it." H. L. Goudge, *The First Epistle to the Corinthians with Introduction and Notes* (London: Methuen & Co, 1903) 56.

What is unclear in Calvin's formulation is the nature of the contamination feared. The Christian partner's piety which overcomes the non-Christian's impiety is a moral-religious category. At the same time the pollution which is feared, yet blocked by such piety is according to Calvin at least partly expressed in physical terms such as "the use and intercourse of the marriage bed."

A particularly illuminating proposal is put forward by Gillihan, who argues that Paul borrows Jewish betrothal language where the same expression "to sanctify" (—ב קדשׁ Piel cf. Paul's ἁγιάζω ἐν) is used in the sense of "to betroth," which presupposes the pre-marital status of the future spouses as eligible for marriage.[374] This insight he applies to the Corinthian situation.

> A pressing concern of the members of the Corinthian congregation seems to have been that they not be in forbidden marriages; for this to happen both partners had to be sanctified, that is, legally eligible. By ruling that the unbelieving spouse is sanctified by the believer, Paul effectively ruled that mixed marriages are, in fact, licit. Thus, in 7:14 the meaning of ἡγίασται is "is sanctified" in the sense of "is eligible" for licit marriage to a believer.[375]

Hayes, who is fundamentally in agreement with Gillihan's main argument, points out the difference between Paul and rabbinic betrothal terminology underlining thereby the instrumental role of the believer.

> Paul also employs an instrumental preposition (ἐν) when he writes that the unbelieving spouse becomes betrothed (is rendered eligible for a valid marriage) *by* or *through* the believing spouse.
>
> However, in the rabbinic cases, the object of the instrumental preposition is always the legal mechanism—the item or act—by which the betrothal becomes valid: an act of cohabitation, a gift of a certain minimum value, or a written document, for example. In rabbinic sources the object of the instrumental preposition is never the spouse. One may become legally betrothed *to* (*l-*) a person but not *by* (*b-*) that person. Yet Paul does not say that the unbeliever becomes eligible for licit marriage (ἡγίασται) *to* the believer. He says that the unbeliever becomes eligible for licit marriage *by* the believer. [...] It would seem that Paul really does mean to say that the unbeliever is sanctified in the sense of *being made holy* (and *therefore* fit for union with a believer) by his or her association with the believer.[376] [emphasis hers]

The main objection to this view is that Jewish betrothal language might be too obscure for Gentile readers of Paul's letter to understand. While this is a

---

[374] Gillihan, "Jewish Laws," 718. See also Collins who observes in passing the similarity between Jewish betrothal language and Paul's formulation in 1 Cor 7:14. Collins, *First Corinthians*, 266.
[375] Gillihan, "Jewish Laws," 716.
[376] Hayes, *Gentile Impurities*, 95.

valid point, there are also other examples where Paul uses obscure illustrations from Jewish Haggadah, such as the reference to the ἀκολούθουσα πέτρα (1 Cor 10:4), the rock that followed the Israelites in the wilderness, mentioned also in *t. Sukkah* 3:11.[377] Moreover, if this was a specific concern of some people rather than a widespread and severe problem then it is even possible that the questioners were themselves Jewish Christians. Gillihan and Hayes particularly note the Jewish concern of the time that illicit marriages (including exogamy) generate moral impurity.[378] If so, then Paul responded to them with terminology that was particularly apt. In any case, even if they were not Jewish, we have seen the way exogamy was viewed as somehow polluting even within the Gentile-Hellenistic world, which would have made the apostle's response intelligible.

The advantage of this proposal is that it allows for a distinction between a mixed marriage as set out in 1 Cor 7:12–16 and one where a Christian knowingly enters into marriage with a non-Christian. It is the licitness and acceptability of the marital union for a Christian that drives the process of "sanctification" rather than merely the status of a Christian as a Christian.

13.3 How Sanctification Is Transmitted

Theories abound concerning the mode in which sanctification is communicated in 1 Cor 7:14 and it is difficult to put the various scholarly views into categories as there is considerable overlap between the ideas. Neither can the mode of transmission be ordered neatly according to the way scholars view the nature of holiness. Nevertheless, for the sake of convenience I shall group them in five different categories: sanctification as (1) "physical contagion," (2) as a "sphere," (3) by "association," (4) as "moral influence" and (5) by "ascription." As a general trend, a "ritual" view of holiness often corresponds with "physical contagion" as a means by which it is seen to spread; while in the case of the "moral influence" or the "ascription" theory, transmission of holiness is conceived as more abstract.

---

[377] Gillihan, "Jewish Laws," 742 fn.96.

[378] Ibid., 727–28., Hayes, *Gentile Impurities*, 92. Hayes highlights the perspective of some Second Temple literature (*Jubilees*, 4QMMT), which understood illicit sexual unions including intermarriage as *zĕnût* (Gr. *porneia*) and she takes Paul's use of *porneia* in this sense in 1 Cor 6:15–20. Ibid., 92–93. (See also Ibid., 250 n.2.) She describes the impurity that Paul is concerned about in intermarriage as "carnal impurity," that is, the contamination that comes from the marital union of an impure (non-Christian) and a pure (Christian) body. Hayes bases this on the analogy of the "genealogical impurity" that she discerns in Ezra 9:2 but notes that Paul's focus is on "bodies" rather than "seeds." However, this seems to read too much into the passages in question (esp. 1 Cor 6:15–20). It is better to take the meaning of *porneia* in 1 Cor 6:15–20 as "sexual immorality" indicating in this particular case sexual intercourse with a prostitute (πόρνη) rather than in the sense of intermarriage between a believer and an unbeliever. See also Gillihan, "Jewish Laws," 728 fn.52 for a brief but useful comment.

The physical contagion idea echoes ways in which ritual impurity is understood in the Old Testament and conceives of sanctification in 1 Cor 7:14 to work in a similar transferable way.[379] A step away from the explicitly "physical" view envisages holiness as a "sphere," in which the unbeliever's ability to contaminate is blocked,[380] and the believer may influence his or her spouse in a way that leads to salvation.[381] Some also link this notion with family solidarity.[382] A number of scholars speak about "holiness by association"[383] some of whom, like Barrett, explicitly argue against a physical or quasi-physical view.[384] I have already discussed the moral influence theory (see §13.2.2 on p.190), which detaches the communication of holiness completely from any physical ideas of "contagion." Finally, the notion of "ascription" [*Zuordnung*] originating with Delling replaces the notion of transmission.[385] The "holy" status of the unbeliever is attributed by virtue of the status enjoyed by the Christian spouse. It is *as if* the unbeliever belonged or was in the covenant. Although the actual words "ascribed holiness" are not used by commentators, a "relational" understanding of holiness such as "belonging to God" (Thrall) could equally fit in with this idea (see also §13.2.3). A more obvious example for ascription is the view that understands holiness to refer to the marriage (e.g., Calvin, Gillihan, Hayes).

It is difficult to decide on how one should view the way in which holiness is communicated and much depends on how one understands the nature of holiness in the first place. No matter which solution one chooses, the common

---

[379] E.g., Richard B. Hays, *First Corinthians* (Interpretation; Louisville KY: John Knox Press, 1997) 121; Hans Conzelmann, *1 Corinthians: A Commentary on the First Epistle to the Corinthians* (trans. James W. Leitch; Hermeneia; Philadelphia PA: Fortress, 1975) 121.

[380] E.g., Archibald Robertson and Alfred Plummer, *A Critical and Exegetical Commentary* (ICC; Edinburgh: T&T Clark, 1911) 141–2; David E. Garland, *1 Corinthians* (BECNT; Grand Rapids MI: Baker Academic, 2003) 288.

[381] Robertson and Plummer, *A Critical and Exegetical Commentary on the First Epistle of St Paul to the Corinthians*, 141–42; Brian S. Rosner, *Paul, Scripture and Ethics: A Study of 1 Corinthians 5–7* (Leiden: Brill, 1994) 170.

[382] Rosner, *Paul, Scripture and Ethics*, 170; James Moffatt, *The First Epistle of Paul to the Corinthians* (MNTC; London: Hodder & Stoughton, 1938) 82. Also Garland, who cites Rosner on this (*1 Corinthians*, 289). Thrall equally mentions family solidarity although the way she works this out is not in terms of a power-sphere or influence but as a kind of representation (*The First & Second Letters*, 53).

[383] Evans, *The Epistles of Paul*, 96; Collins, *First Corinthians*, 266.

[384] Barrett, *A Commentary on the First Epistle*, 165. Thrall might be another example for this view, although she does not explicitly describe her theory of holiness as association.

[385] Gerhard Delling, "Nun aber sind sie heilig," in *Studien zum Neuen Testament und zum hellenistischen Judentum: Gesammelte Aufsätze 1950–1968* (ed. Ferdinand Hahn et al.; Göttingen: Vandenhoeck & Ruprecht, 1970) 92–93, cited in Hans Conzelmann, *1 Corinthians: A Commentary on the First Epistle to the Corinthians, Hermeneia* (trans. James W. Leitch; Philadelphia PA: Fortress Press, 1975), 122, fn.33.

denominator in all these (except perhaps Murphy-O'Connor's) is that the Christian spouse and his or her holy status play a decisive role in dealing with the feared impurity of the unbeliever. Holiness is thus more powerful than impurity.

At this point, some commentators become somewhat triumphalistic. For instance, Goudge writes that "The teaching is a witness to the power of grace. Ezra might demand the putting away of heathen wives (Ezra x.), since among the Jews it could not be hoped that good would triumph over evil; in the Church it is otherwise."[386] Similarly Conzelmann argues (without the negative comparison with Ezra) that "Through the believing partner, the marriage between a pagan and a Christian is withdrawn from the control of the powers of the world. In living together with the world, the "saints" are the stronger party."[387]

Along similar lines Christian teachers or preachers sometimes trace this reversal to Jesus' attitude to the unclean, his willingness to touch the leper in order to heal while not getting contaminated himself, etc. I am not convinced, however, that this adequately explains what is happening. First, we do not know whether touching in the process of healing uncleanness was in any way unique to Jesus or if other healers of the time were doing that as well. It does not occasion surprise or comment from the crowds in the Gospels, although this argument from silence is not conclusive. Secondly, there is no indication that Jesus was unaffected by touching the ritually unclean. For all we know, he may have become ritually unclean, but, as we have seen, this was considered a minor impurity, not sinful and easily rectified. Thirdly, even if we assume that Jesus' holiness was unaffected by uncleanness, it is not clear whether this is due to his status as Son of God and therefore a unique phenomenon or one that is shared by Christians who follow him. Finally, a major objection to all of these suggestions is that it assumes an automatic immunity and positive influence by virtue of the Christian status, whereas in 2 Cor 6:14–7:1 Christians are specifically called to be separate and warned against exposing themselves to the adverse influence and effects of unbelievers.

However, the fact remains that in 1 Cor 7:14 holiness is claimed to be more powerful than impurity and it is necessary at this point to ask where Paul could have found precedent for such a view.

13.4 The Precedent for Paul's Thinking

The predominant scholarly view is that Paul's interpretation in 1 Cor 7:14 is unique in that it overturns the OT idea of defilement threatening holiness and argues instead that the latter overpowers the former.

First, there are those who find the parallel to Paul's thinking in proselyte baptism. While this view is echoed by several commentators, Jeremias

---

[386] Goudge, *The First Epistle*, 56.
[387] Conzelmann, *1 Corinthians*, 122.

is the most prominent representative of it and his concise explanation is worth quoting here.[388]

> Judaism distinguishes between children who were begotten and born "not in holiness" (i.e. before conversion to Judaism), and children who were begotten and born "in holiness" (i.e. after conversion to Judaism). The former were baptized when the parents changed their religion; the latter were not. [...] Anyone who was born "in holiness" did not need the baptismal bath. This terminology of the law concerning proselytes is adopted in I Cor. 7.14c, when Paul says that the children of Christian parents are not "unclean," but "holy."[389]

The objection against this view is that the children are effectively considered "holy" if they had been born *after* the parents have converted, whereas the issue in 1 Cor 7:14 is precisely the fact that one parent is not a Christian.

A second possible source for the logic of 1 Cor 7:14 is suggested by Martin building on Sanders' work and claiming that holiness may be transmitted by proximity.[390] He refers to the technique discussed by the rabbis whereby drawn water may be purified by contact with pure water. Gillihan in his critique, however, notes that the analogy is misleading because the actual process of purification is not by mere contact but by commingling (ערוב) to the point where the two types of water are indistinguishable (cf. *m. Miqwa'ot* ch.6). The analogy with 1 Cor 7:14 breaks down because Paul does not talk about purification but sanctification and the believer need not join the community of believers to be sanctified.[391]

An example for the idea that the "holy" can somehow "purify" the "unholy" is presented by Deming, who mentions Philo's reflection on the significance of the fact that Levitical cities were granted for fugitives, although Deming does not actually quote Philo.[392]

> But it is worth while to consider, in no passing manner, why he granted the cities of the Levites to fugitives, thinking it right that even these, who appear entirely impious, should dwell with the most holy of men. Now these fugitives are they who have committed, unintentionally, homicide.

---

[388] Others who refer to the analogy of proselyte baptism with agreement are, e.g., Rosner, *Paul, Scripture and Ethics*, 170; Moffatt, *The First Epistle of Paul*, 82; Collins, *First Corinthians*, 267; scholars against it, e.g., Barrett, *A Commentary on the First Epistle*, 165; Deming, *Paul, Scripture and Ethics*, 130–31. fn.94.

[389] Joachim Jeremias, *Infant Baptism in the First Four Centuries* (London: SCM Press, 1960), 46–47 cited in Gillihan, "Jewish Laws," 739. For a critique on Jeremias see Gillihan, "Jewish Laws," 740.

[390] Dale B. Martin, *The Corinthian Body* (New Haven CT: Yale University Press, 1995) 293 n.57; E. P. Sanders, *Judaism: Practice and Belief 63 BCE—66 CE* (Philadephia PA: Trinity Press International, 1992) 226.

[391] Gillihan, "Jewish Laws," 738–39 fn.84.

[392] Deming, *Paul, Scripture and Ethics*, 140.

> First of all, therefore, we must repeat what is consistent with what has been said, that the good man is the ransom of the worthless one, so that they who have sinned will naturally come to those who have been hallowed, for the sake of being purified; [...].[393]

This is an interesting, though at a closer inspection, not so convincing example. Philo places purification in parallel with "ransom." Earlier he talks about the wise man as a physician of the soul, who can help "preserve those who are not on the point of being utterly destroyed by the wickedness in them."[394] Thus, it seems that the sense of what he is saying has more to do with "moral" reform or improvement of the "worthless" through good example on the one hand, and intercession of the wise for the sparing of the "wicked" on the other (e.g., Abraham's intercession for Sodom), rather than with what is at issue in 1 Cor 7:14.

A fourth way of thinking that is much closer to the issue of mixed marriages, and to my mind more convincing, is suggested by Gillihan. As described earlier, he understands "sanctification" as language referring to the licitness of the marital union and finds an analogy for this in the similarity of the betrothal idiom. The underlying logic can be expressed in the simple formula: "'saint' (male or female member of the holy community) + legal ('sanctified') partner → holy offspring; 'saint' + illegal partner → defiled, impure offspring, *mamzerim*."[395] Gillihan argues that the decisive factor for Paul is the Lord's command not to divorce, which in effect makes the mixed marriage contracted before the conversion of the Christian spouse retrospectively valid. In his words,

> We might say that the Pharisaic/rabbinic betrothal idiom has come under the influence of the commandment of the Lord against divorce, so that licitness of marriage is now judged on the basis of the indissolubility of the marital bond (by the believer) rather than on the basis of the premarital status of each spouse.[396]

There is one other aspect worth considering here, which chimes in with Gillihan's solution, although it may not be a direct precedent for Paul's thinking. Nevertheless a Christian reader may find the comparison illuminating. Milgrom in discussing the priestly purity system notes a peculiar fact about the sin (חטאת) and guilt (אשם) offerings, which are commanded to be eaten by the priests. In discussing the significance of this Milgrom says,

> Because the purification and reparation offerings are exclusively expiatory and the cereal offering, partially so [...], there is a strong possibility that they had to be eaten by the priests in order to complete the expiatory process. But the purification offering, uniquely among the piacular *[sic]* sacrifices, absorbs the impurities of the sanctuary and hence presents a

---

[393] Philo, *Sacrifices* xxxviii (128).
[394] Ibid., xxxvii (121–23).
[395] Gillihan, "Jewish Laws," 738.
[396] Ibid., 719.

> potential danger to its priestly handlers, not to speak of its priestly consumers. [...]
>
> Moreover, it is precisely because the purification offering is associated with impurity that its ingestion by the priest becomes so crucial. The priest is the personification of holiness, the *ḥaṭṭā't* is the embodiment of impurity. In the Priestly symbolic system (fully developed in H), holiness (*qĕdûšâ*) stands for life whereas impurity (*ṭum'â*) stands for death [...]. When the priest consumes the *ḥaṭṭā't* he is making a profound theological statement: holiness has swallowed impurity; life can defeat death. This symbolism carries through all of the rites with the purification offering. The priest is unaffected by daubing blood on the altar, though the blood is absorbing impurity (4:13–21, 22–35; [...]). The trepidation of the high priest feels when entering the adytum on Yom Kippur is not due to the virulent impurity that has been implanted there but, to the contrary, because of the virulent holiness of the Ark (16:2, 13). Indeed, not only does he effect the removal of all the sanctuary's impurities, he also transfers them (together with Israel's sins) onto the head of a live goat by means of a hand-leaning ritual—yet he emerges unscathed [...].[397]

We see then that there is precedent for the holy to overcome the impure even within the OT system but there is an added condition. After all, the priests can be defiled in the same way as the people when they are outside the temple. It is worth quoting Milgrom again.

> Impurity pollutes the sanctuary, but it does not pollute the priest *as long as he serves God in the sanctuary*. H applies this teaching to the people at large. As long as they live a life of holiness and serve God by obeying his commandments, they can overcome the forces of impurity-death.[398]

This is where the comparison with the case in 1 Cor 7:12–16 becomes interesting. Namely, Christians in an intermarriage described in 1 Cor 7:12–16 are in this situation through no fault of their own. In staying within the marriage and thereby complying with the principles set out by Jesus concerning it, believers are doing right and thus they (as well as the offspring) are protected. Such a view, however, does not allow for triumphalism, since this kind of "immunity" is only granted to those within the will of God. Thus Christians who marry a non-Christian cannot expect to be protected from the consequences of their disobedience (1 Cor 7:39; 2 Cor 6:14–7:1) and do well to heed the warning against alliances that might jeopardize their relationship to God.

13.5 A Clash of Laws: The Priorities

The last two analogies, Gillihan's suggestion of Jewish betrothal language, as well as the one from the priestly purity system highlight the

---

[397] Jacob Milgrom, *Leviticus 1–16: A New Translation with Introduction and Commentary* (AB 3; New York: Doubleday, 1991) 638.
[398] Ibid., 638–9.

importance of marriage as the key aspect of this NT passage. It is the high view of marriage which makes Paul take this unusual understanding of "sanctification" in Gillihan's construal and it is the obedience to God's will in marriage which provides the "immunity" from impurity in the analogy with the priestly purity system. This emphasis on marriage would explain what motivates Paul to defend such "intermarriages" when we have seen that the fear of exogamy is a general concern both in the Gentile Hellenistic and the Jewish world of the time and we would expect it to be a threat for the new Christian minority as well.

It also fits in well with the overall thrust of the chapter, which is primarily concerned with avoiding rash disruptions to existing ties and obligations rather than with intermarriage per se or even religious distinctiveness. The drift of Paul's argument in 1 Cor 7 is best summed up in the statement of v.24: "Brethren, each one is to remain with God in that condition in which he was called." (NASV) Thus he counsels against couples living as if they were not married (depriving one another) (vv.1–7), against the widows and the unmarried getting married (again) unless they feel compelled by their drive (vv.8–9) and the married getting a divorce (vv.10–11); a warning of which our passage is a special sub-case (vv.12–16). He even widens the scope of this concept encompassing other aspects such as slavehood (vv.21–24). The apostle affirms prior commitments and obligations entered into before conversion even as he cautions against taking on further ones. The guiding principle, however, remains his wish that the Corinthians might be "free of concern" (ἀμερίμνους—v.32) and that they might have "undistracted devotion to the Lord" (εὐπάρεδρον τῷ κυρίῳ ἀπερισπάστως—v.35).

As argued earlier, 1 Cor 7:12–16 is unlikely to have been intended as a direct reflection on Ezra 9–10, yet canonically it still functions in this way. The call for religious distinctiveness is in tension with the high view of marriage that Jesus advocates in such passages as Matt 19:19 and parallels. The way the difficulty is dealt with suggests the underlying priority in Ezra 9–10 and in 1 Cor 7:12–16. The former opts for religious distinctiveness over marriage, while the latter places stronger emphasis on safeguarding the marriage. The priority of each drives the argument and conversely the direction the argument takes indicates the priority.

When there is a clash of laws, one has to take precedence and it is up to the discernment of the decision-maker which one is seen to be weightier. The examples in Scripture are numerous. The incest of Tamar with her father-in-law, Judah, is seen in the story as the lesser evil compared to his unfulfilled obligation to give her his son in levirate marriage (Gen 38). When Jephthah made a foolish vow he considered it irrevocable even if it meant the human sacrifice of his own daughter (Judg 11:29–40), while Saul's men prevailed upon the king to spare his son Jonathan's life even though he unknowingly broke Saul's enforced vow (1 Sam 14:43–46). Jeremiah considered lying to the king's officials preferable to betraying a weak and fearful ruler to their suspicions (Jer 38:24–28). The examples perhaps best known from the NT are the ones Jesus cites in his arguments with the Pharisees: David and his men eating the Bread of the Presence unlawfully to preserve life (1 Sam 21:1–6 cf. Matt 12:3–4), saving an animal from the pit on the Sabbath (Matt 12:11; Luke 14:5) and the priests working in the temple on the Sabbath (Matt 12:5). In the first two the well-being of God's creatures overrules religious principles, in the last one religious duties to God (serving in the temple) take precedence over the rest principle for humans.

What motivates Paul's decision to choose keeping the marriages together as his priority? Clearly, Jesus' divorce sayings have something to do with it but there is also another aspect to the question which is driven primarily by the church's calling in contrast to that of Israel. The latter's primary concern was to be holy, set apart, while the former was given the mission to go and make disciples of all the nations (Matt 28:19). A part of such an active commission was also an attitude that aimed at attracting rather than unnecessarily antagonizing those it wanted to reach. Thus there are a number of admonitions that concern behavior toward outsiders, such as leading a quiet lifestyle and earning a living "so that you will behave properly toward outsiders and not be in any need." (1 Thess 4:11–12). Similarly Col 4:5 instructs its readers, "Conduct yourselves with wisdom toward outsiders, making the most of the opportunity."

We see this same concern in 1 Cor 7:15, where Paul frees the believer from the obligation to keep the marriage together if the unbeliever wants to divorce (v.15) with the principle that "God has called us to peace." This same principle is expressed in Rom 14 where the apostle advises his readers concerning matters of conscience regarding the distinction between clean and unclean foods. In his concluding remarks he then says, "So then we pursue the things which make for peace and the building up of one another." (Rom 14:19) While the Romans text discusses not causing stumbling for the weaker believers, 1 Cor 17:15 has a similar concern toward the unbeliever who may be alienated by the unbending attitude of the Christian, either by not letting the unbeliever go or by rejecting him or her. Of course, Paul takes an interest in the welfare of both parties and his advice is meant to free the Christian from worry. Thus we see a flexibility built into Paul's reply which provides a stark contrast to the rigidity of the Ezran solution.

While we can only speculate on Paul's possible response to a situation similar to Ezra 9–10, commentators generally agree that he is unlikely to have advised divorce even then. If this is so, then Paul's prioritizing is not entirely dependent on the Corinthians' innocence and may have a wider significance. In fact, if we re-think the categories, there is a meaningful lesson to be learnt from the comparison with Ezra. Rather than simply seeing the priorities as religious distinctiveness versus the sanctity of the marriage, it may be understood as the clash between the pledge made to God (in this case religious distinctiveness, being holy, etc.) and to other people (to the spouse, i.e., no divorce; and living in peace with an unbeliever, i.e., allowing him or her to leave the marriage).[399] By contrast, in the Ezran solution there is no recognition that there might be another commitment that clashes with the religious one. This is typically a problem in zealous individuals (such as young Christians) or groups (for instance, sects), which often do not give validity to any other consideration beyond faithfulness to God. Perhaps in an age like ours when humanistic concerns are central and religious reasons are often considered suspicious what might be seen as a "humane" treatment of the intermarriages in question is particularly appealing. Yet paradoxically, even though an outward-looking missional consideration focuses on humans, ultimately it has God and his love for the world at its centre and in this sense it is different from modern humanistic concerns which exclude God from the equation altogether. This God-centeredness that incorporates human-centeredness should also make us ponder the fact that true God-centeredness does not make one less but more human and more concerned with the well-being of the world that God loves.

13.6   2 Cor 6:14–7:1

The one text in the NT that seems closest to the separatist tendencies of Ezra 9–10 is 2 Cor 6:14–7:1. It is also one that has a rather strong polemic very different in tone from the peaceable tenor of 1 Cor 7:12–16. In fact, it does not seem to fit very well with its surrounding context either. 2 Cor 6:13 finishes off with Paul's request to the Corinthians to open their hearts to him and picks up the same thread of thought in 7:2 again. The intervening verses call for what seems like rigid separation, which, as many observe, are strongly reminiscent of the vocabulary and separatist ideas of Qumran.[400]

This break in the flow of Paul's argument has led to questions about the Pauline authorship of 2 Cor 6:14–7:1 and about the way the text fits or does not fit with its context.[401] Apart from authorship and contextual integration, the two

---

[399] The marriage commitment actually incorporates both areas in that it may be seen as a vow made before God and therefore holy, as well as a commitment to the spouse. Yet Paul's concern is primarily focused on the people involved.

[400] E.g., J. A. Fitzmyer, "Qumrân and the Interpolated Paragraph in 2 Cor. 6.14–7.1," *CBQ* 23 (1961), 271–80; J. Gnilka, "2 Cor. 6.14–7.1 in the Light of the Qumran Texts and the Testaments of the Twelve Patriarchs," in *Paul and Qumran: Studies in New Testament Exegesis* (ed. J. Murphy-O'Connor; Chicago: The Priory, 1968) 48–68; N. A. Dahl, "A Fragment and its Context: 2 Corinthians 6.14–7.1," in *Studies in Paul: Theology for the Early Christian Mission* (Minneapolis MN: Augsburg, 1977) 62–69. Against a Qumranic influence Jerome Murphy-O'Connor found parallels between 2 Cor 6:14–7:1 and Philo ("Philo and 2 Cor 6.14–7.1," *RB* 95 [1988] 55–69). Others take a mediating position recognising the influence of Qumran and positing that Paul is using here a tradition composed by a Christian of Essene background. E.g., Ralph P. Martin, *2 Corinthians* (WBC 40; Waco TX: Word, 1986) 193.

[401] Generally those who hold to a Pauline authorship attempt to show the passage's integration, while those who consider the text non-Pauline are more likely to see it as an

main questions regarding the meaning of the text are who the "unbelievers" (ἄπιστοι) are and what the "unequal yoking" (ἑτεροζυγοῦντες) refers to.[402] There is no scope within this book to explore all these questions, thus I confine myself here to some general comments and a specific consideration whether the passage refers to intermarriage at all.

First, authorship does not make much difference for my considerations as I am reading the text within its present canonical context rather than in isolation although my own preferred view is that the passage is Pauline despite

---

interpolation. Among those who hold a non-Pauline authorship are Fitzmyer, Gnilka, Dahl (see fn.400), H. D. Betz takes the extreme position that the text is actually anti-Pauline ("2 Cor. 6.14–7.1, An Anti-Pauline Fragment?," *JBL* 92 [1973] 88–108). Scholars who argue for Pauline authorship are, e.g., Margaret E. Thrall, "The Problem of II Cor. VI.14–VII.1 in Some Recent Discussion," *NTS* 24 (1977) 132–48; Gordon D. Fee, "II Corinthians VI.14–VII.1 and Food Offered to Idols," *NTS* 23 (1977) 140–61. An in-between view is held by some who argue that Paul is using here a pre-existent tradition or fragment. E.g., V. P. Furnish, *II Corinthians* (AB 32A; Garden City NY: Doubleday, 1984) 359–83; Martin, *2 Corinthians*, 189–212; F. G. Lang, *Die Briefe an die Korinther* (NTD 7; Göttingen: Vandenhoeck & Ruprecht, 1986) 308–11 and Jerome Murphy-O'Connor, "Relating 2 Corinthians 6.14–7.1 to Its Context," *NTS* 33 (1987) 272–75.

[402] The dominant view re the ἄπιστοι is that the word has the technical sense of non-Christian (cf. 1 Cor 6:6; 7:12–15; 10:27; 14:22–24, etc.). Representatives are, e.g., Furnish, *II Corinthians*, 359–83; Fee, "II Corinthians VI.14–VII.1," 140–61; H. Windisch, *Der zweite Korintherbrief* (Göttingen: Vandenhoeck & Ruprecht, 1924) 211–20; F. F. Bruce, *1 and 2 Corinthians* (NCB; Grand Rapids MI: Eerdmans, 1971) 213–16; Thrall, "The Problem of II Cor. VI.14–VII.1" 132–48; P. E. Hughes, *The Second Epistle to the Corinthians* (NICNT; Grand Rapids MI: Eerdmans, 1962) 241–60. Other views take the referent of the word to be the false apostles/Paul's opponents (e.g., N. A. Dahl, "A Fragment and its Context: 2 Corinthians 6.14–7.1," in *Studies in Paul: Theology for the Early Christian Mission* [Minneapolis MN: Augsburg, 1977] 62–69), the untrustworthy among the Corinthian Christians (J. D. M. Derrett, "2 Cor. 6, 14ff. a Midrash on Dt 22,10," *Bib* 59 (1978) 231–50) or the immoral who live like non-Christians (e.g., R. H. Strachan, *The Second Epistle of Paul to the Corinthians* [5th ed.; MNTC; New York: Harper, 1948] xv, 3–4; J. C. Hurd, *The Origin of 1 Corinthians* [2nd ed.; Macon: Mercer University Press, 1983] 235–39). Re the meaning of ἑτεροζυγοῦντες the most common position takes it to refer to mixed marriages although not necessarily exclusively so (e.g., Martin, *2 Corinthians*, 197; A. Plummer, *A Critical and Exegetical Commentary on the Second Epistle of St Paul to the Corinthians* [ICC 34; Edinburgh: T&T Clark, 1915] 206; Strachan, *The Second Epistle of Paul*, 5; Thrall, *The First and Second Letters of Paul*, 156; Hughes, *The Second Epistle*, 245). Other suggestions include eating meat sacrificed to idols in pagan temples or in a pagan's home (e.g., Hughes, *The Second Epistle*, 246; Martin, *2 Corinthians*, 197; Bruce, *1 and 2 Corinthians*, 214), visiting temple prostitutes (e.g., Barrett, *A Commentary on the Second Epistle to the Corinthians* [London: A&C Black, 1973] 196; Murphy-O'Connor, "Philo and 2 Cor 6.14–7.1," 68), taking lawsuits to pagan judges (e.g., Barrett, *A Commentary on the Second Epistle*, 196, Hughes, *The Second Epistle*, 245; Martin, *2 Corinthians*, 189), business partnerships with unbelievers (e.g., Windisch, *Der zweite Korintherbrief*, 214, Martin, *2 Corinthians*, 197).

the difficulties of incorporation into the flow of Paul's argument before and after. Secondly, I am inclined to opt for the position that the text can be integrated into the context (even if the transition is not entirely smooth). Namely, it is hard to see why an editor would insert such a passage into the middle of an argument that has no relation to it.[403]

Among the integration theories Webb's detailed study is particularly interesting as it examines the links not only with the passage's immediate context in chapter 6 but also within the larger unit of 2 Cor 2:14–7:4.[404] He traces the theme of exodus and new covenant throughout and concludes that the flow of thought makes logical sense despite the seeming contradiction between opening the heart to Paul and separation. His synthesis is worth quoting in full:

> New covenant and exilic return imagery thread the pieces together: as a servant of the new covenant, Paul stands between God and the Corinthians with a message of "new things" patterned after the exodus paradigm and centered on the restoration of the cosmos to God (5.16–21). He expresses the urgent need that "now" is the time for their reception/home coming (6.1–2). He has cleared away any obstacles in their path (6.3–10). He has "enlarged his heart" in anticipation of their return and calls on them to do likewise (6.11–13; cf. 7.2–4). And finally, like the *"ebed"* [i.e. the Isaianic Servant], he prompts their return with the cry for a new exodus ("Come out from...") and with promises related to their home coming (6.14–7.1)— just as he will welcome them as his children, so will their covenant God make them his sons and daughters. Through skillful use of return traditions, both inside and outside the fragment, Paul effectively parallels the Corinthians' need to return to him as apostle with their need to return to God.[405]

Put this way, there are some striking similarities between Ezra 9–10 and 2 Cor 6:14–7:1. In §3.2.2 of Ezra 9–10 and its context I noted resonances of the first exodus out of Egypt and a similar call for "coming out from Babylon" and separation for the sake of preserving the covenant. Both OT and NT texts above are anxious about idolatry and a compromised allegiance to God.

The next question to clarify is whether the "unequal yoking" (ἑτεροζυγοῦντες) in 2 Cor 6:14 is a reference to intermarriage. In fact, among the interpretations advocated for the "unequal yoking" the most enduring one is that it is to do with intermarriage (see fn.402). This view is supported by a number of considerations. First, the imagery of yoking is a familiar one for marriage (see examples in §13.1) and is certainly a close bond that could adversely impact the believer if he or she is married to a non-Christian. Secondly, the obvious connection between the unequal yoke and idolatry in 2 Cor 6:14, 16 makes intermarriage a likely interpretative option, since the

---
[403] This is an argument often advanced against treating the passage as an interpolation. E.g., Martin, *2 Corinthians*, 194; Fee, "II Corinthians VI.14–VII.1," 142.
[404] Webb, *Returning Home*.
[405] Ibid., 158.

association of intermarriage and idolatry is a well-known one that surfaces most prominently in Solomon's and Ahab's story in 1 Kings and is hinted at in Ezra 9–10 as well. Thirdly, it has a long-standing tradition in Christian interpretation, which does not necessarily make it right but certainly adds weight to its claim.

On the other hand, the most obvious difficulty with it is that it makes the passage even more out of place within its immediate and wider context. Why this sudden jump from an appeal to the Corinthians to open their hearts to the question of intermarriage? Moreover, this is not an issue that is raised elsewhere in the Corinthian correspondence and as I mentioned earlier in agreement with Webb, the tone of 1 Cor 7 is conciliatory, which makes it unlikely that intermarriages were a serious problem in Corinth.

Moreover, as Webb rightly argues, it seems that the Corinthians are already in such unacceptable partnerships with unbelievers. For one thing, the effects are felt by Paul prior to his warning (they are restrained toward him—6:12) and Paul's appeal to cleanse themselves (7:1) again implies an already existing association. If the issue is intermarriage, then the logic of Paul's argument would demand divorce ("come out of their midst"—6:17).[406] This, however, is highly unlikely considering the high view of marriage in Jesus' divorce sayings and the solution suggested in 1 Cor 7:12–14, which is at pains to avoid divorce.

Although there are some good reasons why one should consider the "unequal yoke" to be about intermarriage, there are also serious arguments speaking against it. It is more probable from the overall Corinthian correspondence that the problem is connected to idolatry in the form of participation in pagan temple feasts and sexual immorality with temple prostitutes, since these are recurring issues in Corinth and Paul deals with them elsewhere using similar language and arguments (incompatibility of union with the Lord and with demons: 1 Cor 10:14–22; temple imagery in connection with sexual immorality: 1 Cor 6:12–20).[407]

Despite my argument that 2 Cor 6:14–18 is not about intermarriage if interpreted within its present context of 2 Corinthians, I wish to retain the appeal of v.14 to intermarriage in another sense. Namely, the admonition not to be in union with unbelievers that jeopardize the believer's covenant relationship with God is a general principle that may be applied more widely than just in the specific cases envisaged within the Corinthian context as we know it. Thus *exegetically* the interpretation of the unequal yoke as intermarriage does not seem feasible but *applicationally* it may be included among the unacceptable

---

[406] This, I believe, is Webb's strongest argument against the "unequal yoke" referring to intermarriage (Ibid., 207).

[407] Ibid., 204, 210. A further reinforcement for Webb's view that the yoking is a reference to temple prostitution and idolatry is the use of the Hebrew verb צמד in Num 25:3 (lit. "they yoked themselves to Baal-Peor"), although the LXX's use of τελέω does not bear out the connection. I thank Robert Hayward for drawing my attention to the use of the Hebrew צמד here. Personal communication.

alliances. However, the canonical constraints need to be born in mind; namely that divorce is most likely not envisaged in such a case despite the call in v.17 to "come out of their midst." Thus we have here a counter-point to the peaceable tone of 1 Cor 7:12–16, which does draw a line for separation and rejects compromise.

13.7 Conclusion

The discussion on 2 Cor 6:14–7:1 shows that religious distinctiveness continues to be important, however its relationship with intermarriage becomes more nuanced such that in the special case where one spouse becomes a Christian after the marriage (1 Cor 7:12–16) the direction of influence is reversed. Thus it is not the Christian spouse who is contaminated but the non-Christian who is sanctified. In my assessment of various options as to the nature of sanctification I found a relational view or one that expressed the licitness of the marriage more convincing than a "ritual" or "moral" understanding. I suggested that the precedent for Paul's thinking may lie in Jewish betrothal language (Gillihan). I also argued that there might be a parallel for the reversal of the direction of influence evident in 1 Cor 7:12–16 in the priestly purity system where the priests serving in the temple enjoyed immunity from impurity despite handling and even eating sacrifices that absorbed impurity. By analogy, those Christians who inadvertently found themselves exposed to "non-holy/impure" influences through their marriage were protected by virtue of their position as being in the will of God. This, however, should in no way lead to Christian triumphalism as Paul's severe warning in 2 Cor 6:14-7:1 demonstrates. Paul's reasoning and concession in 1 Cor 7 were most likely driven by Jesus' high view of marriage and by the church's calling for mission while the Ezran priority was obviously religious distinctiveness and holiness expressed in separation. I also suggested that if one re-conceptualizes the priorities as commitment to God versus to other people (the spouses) then there may be a lesson learnt from the way Paul takes into consideration the human element while not forgetting faithfulness to God, while the Ezran solution does not recognize any other allegiance than the one due to God.

14

Insights from Anthropology and a Contemporary Case Study

So far, I have attempted to explore interpretations of Ezra 9–10 from various angles looking at both the interpretative traditions within Christianity and Judaism and the text's place within the wider canon. In this chapter I shall go further and consider what our contemporary world, its understanding and solutions might bring to this ancient story. In order to do this I shall consider how the "holy seed" rationale functions and what its focus of interest is in anthropological terms building on Mary Douglas' work. Further, I shall look at the Roman Catholic position on intermarriage and compare its resolution and focus with the Ezran view. The reasons for these particular choices are as follows.

Although anthropology is often utilized in throwing light on exegetical issues and these explorations might have found a place in the first half of the book, my decision to include them here is based on two arguments. First, Part I stays broadly within the world of the text and its categories and it felt to me more logical to move from the ancient text, interpretations, traditions and solutions toward the contemporary world, its interpretation and solutions gradually broadening the circle. Secondly, I am using anthropological insights specifically to enhance a Christian reading and application of the Ezran story rather than to throw light on exegetical issues within the text. Thus again, it made sense to include these observations here in the second part of the book where I am reflecting on the implications of the story's meaning for Christians today.

Evaluating anthropological insights on Ezra 9–10 could be the subject of a book in itself and it is not my purpose here. My aim is to construct a hermeneutical framework for reading difficult texts. Thus what I wish to demonstrate through an example is how contemporary insights in our understanding of the world may illumine the reading of this difficult ancient story. Undoubtedly there is much more out there that I could have chosen to engage with but my intention within the limitations of this book is to illustrate rather than treat exhaustively.

For a Christian biblical scholarship that is predominantly Protestant in its roots my choice of the RC position on intermarriage may seem an unusual one. The reason for this is that I wanted to consider how contemporary mainstream Christianity deals with the dilemma of intermarriage that was comparable to the rabbinic and the Ezran solution. The Protestant position is by its very nature more fragmented, informal and individualistic, as well as more difficult to trace without an obvious written source for guidelines. Thus the extent to which Protestants criticize mixed marriages varies and the way such marriages are defined (i.e., who counts as an "unbeliever") is vague since it focuses on an internal state of "faith" rather than on external signs and expressions of that faith. Further, disapproval is expressed in informal ways without any long-established written church policy and does not, on the whole, have any automatic consequences for either the "believer" in the marriage or the children. Much is left to the conscience of the individuals in question. Neither are there any safeguards put in place for the protection of the Christian/believing spouse or the children from the adverse effects of an "unbelieving" partner/parent. Thus, it seems more fruitful to compare the Ezran position with that of the Roman Catholic Church since its criteria and policies are more tangible. Again, the selection of one solution among many options is due to the purpose of my inquiry, which is illustrative rather than exhaustive.

14.1 The "Holy Seed" Rationale: A Hedge

I have already shown in my exegesis (see Chapter 7 esp. §7.5) that the "holy seed" argument was a secondary reason to bolster the "moral-religious" motivation for separation. I wish to reflect further on this and propose that the holy seed argument functions in Ezra 9–10 as "a hedge around the Law," an extra boundary to protect Israel's religious concerns. Mary Douglas in her book *Purity and Danger* explores the connection between moral and "pollution" rules.[408] She reasons that moral situations are often hard to define by which she means that what is morally right or wrong is not always clear-cut and black-and-white but involves a lot of grey areas, whereas pollution rules are unequivocal. She theorizes that pollution beliefs can support the moral code in four ways.

> (i) When a situation is morally ill-defined, a pollution belief can provide a rule for determining *post hoc* whether infraction has taken place, or not.
>
> (ii) When moral principles come into conflict, a pollution rule can reduce confusion by giving a simple focus for concern.

---

[408] Mary Douglas, *Purity and Danger: An Analysis of Concepts of Pollution and Taboo (London: Routledge and Keegan Paul, 1966; repr., London: Routledge Classics, 2002)* (London & New York: Routledge Classics, 2002), 160–172.

(iii) When action that is held to be morally wrong does not provoke moral indignation, belief in the harmful consequences of a pollution can have the effect of aggravating the seriousness of the offence, and so of marshalling public opinion on the side of the right.

(iv) When moral indignation is not reinforced by practical sanctions, pollution beliefs can provide a deterrent to wrongdoers.[409]

Although Douglas does not apply these insights to EN, the "holy seed" rationale can be seen in Ezra 9:2 as a means to buttress the "moral" case, namely that intermarriage with foreigners will lead to apostasy and other "moral" evil. It is unclear what the spiritual status of these "foreign" wives was and ambiguous to what degree they could and would influence their husbands for the worse, if at all. Israel of course had plenty of discouraging examples among her kings whose idolatrous practices, divided loyalties or ultimately their apostasy drew down YHWH's judgment of exile on the nation's head. At the same time, the legislation directly mentioning a ban on intermarriage does not discuss mixed marriages with *all* foreigners, only with the seven Canaanite nations (Exod 34:12–16; Deut 7:1–3); neither does it provide guidance as to what needs to be done once intermarriages occur. Thus the case for moral ambiguity is set. The shifting of the moral issue onto the ground of holiness as physical separation makes the ambiguous area into a question of "yes" or "no." It is more difficult to gauge one's moral commitment and much easier to decide on the issue of physical descent, which allows the problem to be dealt with in a "black-and-white" albeit ruthless fashion.

Further, as Douglas notes, pollution beliefs can marshal "public opinion on the side of the right" especially when morally wrong action does not provoke suitable indignation. Again, Douglas does not relate these observations to the Postexilic Period and the narrative of EN, yet the recurring problem of weakened allegiance to YHWH seen as a result of foreign influences suggests that conviction in this respect was flagging and required reinforcement. The lack of internal commitment created the need for firmer external boundaries.

It is easy to understand how the exiles came to be a community characterized by the above: Israel collapsed as an independent nation with an identity as God's people, and went through the shock of captivity and a sense of abandonment. The fragmentation of who they were and the danger to their distinctiveness evoked an unbending response and the erection of inflexible boundaries typical of threatened minorities. Some scholars show sympathy for such strict separation, as we see in Williamson's remark when he comments on the renewed problem of intermarriage in Neh 13:23–29: "From a position of strength and security it is possible to extend a hand of welcome and forgiveness to those outside. From a position of weakness both parties would sink

---

[409] Ibid., 165.

together."⁴¹⁰ While the reaction of the exiles is understandable, the story may also serve as an object lesson.

Although the issue in Ezra 9–10 is described in terms that are corporate rather than individual, Christian readers might think analogically of that "first love" often seen in individuals who have recently embraced the Christian faith. In their zeal to God they may not realize whom they hurt and may also show the rigidity of immaturity, of boundaries that are not yet firmly in place and are therefore inflexible to a degree that not only keeps bad influences out but does not allow good in. What seems like the only acceptable course of action for such early zeal proves in the long term to be a mistake. It takes maturity and a long engagement with difficult questions to create healthy boundaries.

The temptation to shift the emphasis from a less clear-cut "moral" issue onto something unambiguous is an ongoing one. Making something taboo that has a potential for a negative influence but is not wrong in itself saves one the trouble to select and choose and consider what is morally appropriate or inappropriate in each individual case. The system of holiness expressed in physical separations in Israel's religious beliefs cannot, indeed should not, be reduced to this one aspect. However, in this particular instance the exiles used the argument from the "holy seed" to set a rigid boundary which went beyond the underlying moral concern in an effort to make sure that the latter was not jeopardized.

Clearly, the aim would be ultimately to develop moral discernment; yet what about times when moral discernment is defective or moral conviction is weak? In such instances a boundary set further away from temptation may protect from sin and its inevitable consequences and allow time for internal convictions and discernment to develop. At the same time how long is it legitimate, if at all, to keep such rigid boundaries? The danger is that such protection may become a constraint and a limitation keeping those it ostensibly protects in a position of weakness and never allowing "moral muscle" to develop in an interaction with the world.

14.2 The Focus of Protection

If the "profanation-holiness" issue is a means by which moral law is supported and reinforced then it is also worth considering where the focus of the "holy seed" rationale is, that is, what it wants to protect. In the "moral defilement" argument of Deut 7, which is hinted at in Ezra 9:1 and directly quoted in 9:12, the adverse effects on the spouse are emphasized (Deut 7:3–4) although the consequences for the descendants are possibly implied.⁴¹¹

---

⁴¹⁰ H. G. M. Williamson, "Ezra and Nehemiah," in *New Bible Commentary: 21ˢᵗ Century Edition* (ed. D. A. Carson, et al.; Leicester: IVP, 1994) 441.

⁴¹¹ The Hebrew of Deut 7:3 addresses the Israelites in the 2ⁿᵈ person singular not to intermarry with the Canaanites (לא תתחתן בם), continuing the admonition to them as parents not to let their children intermarry with them either using the singular "your son"

Nehemiah in his example of Solomon in Neh 13:26 equally speaks of the influence on the king rather than the effects on his offspring although what he notices about the intermarriages with the Ashodites, etc. in the first place is that the children do not speak Hebrew any more (v.24). In the New Testament there is only one direct command regarding a Christian's choice of marriage partner ("only in the Lord" μόνον ἐν κυρίῳ—1 Cor 7:39), which is generally taken to mean that a Christian should only marry another Christian. However, there is no explanation as to why this should be so. The other NT text that speaks explicitly of marriage with an unbeliever (1 Cor 7:12–16) is, as we have seen on p. 183, somewhat of a special case in that the conversion of one spouse to Christianity is subsequent to the marriage. From Paul's justification it seems that the children's status would be affected by an "unsanctified" spouse (v.14), but it is unclear if the Corinthians' possible question on this head was fuelled by a fear for the impact on the believer or on the children or both. Another text we noted as speaking of close association if not necessarily or exclusively against intermarriage is 2 Cor 6:14–18, which if applied to intermarriage is also focusing on the spouse.

The Ezran "holy seed" argument has implications for both parents and children, yet to some extent these are more serious for the latter. While the MT is ambiguous whether the exiles actually went through with the divorces,[412] it is not in question that the children belong with the foreign mothers and are to be sent away with them (Ezra 10:3, 10:44). In fact, as we have seen (p.162), the rabbinic tradition derives the basis for matrilineal descent from this story (*Gen. Rab.* 7:2). The logic of the "holy seed" rationale implies that by mixing the holy seed with profane the children can no longer be called holy.

In discussing the legal background for the "holy seed" rationale I argued that it is partly based on Deut 22:9. There it is not the vine or the other plant which is explicitly profaned by the mixing but the *fruit* of both. Similarly, the high priestly rule of marriage (to marry a virgin of Israel—Lev 21:14) explains the need for such a regulation reasoning that the offspring, the "seed," must be safeguarded from profanation (ולא־יחלל זרעו—v.15). Likewise, Deut 23:4–7[3–6] is concerned with the descendants rather than the Israelite parent.

(בנך) and "your daughter" (בתך). V.4 continues to employ the singular "your son" (בנך) outlining the consequences of such a marriage in the ensuing apostasy "it will turn your son away from me" (כי־יסיר את־בנך מאחרי). It is unclear if the referent of "your son" is the husband in such a marriage or if it is used as a more generic term for him as well as his descendants. Interestingly, the Hebrew יסיר is 3rd masc sing in form when one would expect the feminine תסיר ("she will turn"). The "agent" of the turning away thus seems to be the marriage itself.

[412] The MT simply reads כל־אלה נשאו נשים נכריות ויש מהם נשים וישימו בנים ("And all these had married foreign wives, and some of them had wives by whom they had children"—NASV). 1 Esd 9:36 on the other hand makes the divorces unambiguous: "All these had married foreign women, and they put them away together with their children."—NRSV).

My point here is that if we accept Douglas' theory that pollution rules may support moral ones when the conviction for the latter is weak or the issue is ambiguous then the focus of the "holy seed" rationale may also pinpoint the exiles' underlying concern for the effects of such marriages on the children as much as if not more than on themselves. This seems a common sense and reasonable perspective: children are more vulnerable to harmful influences and are more in need of protection than adults.

Yet, a closer look at the "holy seed" rationale makes it clear that the measure is preventative and a deterrent; the effects on the offspring are final. Thus it shows the irreversible consequences of intermarriage. While the reasoning fulfils the function that Douglas assigns to pollution rules in relation to "moral" ones, yet, as I have argued in §7.3, it does not fit neatly into either category but incorporates aspects of both.[413] It is the "moral" impurity of the foreign women that is the issue but the way its effects are communicated to the children is through the sexual act, which reminds one of the contact-contagion of "ritual" impurities. The rationale is built up in such a way that it combines the worst of both impurities: the contagious nature of the latter with the serious, sinful aspect of the former.

Thus while the exiles' reasoning teaches an object lesson about the more intangible effects of foreign worship and its far-reaching consequences for the offspring, it also creates its own difficulty not only for the marriage itself and the foreign spouse but also for the children. The logic of the argument makes profanation permanent and the children tainted and irretrievably lost to Israel. The solution the exiles found could function as a possible deterrent but it had no means of protecting the children; it could only push them away completely without the possibility of integration.[414]

Here again, Mary Douglas' anthropological work is invaluable. Reflecting on the effectiveness of purity rules to bolster the "moral" cause she shows that in some instances such beliefs can get out of hand and achieve the

---

[413] Jonathan Klawans classes it with "moral" purity although he notes the peculiar nature of it (*Impurity and Sin in Ancient Judaism* [New York: Oxford University Press, 2000] 43–45). Christina E. Hayes on the other hand invents a whole new category for it, which she calls "genealogical purity" (*Gentile Impurities and Jewish Identities: Intermarriage and Conversion from the Bible and the Talmud* [New York: Oxford University Press, 2002] 7).

[414] In contrast, rabbinic Halakah allows conversion of a Gentile and thus makes integration possible either on the level of a Gentile spouse or that of the Gentile offspring (from a mixed marriage between a Gentile woman and a Jewish man). If the offspring is of a Jewish mother and a Gentile father the child is Jewish by law although certain marriage restrictions apply. According to an older law such an offspring is a *mamzer* and cannot marry a Jew (*m. Yebam.* 69b), only another *mamzer*, a convert, or in the case of a man a non-Jewish female slave. Others, however, treat such a person as a Jew by law and only restrict his or her marriage into the priestly family (*b. Yebam.* 45a). See Louis M. Epstein's discussion (*Marriage Laws in the Bible and the Talmud* (Cambridge MA: Harvard University Press, 1942], 194–197).

opposite of what they aim to do. She remarks on the example of the Bemba, a tribe where adultery was thought to lead to defilement. She observes, however, that instead of strengthening the marriage, such pollution beliefs actually backfired by leading to divorce and remarriage with others in an effort to avoid the effects of pollution.[415] It is ironic that the exiles' insistence on protecting their own and their children's allegiance to God led down a route that could only disown children from such marriages.

14.3 A Case Study and Comparison

The Ezran text as well as the overall biblical witness testifies to a dual perspective: the effects of intermarriage on both the Israelite/believing spouse and the children. How does the question look in postbiblical mainstream Christianity today? For reasons explained in the introduction of this chapter I have chosen to use the RC position rather than any Protestant one for comparison. Although Vatican II has led to some minor changes in the perception of intermarriage (see at the end of my summary below), the earlier *Catholic Enyclopedia* (1913) gives a good account of the present RC position as follows.[416]

Roman Catholic terminology speaks of various impediments to marriage, among them Disparity of Worship (*Disparitas Cultus*). In its "perfect" sense this means the marriage of a baptized Catholic[417] with an unbaptized (unbelieving) person, while an "imperfect disparity" means that both parties are baptized but there is a disparity in faith such that one is a Catholic and the other is not. The latter disparity is also known as mixed religion (*mixta religio*) and such marriages are valid although illicit and sinful unless dispensation intervenes. On the other hand, in the former case of perfect disparity of worship the impediment makes the marriage null and void unless dispensation is granted.

The reason for having baptism as the basis for this "diriment [i.e., absolute] impediment" are as follows:

- it is an external ceremony, easy of recognition and proof, and

- it is a sacrament which imprints an indelible character upon the soul of the receiver and so presents a personal religious condition which is fixed and unchangeable.

Personal faith, on the contrary, viewed either as the internal assent of the mind or as the outward profession of the internal act, is subject to change and not always easy of demonstration, and hence could not afford a certain and immovable foundation. The primary reason why Catholics are

---

[415] Douglas, *Purity and Danger*, 170–171.
[416] "Disparity of Worship," *The Catholic Encyclopedia* (1913), n.p. [cited 22 May 2009]. Online: http://www.newadvent.org/cathen/05037b.htm
[417] For convenience, I am using "Catholic" here and in the ensuing discussion to mean Roman Catholic.

debarred from intermarriage with unbaptized persons is because the latter are not capable of receiving the Sacrament of Matrimony, as baptism is the door to all the other sacraments.[418]

At the same time, the *Encyclopedia* argues that the baptized Catholic who enters into such a marriage with dispensation more than likely does not receive the sacrament or its concomitant graces either although the Catholic Church is undecided on this question. Nevertheless the conclusion is considered both tenable and probable.

The origins of this impediment, as the *Encyclopedia* observes, are derived from Deut 7:3 in the OT (the threat of apostasy) and 1 Cor 7:39 and 2 Cor 6:14 in the New. Somewhat oddly, it seems to assume that Paul allowed intermarriages with non-Christians because of the small number of Christians with the hope that the unbelieving party will convert. Although the reason for the above is not spelt out, presumably this is based on 1 Cor 7:12–16, which is understood to mean marriage between a believer and an unbeliever rather than the marriage of two unbelievers one of whom subsequently becomes a Christian.

Significantly, dispensation from such impediment is only granted in the Catholic Church on certain conditions and guarantees and these have been slightly relaxed after Vatican II. In the pre-Vatican II understanding the unbaptized person was required to give written confirmation that he or she would not hinder the Catholic partner's practice of faith and promise to allow the children to be baptized and reared in the Catholic faith. Similarly, the Catholic spouse promised to practice his or her own faith, have the children baptized and brought up in the Catholic faith and work on the conversion of the unbaptized spouse.

Following the Second Vatican Council, the above was modified in the Apostolic Letter of Pope Paul VI on Mixed Marriages ("Matrimonia Mixta," 1970). It reworded the conditions for dispensation (later incorporated into Canon Law 1125 in the new Code of Canon Law of 1983) to something less than a firm written commitment to have the children baptized and brought up in the Catholic Church.

> To obtain from the local Ordinary dispensation from an impediment, the Catholic party shall *declare* that he is ready to remove dangers of falling from the faith. He is also gravely bound to make *a sincere promise to do all in his power* to have all the children baptized and brought up in the Catholic Church.[419] [italics mine]

The same letter also expressed a diminished censure toward baptized non-Catholics along the lines of the new ecclesiology of Vatican II.

---

[418] "Disparity of Worship," http://www.newadvent.org/cathen/05037b.htm
[419] "Matrimonia Mixta: Apostolic Letter of Pope Paul VI on Mixed Marriages (1970)," n.p. [cited 24 May 2009]. Online: http://www.catholicdoors.com/misc/marriage/mixed.htm

Insights from Anthropology and Some Contemporary Solutions 215

> Neither in doctrine nor in law does the Church place on the same level a marriage between a Catholic and a baptized non-Catholic, and one between a Catholic and an unbaptized person for, as the Second Vatican Council declared, men who, though they are not Catholics, "believe in Christ and have been properly baptized are brought into a certain, though imperfect, communion with the Catholic Church." [*Decree on Ecumenism, Unitatis Redintegratio, 3, AAS (1965), P. 93. Cf. Dogmatic Constitution on the Church, Lumen Gentium, AAS 57 (1965), pp. 19–20.*][420]

There are several observations to be made by way of comparison with the Ezran situation. First, it is worth noting that in both solutions (RC and Ezra) intermarriage is a serious issue although it is expressed in different ways. The Ezran answer does not seem to question the validity of the intermarriages but neither does it permit its continuation and demands divorce and the sending away of the children as foreign. Catholicism, on the other hand, considers such a marriage null and void from the outset unless there are some guarantees safeguarding the believing spouse and offspring.

Secondly, both are concerned with religious allegiance although the strategies used to protect it are again different. The "holy seed" rationale in the Ezran view can only deal with the crisis by erecting an impermeable boundary between foreigners and Israelites. On the other hand, the Catholic solution offers a way out by putting forward a minimal and an ideal solution. Minimally, the religious commitments of the baptized Catholic parent and children must be protected for the marriage to be acknowledged at all; ideally, however, conversion and baptism of the unbelieving spouse is best, because it eliminates the root of the original difficulty. In the Catholic position inward change is linked to outward, visible signs and procedures that are recognizable and demonstrable.

Thirdly, the focus of concern in the case of intermarriages is similar in the two cases. The Ezran solution centers attention on both the Israelite entering into marriage and on the offspring and demands unconditional separation from the foreign spouses, which would preclude any further influence on the Israelite and the procreation of (further) foreign children.[421] Likewise, the Catholic position is concerned with the effects of an unbaptized (unbelieving) partner on both the baptized Catholic and the children. This is illustrated by the fact that the dispensation from the impediment requires guarantees to protect the religious allegiance of both.

The particular emphasis of the Catholic view here is further demonstrated in the focus of the unbaptized spouse's lingering impact even when certain preconditions are met. The lack of baptism on the part of the

---

[420] "Matrimonia Mixta," http://www.catholicdoors.com/misc/marriage/mixed.htm See also "The Code of Canon Law (1983)," n.p. [cited 24 May 2009]. Online: http://www.catholicdoors.com/misc/marriage/canonlaw.htm

[421] The Ezran case is specifically related to children born of foreign women and it is not clear how the exiles would have dealt with children where the father was foreign.

unbelieving spouse makes Catholic intermarriage less than what it could be even for the baptized Catholic, since the union lacks the unity of experience as sacrament as well as its graces and it is even doubtful whether the believer individually receives these. Thus the idea of marriage as sacrament expresses the view that disparity of worship affects the Catholic spouse even if he or she is allowed to practice his or her faith. Clearly, the missing sacramental aspect of a marriage is more subtle and less demonstrable. Nevertheless, it signals the more intangible disparity between husband and wife who do not share a common faith.

This difference that goes beyond the primary need to protect believing spouse and children goes back perhaps to the NT's idea of marriage. Eph 5:22–33 uses the analogy of Christ's love for the church and applies it to the relationship between husband and wife modeling their role in marriage on the way Christ relates to the church and vice versa. This association of Christ and church with husband and wife raises marriage out of the mere commonplace, prosaic reality onto a different level.

We see then that the Ezran and the Catholic treatment of the issue share a concern for both the offspring and the spouse although the terminology that expresses the disparity of the marriage partners in particular is different. Thus the Catholic discourse operates with the idea of marriage as sacrament while the Ezran thinking uses the language of holiness/unholiness to convey the same.

In terms of the solution offered to the problem of intermarriage, Ezra bans any integration of a foreigner into Israel and excludes potential children of mixed descent, while Catholicism proposes ideally conversion or minimally a safeguard to protect the faith commitment of the believing spouse and any children. In the sense of making the boundary between believer and unbeliever more permeable the RC position is somewhat similar to rabbinic Judaism though clearly there are differences in the measures advocated.

14.4 Conclusion

The above exploration into anthropological perspectives provided a model for understanding the way the "holy seed" rationale meant to function. Based on the observations of Mary Douglas regarding the way purity laws might work in other cultures I suggested that the exiles' reasoning formed a "hedge" around the primary deuteronomic law (Deut 7:3) and that it was meant to reinforce the conviction for the latter through its tangible, black-and-white categories. I reflected on the need for boundaries for protecting religious allegiance and on the drawbacks of an inflexible boundary like the exiles'. I also argued that the focus of protection in the Ezran case was both the spouses and the children but that the impermeable boundary the exiles created backfired in relation to the latter in the sense that it could only exclude but not protect the offspring of such mixed marriages. The RC model for safeguarding religious allegiance in intermarriage is a contemporary Christian alternative to the Ezran solution and it reflects some of the NT's perspective on the question. Its dual focus to protect the religious allegiance of believing spouse and children can be traced back to a similar concern in the NT and its graded view on the effects of such a marriage with a secondary impact on the quality of the marriage itself demonstrates something of the elevated NT view of the marital union (e.g., Eph 5:22–33; Matt 19:1–9).

15

Conclusion

In the light of all that has gone before, how then do we read Ezra 9–10 as Christian Scripture with profit? My explorations into comparing Christian readings of the text with Jewish ones in Chapter 11 highlighted the underlying presuppositions for both, which lead onto particular tension points for Christians. The latter see narrative as having a controlling function in a way that is not the case for Jews, for whom this story is simply an illustration of a certain solution to a legal problem. Added to this is the basic conviction on the Christian side that all Scripture is equally authoritative, whereas in Jewish thinking the Writings to which EN belong do not have the same authority as the Pentateuch, particularly its legal portions.

The combination of scriptural authority and the primacy of narrative in Christian interpretation leads to an often tacit assumption that stories are there as positive examples to be followed or negative ones acting as deterrents. This then creates a tension because on the one hand, Christian readers would want to say that this is not an example to follow, yet there are elements to the story, which one would want to affirm such as faithfulness in being a holy people to God. Added to this is the fact that there is no obviously negative judgment passed on it by the author, so that the Christian reader is left with some uncertainty as to which category the story fits into. Jewish readers, on the other hand, do not see a tension because, as we have noted, they understand the story in different terms. I am not suggesting that Christians should give up their convictions and follow a Jewish model in order to eliminate the tension, but it is worth considering whether the Christian belief in authority and the primacy of narrative really demand one to read stories such as Ezra 9–10 within the framework of "positive example to follow/negative example to avoid." In fact the conclusion, it seems to me, is not at all inevitable.

A story may be authoritative and instructive even if the lessons learnt from it are more indirect than a straightforward "do" or "do not" and cannot immediately translate themselves into action. This is, of course, not a new idea and those who advocate literary-narrative readings often point out that stories affect the reader's thinking in more subtle and profound ways than through commands couched in a didactic moral tale.[422] Understanding Ezra 9–10 as a story which shapes our thinking as we reflect and meditate on it opens up the meaning of authority to involve an active engagement with teaching for the renewing of the mind (Rom 12:1–2) rather than a simple assent to an order issued from on high. Here, the Jewish attitude of probing, questioning and involvement as discussed in Chapter 2 is something that Christians may learn from and adapt to their own perspective and practice. Similarly, as mentioned in the same chapter, seeing the creational aspects of the law may help with the recognition that God wants obedience not only out of gratitude for his redeeming grace but also in full recognition that his instructions are good and woven into the pattern of the created order. All these considerations feed into the reflection that God's way of renewing his people is perhaps a slower and more painstaking process of inner transformation than the quick fix of simple solutions and straightforward orders.

Even if the story does not invite emulation and has a more indirect way of instruction, it is still necessary to evaluate what to make of the exiles' action when there is no explicit judgment made by the writer/editor. Here, I believe, a long view on the development of the solutions regarding intermarriage helps put the question into perspective. This is based on the idea discussed in Chapter 12 that different generations have to revisit difficult questions and re-appropriate general principles within their own setting. Thus there is a constant re-evaluation and re-contextualization of what it means to be faithful to God's requirements. Fishbane calls this "inner-biblical exegesis" and Davis speaks of "critical traditioning," the idea that the canon preserves this process of sifting and re-thinking and builds or transforms earlier traditions without eliminating them from the canon. This development is further continued beyond the canon in "tradition" as well. As mentioned in §12.1.2 I am hesitant to speak of mistakes where Scripture leaves the question ambiguous though I find Davis' idea helpful overall.

Within this framework looking at the question of intermarriage both within EN, the wider OT and the NT, as well as rabbinic tradition (Chapter 11) suggest three things. First, even within EN there is more than one solution offered to the intermarriage crisis and the issue of distinctiveness, which relativizes the Ezran solution and may ease the tension that the modern reader might feel in encountering the story. Secondly, and this may seem self-evident, the history of developing the ban on intermarriage suggests that distinctiveness is important and marriage to a person without the same religious commitment/faith presents dangers for the people of God that should not be

---

[422] It is interesting in this respect that the trio most well known for helping the rediscovery of the power of narrative in biblical studies are three Jewish scholars (Alter, Sternberg & Bar-Ephrat) perhaps because they are less predisposed to a didactic and deductive approach to stories.

taken lightly. Thirdly, the Ezran solution or more specifically its "holy seed" rationale and consequent requirement for divorce proved to be a dead end in the long term and not a viable way for dealing with the crisis.

What then might be learnt from the Ezran intermarriage crisis? First, the exiles' attitude is certainly commendable inasmuch as they take sin seriously. Far from the accusation of legalism leveled against the Postexilic Period in older scholarly works the returnees do not see themselves as people who needed to earn God's grace. Rather, precisely because they have experienced his forbearing patience and help despite their own unfaithfulness and sin they want to make a firm commitment to him (Chapter 3). Grace does not foster in them complacency because they recognize from their own experience that recurring and highhanded disobedience eventually brings judgment. The balance between grace and justice is a difficult one, but perhaps Ezra 9–10 is a wake-up call for Christians who preach grace without the need for commitment and obedience.

Coupled with the issue of legalism is the charge of interpreting laws in a rigid manner adhering to the letter of the law while ignoring its spirit. My own detailed exegesis suggests, however, that the exiles' approach was flexible, taking precisely the spirit of the law rather than its letter and extending the law from the historic Canaanite nations to all those who commit the kind of abominations associated with them. Further, we may note that the combination of various deuteronomic laws leads to a re-appropriation of the *ḥērem* law as divorce. Although we find this still cruel and unacceptable, it is actually a milder treatment of the question than the original extermination. Earlier material is re-contextualized in a new setting and it demonstrates exactly the kind of lively engagement with God's instruction that is continued in the approach of Judaism. Yet, flexibility does not mean a free and random association of ideas where anything goes, nor is it an excuse to find a back door to a difficult verdict.

So far, my own estimate is not new, other Christian commentators make these two points too although I believe that my exegesis puts flesh on the bones in a way standard commentaries do not have space for. However, no matter how positive some of these considerations may be, most modern readers feel uncomfortable with the way the women are rejected and expelled and this needs to be explored further. Where exactly did the exiles go wrong in their reasoning? Here a scriptural example of dealing with the same or similar crisis may help highlight what is missing from the Ezran solution and my own explorations used 1 Cor 7 for this.[423] A NT example may be useful for a Christian reader to reveal the continuities and discontinuities with the OT.

As mentioned at the beginning of Chapter 13 the Corinthian scenario differs from the Ezran one. Most obviously the exiles' intermarriage is considered sinful whether it was committed in ignorance or not, whereas the Corinthians are innocent of any wrongdoing. This may go some way to explain Paul's conciliatory tone and his novel idea that the holy positively affects the

---

[423] Although the example is a NT one, this in no way implies that the OT gets it wrong while the New gets it right.

unholy rather than the latter profaning or defiling the holy. There is also some discontinuity in the way Paul thinks of purity and impurity, which on my understanding, is more relational and metaphorical and further removed from ritual ways of thinking and physical contact contagion. This is probably due to the larger framework of thinking about purity in the light of Jesus' actions and teaching and the church's developing understanding at this stage which was being shaped by the inclusion of the Gentiles among God's people. The reversal of the direction of influence from holy to unholy is connected to the Corinthians' innocence in the matter of intermarriage and this aspect of the story cannot help us with the Ezran predicament.

However, in another respect there is something to learn from the comparison of the two stories, namely from the clash of priorities in both which is resolved differently in each case. I have noted in §13.5 that Paul chooses the priority of keeping the marriages together and this is very likely driven by Jesus' teaching on marriage and divorce as well as the church's call and concern for mission.[424] It may seem that the Corinthian situation is too much of a special case to help us but when we consider that Paul would probably have not advised divorce even in the Ezran scenario then his prioritizing may not depend entirely on the Corinthians' innocence. In fact, I suggested that if the categories are re-thought as a clash between the commitment made to God and to human beings then there is a lesson to be learnt from Paul's argument in relation to the Ezran story.

Paul navigates masterfully between priorities. Clearly, distinctiveness as a Christian is important and so Christians should marry "only in the Lord" (1 Cor 7:39), that is, to another Christian. This same principle is also expressed in 2 Cor 6:14–7:1 in the admonition not to be yoked together with unbelievers. At the same time, the marriage commitment is binding as long as the spouse lives (v.39), even if he or she is an unbeliever. Divorce then is not an option for a believer. Yet, no matter how important marriage is, the Christian should not shackle the non-Christian if he or she wants to leave (v.15). Thus the high commitment to marriage gives way to another principle, living at peace with an unbeliever.

In this way Paul manages to keep the two priorities together recognizing that faithfulness to God also involves and incorporates faithfulness to other people and the two cannot and should not be separated in the way it is done in the Ezran story. Neither should one disregard commitment to God as the modern/postmodern age does, which tends to prioritize humanistic concerns without considering religious allegiance as a valid priority. Clearly these thoughts raise larger questions regarding a number of OT narratives which our modern era has particular trouble with precisely because they put allegiance to God first even when it is to the detriment of other human beings (e.g., the

---

[424] This is not to suggest that only a mission focus may make a balanced view possible since the rabbinic answer has also done away with the holy seed rationale and achieved a viable and fair solution.

"sacrifice" of Isaac in Gen 22 or the *ḥērem* law in Deut 7). This is an area that could do with further examination although the present book does not allow space for considering to what extent these stories are similar to or different from Ezra 9–10 and how they might be evaluated in the light of the discussion above.

Apart from the commitment to God and considerations for others, there is also another lesson emerging from the story that has to do with responsibility. Paul calls Christians to take responsibility for their own beliefs and do not force others to pay the cost of their conviction (i.e., force the unbeliever to remain in the marriage for the sake of the Christian's beliefs on this—1 Cor 7:15). Neither should they shoulder responsibility for their spouse's conversion and force him or her to remain in the marriage with the hope that they may be saved through staying (v.16). One cannot take over other people's lives and here mission focus must take a back seat and allow the unbeliever freedom of choice.

Taking responsibility for oneself but not taking on undue responsibility for others is part of healthy boundary maintenance: where one ends and where the other person begins, as well as how one draws the boundary: what influences one lets in and keeps out.

How do these questions look in the Ezran story? We have already seen that in the exilic thinking demonstrated in Ezra 9–10 there is no room for considering the plight of the women, only the religious commitment to holiness. In §14.1 I suggested further that the exiles' concern to obey God leads them into creating an extra hedge around the law through the holy seed rationale. In an effort to make a difficult and somewhat ambiguous situation into a clear-cut issue of black-and-white, they bolster the religious-moral concern of distinctiveness with purity language and the effects of this move, as the history of the idea demonstrates, has unforeseen negative implications of zealotry that mainstream Judaism did away with. When the hedge erected to protect the law becomes equated with the law, it ceases to function right.

The urge to create extra barriers of protection around a central concern and then mistake the barrier for the main issue is also a danger for Christians, particularly if it is felt that the central concern is under threat. One only needs to think of particular *shibboleths* within Christian groups where commitment to God is measured by holding certain views or doing or abstaining from certain practices. This is not to suggest that there is no connection between those views/practices and faithfulness to God; there very often is. After all, in the Ezran situation foreignness on the most part meant not worshiping YHWH but other gods and the latter would have inevitably carried with it a different world view and lifestyle clashing with the former. Having an extra and external hedge or barrier may be helpful and, in the case of people particularly vulnerable to danger, essential. Yet, maturity requires an awareness that there is a gap between the hedge and the main concern, which the hedge is meant to protect.

This principle also connects to responsibility. Extra hedges can take people's responsibility away in developing discernment and making wise decisions for themselves and thus barriers can keep them in a state of childhood. Transition needs to happen in gradual stages with a recognition that the freedom to make choices will bring the danger of making mistakes. Yet, wise parents can limit the sphere of responsibility, so that errors of judgment do not cause irreparable damage gradually widening the circle as the child becomes better able to navigate between choices.

For a postmodern, Western world the Ezran intermarriage crisis brings a different and more subtle challenge. After all, this culture is rather permissive and tries to remove barriers rather than erect them. When it comes to central concerns seemingly anything goes. Paradoxically, however, the Western world's emphasis on freedom, equal rights and the fight for no discrimination creates its own protective hedges that set off an alarm when these are breached. Thus many are quick to see racism in Ezra 9–10 despite the fact that several aspects of the story do not fit this theory. My own explorations in the exegetical part of this book suggest that while descent is important, it is not everything. Those who belong to Israel but do not comply with the community's decision in the story are to be excluded and in that sense their continued inclusion is not automatic but contingent on faithfulness. Further, the women's exclusion is not based on genetic inferiority, neither is there any trace in the story that the exiles are a superior people. If anything, Ezra's prayer (Ezra 9:5–15) and the community's rehearsal of their past history (Neh 9) speak of God's graciousness to an undeserving and sinful people. The language reflects moral-religious reasoning both in Israel's past and present sin and it is implied in the laws (Deut 7; 23:4–7[3–6]; Lev 18:3; 24–30) they draw on (Chapter 4). Admittedly the second half of the argument with the holy seed rationale brings in purity language, but a closer look at the vocabulary used such as 'āšām and ma'al seem to be employed in the service of covenant breaking rather than sacrilege (Chapter 7).

When some central concerns are seen to be threatened, such as we see in the postmodern fear of discrimination, it is easy to pin on the label and dismiss the story as of no benefit. However, once Christian readers start examining the narrative closer it forces them to consider different angles. Returning to the initial thought of this chapter, this is not a straightforward example for imitation but not one to condemn out of hand either. Yes, the expulsion of the women is cruel and in that culture would have been deeply shameful, a loss of face. Moreover, the various examples of treating such a crisis in EN, in Scripture overall, as well as in Christian and Jewish thinking beyond the Bible, suggest that there have been better long-term answers to the problem. There are also valuable lessons to be learnt when these are compared with the Ezran solution, lessons about responsibility and boundaries and what it takes to rear and train people to be both in the world but not of it. Yet the story also challenges our cultural norms and priorities. Do we put a lesser value on religious commitment than we should? Reading pre-moderns such as Josephus or the Puritans, Henry and Scott, it seems that they did not see the wrong done to the wives in the same light perhaps because religious commitment had a higher priority for them than for us today. If they had a blind spot when it came to human considerations, do we have a blind spot when it comes to what is due God? It should be clear from what has gone before that I do not advocate the

Ezran solution. Yet, there is something provoking about the story, like Jesus' harsh sayings about cutting off limbs and gouging out eyes that offend. Despite their excess or perhaps precisely because of it they goad us out of complacency, of knowing better, and force us to consider our priorities.

This book started out by raising the question how difficult OT texts such as the controversial story of Ezra 9–10 could be read with profit from a Christian perspective. The intervening chapters mapped out various aspects that may help interpretation although I recognize that some of these could in themselves be the subject of a book (such as anthropological perspectives). My aim, however, was simply to demonstrate how these considerations may give depth to our understanding and application rather than treat each of these areas exhaustively. In conclusion, then, I suggest that a Christian approach to reading problem texts would benefit, beyond a detailed exegesis, from mapping out the larger Christian frame of reference through the contrast with Jewish perspectives, the spelling out of constraints placed on an OT text by canon and tradition, a closer examination of continuities and discontinuities with the NT through the use of NT texts which address similar concerns, and possibly drawing on insights from our own time outside the biblical interpretative disciplines from such areas as anthropology and a comparison with contemporary answers to questions posed by the ancient text.

Bibliography

Ackroyd, Peter R. *I & II Chronicles, Ezra, Nehemiah: Introduction and Commentary*. London: SCM, 1973.

Allen, Leslie C., and Timothy S. Laniak. *Ezra, Nehemiah, Esther*. NIBCOT 9. Peabody MA: Hendrickson, 2003.

Alon, Gedalyahu. "The Levitical Uncleanness of Gentiles." Pp. 146–189 in *Jews, Judaism and the Classical World: Studies in Jewish History in the Times of the Second Temple and Talmud*. Translated by Israel Abrahams. Jerusalem: Magnes, 1977.

Alt, Albrecht. "Die Ursprünge des israelitischen Rechts." Vol. 86/1 of *Berichte über die Verhandlungen der Sächsischen Akademie der Wissenschaften zu Leipzig Philologisch-historische Klasse*. Leipzig: S. Hirzel, 1934.

Anderson, Bernhard W. *The Living World of the Old Testament*. 2nd ed. London: Longman, 1966.

Anderson, Bernhard W., and Steven Bishop. *Contours of Old Testament Theology*. Minneapolis MN: Fortress, 1999.

Averbeck, Richard E. "גאל." Pp. 794–95 in vol. 1 of *New International Dictionary of Old Testament Theology and Exegesis*. Edited by Willem A. VanGemeren. Grand Rapids MI: Zondervan, 1997.

———. "טהר." Pp. 338–53 of vol. 2 of *New International Dictionary of Old Testament Theology and Exegesis*. Edited by Willem A. VanGemeren. Grand Rapids MI: Zondervan, 1997.

Barr, James. *Biblical Faith and Natural Theology: the Gifford Lectures for 1991, Delivered in the University of Edinburgh*. Oxford: Clarendon, 1993.

Barrett, C. K. *A Commentary on the First Epistle to the Corinthians*. 2nd ed. London: A&C Black, 1971.

———. *A Commentary on the Second Epistle to the Corinthians*. London: A&C Black, 1973.

Batten, Loring W. *A Critical and Exegetical Commentary on the Books of Ezra and Nehemiah*, ICC. Edinburgh: T&T Clark, 1913.

Bauer, W., et al. *A Greek-English Lexicon of the New Testament and Other Early Christian Literature*. 3rd ed. London: Chicago University Press, 2000.

Berlin, Adele and Marc Z. Brettler, eds. *The Jewish Study Bible*. Oxford: Oxford University Press, 1999.

Betz, H. D. "2 Cor. 6.14–7.1, An Anti-Pauline Fragment?" *JBL* 92 (1973) 88–108.

Blenkinsopp, Joseph. *Ezra–Nehemiah: A Commentary*. London: SCM, 1988.

———. *Judaism: The First Phase. The Place of Ezra and Nehemiah in the Origins of Judaism*. Grand Rapids, MI: Eerdmans, 2009.

The Book of Common Prayer (1662). No pages. Cited 10 June 2009. Online: http://www.cofe.anglican.org/worship/liturgy/bcp/texts/

Brettler, Marc Z. "Biblical Authority: A Jewish Pluralistic View." Pp. 1–9 in *Engaging Biblical Authority: Perspectives on the Bible as Scripture*. Edited by William P. Brown. Louisville KY: Westminster John Knox, 2007.

Brockington, L. H. *Ezra, Nehemiah and Esther*, CB. London: Nelson, 1969.

Brown, F., S. R. Driver and C. A. Briggs, eds. *The New Brown-Driver-Briggs-Gesenius Hebrew And English Lexicon with an Appendix Containing the Biblical Aramaic*. Lafayette IN: Associated Publishers and Authors, 1978.

Bruce, F. F. *1 and 2 Corinthians*. NCB. Grand Rapids MI: Eerdmans, 1971.

Brueggemann, Walter. *Theology of the Old Testament: Testimony, Dispute, Advocacy*. Minneapolis MN: Fortress, 1997.

Calvin, John. *Commentary on the Epistles of Paul the Apostle to the Corinthians*. Translated from the original Latin and collated with the author's French version by John Pringle. Grand Rapids MI: Baker, 2005.

Carmichael, Calum M. "Forbidden Mixtures in Deuteronomy XXII 9–11 and Leviticus XIX 19." *VT* 45 (1995) 433–448.

Childs, Brevard S. *Biblical Theology in Crisis*. Philadelphia PA: Westminster, 1970.

———. "Critique of Recent Intertextual Canonical Interpretation." *ZAW* 115 (2003) 173–184.

———. *Introduction to the Old Testament as Scripture*. London: SCM, 1979.

———. *Isaiah*. Louisville KY: Westminster John Knox, 2001.

———. *The New Testament as Canon: An Introduction*. Philadelphia PA: Fortress, 1985.

Clements, Ronald E. *Old Testament Theology: A Fresh Approach*. London: Marshall, Morgan & Scott, 1978.

Clines, David J. A., ed. "גאל." Pp. 295–96 in vol. 2 of *The Dictionary of Classical Hebrew*. Sheffield: Sheffield Academic, 1995.

———. *Ezra, Nehemiah, Esther*. NCB. Grand Rapids MI: Eerdmans / London: Marshall, Morgan & Scott, 1984.

———. "Nehemiah 10 as an Example of Early Jewish Biblical Exegesis." *JSOT* 21 (1981) 111–117.

"The Code of Canon Law (1983)." No pages. Cited 24 May 2009. Online: http://www.catholicdoors.com/misc/marriage/canonlaw.htm

Coggins, R. J. *The Books of Ezra and Nehemiah*. Cambridge: Cambridge University Press, 1976.

Collins, Raymond F. *First Corinthians*, Sacra Pagina 7. Collegeville MN: The Liturgical Press, 1999.

Conzelmann, Hans. *1 Corinthians: A Commentary on the First Epistle to the Corinthians*. Translated by James W. Leitch. Hermeneia. Philadelphia PA: Fortress, 1975.

Cranfield, Charles E. B. "Has the Old Testament Law a Place in the Christian Life? A Response to Professor Westerholm." Pp. 109–124 in *On Romans and Other New Testament Essays*. Edinburgh: T&T Clark, 1998.

Dahl, N. A. "A Fragment and its Context: 2 Corinthians 6.14–7.1." Pp. 62–69 in *Studies in Paul: Theology for the Early Christian Mission*. Minneapolis MN: Augsburg, 1977.

Daiches, Samuel. *The Jews in Babylonia in the Time of Ezra and Nehemiah according to Babylonian Inscriptions*. London: Jews' College, 1910.

Davis, Ellen F. "Critical Traditioning: Seeking an Inner Biblical Hermeneutic." Pp. 163–180 in *The Art of Reading Scripture*. Edited by Ellen F. Davis and Richard B. Hays. Grand Rapids MI: Eerdmans, 2003.

———. "The Soil That Is Scripture." Pp. 36–44 in *Engaging Biblical Authority: Perspectives on the Bible as Scripture*. Edited by William P. Brown. Louisville KY: Westminster John Knox, 2007.

Davies, T. Witton. *Ezra, Nehemiah and Esther*. Edinburgh: Jack / London: Caxton, 1909)

Deming, Will. *Paul on Marriage and Celibacy: The Hellenistic Background of 1 Corinthians 7*. 2nd ed. Grand Rapids MI: Eerdmans, 2004.

Derrett, J. D. M. "2 Cor. 6, 14ff. a Midrash on Dt 22,10." *Bib* 59 (1978) 231–50

"Disparity of Worship." In *The Catholic Encyclopedia (1913)*. No pages. Cited 22 May 2009. Online: http://www.newadvent.org/cathen/05037b.htm

Douglas, Mary. *Natural Symbols*. 2nd ed. London: Routledge Classics, 2007.

―――. *Purity and Danger: An Analysis of Concepts of Pollution and Taboo*. London: Routledge and Keegan Paul, 1966. Repr., London: Routledge Classics, 2002.

Driver, S. R. *A Critical and Exegetical Commentary on Deuteronomy*. ICC. Edinburgh: T&T Clark, 1902.

Eichrodt, Walther. *Theology of the Old Testament*. 2 volumes. Translated by J. A. Baker. London: SCM, 1967.

Epstein, Louis M. *Marriage Laws in the Bible and the Talmud*. Cambridge MA: Harvard University Press, 1942.

Eskenazi, Tamara C. *In an Age of Prose: A Literary Approach to Ezra–Nehemiah*. SBL MS 36. Atlanta GA: Scholars Press, 1988.

Eskenazi, Tamara C., and Eleanore P. Judd. "Marriage to a Stranger in Ezra 9–10." Pp. 266–285 in *Second Temple Studies: 2. Temple Community in the Persian Period*. Edited by Tamara C. Eskenazi and Kent H. Richards. JSOT SS 175. Sheffield: JSOT Press, 1994.

Evans, Ernest. *The Epistles of Paul the Apostle to the Corinthians in the Revised Version with Introduction and Commentary*. The Clarendon Bible. Oxford: Clarendon, 1930.

Fee, Gordon D. "II Corinthians VI.14–VII.1 and Food Offered to Idols." *NTS* 23 (1977) 140–61.

―――. *The First Epistle to the Corinthians*. Grand Rapids MI: Eerdmans, 1987.

Fensham, F. C. *The Books of Ezra and Nehemiah*. Grand Rapids MI: Eerdmans, 1982.

Fishbane, Michael. *Biblical Interpretation in Ancient Israel*. Oxford: Clarendon, 1985.

―――. "Inner-Biblical Exegesis: Types and Strategies of Interpretation in Ancient Israel." Pp. 3–18 in *The Garments of Torah: Essays in Biblical Hermeneutics*. Bloomington: Indiana University Press, 1989.

Fitzmyer, J.A. "Qumrân and the Interpolated Paragraph in 2 Cor. 6.14–7.1." *CBQ* 23 (1961) 271–80.

Fretheim, Terence E. "Law in the Service of Life: A Dynamic Understanding of Law in Deuteronomy." Pp. 183–200 in *A God So Near: Essays on Old Testament Theology in Honor of Patrick D. Miller*. Edited by Brent A. Strawn and Nancy R. Bowen. Winona Lake IN: Eisenbrauns, 2003.

Frymer-Kensky, Tikva. "Pollution, Purification, and Purgation in Biblical Israel." Pp. 399–414 in *The Word of the Lord Shall Go Forth: Essays in Honor of David Noel Freedman in Celebration of His Sixtieth Birthday*. Edited by Carol L. Meyers and M. O'Connor. Winona Lake IN: Eisenbraun, 1983.

Furnish, V. P. *II Corinthians*. AB 32A. Garden City NY: Doubleday, 1984.

Garland, David E. *1 Corinthians*. BECNT. Grand Rapids MI: Baker Academic, 2003.

Gillihan, Yonder M. "Jewish Laws on Illicit Marriage, the Defilement of Offspring, and the Holiness of the Temple: A New Halakic Interpretation of 1 Corinthians 7:14." *JBL* 121/4 (2002) 711–744.

Gnilka, J. "2 Cor. 6.14–7.1 in the Light of the Qumran Texts and the Testaments of the Twelve Patriarchs." Pp. 48–68 in *Paul and Qumran: Studies in New Testament Exegesis*. Edited by Jerome Murphy-O'Connor. Chicago IL: The Priory, 1968.

Goldingay, John. "Justice and Salvation for Israel and Canaan." Pp. 169–87 in *Reading the Hebrew Bible for a New Millennium: Form, Concept, and Theological Perspective, Studies in Antiquity & Christianity I*. Edited by Wonil Kim et al. Harrisburg PA: Trinity International, 2000.

———. *Old Testament Theology*. 3 volumes. Downers Grove, IL: IVP Academic, 2003–2009)

Goudge, H. L. *The First Epistle to the Corinthians with Introduction and Notes*. London: Methuen & Co, 1903.

Grabbe, Lester L. *Ezra–Nehemiah*. London: Routledge, 1998.

Gray, G. B. *A Critical and Exegetical Commentary on the Book of Isaiah 1–39*. ICC. Edinburgh: T&T Clark, 1912.

Greenberg, Moshe. "Herem." Pp. 344–350 in vol. 8 of *Encyclopaedia Judaica*. Edited by C. Roth. Jerusalem: Keter, 1971.

———. "On the Political Use of the Bible in Modern Israel: An Engaged Critique." Pp. 461–72 in *Pomegranates and Golden Bells: Studies in Biblical, Jewish and Near Eastern Ritual Law and Literature*. Edited by David P. Wright, David Noel Freedman, and Avi Hurvitz. Winona Lake IN: Eisenbrauns, 1995.

Grosheide, F. W. *Commentary on the First Epistle to the Corinthians: The English Text with Introduction, Exposition and Notes*. NICNT. Grand Rapids MI: Eerdmans, 1953.

Grüneberg, Keith N. *Abraham, Blessing and the Nations: A Philological and Exegetical Study of Genesis 12:3 in its Narrative Context*. BZAW 332. Berlin: Walter de Gruyter, 2003.

Gunton, Colin E. *Christ and Creation*. Carlisle: Paternoster / Grand Rapids MI: Eerdmans, 1992.

———. *The One, the Three and the Many: God, Creation and the Culture of Modernity: the Bampton Lectures 1992*. Cambridge: Cambridge University Press, 1993.

Hartley, John E. *Leviticus*. WBC 4. Dallas TX: Word, 1992.

Hayes, Christine E. *Gentile Impurities and Jewish Identities: Intermarriage and Conversion from the Bible and the Talmud*. New York: Oxford University Press, 2002.

———. "Intermarriage and Impurity in Ancient Jewish Sources." *HTR* 92/1 (1999) 3–36.

Hays, Richard B. *First Corinthians*. Interpretation. Louisville KY: John Knox, 1997.

Hengel, Martin. *Judaism and Hellenism: Studies in their Encounter in Palestine during the Early Hellenistic Period*. Translated by John Bowden. 2 volumes. London: SCM, 1974.

Henry, Matthew and Thomas Scott. Joshua to Esther. Vol. 2 of *A Commentary upon the Holy Bible from Henry and Scott: With Occasional Observations and Notes from Other Writers*. London: The Religious Tract Society, 1834.

Heschel, Abraham J. *God in Search of Man: A Philosophy of Judaism*. New York: Farrar, Straus & Giroux, 1955.

Hoffman, Yair. "The Deuteronomistic Concept of the Herem." *ZAW* 111 (1999) 196–210.

Holmgren, F. C. *Israel Alive Again: A Commentary on the Books of Ezra and Nehemiah*. ITC. Grand Rapids, MI: Eerdmans, 1987.

Horbury, William. "Extirpation and Excommunication." *VT* 35/1 (1985) 13–38.

Hughes, P. E. *The Second Epistle to the Corinthians*. NICNT. Grand Rapids MI: Eerdmans, 1962.

Hurd, J. C. *The Origin of 1 Corinthians*. 2nd ed. Macon: Mercer University Press, 1983.

Instone-Brewer, David. *Divorce and Remarriage in the Bible: The Social and Literary Context*. Grand Rapids MI: Eerdmans, 2002.

Janzen, David. *Witch-hunts, Purity and Social Boundaries: The Expulsion of the Foreign Women in Ezra 9–10*. JSOT SS 350. Sheffield: Sheffield Academic, 2002.

Japhet, Sara. "The Composition and Chronology in the Book of Ezra–Nehemiah." Pp. 189–216 in *Second Temple Studies: 1. Persian Period*. Edited by Philip R. Davies. JSOT SS 117. Sheffield: JSOT Press, 1991.

———. "Sheshbazzar and Zerubbabel. Against the Background of the Historical and Religious Tendencies of Ezra–Nehemiah." *ZAW* 94 (1982) 66–98.

———. "The Supposed Common Authorship of Chronicles and Ezra–Nehemiah Investigated Anew." *VT* 18 (1968) 330–371.

Jenson, Robert W. "Scripture's Authority in the Church." Pp. 27–37 in *The Art of Reading Scripture*. Edited by Ellen F. Davis and Richard B. Hays. Grand Rapids MI: Eerdmans, 2003.

Josephus, Flavius. *The Complete Works*. Translated by William Whiston. Nashville TN: Nelson, 1998.

Kaiser, Otto. *Isaiah 1–12*. Translated by R. A. Wilson. London: SCM, 1972.

Kaufmann, Yehezkel. *From the Babylonian Captivity to the End of Prophecy*. Vol. 4 of *History of the Religion of Israel*. New York: Ktav, 1977.

Keener, Craig S. *1–2 Corinthians*. NCBC. Cambridge: Cambridge University Press, 2005.

Keil, C. F. *The Books of Ezra, Nehemiah, and Esther*. Translated by Sophia Taylor. Edinburgh: T&T Clark, 1873.

Kidner, Derek. *Ezra and Nehemiah: An Introduction and Commentary*. TOTC. Leicester: IVP, 1979.

Klawans, Jonathan. *Impurity and Sin in Ancient Judaism*. New York: Oxford University Press, 2000.

———. "Notions of Gentile Impurity in Ancient Judaism." *AJS Review* 20/2 (1995) 285–312.

———. *Purity, Sacrifice, and the Temple: Symbolism and Supersessionism in the Study of Ancient Judaism*. New York: Oxford University Press, 2006.

Klein, Ralph W. "The Books of Ezra and Nehemiah." Pp. 661–852 in vol. 3 of *The New Interpreter's Bible: A Commentary in Twelve Volumes*. Choon-Leong Seow et al. Nashville TN: Abingdon, 1999.

Koehler, Ludwig. *Old Testament Theology*. Translated by A. S. Todd. London: Lutterworth, 1957.

Koehler, Ludwig, and Walter Baumgartner (eds.), *The Hebrew and Aramaic Lexicon of the Old Testament*. Translated and edited by M. E. J. Richardson. 2 volumes. Leiden: Brill, 1994.

Lang, F. G. *Die Briefe an die Korinther*. NTD 7. Göttingen: Vandenhoeck & Rupprecht, 1986.

Lash, Nicholas. "What Might Martyrdom Mean?" Pp. 75–92 in *Theology on the Way to Emmaus*. London: SCM, 1986.

Levenson, Jon D. "The Eighth Principle of Judaism and the Literary Simultaneity of Scripture." Pp. 62–81 in *The Hebrew Bible, the Old Testament, and Historical Criticism: Jews and Christians in Biblical Studies*. Louisville, KY: Westminster John Knox, 1993.

———. "Theological Consensus or Historicist Evasion? Jews and Christians in Biblical Studies." Pp. 82–105 in *The Hebrew Bible, the Old Testament, and Historical Criticism: Jews and Christians in Biblical Studies*. Louisville, KY: Westminster John Knox, 1993.

———. "Theologies of Commandment in Biblical Israel" *HTR* 73 (1980) 17–33.

———. "Why Jews Are Not Interested in Biblical Theology." Pp. 33–61 in *The Hebrew Bible, the Old Testament, and Historical Criticism: Jews and Christians in Biblical Studies*. Louisville, KY: Westminster John Knox, 1993.

Levine, Baruch A. *Leviticus*. JPS Torah Commentary. Philadelphia PA: JPS, 1989.

Lipton, Diana. "The Furnace of Desire: Forging Identities in Foreign Bedrooms." Pp. 214–264 in *Longing for Egypt and Other Unexpected Biblical Tales*. HBM 15. Sheffield: Sheffield Phoenix, 2008.

———. "Terms of Endearment: A (Very) Fresh Look at Biblical Law." Pp. 172–213 in *Longing for Egypt and Other Unexpected Biblical Tales*. HBM 15. Sheffield: Sheffield Phoenix, 2008.

Lockwood, Gregory J. *1 Corinthians*. Concordia Commentary. Saint Louis MO: Concordia, 2000.

Lohfink, N. "חֵרֶם חָרַם" Pp. 180–199 in vol. 5 of *Theological Dictionary of the Old Testament*. Edited by G. Johannes Botterweck, Helmer Ringgren, and Heinz-Josef Fabry. Translated by David E. Green. Grand Rapids MI: Eerdmans, 1986.

Lohr, Joel N. *Chosen and Unchosen: Conceptions of Election in the Pentateuch and Jewish-Christian Interpretation*. Siphrut 2. Winona Lake IN: Eisenbrauns, 2009.

Luther, Martin. *Small Cathecism*. No pages. Cited 10 June 2009. Online: http://bookofconcord.org/smallcatechism.php

Maccoby, Hyam. "Holiness and Purity: The Holy People in Leviticus and Ezra–Nehemiah." Pp. 153–170 in *Reading Leviticus: A Conversation with Mary Douglas*. Edited by John F. A. Sawyer. Sheffield: Sheffield Academic, 1996.

———. *Ritual and Morality: The Ritual Purity System and its Place in Judaism*. Cambridge: Cambridge University Press, 1999.

Martin, Dale B. *The Corinthian Body*. New Haven CT: Yale University Press, 1995.

Martin, Ralph P. *2 Corinthians*. WBC 40. Waco TX: Word, 1986.

"Matrimonia Mixta: Apostolic Letter of Pope Paul VI on Mixed Marriages (1970)." No pages. Cited 24 May 2009. Online: http://www.catholicdoors.com/misc/marriage/mixed.htm

May, Alistair S. "*The Body for the Lord:*" *Sex and Identity in 1 Corinthians 5–7*. London: T&T Clark International, 2004.

McCarthy, Dennis J. *Treaty and Covenant: A Study in Form in the Ancient Oriental Documents and in the Old Testament*. Rome: Biblical Institute, 1981.

McConville, J. G. Ezra, *Deuteronomy*. AOTC 5. Leicester: Apollos / Downers Grove IL: IVP, 2002.

———. *Nehemiah and Esther*. DSB. Edinburgh: St Andrew, 1985.

———. "The Shadow of the Curse: A Key to Old Testament Theology," *Evangel* 3/1 (1985) 2–5.

Mendenhall, George E. "Ancient Oriental and Biblical Law." *The Biblical Archaeologist* 17/2 (1954) 25–46.

———. "Covenant Forms in Israelite Tradition." *The Biblical Archaeologist* 17/3 (1954) 49–76.

Meyer, Eduard. *Die Entstehung des Judenthums: eine historische Untersuchung*. Halle: Max Niemeyer, 1896.

Milgrom, Jacob. "The Concept of Ma'al in the Bible and the Ancient Near East." *JAOS* 96/2 (1976) 236–247.

———. *Cult and Conscience: The Asham and the Priestly Doctrine of Repentance*. Leiden: Brill, 1976.

———. "Law and Narrative and the Exegesis of Leviticus XIX 19." *VT* 46/4 (1996) 544–548.

———. *Leviticus 1–16: A New Translation with Introduction and Commentary*. AB 3. New York: Doubleday, 1991.

———. *Leviticus 17–22: A New Translation with Introduction and Commentary*. AB 3A. New York: Doubleday, 2000.

———. "Religious Conversion and the Revolt Model for the Formation of Israel." *JBL* 101/2 (1982). 169–176

Mishnah (Hebrew). No pages. Cited 22 Sep 2007. Online: http://www.mechon-mamre.org/b/h/h2a.htm

Moberly, R. W. L. *The Bible, Theology and Faith*. Cambridge: Cambridge University Press, 2000.

———. "'Holy, Holy, Holy': Isaiah's vision of God." Pp. 122–140 in *Holiness Past and Present*. Edited by Stephen C. Barton. London: T&T Clark / New York: Continuum, 2003.

———. "Is Election Bad for You?" Pp. 95–111 in *The Centre and the Periphery : A European Tribute to Walter Brueggemann*. Edited by Jill Middlemas, David J. A. Clines, and Else Holt. Sheffield: Sheffield Phoenix, 2010.

———. *The Old Testament of the Old Testament: Patriarchal Narratives and Mosaic Yahwism*. Minneapolis MN: Fortress, 1992.

———. *The Theology of the Book of Genesis*. Cambridge: Cambridge University Press, 2009.

———. "Toward an Interpretation of the Shema." Pp. 124–144 in *Theological Exegesis: Essays in Honor of Brevard S. Childs*. Edited by C. Seitz and K. Greene-McCreight. Grand Rapids, MI: Eerdmans, 1999.

Moffatt, James. *The First Epistle of Paul to the Corinthians*. MNTC. London: Hodder and Stoughton, 1938.

Morris, Leon. *The First Epistle of Paul to the Corinthians: An Introduction and Commentary*. 2nd ed. TNTC. Leicester: IVP / Grand Rapids MI: Eerdmans, 1985.

Murphy-O'Connor, Jerome. "Philo and 2 Cor 6.14–7.1." *RB* 95 (1988) 55–69.

———. "Relating 2 Corinthians 6.14–7.1 to Its Context." *NTS* 33 (1987) 272–75.

———. "Works without Faith in I Cor., VII, 14" *RB* 84 (1977) 349–361.

Myers, J. M. *Ezra, Nehemiah*. AB 14. New York: Doubleday, 1965.

Najman, Hindi. "Ezra." Pp. 1666–87 in *The Jewish Study Bible*. Edited by Adele Berlin and Marc Z. Brettler. Oxford: Oxford University Press, 1999.

Neusner, Jacob. *Making God's Word Work: A Guide to the Mishnah*. New York: Continuum, 2004.

Nicholson, Ernest W. *God and His People: Covenant and Theology in the Old Testament*. Oxford: Clarendon, 1986.

———. "The Meaning of the Expression עם הארץ in the Old Testament." *JSS* 10 (1965) 59–66.

North, Robert. "Ezra and Nehemiah." Pp. 384–398 in *The New Jerome Biblical Commentary*. Edited by Raymond E. Brown, Joseph A. Fitzmyer, and Roland E. Murphy. London: Geoffrey Chapman, 1989.

Noth, Martin. "The Laws in the Pentateuch: Their Assumptions and Meaning." Pp. 1–107 in *The Laws in the Pentateuch and Other Studies*. Translated by D. R. AP-Thomas. (Edinburgh: Oliver & Boyd, 1966.

Olyan, Saul M. "Purity Ideology in Ezra–Nehemiah as a Tool to Reconstitute the Community." *JSJ* 35/1 (2004) 1–16.

Palestinian Talmud (Hebrew). No Pages. Cited 22 Sep 2007. Online: http://www.mechon-mamre.org/b/r/r2a04.htm

Rosenbaum, M., and A. M. Silbermann, eds. *Pentateuch with Targum Onkelos, Haphtaroth and Prayers for Sabbath and Rashi's Commentary*. London: Shapiro, Vallentine & Co, 1946.

Parry, John. *The First Epistle of Paul the Apostle to the Corinthians in the Revised Version with Introduction and Notes*. Cambridge: Cambridge University Press, 1916.

Philo of Alexandria. *The Works of Philo: Complete and Unabridged*. Translated by C. D. Yonge. Peabody MA: Hendrickson, 1993.

Plummer, A. *A Critical and Exegetical Commentary on the Second Epistle of St Paul to the Corinthians*. ICC 34. Edinburgh: T&T Clark, 1915.

Porten, Bezalel. *Archives from Elephantine: The Life of an Ancient Jewish Military Colony*. Berkeley: University of California Press, 1968.

Porter, J. R. *Leviticus*. Cambridge: Cambridge University Press, 1976.

Preuss, Horst D. *Old Testament Theology*. Translated by Leo G. Perdue. 2 volumes. Edinburgh: T&T Clark, 1995–96.

———. "תּוֹעֵבָה tôʻēbâ תעב tʻb" Pp. 591–604 in vol. 15 of *Theological Dictionary of the Old Testament*. Edited by Johannes G. Botterweck, Helmer Ringgren, and Heinz-Josef Fabry. Translated by David E. Green. Grand Rapids MI: Eerdmans, 2006.

Qimron, Elisha, and John Strugnell, eds. *Miqsat Ma'ase Ha-Torah*. Vol. 5 of *Qumran Cave 4*. DJD 10. Oxford: Clarendon, 1994.

Quell, G. "σπέρμα" Pp. 536–543 in vol. 7 of *Theological Dictionary of the New Testament*. Edited by Gerhard Kittel, and Gerhard Friedrich. Translated by Geoffrey W. Bromiley. Grand Rapids MI: Eerdmans, 1971.

Rad, G. von. *Old Testament Theology*. 2 volumes. Translated by D. M. G. Stalker. London: SCM, 1975.

Bibliography

Rendtorff, Rolf. *The Canonical Hebrew Bible: A Theology of the Old Testament.* Translated by David E. Orton. Leiden: Deo, 2005.

———. "Old Testament Theology: Some Ideas for a New Approach." Pp. 1–16 in *Canon and Theology: Overtures to an Old Testament Theology.* Translated by Margaret Kohl. Edinburgh: T&T Clark, 1993.

———. "Rabbinic Exegesis and the Modern Christian Bible Scholar." Pp. 17–24 in *Canon and Theology: Overtures to an Old Testament Theology.* Translated by Margaret Kohl. Edinburgh: T&T Clark, 1993.

———. "Toward a Common Jewish-Christian Reading of the Hebrew Bible." Pp. 31–45 in *Canon and Theology: Overtures to an Old Testament Theology.* Translated by Margaret Kohl. Edinburgh: T&T Clark, 1993.

Ringgren, Helmer, "גָּאַל gāʾal; גֹּאֵל gōʾēl; גְּאֻלָּה geʾullāh." Pp. 350–55 in vol. 1 of *Theological Dictionary of the Old Testament.* Edited by G. Johannes Botterweck, Helmer Ringgren, and Heinz-Josef Fabry. Translated by John T. Willis. 2nd ed. Grand Rapids MI: Eerdmans, 1977.

———. "טָהֵר ṭāhar; טָהוֹר ṭāhôr; טֹהַר ṭōhar; טָהֳרָה ṭohºrâ." Pp. 287–96 in vol. 5 of *Theological Dictionary of the Old Testament.* Edited by G. Johannes Botterweck, Helmer Ringgren, and Heinz-Josef Fabry. Translated by David E. Green. Grand Rapids MI: Eerdmans, 1986.

Rivkin, Ellis. *A Hidden Revolution.* Nashville TN: Abingdon, 1978.

Robertson, Archibald, and Alfred Plummer. *A Critical and Exegetical Commentary on the First Epistle of St Paul to the Corinthians.* ICC. Edinburgh: T&T Clark, 1911.

Rosner, Brian S. *Paul, Scripture and Ethics: A Study of 1 Corinthians 5–7.* Leiden: Brill, 1994.

Rudolph, Wilhelm. *Esra und Nehemia mit 3.Esra.* HAT 20. Tübingen: Mohr Siebeck, 1949.

Ryle, H. E. *The Books of Ezra and Nehemiah with Introduction, Notes and Maps.* Cambridge: Cambridge University Press, 1897.

Sanders, E. P. *Judaism: Practice and Belief 63 BCE—66 CE.* Philadephia PA: Trinity International, 1992.

———. *Paul and Palestinian Judaism: A Comparison of Patterns of Religion.* London: SCM, 1977.

Sanders, James. *Canon and Community.* Philadelphia PA: Fortress, 1984

———. *Torah and Canon.* Philadelphia PA: Fortress, 1972.

Satterthwaite, P. E. and D. W. Baker. "Nations of Canaan." Pp. 596–604 in *Dictionary of the Old Testament: Pentateuch*. Edited by T. Desmond Alexander & David W. Baker. Downers Grove, IL: IVP, 2003.

Schäfer-Lichtenberger, Christa. "Bedeutung und Funktion von Herem in biblisch-hebräischen Texten." *BZ* 38 (1994) 270–275.

Schmitt, Götz. *Du sollst keinen Frieden schliessen mit den Bewohnern des Landes: Die Weisungen gegen die Kanaanäer in Israels Geschichte und Geschichtsschreibung*. BWANT 91. Stuttgart: Kohlhammer, 1970.

Schneider, Heinrich. *Die Bücher Esra und Nehemia*. Bonn: Peter Hanstein, 1959.

Schürer, Emil. *Geschichte des jüdischen Volkes im Zeitalter Jesu Christi*. 2 volumes. Leipzig: J. C. Hinrich, 1901–1911.

Smith-Christopher, Daniel L. "Ezra and Nehemiah." Pp. 155–159 in *Theological Bible Commentary*. Edited bz Gail R. O'Day and David L. Petersen. Louisville KY: Westminster John Knox, 2009.

Southwood, K. E., *Ethnicity and the Mixed Marriage Crisis in Ezra 9–10*. Oxford Theological Monograph Series. Oxford: Oxford University Press, 2012. [forthcoming]

Stendhal, Krister. "Biblical Theology, Contemporary." Pp. 67–106 in *Reading the Bible in the Global Village*. Edited by H. Räisänen et al. Helsinki: SBL, 2000.

Strachan, R. H. *The Second Epistle of Paul to the Corinthians*. 5th ed. MNTC. New York: Harper, 1948.

Targum Pseudo-Jonathan (Aramaic). No pages. Cited 22 Sep 2007. Online: http://cal1.cn.huc.edu

Thiselton, Anthony C. *The First Epistle to the Corinthians: A Commentary on the Greek Text*. Grand Rapids MI: Eerdmans / Carlisle: Paternoster, 2000.

Thrall, Margaret E. *The First and Second Letters of Paul to the Corinthians*. CBC. Cambridge: Cambridge University Press, 1965.

———. "The Problem of II Cor. VI.14–VII.1 in Some Recent Discussion." *NTS* 24 (1977) 132–48.

Tigay, Jeffrey H. *Deuteronomy*. JPS Torah Commentary. Philadelphia PA: JPS, 1996.

Torrey, C. C. *Ezra Studies*. New York: Ktav, 1970.

Van Seters, J. "The Terms 'Amorite' and 'Hittite' in the Old Testament." *VT* 22 (1972) 64–81.

Vermes, Geza. "Leviticus 18:21 in Ancient Jewish Bible Exegesis." Pp. 108–124 in *Studies in Aggadah, Targum, and Jewish Liturgy in Memory of Joseph Heinemann*. Edited by Jacob J. Petuchowski and Ezra Fleischer. Jerusalem: Magnes, 1981.

Washington, Harold C. "Israel's Holy Seed and the Foreign Women of Ezra–Nehemiah: A Kristevan Reading." *BI* 11 (2003) 427–437.

Watts, John D. W. *Isaiah 1–33*. Rev. ed. WBC 24. Nashville TN: Nelson, 2005.

Webb, William J. *Returning Home: New Covenant and Second Exodus as the Context for 2 Corinthians 6.14–7.1*. JSNT SS 85. Sheffield: JSOT Press, 1993.

Wellhausen, Julius. *Prolegomena to the History of Israel*. Translated by J. Sutherland Black and Allan Menzies. Edinburgh: A&C Black, 1885.

Wenham, Gordon. *The Book of Leviticus*. NICOT. Grand Rapids MI: Eerdmans, 1979.

Westermann, Claus. *Elements of Old Testament Theology*. Translated Douglas W. Stott. Atlanta GA: John Knox, 1982.

———. *Handbook to the Old Testament*. Edited and translated by Robert H. Boyd. London: SPCK, 1969.

The Westminster Shorter Catechism. No pages. Cited 10 June 2009. Online: http://www.ccel.org/creeds/westminster-shorter-cat.html

Wijk-Bos, Johanna W. H. *Ezra, Nehemiah, and Esther*. Louisville, KY: Westminster John Knox, 1998.

Wildberger, Hans. *Isaiah 1–12*. Translated by Thomas H. Trapp. Minneapolis MN: Fortress, 1991.

Williamson, H. G. M. *The Book Called Isaiah: Deutero-Isaiah's Role in Composition and Redaction*. Oxford: Clarendon, 1994.

———. "Ezra and Nehemiah." Pp. 424–441 in *New Bible Commentary: 21st Century Edition*. Edited by Carson, D. A. et al. Leicester: IVP, 1994.

———. *Ezra, Nehemiah*. WBC 16. Nashville TN: Nelson, 1985.

Windisch, H. *Der zweite Korintherbrief*. Göttingen: Vandenhoeck & Rupprecht, 1924.

Wolff, Hans Walter. *The Old Testament: A Guide to Its Writings*. Translated by Keith R. Crim. London: SPCK, 1974.

Wright, Christopher. *Deuteronomy*. NIBCOT 4. Peabody MA: Hendrickson, 1996.

Wright, David P. "The Spectrum of Priestly Impurity." Pp. 150–181 in *Priesthood and Cult in Ancient Israel*. Edited by Gary A. Anderson and Saul M. Olyan. JSOT SS 125. Sheffield: Sheffield Academic, 1991.

———. "Unclean and Clean (OT)." Pp. 729–41 in vol. 6 of *Anchor Bible Dictionary*. Edited by David Noel Freedman. New York: Doubleday, 1992.

Zenger, Erich, et al. *Einleitung in das Alte Testament*. 6th ed. Stuttgart: Kohlhammer, 2006

Zimmerli, Walther. *Old Testament Theology in Outline*. Translated by David E. Green. Edinburgh: T&T Clark, 1978.

Index of Biblical Citations

Gen
1	89
1:1	11
1:11	82
2:24	109, 154, 167, 190
2:25	110
3:24	14
4:10-13	13
6:1-6	89, 96
6:11-12	96
12:1-3	23, 144
12:3	37, 146, 147
12:7	82, 144
12:7-8	177
13:5-6	147
13:15-16	82
13:18	177
15:3-5	82
15:5	22
15:6	23
15:16	41
16:10	82
17:1	24
17:5	21
17:7-10	82
17:9-14	24
17:20	147
18:19	13
18:25	13
19:30-38	37
22	16, 222
22:1-19	23
22:17	22
22:18	147
23:7	46
23:12-13	46
26	147
26:4	144, 147
26:5	13
26:14	147
26:25	177
28:18	177
30:27	147
31:7	35
33:20	177
34	93, 150, 166
34:9	75
38	200
38:9-10	110
39:5	147
42:6	46
47:23	82
49:6	55, 90

Exod
3:5	138
3:21-22	39
6:4	22
12:2	11
12:15	78
12:38	52–53, 55, 137
13:11	41
13:21-22	26
19:5	22
19:5-6	24
19:6	137, 144, 145, 146
19:8	165
19:12-13	96
19:13	184
20:2	38, 75
20:5-6	172
20:11	13
22	60
22:19[20]	60–61, 63, 64, 66, 67
22:21	150
23:33	75
25:11	120
25:17	120
25:22	14
25:29	120

25:31	120	19:19	87, 92, 95, 106, 124, 143, 166
28:6	91	19:20-22	102, 103, 120, 163
28:15	91	19:31	99
29:37	184	20	90, 110, 114
30:26-29	184	20:1-3	99, 111
32	27	20:2	46
32:13	22	20:2-3	93
34:6	24	20:3	107
34:11-16	31, 58	20:7	137
34:14-16	209	20:21	39
34:16	32	20:24-26	31, 89
34:28	22, 165	21	111, 114
39:29	91	21:4	107
40:34	26	21:6	86, 107
		21:7	92, 100, 107, 109, 120
Lev		21:7-9	111
4:2	101	21:7-15	91, 92, 95, 97, 113, 124
4:13	101	21:9	93, 111, 114, 121, 125
4:22	101	21:12	107
5:14-16	72, 87, 97, 100, 101	21:13-15	111
5:17-19	101	21:14	92, 106, 110, 211
5:18	101	21:14-15	106, 111, 114, 120
6:11	184	21:15	92, 104, 106, 107, 112, 114, 121, 125, 177
6:20	184	21:19-22	103
7:14	100	21:20-22	163
10:10	31, 89	21:21	82
11:1-47	98	22:4	82
11:47	31, 89	22:9	107
12:1-8	98	22:14-15	111
13:1-14:32	98	26:14	100
15:1-33	98	26:32-33	100
15:16	82	26:40	100
15:18	108	26:42	22
16:28	98	27	58, 68
18	36, 39, 40, 90, 110, 114, 117	27:1-8	61, 101
18:3	38, 40, 43, 56, 74, 81, 124, 223	27:21	58, 66, 77
18:21	39, 93, 94, 124, 180	27:28	58, 60–62, 66, 73, 77
18:22	34, 113	27:28-29	67
18:24-30	39, 97, 99, 111, 223	27:29	60–61, 64
18:26	38		
18:26-30	39, 92	Num	
18:27	38	1:18	162
18:29	38		
18:30	38		

4:15	96, 111	4:23	22
6:5	86	4:37	82
11:4	52–53, 55, 138	4:44	82
11:17	25	4:45	82
14:4	27	4:46	82
14:9	46	5:6	38, 75
14:22	35	5:14	12
17:5[16:40]	82	5:15	13
18:4	77	6:10	22
18:11	112	6:11	66
18:14	61	6:12	38, 75
19:8	98	6:12-15	66
19:10-22	98	7	41, 42, 52, 58, 59, 62, 69, 71, 72, 81, 83–84, 87, 93, 95, 105, 124, 125, 137–38, 148, 158, 172, 175, 210, 222, 223
19:13	113		
19:20	113		
21:2-3	66		
22	36	7:1	35, 40
22:24	88	7:1-2	86
25	37, 117–18, 121	7:1-3	31–32, 33, 34, 43, 54, 56, 57, 58, 70, 72, 77, 79, 81–84, 96, 100, 105, 115, 124, 209
25:1	117		
25:3	205		
25:12	118	7:2	62, 70
31:16	37, 100	7:2-3	62
35:33-34	99, 111	7:2-4	86
Deut		7:3	34, 49, 54, 56, 163, 165, 166, 178–79, 179, 210, 214, 216
1	27		
1:3	82	7:3-4	71, 210
1:8	22, 82	7:3-6	75
1:33	25	7:4	34, 64, 72, 163, 166
2:4	82	7:6	48, 81, 82, 86–87, 92, 137
2:5	64	7:6-7	143–44, 147–48
2:9	64	7:9-10	172
2:19	64	7:20	62
2:28-29	36	7:23	62
2:31	64	7:24	62
2:34	63	7:25	86
2:35	66	7:25-26	34, 65, 81, 92, 113
2:37	36	7:26	72–74, 92
3:2	64	8:3	25
3:3	63	8:27	66
3:7	66	9:5-6	22
4:5-8	30	9:12-13	82
4:6	82, 148	9:18	165
4:13	22	9:26	82

10:11	82	23:4-7[3-6]	37, 43, 44, 48, 54, 77, 81, 115, 124, 134, 211, 223
10:13	7		
10:15	82		
11:9	82	23:4-9[3-8]	31–32, 33, 34, 35, 54, 77, 79, 83
11:31	75		
12:10	75	23:5[4]	37
12:29	75	23:5-6[4-5]	55
13:2-12[1-11]	60	23:7[6]	34
13:6-7[5-6]	62	23:8[7]	35, 40
13:10-11[9-10]	62	23:8-9[7-8]	38, 52
13:13-16[12-15]	60	23:18[17]	82
13:13-18[12-17]	61, 62–63, 65, 72, 79, 80	24:1	110
		24:1-4	75–76, 79, 109, 152, 167
13:15[14]	34		
13:16-17[15-16]	66	24:7	82
13:17-18[16-17]	62	24:17-21	110
13:18[17]	72, 73	25:5-10	109
14:2	82, 86, 137	25:16	34
14:3	34	25:19	64–65
14:21	86, 137	26:19	30
17:2	22	27:15-26	55
17:3-4	113	27-28	7
17:16	82	28:9	30
18:3	82	28:10	47
18:9-10	34	28:15-68	55
20	63	28:33	23
20:10-18	35, 65–66	28:47-48	23
20:16-18	63	29:9	22
20:18	64	29:11[12]	24, 55, 103–4, 115, 120
21:10-14	35, 63, 83		
21:18-21	167	29:13-14[14-15]	103
22:9	90–91, 97, 106, 211	29:16[17]	103
22:9-11	87–89, 92, 95, 106, 124	30:20	22, 75
		31:16	22
22:10	186	31:19	82
22:13-23:2[22:30]	37	31:22	82
22:28-29	108	31:23	82
23	39, 40, 42, 52, 83, 95	33:10	65
23:4[3]	34–36	34:4	22
23:4-7[3-6]	56–57		
23:2-9[1-8]	54–55	Josh	
23:4[3]	40, 134, 135, 168–69	4:24	47
23:4-6[3-5]	52, 150	6:17	62
		6:18	62, 72–73
		6:19	73

6:21	66
6:24	66
7	63
7:1	62
7:12	72–73
8:24	63
10:1	66
10:28	63, 66
10:35	63
10:35-40	66
10:37	63
10:39	63
11:11	63
11:12	63
11:14	63, 66
11:21	66
15:13	70
16:10	70
17:12	70
23:7	55
23:12	55
23:12-13	70

Judg

1:17	66
2:1-3	70
2:21-3:6	70
11:29-40	200
11:39	110
21	68, 78, 80
21:5	63, 65
21:10-11	65, 78
21:11	63, 66
21:12	110

1 Sam

6:19	111
7:9	65
14:43-46	200
15	64–66, 68, 71
15:2-3	65
15:3	63
15:21	62, 72
21:1-6	201
21:6	168
26:23	23

2 Sam

6:6-7	96, 111, 184
11:3	70
13:13	108
17:19	163
22:51	82
24:16	70

1 Kgs

2:33	82
5:15-26[1-12]	138
5:27-32[13-18]	44
8:10-12	26
8:21	22
8:43	47
8:53	47
8:60	47
9:21	66
11	56
11:1	41, 51
11:1-2	42, 52, 165
11:1-8	87
11:1-11	54, 56, 57, 80, 115, 124
11:1-13	38
11:2	54
11:39	82
12:19	103
14:24	34
16:30-33	51
20:42	62, 64, 66
21:25	51

2 Kgs

3:5	103
16:3	34
17	44
17:8	39
19:11	64
21:2	34
23:13	34
24:2	36
24:14	46
25:6	46
25:12	46

Isa		3:1-3	167
1:4	85	3:6-10	108
1:9	85	3:8	167
1:13	35	3:13	103
1:28	103	5:1	23
2:3	30, 33, 148	6:13-15	34
5:5	88	7:9-10	34
5:7	88	12:10	88
6:12-13	85	22:9	22
6:13	84–85, 95	24	48
11:6-7	13	24:8	38
11:8	13	25:9	64
11:15	64	32:35	34
24:5	22	33:20	13
24-27	133	38:24-28	200
30:2-3	38	43:5-7	46
33:8	22	44:4	34, 113
34:2	64	44:8	38
34:5	62, 64	44:15-19	49
34:6	65	50:21	64
37:11	64	50:26	64
40-55	39	51:3	64
41:24	34	Ezek	
42:6	144, 145, 146	1:5-11	91
43:28	64	2:3	103
45:1	146	5:9	34
45:14	146, 148	11:15	48
49:6	146	13:5	88
51:4	30, 146	16	108
52:11	188–89	16:26	38
52:11-12	31	16:47	34
53	146	16:50	22
54:4	109	17:15	103
56:3-8	150	17:19	22
56:6-8	146	18	172
59:3	115	18:2	112
59:4	23	18:3	34
61:5-6	146	20:4	35
63:3	116	20:7-10	38
63:10	25	22:11	34, 113
65:17	13	22:30	88
65:25	13	23:19	38
Jer		23:27	38
2:3	86–87, 95	23:39	107

25:12-14	41	13:1	114
31:12	47	Mal	
33:26	34	1:4	41
35:15	41	1:7	116
36:5	41	1:7-12	118
36:17	113	1:8	93
36:25	114	1:11	133
41:25	14	1:12	116
42:14	184	1:13	26
42:20	89	1:13-14	93
43:7-8	107	2	118
44:6-8	35	2:4-5	118
44:19	184	2:8-9	118
44:22	108, 110, 179	2:10-16	152–53
44:29	62, 77	2:11	85, 118, 150
46:20	184	2:14	85, 95
47:1-12	14	2:16	152, 154, 170

Hos
1:9	144
2:21-22[19-20]	23
6:7	23
7:11	38
7:13	104
8:1	104
11:1-7	167

Jonah
3:5-9	135
3:7-8	135

Mic
4:2	30
4:13	67

Zeph
3:1	116
3:20	47

Hag
1:2	26
1:2-4	93
1:3-4	51
2:11-13	184
2:13-14	93

Zech
8:20-23	148

Ps
19	12
22:24[23]	82
25:10	22
32:8	25
51:19[17]	65
55:21[20]	23
78:10	22
78:14-16	25
78:24	25
78:37	23
80:8-11[7-10]	88
80:13[12]	88
89:25[24]	23
92:3[2]	23
98:3	23
105:6	82
105:9	22
105:11	22
105:39-45	25
106:27	86, 95
106:33	25
106:34-36	86
106:35	95
119	12
119:105	25
137:7	41

Job	
19:3	35
Prov	
11:1	34
12:17	23
27:22	163
Ruth	
1:4	31
1:13	109
1:16	84
1:16-17	149
1:20	109
4:18-22	134
Song	
8:11-12	90
Eccl	
12:12	30
Lam	
1:8-9	113
1:17	113
1:19	113
4:14	115
Esth	
3:1	71
7:10	71
8:17	47
9:6-10	71
9:14	71
Dan	
1:8	116
2:37	30
2:44	30
4:3	30
4:34	30
6:26	30
11:44	64
Ezra	
1	31
1-6	151
1:2	30
1:6	39
1:8	31
2	48, 82, 132, 138
2:40	132
2:59	83
2:62	48, 83, 117
2:62-63	87
3	43
4	150
4:1	44, 47
4:1-2	43–44, 114
4:1-4	174
4:2-3	132
4:3	43
4:4	46
4:8-16	44
4:15	25
4:19	25
5:11	30
5:12	30
6:7	42
6:14	42
6:19	47
6:21	31, 47, 134, 137, 149–51, 174
7	30
7-8	5, 124
7-10	70
7:1-5	31, 82, 161, 173
7:3	136
7:9	29
7:10	30, 118, 129, 136, 165, 173
7:14	30
7:15-23	30
7:25	30, 118, 129
7:26	78
8	31, 33, 48, 136, 173
8:1-14	82
8:15	132
8:24	90
8:25	39
8:28	31
8:31	31
8:35	47
8:36	29, 30

Index of Authors and Subjects

9   20, 33, 39, 52, 53, 69, 72, 86, 88, 90, 106, 133, 134, 145, 150, 155, 158
9-10   4–5, 9, 11, 15, 18, 20–21, 29, 31, 33, 43, 47–51, 54–57, 58–59, 68–69, 71–80, 83–84, 92, 93, 97, 101, 104–8, 113–15, 118, 121, 123–25, 129–30, 131, 137–38, 139, 142, 144, 149–58, 160, 162–69, 170, 173–77, 178, 180, 182–83, 185, 200–201, 202–5, 207, 208, 210, 218–20, 222–24
9:1   31, 33, 34–36, 38–42, 45, 52, 56, 58, 72, 77, 81–82, 124, 137, 210
9:1-2   55, 73, 93, 124, 136, 173
9:2   20, 31–32, 44, 48, 51, 52, 72, 75, 81–82, 84–88, 90–91, 92, 93, 95, 96, 97, 100, 103, 105, 106, 113, 120, 143, 151, 160, 183, 194, 209
9:4   87, 97, 100, 103
9:5-15   136, 223
9:6   103
9:6-15   147
9:7   103
9:8-9   134
9:9   22, 88
9:10   100
9:10-12   76
9:11   39, 72, 81, 113
9:11-12   43
9:12   22, 31, 32, 34, 39, 49, 54, 75, 210
9:13   103, 134
9:14   31, 81, 100, 137, 173
9:15   51, 90, 103
10   20, 76, 78, 142, 150, 154, 156, 196
10:1   136
10:2   31, 72, 75, 87, 97, 100, 103, 136, 153
10:2-3   173
10:3   48, 50, 75, 76, 129, 132, 162, 165–66, 173, 211
10:6   87, 97, 100, 103, 165
10:7   47
10:7-8   138
10:8   48, 58, 61, 74, 77–80, 160, 176
10:9   29
10:10   87, 103
10:11   72, 134
10:12-14   165
10:13   76, 103
10:15   20
10:16   20, 47, 76
10:18   105
10:19   76, 87, 97, 100, 103, 104–5, 163
10:21   134
10:44   31, 160, 174, 211

Neh
1:3   88
1:4   30
1:5   30
1:8   100
2:4   30
2:19   36, 42
2:20   30, 44, 174
3   48
3:1-3   133
3:33[4:1]   88
3:33-4:17[4:1-13]   44
4:1[4:7]   41, 88
4:1-8[7-14]   36
4:6[12]   35
4:7[13]   42
5   29, 51
5:1-5   93
5:1-13   9
6:1   41
6:17-19   44
6:18   36, 49
6:21   54
7   48, 82, 138
7:1   88

7:43	132	10:29[28]	137, 149, 174
7:73	29	10:29-30[28-29]	134
8	5, 20, 28, 29, 136, 142	10:29-40[28-39]	55
8	135–36	10:30[29]	23, 28, 55, 103, 115
8:1	165	10:31[30]	27, 28, 115, 174
8:2	118	10:32-39[31-38]	28
8:8	118	11	48
8:9-11	136	12	48
8:9-12	20	12:1-26	82
8:13	118	13	26, 55–57, 108, 117, 119, 134, 174
8:13-18	28		
8:14	29	13:1	42
9	5, 20, 21, 23, 25, 27, 29, 32, 75, 123, 223	13:1-3	28, 52–53, 54, 77, 149–50, 174
9	134–35	13:3	55, 119
9:1	20, 136	13:4-5	36, 93
9:2	20, 82, 132, 174	13:4-9	28, 44
9:3	136	13:9	119
9:5-37	147	13:10	93
9:6	30	13:10-14	28, 51
9:7	21	13:11	120
9:8	21–22	13:13	120
9:10	24	13:15-16	93
9:11	24	13:15-18	27, 28, 44
9:12	25	13:15-22	51
9:13	21	13:17-18	174
9:13-14	25	13:22	119, 120
9:14	21	13:23	42, 54–55
9:15	22, 25	13:23-27	117, 118, 132, 175
9:16	24	13:23-29	28, 93, 119, 121, 209
9:17	24	13:23-30	115
9:22	22	13:23-31	52, 54–55, 56–57, 97, 115, 118, 121, 174
9:23	22		
9:24	22–23	13:24	44, 54, 211
9:25	22	13:25	31, 55, 103
9:27	23	13:26	51, 54, 56, 211
9:28	23	13:27	100, 115
9:30	22–23	13:28	133, 174
9:31	24	13:28-31	118
9:32	21	13:29	55, 83, 115–16, 118–19
9:35	22–23	13:30	115, 118–20
9:36	22–23	13:31	120
9:37	23	1 Chr	
10	5, 20, 21, 28–29, 174	1:27	21
10:1[9:38]	21		

Index of Authors and Subjects

2-3	21
3:17-19	42
4:41	64, 71
4:43	64, 71
5:25	47
6	21

2 Chr

2:1[2]	44
2:17[18]	44
6:33	47
11:21	31
12:1-2	100
13:9	47
13:21	31
15:12	78
15:13	78–80
15:14	78
18:1	75
20:23	64
24:3	31
28:22-25	100
29:5	113
32:13	47
32:14	47, 64
32:19	47
33:19	100
36:13	103
36:19	42

Matt

5:13-16	155
5:31-32	152
5:31-35	170
12:3-4	201
12:5	201
12:11	201
19:1-9	169, 170, 217
19:4-5	167
19:6	109
19:8	109, 154
19:9	152
19:19	200
21:33	88
28:19	201

Mark

10:2-12	167, 170

Luke

14:5	201

John

4	145

Acts

4:13	145
8:37	191
10	99
15	180
16:31	8
16:34	191
17:26	155
22:3	187

Rom

1:7	184
4	146
6:19	184
10:14	8
11:16	191
12:1-2	184, 219
14	201
14:19	201

1 Cor

1:2	184
5:1-5	184
6:6	203
6:9-10	10
6:12-20	184, 205
6:13-19	189
6:15-20	194
7	185, 187, 205, 220
7:10-16	152
7:12	183
7:12-13	155, 161, 183
7:12-14	205
7:12-15	203
7:12-16	5, 129, 169, 170, 182–84, 187, 194, 199–200, 202, 206, 211, 214
7:14	183, 188–98, 211

7:15	183, 201, 222	6:17	188
7:16	222	7:2	202
7:24	200	7:2-4	204
7:39	183–84, 199, 211, 214, 221		

Gal

2:11-14	99
3-4	146
3:15-18	177
3:28	155
5:14-24	10
6:7-8	10

9:1-14	184
10:4	194
10:14-22	205
10:27	203
14:22-24	203

2 Cor

1:12	184
2:14-7:4	204
5:16-21	204
6:1-2	204
6:3-10	204
6:11-13	204
6:13	202
6:14	186, 204–5, 214
6:14-7:1	130, 182, 185, 189, 192, 196, 199, 202, 204, 206, 221
6:14-16	189
6:14-18	205, 211
6:16	204

Eph

5:22-33	216–17

Phil

1:27	8

Col

4:5	201

1 Thess

3:3	184
4:3-5	184
4:11-12	201

Jas

2:14-26	10

Index of Authors and Subjects

abominations 34–35, 38–39, 40, 41, 43–45
Ackroyd, P. R. 28
Allen, L. C. 25, 26, 28, 45, 144, 150, 152, 157
Alon, G. 99, 114
Alt, A. 60
Anderson, B. W. 98, 135
Averbeck, R. E. 116, 118
Baker, D. W. 36, 192, 195
Barr, J. 12
Barrett, C. K. 184, 195, 197, 203
Batten, L. W. 4, 54, 77, 117, 119
Berlin, A. 165

Betz, H. D. 203
biblical authority 171–72, 175–76, 218–19
   and rabbinic tradition 178
   and the church 177–78
   Halakah vs Haggadah 166–68
   Law/Torah 14, 17, 75, 137, 165
   Writings 162, 166
Blenkinsopp, J. 21, 23, 28, 29, 40, 45, 50, 54, 77, 78, 174, 175
Brettler, M. Z. 165, 171–72, 175
Bright, J. 10
Brockington, L. H. 175
Bruce, F. F. 203

Index of Authors and Subjects

Brueggemann, W. 135, 136, 148
Calvin, J. 192-93, 195
Carmichael, C. M. 90
Childs, B. S. 59, 84, 136, 173
Clements, R. E. 132
Clines, D. J. A. 21, 24, 25, 26, 27, 143, 144, 147, 152, 158
Coggins, R. J. 28
Collins, R. F. 188, 193, 195, 197
conversion 84, 95, 111, 149-51
Conzelmann, H. 195-96
covenant
  Abrahamic 21-22, 23, 24
  'ămānâ/běrît 23
  broken 22, 24, 27
  curses 23-24, 55
  Davidic 24-25
  God's commitment 23, 28
  Mosaic 22-23
  new 204
Cranfield, C. E. B. 8, 9, 15
Dahl, N. A. 202, 203
Daiches, S. 40
Davis, E. F. 167, 173, 175-76, 177, 178, 180, 219
Deming, W. 185-87, 197
Derrett, J. D. M. 203
divorce
  and 2 Cor 6:14-7:1 205-6
  and Neh 13 55
  as witch-hunt 50
  Christian views on 151-54
  in canon 170
  initiating 49
  language of 74-75
  law behind 75-77
Douglas, M. 44, 89, 104, 130, 132, 157, 207, 208-9, 212-13, 216
Driver, S. R. 89
Eichrodt, W. 7, 131, 132-35, 141, 149
Epictetus 186
Epstein, L. M. 75, 164, 212
Eskenazi, T. C. 164

Evans, E. 189, 195
Fee, G. D. 184, 191, 203, 204
Fensham, F. C. 24, 26, 143-46, 148, 151-52
Fishbane, M. 17, 30, 37, 39, 40, 54, 55, 75, 90, 172, 176, 219
Fitzmyer, J. A. 154, 202, 203
Fretheim, T. E. 12, 13
Frymer-Kensky, T. 98, 108
Furnish, V. P. 203
Garland, D. E. 195
Gillihan, Y. M. 184, 187, 193-94, 195, 197-98, 199, 200, 206
Gnilka, J. 202, 203
Goldingay, J. 8, 9, 131, 136-39, 139, 142, 143, 148, 153, 166
Goudge, H. L. 192, 196
Grabbe, L. L. 4, 46
Gray, G. B. 84
Greenberg, M. 65, 66, 69
Grosheide, F. W. 189
Grüneberg, K. N. 146
Gunton, C. E. 12
Halakah/Haggadah 11-12, 15, 17, 166-69
Hartley, J. E. 38
Hayes, C. E. 43, 73-74, 92, 99, 104, 111, 114, 115, 120, 178-80, 189, 193-94, 195, 212
Hays, R. B. 133, 167, 176, 195
Hengel, M. 187
Henry, M. 131, 149, 151, 152, 161, 223
ḥērem
  and idolatry 64
  as extermination 60-61, 62-63
  as sacrifice 64-65
  irrevocable 61
  meaning ambiguous 60, 61-62, 63
  metaphorical 59, 74-75
  of Israelites 65, 78
  of non-Canaanites 63-64, 65
  of property 65-67, 77-79
  Sitz im Leben 68-70

withholding devoted things 72–74
Heschel, A. J. 11–12, 166
Hoffman, Y. 69–70
Holmgren, F. C. 24, 50
holy seed
   and descent 82–83
   and ʿēreb 52–53
   disappearance of 94, 179–80
   focus of 210–12
   function of 83, 93, 208–9
   identity of 105–6
   in rabbinic literature 178–79
   resonances 84–86
Horbury, W. 78
Hughes, P. E. 203
Hurd, J. C. 203
Instone-Brewer, D. 49, 50
Janzen, D. 50, 51
Japhet, S. 25, 164
Jenson, R. W. 167
Josephus, F. 76, 77, 110, 160–61, 223
Judd, E. P. 164
Kaiser, O. 85
Kaufmann, Y. 29, 84, 164
Keener, C. S. 190
Keil, C. F. 52, 77, 87, 119, 120
Kidner, D. 143, 149, 150, 152, 153
Klawans, J. 97–99, 189, 212
Klein, R. W. 142, 150, 151, 152, 153, 156
Koehler, L. 132
Lang, F. G. 203
Laniak, T. S. 25, 45, 144
Lash, N. 141
law
   a clash of priorities 200–201, 221–22
   and covenant 6–8, 10, 15, 135–36
   and creation 12–14, 26–27, 219
   and God's Spirit 25–26
   and repentance 136
   and the nations 30
   as (in)flexible 15, 84, 158, 220
   as engagement 16–18
   as gift 25, 135
   as good 26
   hedge around 208–10, 222
   negative view of 3–4, 132–34
   ritual/cultic/ceremonial 8–9
Levenson 9–10, 12–13
Levenson, J. D. 17, 18, 70, 123, 140
Levine, B. A. 39
Lipton, D. 9, 14–19, 76, 96, 123–24
Lockwood, G. J. 190
Lohfink, N. 60, 61, 64, 65
Lohr, J. N. 62
Luther, M. 10
maʿal
   and ʾāšām 72, 87, 97, 100–105
   as covenant breaking 100, 103–4, 115
   as sancta desecration 86
Maccoby, H. 44, 104, 108, 114
Martin, D. B. 197
Martin, R. P. 202, 203, 204
May, A. S. 184
McCarthy, D. J. 7
McConville, J. G. 37, 64–65, 90, 143, 145, 148, 149, 151, 152, 155–56
Mendenhall, G. E. 7
Meyer, E. 52
Milgrom, J. 38–39, 56, 68, 72, 74, 86–87, 90–91, 92, 95, 96–97, 100–105, 107–10, 111, 112, 113, 115, 120, 125, 134, 135, 164, 184, 198–99
mission 144–49, 155, 201, 221, 222
Moberly, R. W. L. 13, 43, 59, 85, 138, 147, 148, 167, 173, 177
Moffatt, J. 195, 197
Morris, L. 188

Murphy-O'Connor, J.   190,   196, 202, 203
Musonius   186
Myers, J. M.   23, 52
Najman, H.   165, 173, 178
Neusner, J.   45
Nicholson, E. W.   6–7, 46
North, R.   64, 153, 154
Noth, M.   3–4, 7, 133, 141
Olyan, S. M.   98, 104
Parry, J.   191
people(s) of the land(s)   31,   43–44, 45–48, 72
Philo   185, 186, 197, 198, 202–3
Plummer, A.   195, 203
Porten, B.   38
Porter, J. R.   38
Preuss, H. D.   7, 35
profanation/defilement
   gā'al   117
   Hellenistic vs. Jewish   185–88, 185–88
   moral or not   137
   of land   39
   of lineage   56
   of mixed seeds   89
   of priest   107
   of priestly offspring   106, 111–12
   of sacred space   44
   permanent   212
purity/impurity
   'ereṣ nīdâ   113–14
   immunity from impurity   198–99
   in Ezra 9-10   99
   moral   99, 111, 113, 194
   ritual   98–99
   ritual impurity of Gentiles   99, 189
   ṭāhar   118–20
   terminology   98
Qimron, E.   92
Quell, G.   85
racism   129, 143–44, 147, 223

Rad, G. von   7, 132, 133, 135, 141
Rendtorff, R.   131, 139–42
Ringgren, H.   116, 118
Rivkin, E.   167, 168
Robertson, A.   195
Rosenbaum, M.   40, 41
Rosner, B. S.   195, 197
Rudolph, W.   4, 20, 29, 39, 40, 49, 52, 174
Ruth   84, 133, 134–35, 148, 149–51, 168–69
Ryle, H. E.   21, 22
Sanders, E. P.   133, 197
Sanders, J.   173
Satterthwaite, P. E.   36
Schäfer-Lichtenberger, C.   60
Schmitt, G.   62–63
Schneider, H.   27, 78
Schürer, E.   99
Scott, T.   131, 149, 151, 152, 161, 223
Silbermann, A. M.   40
Smith-Christopher, D. L.   142, 143, 157
Southwood, K. E.   46
Stendhal, K.   141
Strachan, R. H.   203
Strugnell, J.   92
Thiselton, A. C.   183, 187, 190
Thrall, M. E.   191, 195, 203
Tigay, J. H.   35, 36
Torrey, C. C.   4, 45
Van Seters, J.   41
Vermes, G.   180
Washington, H. C.   50
Watts, J. D.   85
Webb, W. J.   184, 204–5
Wellhausen, J.   3, 6, 132
Wenham, G.   38, 61, 102
Westermann, C.   132, 135
Whiston, W.   76, 161
Wijk-Bos, J. W. H.   45
Wildberger, H.   84
Williamson, H. G. M.   20, 24, 25, 26, 28, 29, 38, 40, 41, 43, 45, 54,

75, 76, 78, 84–85, 88, 142–43,
144–48, 150, 152, 154, 155, 157,
158, 173, 174, 175, 209–10
Windisch, H. 203
Wolff, H. W. 132

Wright, C. 148
Wright, D. P. 69, 98, 108
Wright, N. T. 133
Zenger, E. 136
Zimmerli, W. 132

www.ingramcontent.com/pod-product-compliance
Lightning Source LLC
Chambersburg PA
CBHW030311080526
44584CB00012B/526